9-11

ARTISTS RESPOND • VOLUME ONE

TABLE OF CONTENTS

Thanks to everyone who donated
their time and energy to the
production of this book.

Published by Chaos! Comics, Dark Horse Comics, and Image

Special thanks to QUEBECOR WORLD MONTREAL,
SUN CHEMICAL INC., UPM-KYMMENE, and KRUGER for
their generous donation of time, labor, and materials

www.comics911.com

9-11 Volume 1, January 2002. Published by Dark Horse Comics, Inc.,
10956 SE Main Street,Milwaukie, Oregon 97222. Text, stories, and art
© 2001, 2002 respective artists and authors. Compilation © 2002 Dark
Horse Comics, Inc., Chaos! Comics, and Image. No portion of this
publication may be reproduced or transmitted, in any form or by any
means, without the express written permission of copyright holder.
Names, characters, places, and incidents featured in this publication
either are the product of the author's imagination or are used fictitiously.

First Edition: January 2002
ISBN: 1-56389-881-0

3 5 7 9 10 8 6 4 2

P. Craig Russell

In Flanders Fields

THE FOLLOWING POEM 'IN FLANDERS FIELDS', FOR GENERATIONS THE MOST WELL KNOWN POEM TO COME OUT OF WORLD WAR I, WAS WRITTEN BY LIEUT.-COL. JOHN McCRAE, A MEMBER OF THE FIRST CANADIAN CONTINGENT, WHO DIED IN FRANCE ON JANUARY 28, 1918, AFTER FOUR YEARS OF SERVICE ON THE WESTERN FRONT. THIS ADAPTATION BY P. CRAIG RUSSELL UTILIZES IMAGES PRIOR TO AND INCLUDING 9/11. LETTERING BY GALEN SHOWMAN · COLORING BY LOVERN KINDZIERSKI AND DIGITAL CHAMELEON.

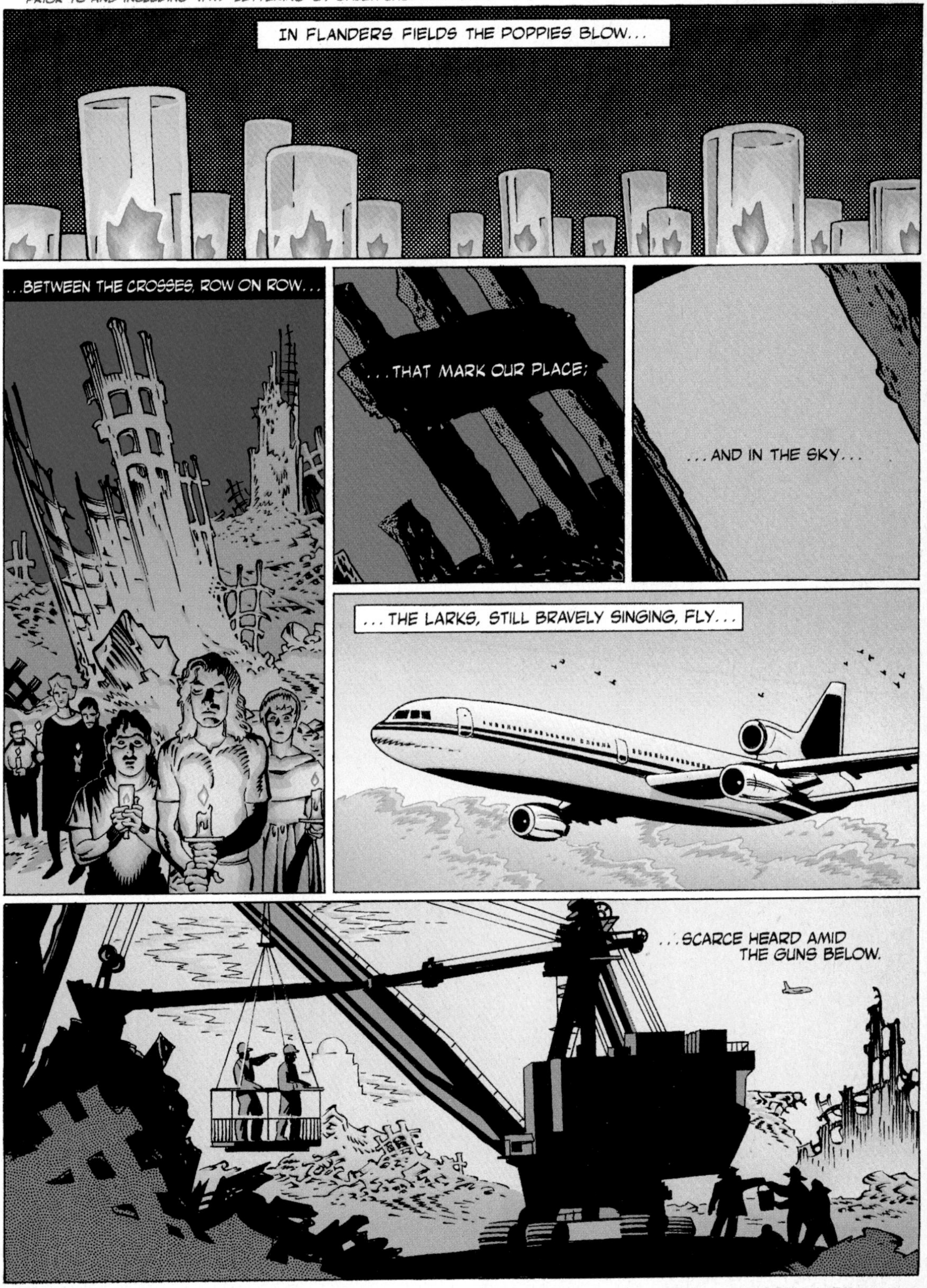
IN FLANDERS FIELDS THE POPPIES BLOW...
...BETWEEN THE CROSSES, ROW ON ROW...
...THAT MARK OUR PLACE;
...AND IN THE SKY...
...THE LARKS, STILL BRAVELY SINGING, FLY...
...SCARCE HEARD AMID THE GUNS BELOW.

WE ARE THE DEAD.

SHORT DAYS AGO
WE LIVED,
FELT DAWN,
SAW SUNSET GLOW,
LOVED AND
WERE LOVED...

...AND NOW WE LIE IN FLANDERS FIELDS.

TAKE UP OUR QUARREL
WITH THE FOE;
TO YOU FROM FAILING HANDS
WE THROW THE TORCH;

BE YOURS TO HOLD IT HIGH.

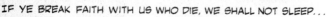

IF YE BREAK FAITH WITH US WHO DIE, WE SHALL NOT SLEEP...

MISSING

MISSING

...THOUGH POPPIES GROW
IN FLANDERS FIELDS.

Eric Powell

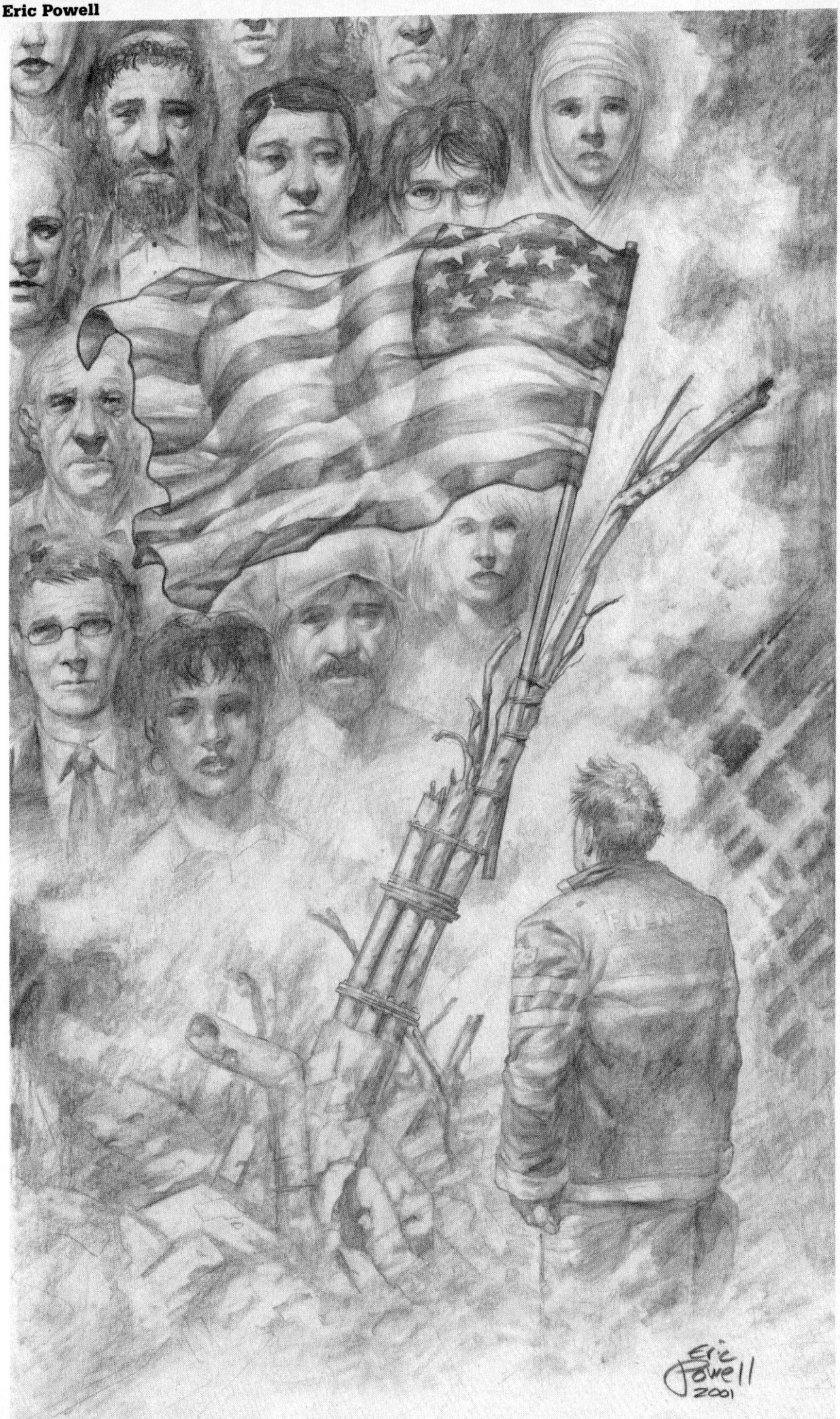
Eric Powell
2001

prayer

i am the son whose mother is lighting a candle
beneath a photograph at a new york city firehouse.

i am the daughter of a man who hijacked a plane in the name of allah.

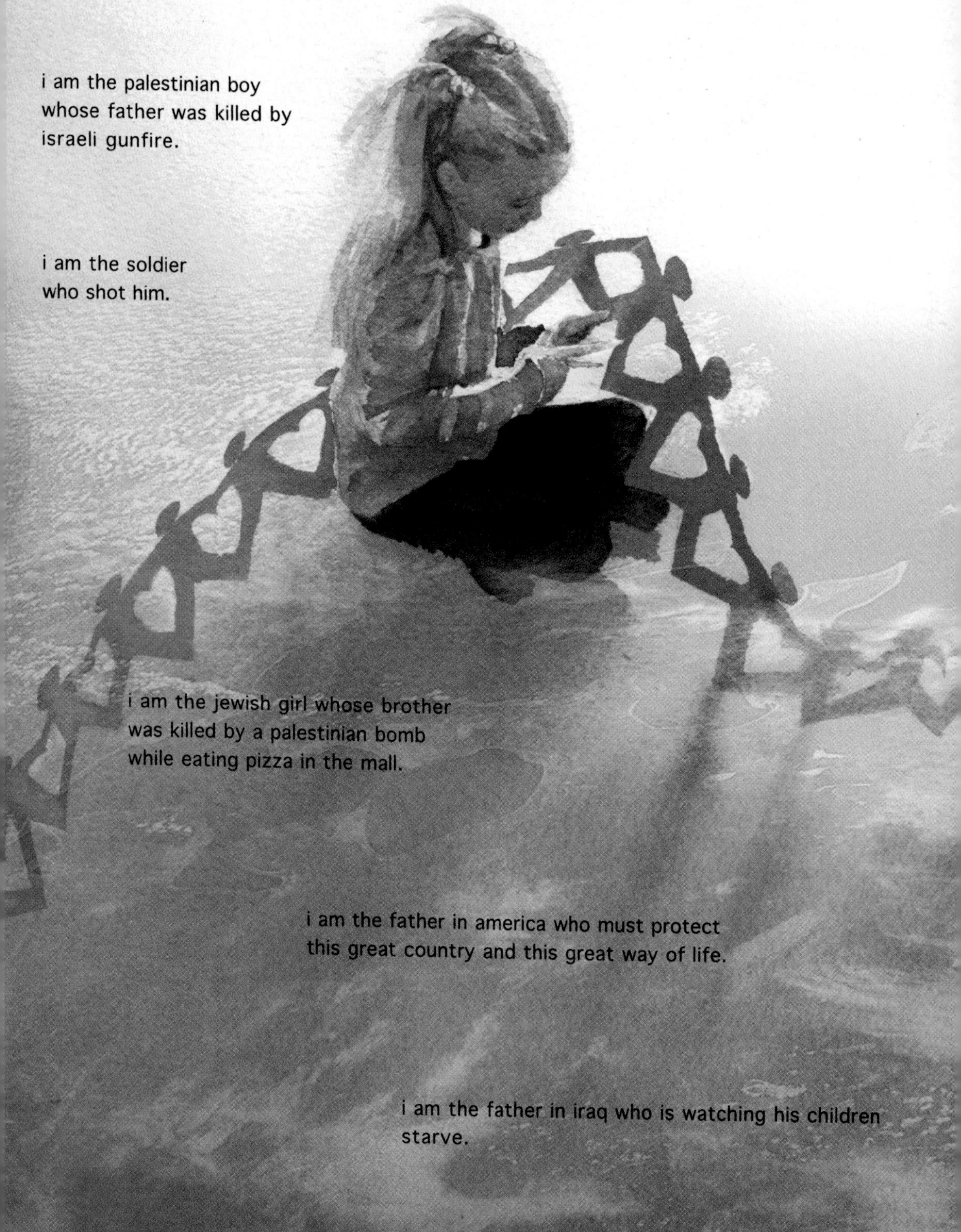

i am the palestinian boy
whose father was killed by
israeli gunfire.

i am the soldier
who shot him.

i am the jewish girl whose brother
was killed by a palestinian bomb
while eating pizza in the mall.

i am the father in america who must protect
this great country and this great way of life.

i am the father in iraq who is watching his children
starve.

i am the daughter who jumped from the burning
world trade center holding my friend's hand.

i am the orphaned afghani
boy who lives in a refugee
camp.

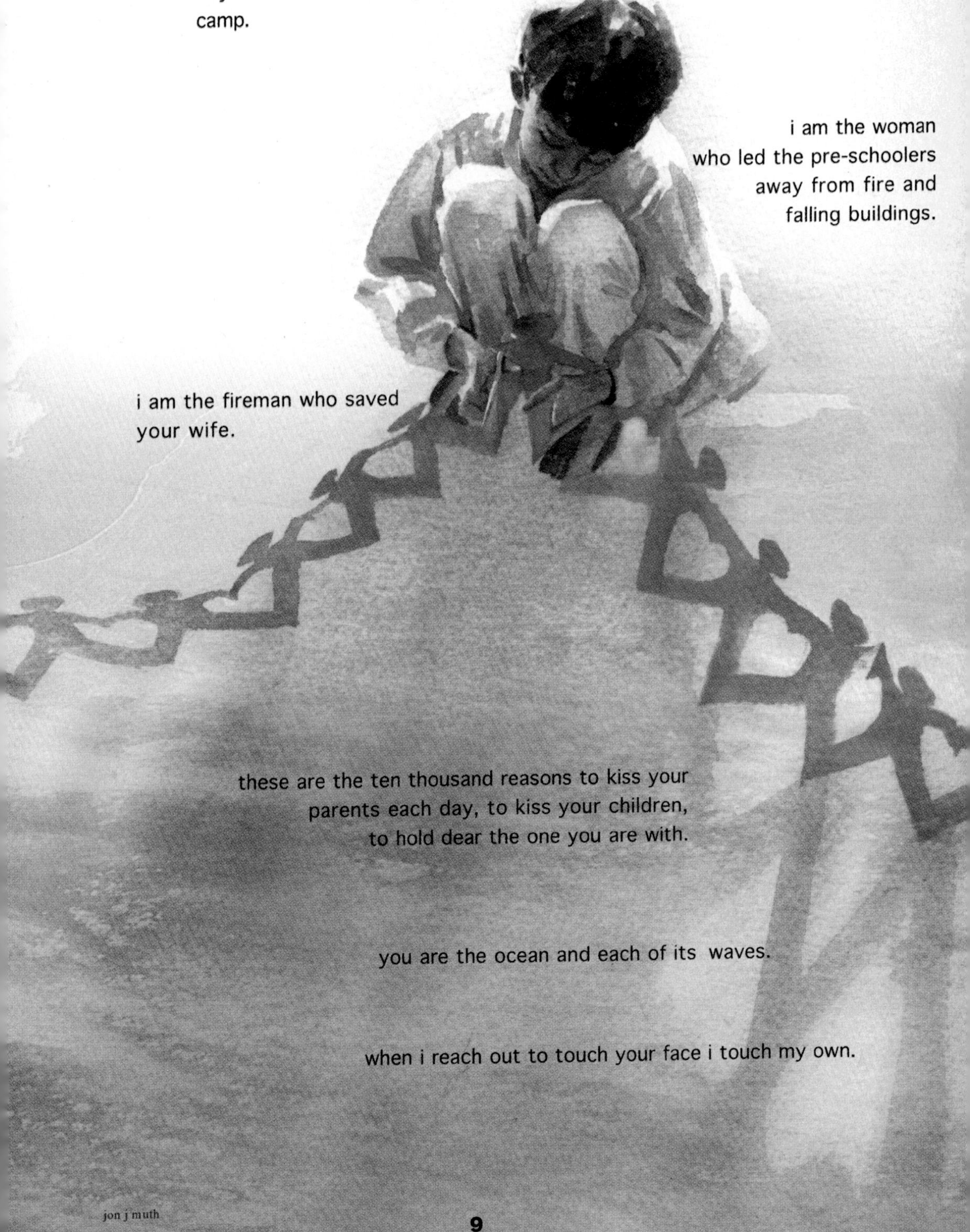
jon j muth

i am the woman
who led the pre-schoolers
away from fire and
falling buildings.

i am the fireman who saved
your wife.

these are the ten thousand reasons to kiss your
parents each day, to kiss your children,
to hold dear the one you are with.

you are the ocean and each of its waves.

when i reach out to touch your face i touch my own.

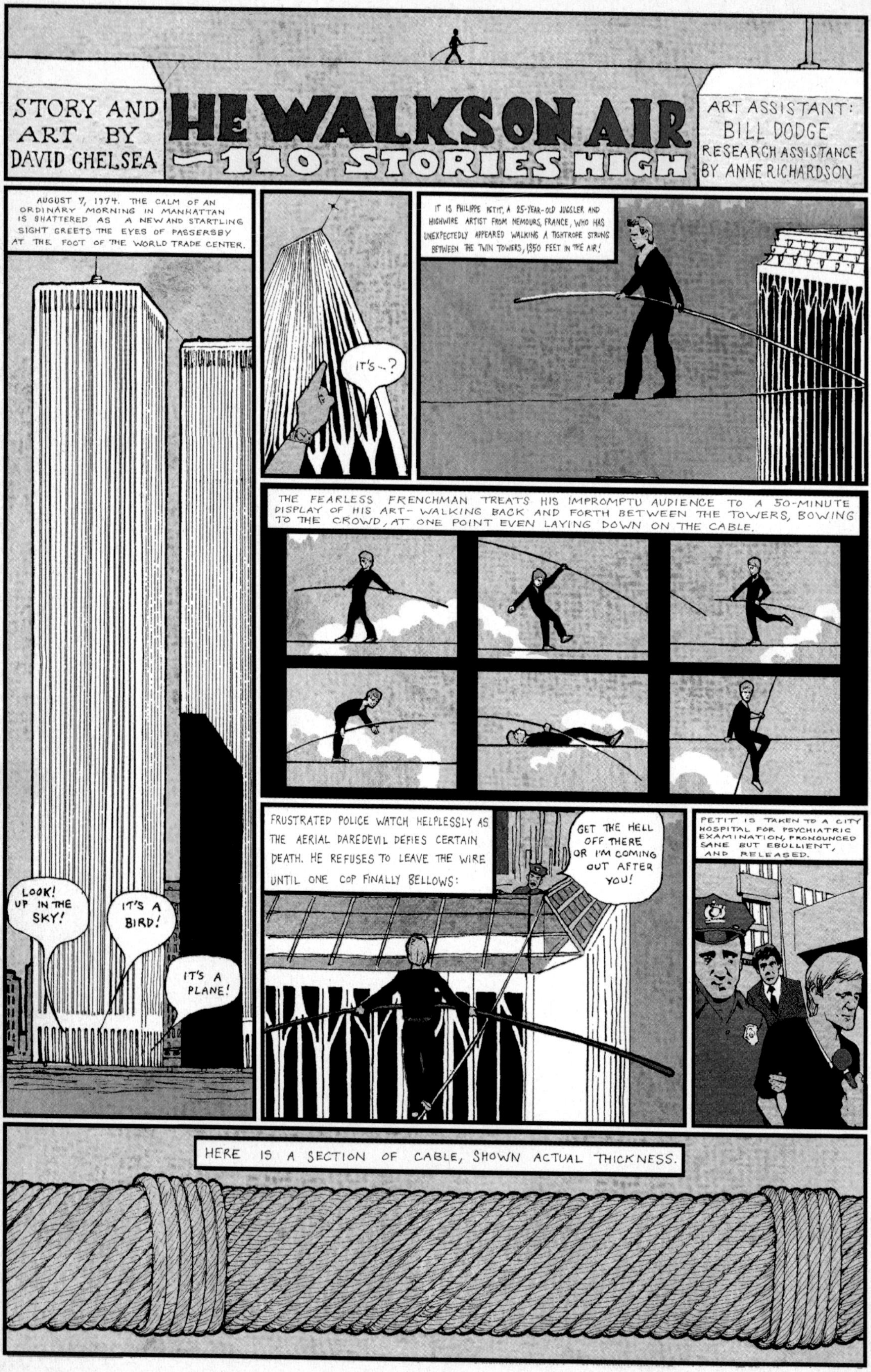
STORY AND ART BY DAVID CHELSEA
HE WALKS ON AIR — 110 STORIES HIGH
ART ASSISTANT: BILL DODGE
RESEARCH ASSISTANCE BY ANNE RICHARDSON
AUGUST 7, 1974. THE CALM OF AN ORDINARY MORNING IN MANHATTAN IS SHATTERED AS A NEW AND STARTLING SIGHT GREETS THE EYES OF PASSERSBY AT THE FOOT OF THE WORLD TRADE CENTER.
LOOK! UP IN THE SKY!
IT'S A BIRD!
IT'S A PLANE!
IT'S...?
IT IS PHILIPPE PETIT, A 25-YEAR-OLD JUGGLER AND HIGHWIRE ARTIST FROM NEMOURS, FRANCE, WHO HAS UNEXPECTEDLY APPEARED WALKING A TIGHTROPE STRUNG BETWEEN THE TWIN TOWERS, 1350 FEET IN THE AIR!
THE FEARLESS FRENCHMAN TREATS HIS IMPROMPTU AUDIENCE TO A 50-MINUTE DISPLAY OF HIS ART- WALKING BACK AND FORTH BETWEEN THE TOWERS, BOWING TO THE CROWD, AT ONE POINT EVEN LAYING DOWN ON THE CABLE.
FRUSTRATED POLICE WATCH HELPLESSLY AS THE AERIAL DAREDEVIL DEFIES CERTAIN DEATH. HE REFUSES TO LEAVE THE WIRE UNTIL ONE COP FINALLY BELLOWS:
GET THE HELL OFF THERE OR I'M COMING OUT AFTER YOU!
PETIT IS TAKEN TO A CITY HOSPITAL FOR PSYCHIATRIC EXAMINATION, PRONOUNCED SANE BUT EBULLIENT, AND RELEASED.
HERE IS A SECTION OF CABLE, SHOWN ACTUAL THICKNESS.

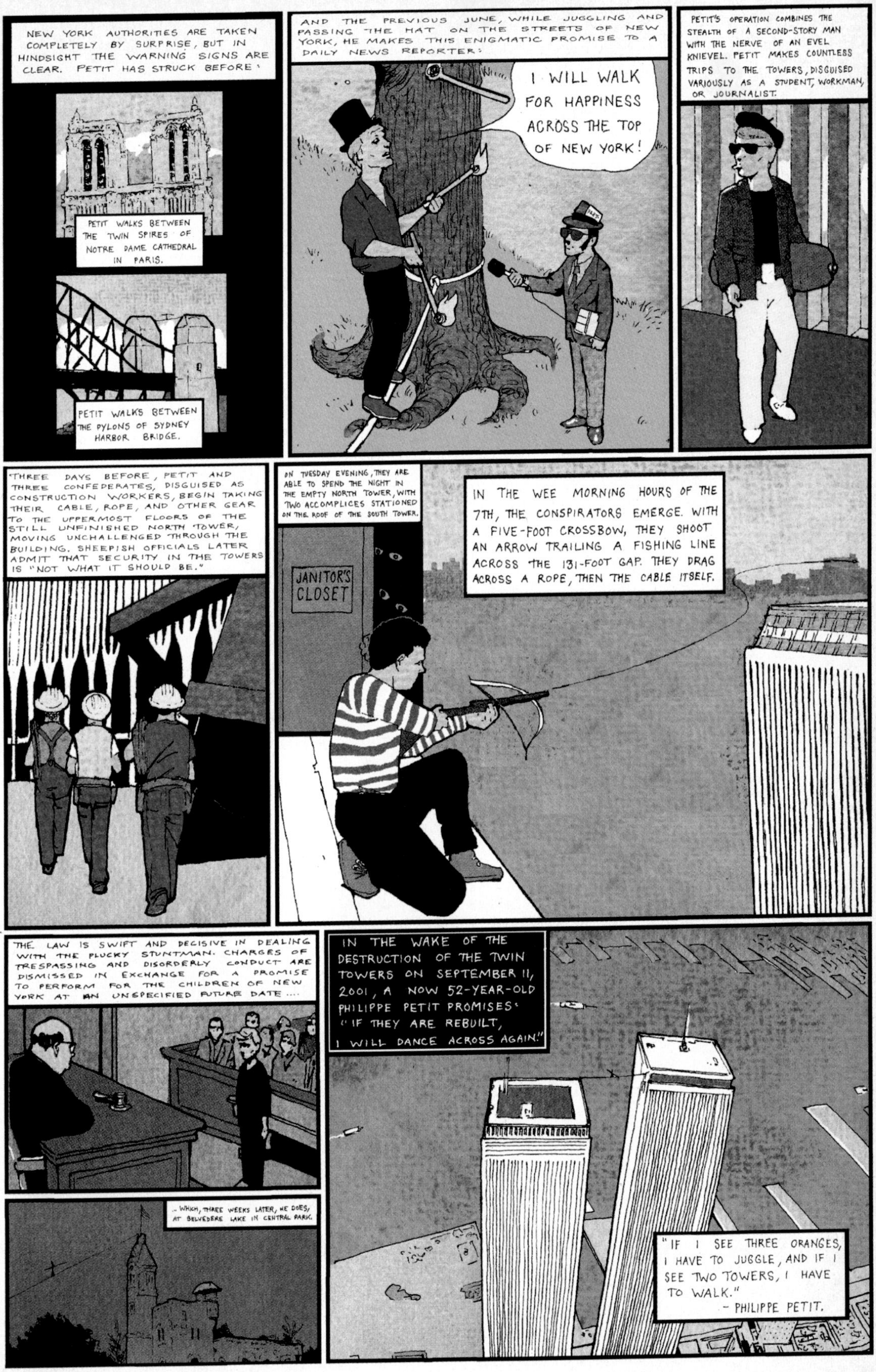
NEW YORK AUTHORITIES ARE TAKEN COMPLETELY BY SURPRISE, BUT IN HINDSIGHT THE WARNING SIGNS ARE CLEAR. PETIT HAS STRUCK BEFORE:
PETIT WALKS BETWEEN THE TWIN SPIRES OF NOTRE DAME CATHEDRAL IN PARIS.
PETIT WALKS BETWEEN THE PYLONS OF SYDNEY HARBOR BRIDGE.
AND THE PREVIOUS JUNE, WHILE JUGGLING AND PASSING THE HAT ON THE STREETS OF NEW YORK, HE MAKES THIS ENIGMATIC PROMISE TO A DAILY NEWS REPORTER:
I WILL WALK FOR HAPPINESS ACROSS THE TOP OF NEW YORK!
PETIT'S OPERATION COMBINES THE STEALTH OF A SECOND-STORY MAN WITH THE NERVE OF AN EVEL KNIEVEL. PETIT MAKES COUNTLESS TRIPS TO THE TOWERS, DISGUISED VARIOUSLY AS A STUDENT, WORKMAN, OR JOURNALIST.
THREE DAYS BEFORE, PETIT AND THREE CONFEDERATES, DISGUISED AS CONSTRUCTION WORKERS, BEGIN TAKING THEIR CABLE, ROPE, AND OTHER GEAR TO THE UPPERMOST FLOORS OF THE STILL UNFINISHED NORTH TOWER, MOVING UNCHALLENGED THROUGH THE BUILDING. SHEEPISH OFFICIALS LATER ADMIT THAT SECURITY IN THE TOWERS IS "NOT WHAT IT SHOULD BE."
ON TUESDAY EVENING, THEY ARE ABLE TO SPEND THE NIGHT IN THE EMPTY NORTH TOWER, WITH TWO ACCOMPLICES STATIONED ON THE ROOF OF THE SOUTH TOWER.
JANITOR'S CLOSET
IN THE WEE MORNING HOURS OF THE 7TH, THE CONSPIRATORS EMERGE. WITH A FIVE-FOOT CROSSBOW, THEY SHOOT AN ARROW TRAILING A FISHING LINE ACROSS THE 131-FOOT GAP. THEY DRAG ACROSS A ROPE, THEN THE CABLE ITSELF.
THE LAW IS SWIFT AND DECISIVE IN DEALING WITH THE PLUCKY STUNTMAN. CHARGES OF TRESPASSING AND DISORDERLY CONDUCT ARE DISMISSED IN EXCHANGE FOR A PROMISE TO PERFORM FOR THE CHILDREN OF NEW YORK AT AN UNSPECIFIED FUTURE DATE....
...WHICH, THREE WEEKS LATER, HE DOES, AT BELVEDERE LAKE IN CENTRAL PARK.
IN THE WAKE OF THE DESTRUCTION OF THE TWIN TOWERS ON SEPTEMBER 11, 2001, A NOW 52-YEAR-OLD PHILIPPE PETIT PROMISES: "IF THEY ARE REBUILT, I WILL DANCE ACROSS AGAIN."
"IF I SEE THREE ORANGES, I HAVE TO JUGGLE, AND IF I SEE TWO TOWERS, I HAVE TO WALK." - PHILIPPE PETIT.

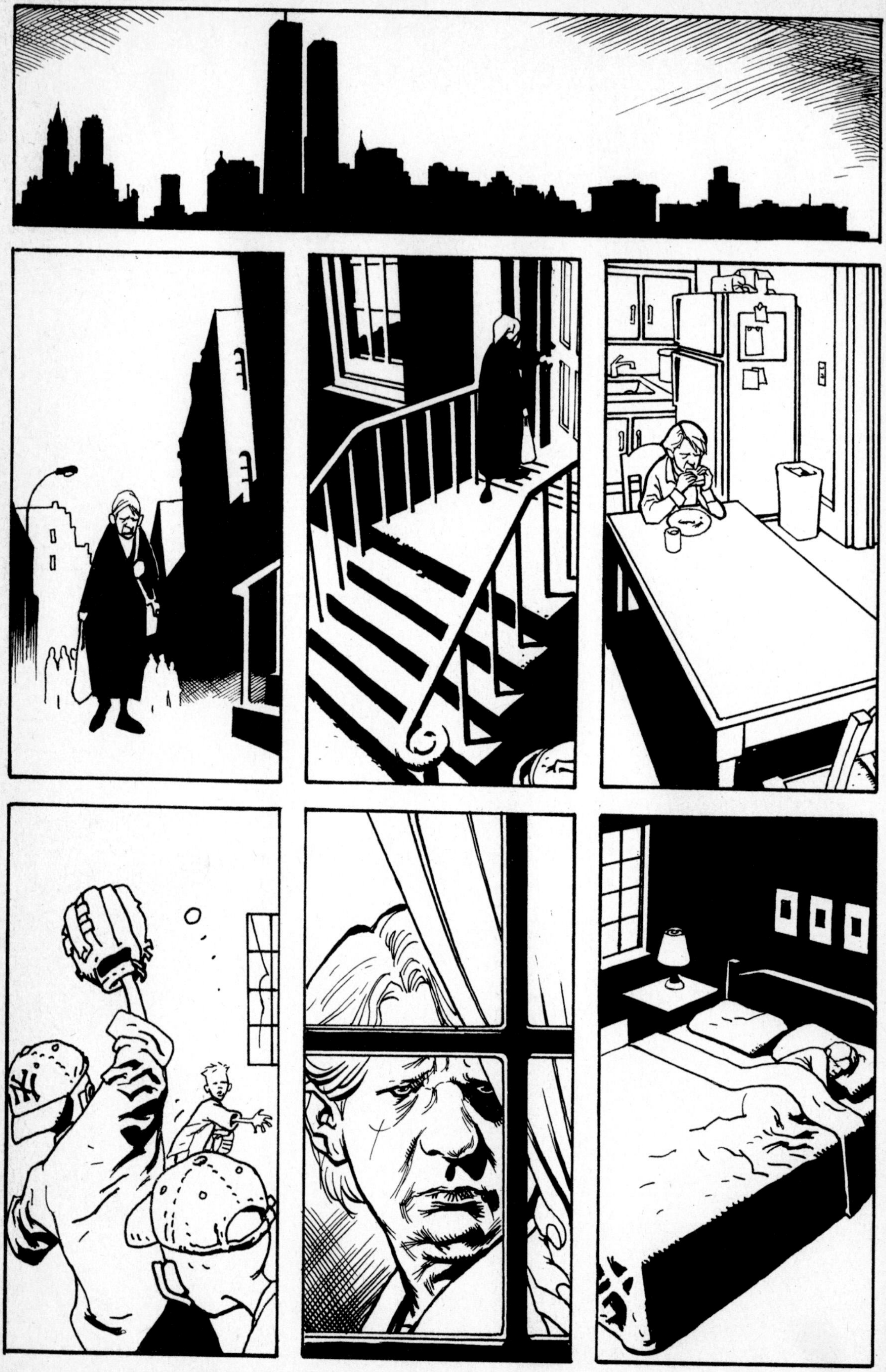

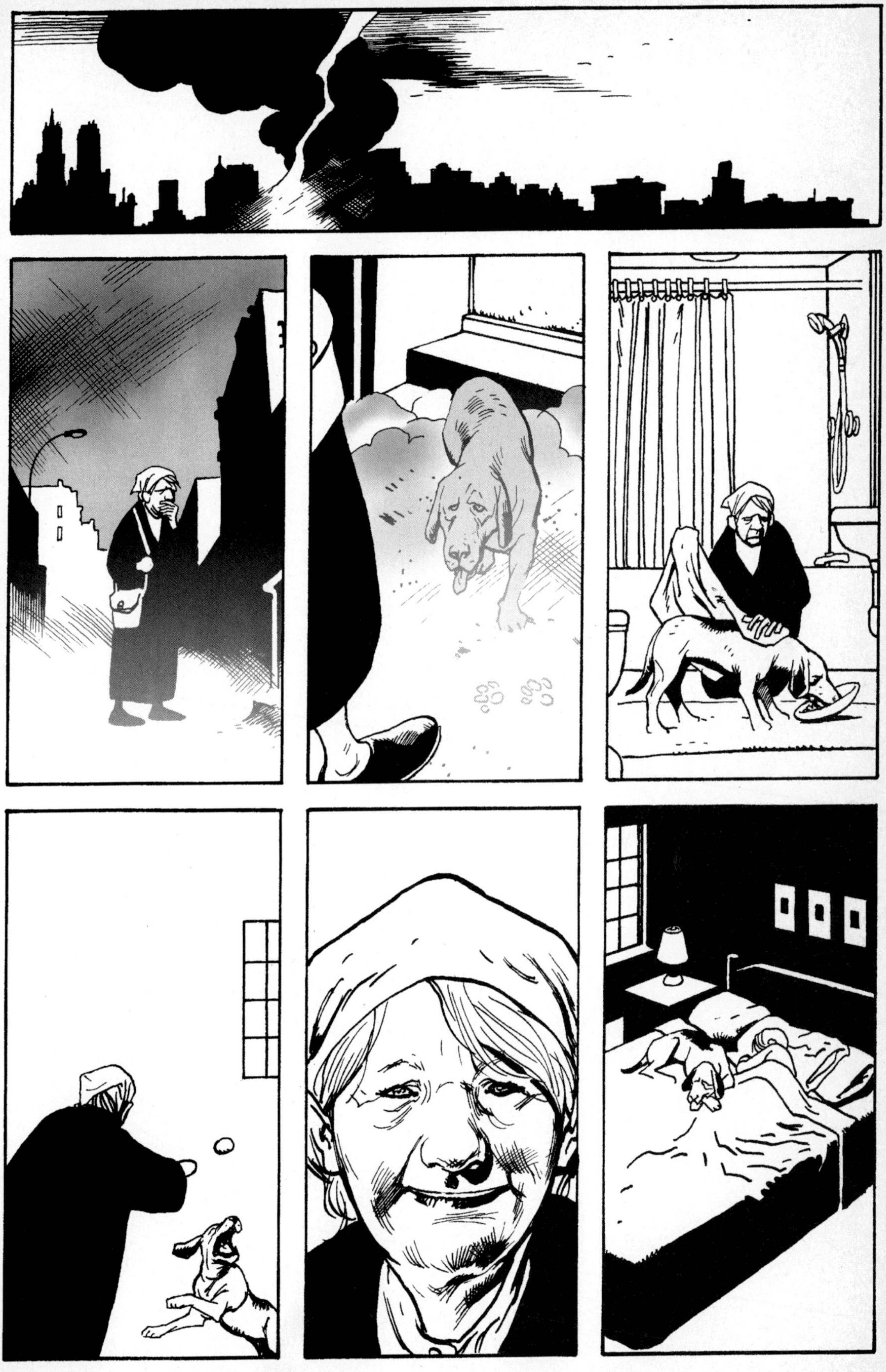

mind THE gap

paul sloboda

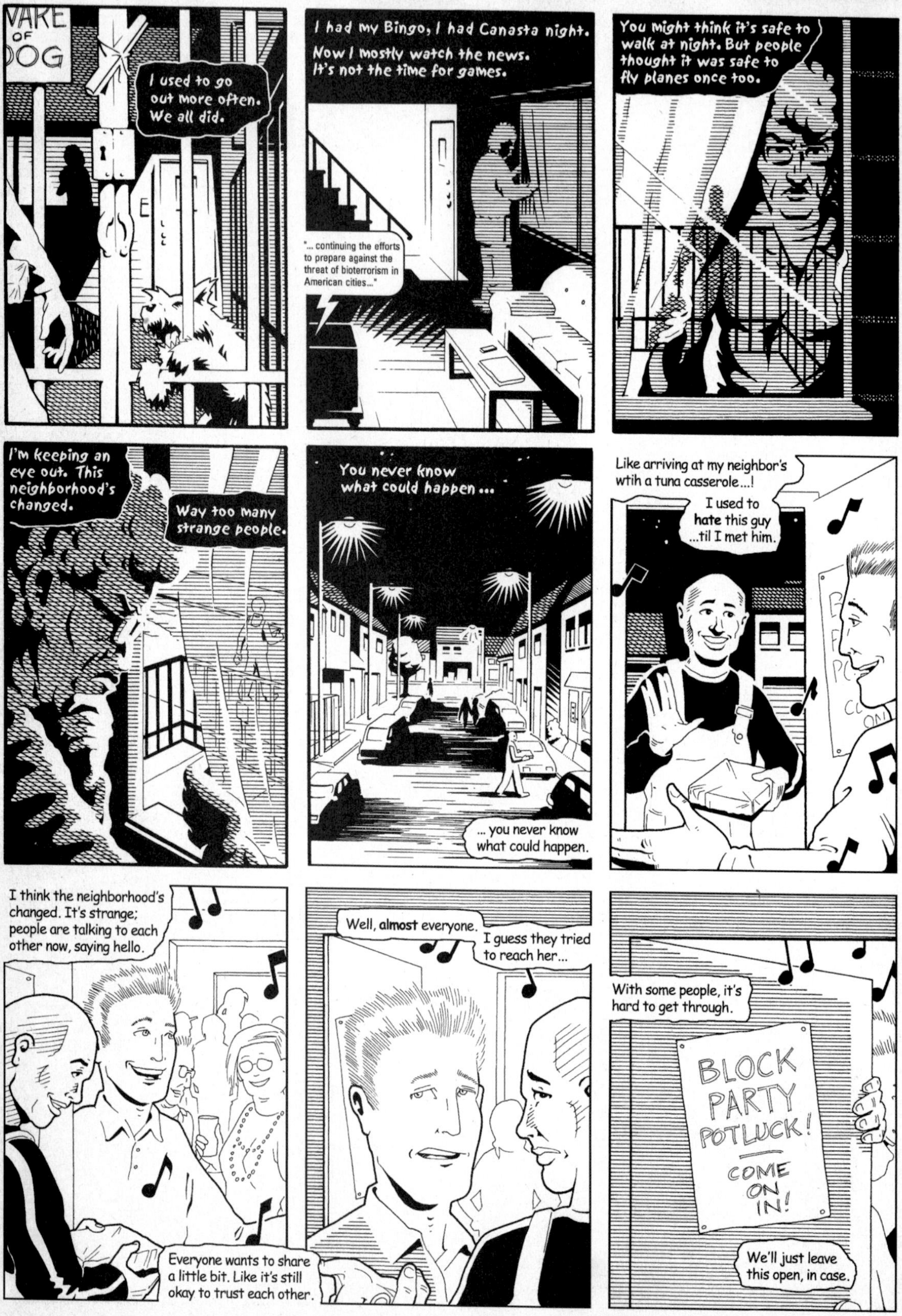
I used to go out more often. We all did.
I had my Bingo, I had Canasta night.
Now I mostly watch the news. It's not the time for games.
"... continuing the efforts to prepare against the threat of bioterrorism in American cities..."
You might think it's safe to walk at night. But people thought it was safe to fly planes once too.
I'm keeping an eye out. This neighborhood's changed.
Way too many strange people.
You never know what could happen ...
... you never know what could happen.
Like arriving at my neighbor's wtih a tuna casserole...!
I used to **hate** this guy ...til I met him.
I think the neighborhood's changed. It's strange; people are talking to each other now, saying hello.
Everyone wants to share a little bit. Like it's still okay to trust each other.
Well, **almost** everyone.
I guess they tried to reach her...
With some people, it's hard to get through.
BLOCK PARTY POTLUCK!
COME ON IN!
We'll just leave this open, in case.

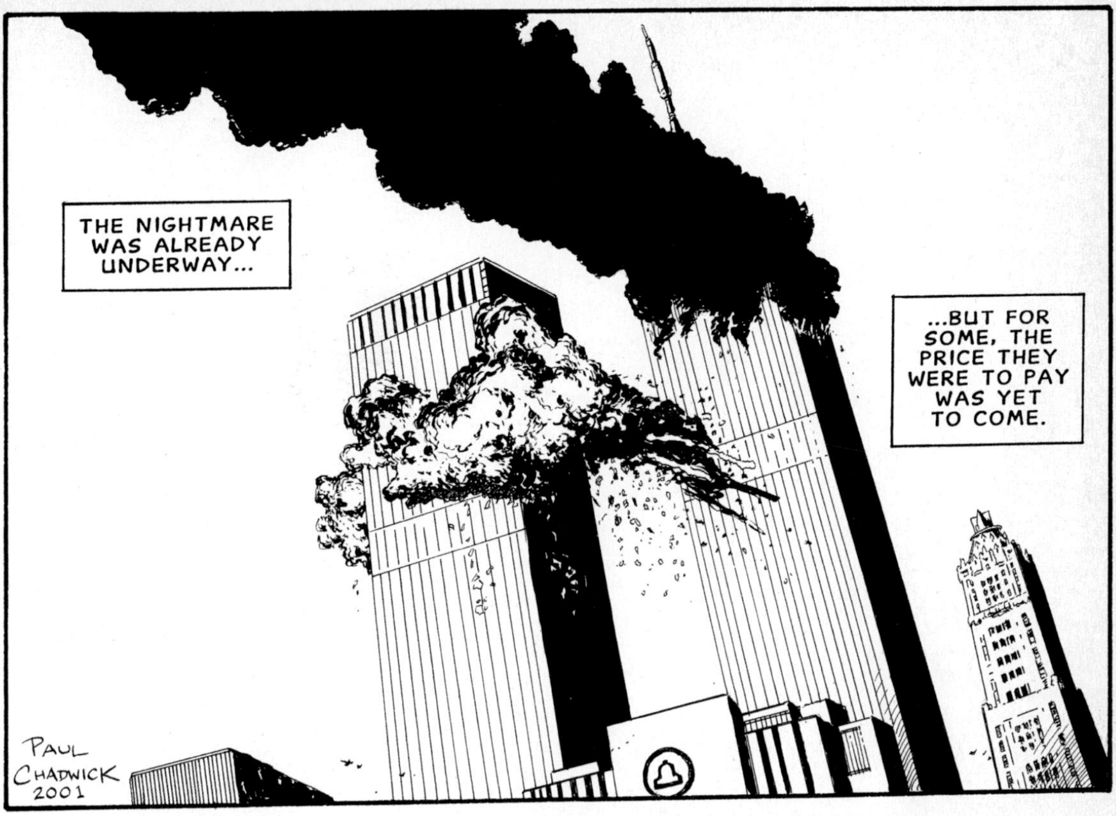
THE NIGHTMARE WAS ALREADY UNDERWAY...
...BUT FOR SOME, THE PRICE THEY WERE TO PAY WAS YET TO COME.
PAUL CHADWICK 2001

THEY WERE TO MAKE WHAT CAN ONLY BE CALLED AN HEROIC...

SACRIFICE

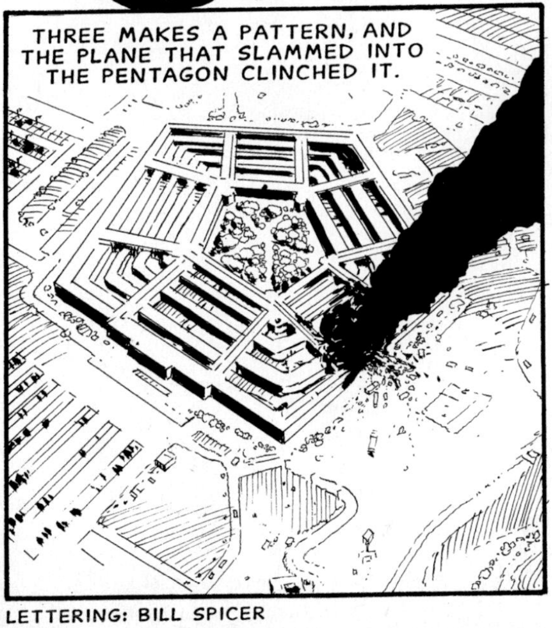
THREE MAKES A PATTERN, AND THE PLANE THAT SLAMMED INTO THE PENTAGON CLINCHED IT.

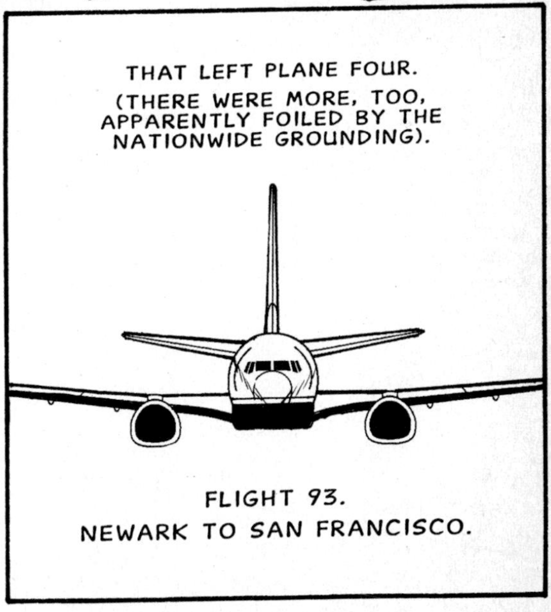
THAT LEFT PLANE FOUR.
(THERE WERE MORE, TOO, APPARENTLY FOILED BY THE NATIONWIDE GROUNDING).
FLIGHT 93. NEWARK TO SAN FRANCISCO.

LETTERING: BILL SPICER

WHAT WE KNOW AT THIS POINT (BEFORE THE 'BLACK BOX' RECORDING HAS BEEN RELEASED) COMES FROM REPORTS OF PASSENGERS' PHONE CALLS.

ONE CALLED HIS MOTHER.

WE'VE BEEN TAKEN OVER.

THERE ARE THREE MEN WHO SAY THEY'VE GOT A BOMB.

MARK BINGHAM, 31, PR FIRM OWNER, RUGBY PLAYER.

ONE SPOKE WITH THE GTE OPERATOR.

WHAT? THE WORLD TRADE CENTER?

TODD BEAMER, 32, ORACLE SALES MANAGER, SUNDAY SCHOOL TEACHER.

AND TWO CALLED THEIR WIVES.

THEY'VE ALREADY KNIFED A GUY.

THOMAS BURNETT, JR., 38, CEO OF THORATEC, A MEDICAL DEVICE MAKER.

WEARING RED HEAD-BANDS...

...A LARGE RED BOX THEY SAY IS A BOMB.

JEREMY GLICK, 31, SALES REP FOR VIVIDENCE, NEW DAD, JUDO CHAMPION.

UNTIL 9-11-01, EXPERT ADVICE ON HIJACKINGS WAS TO COOPERATE.

STAY IN THE BACK AND YOU WON'T BE HURT.

BUT RUMORS OF THE WORLD TRADE CENTER CRASHES WERE ALREADY PASSING IN WHISPERS.

THAT CHANGED THINGS.

BURNETT CALLED FOUR TIMES.

PLEASE! SIT DOWN AND DON'T CALL ATTENTION TO YOURSELF.

NO, DEENA. THERE'S THREE OF US WHO ARE GOING TO DO SOMETHING ABOUT IT.

I LOVE YOU, HONEY.

IN BETWEEN, HE TALKED TO BINGHAM, SITTING NEXT TO HIM, AND OTHERS.

LAST WORDS.

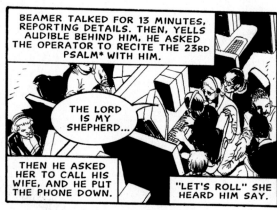

BEAMER TALKED FOR 13 MINUTES, REPORTING DETAILS. THEN, YELLS AUDIBLE BEHIND HIM, HE ASKED THE OPERATOR TO RECITE THE 23RD PSALM* WITH HIM.

THE LORD IS MY SHEPHERD...

THEN HE ASKED HER TO CALL HIS WIFE, AND HE PUT THE PHONE DOWN.

"LET'S ROLL" SHE HEARD HIM SAY.

JEREMY GLICK TOLD HIS WIFE THE MALE PASSENGERS HAD VOTED.

WE DECIDED. WE'RE GOING TO DO IT.

I WANT YOU TO BE HAPPY IN YOUR LIFE. I WILL BE HAPPY FOR YOU...

THEN HE SAID HE'D LEAVE THE PHONE OFF THE HOOK.

LYZBETH GLICK GAVE THE PHONE TO HER FATHER.

I DON'T WANT TO HEAR THE REST.

WHO COULD BLAME HER?

*OR POSSIBLY THE LORD'S PRAYER -- REPORTS VARY.

16

NOBODY KNOWS HOW MANY PEOPLE HELPED. ONE WHO WELL MAY HAVE IS CEE CEE LYLES, FLIGHT ATTENDANT.

BABE, MY FLIGHT'S BEEN HI-JACKED...

SHE'D BEEN A COP.

OR PASSENGER LAUREN GRANDCOLAS.

I LOVE YOU.

WHO KNOWS?

YAAAHHH!!

MAYBE BINGHAM LED. HE'D RECENTLY RUN WITH THE BULLS IN PAMPLONA, SPAIN.

OR GLICK, THE JUDO CHAMPION.

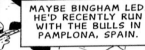
THESE GUYS WEREN'T PUSHOVERS.

OR BEAMER, A FORMER FOOTBALL PLAYER.

BUT THEY STILL HAD TO RUN *SINGLE FILE* AT KNIVES WET WITH BLOOD.

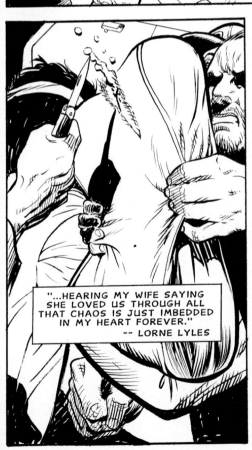
"...HEARING MY WIFE SAYING SHE LOVED US THROUGH ALL THAT CHAOS IS JUST IMBEDDED IN MY HEART FOREVER."
-- LORNE LYLES

"I KNOW WITHOUT A DOUBT THAT THAT PLANE WAS BOUND FOR SOME LANDMARK AND THEY SAVED MANY, MANY MORE LIVES THAN WERE LOST ON THAT PLANE."
-- DEENA BURNETT

A CALLER FROM A RESTROOM SAID HE HEARD AN EXPLOSION AND SAW WHITE SMOKE "COMING FROM THE AIRCRAFT"-- ACCORDING TO ONE REPORT--AND "IN THE CABIN" ACCORDING TO ANOTHER.

SOME HAVE SPECULATED THE PLANE WAS SHOT DOWN. PRESIDENT BUSH *HAD* AUTHORIZED SHOOT-DOWNS BY THIS TIME.

BUT THE F-16s SCRAMBLED FROM LANGLY WERE FLYING PROTECTIVE PATTERNS OVER WASHINGTON, ACCORDING TO AP.

MAYBE THE HIJACKERS *DID* HAVE A BOMB.

MAYBE THE PASSENGERS SEIZED CONTROL ONLY TO BE SHOT DOWN.

IT DOESN'T REALLY CHANGE THE FACT THAT *THEY DECIDED.*

THEY WERE WILLING TO FACE ATTACKERS WHO HAD JUST SLIT THROATS AS THEY WATCHED.

WILLING TO DIE TO SAVE OTHERS.

DIE THEY DID.

ALL 45 ABOARD WERE LOST WHEN THE PLANE CRATERED IN A FIELD OUTSIDE SHANKSVILLE, PA.

NO PIECE BIGGER THAN A CAR DOOR WAS LEFT.

"...WE KNOW THE PLANE...WAS HEADED FOR WASHINGTON.* MR. GLICK AND OTHERS-- MR. BURNETT--WERE VERY COURAGEOUS WHEN THEY MADE THAT DECISION..." -- VICE PRESIDENT CHENEY

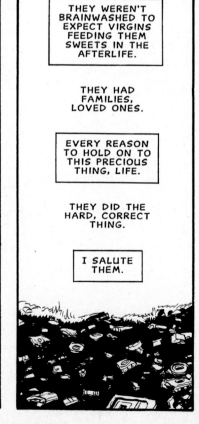

THEY WEREN'T BRAINWASHED TO EXPECT VIRGINS FEEDING THEM SWEETS IN THE AFTERLIFE.

THEY HAD FAMILIES, LOVED ONES.

EVERY REASON TO HOLD ON TO THIS PRECIOUS THING, LIFE.

THEY DID THE HARD, CORRECT THING.

I SALUTE THEM.

*WORSE, THREE NUCLEAR PLANTS WERE DIRECTLY IN ITS PATH.

ZERO DEGREE OF SEPARATION

SCRIPT - 21 Sept 2001: Randy Stradley   **ART - 31 Oct 2001: Dave Gibbons**

MOMENTS AFTER IT HAPPENED, PEOPLE WERE SAYING THE WORLD HAD CHANGED. HAD IT?

IT'S THE NATURE OF OUR EXISTENCE THAT WE VIEW THE WORLD SUBJECTIVELY. EVENTS EITHER AFFECT US, OR THEY'RE HAPPENING TO SOMEBODY ELSE.

AS WE GO THROUGH LIFE, THE SUBJECTIVE "US" EXPANDS TO INCLUDE OUR OWN PERSONAL CIRCLE OF FAMILY AND FRIENDS. WE FEEL THEIR PAIN AS ACUTELY AS WE DO OUR OWN.

BUT WHEN THINGS HAPPEN TO PEOPLE FAR AWAY -- PEOPLE WE DON'T KNOW AND HAVE NEVER MET -- IT HAPPENS TO *THEM*. WE JUST HEAR ABOUT IT. OR SEE IT.

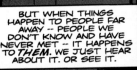

I WATCHED IT HAPPEN ON TELEVISION. WATCHED IT HAPPEN TO OTHER PEOPLE. FROM THE SAFE REMOVE OF THREE THOUSAND-SOME MILES.

TV'S BLAND FRAME PROVIDES NO CONTEXT FOR WHAT IT DISPLAYS -- OR RATHER, THE SAME CONTEXT FOR EVERY-THING IT DISPLAYS. COMEDY, DRAMA, TRAGEDY...ARE ALL PAINTED ON THE SAME CANVAS.

REDUCED TO THAT TWENTY-SEVEN-INCH SCREEN, EVENTS TOOK ON AN AIR OF UNREALITY. LIKE SCENES FROM A MOVIE, THEIR POWER WAS FLEETING. DIS-TURBING, BUT DISTANT. AND, AFTER ALL, HAPPENING TO SOMEBODY ELSE.

MAYBE WE'RE BUILT THIS WAY INTENTIONALLY -- LEST THE WEIGHT OF ALL THE DEATH, DESTRUCTION, MURDER AND CRUEL FIAT IN THE WORLD BREAK OUR HEARTS ON A DAILY BASIS.

I COULD CONCEP-TUALIZE THE MOUNTING HORROR OF THE PASSENGERS ON THE CRASHING PLANES... THE PANIC OF THOSE TRYING TO ESCAPE THE TOWERS...THE DESPERATE HEROICS ON BOARD UNITED FLIGHT 93...BUT THESE PEOPLE WERE UNKNOWN TO ME. I FELT FOR THEM, BUT THEIR PAIN WAS NOT MINE.

AT LEAST NOT AT,THAT MOMENT. BUT THE CUSHIONING NUMBNESS OF SHOCK ONLY LASTS SO LONG...

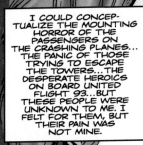

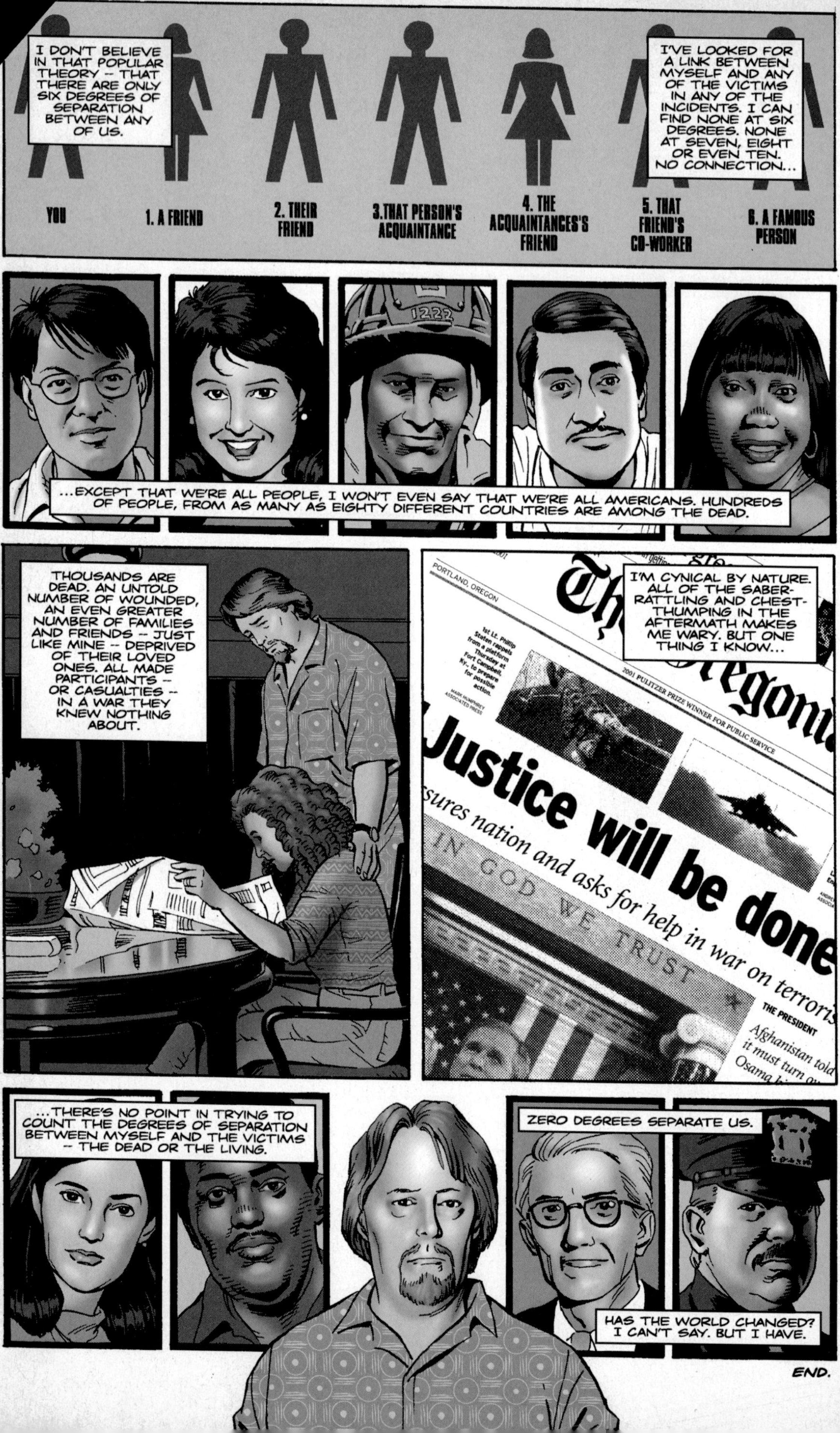
I DON'T BELIEVE IN THAT POPULAR THEORY -- THAT THERE ARE ONLY SIX DEGREES OF SEPARATION BETWEEN ANY OF US.
I'VE LOOKED FOR A LINK BETWEEN MYSELF AND ANY OF THE VICTIMS IN ANY OF THE INCIDENTS. I CAN FIND NONE AT SIX DEGREES. NONE AT SEVEN, EIGHT OR EVEN TEN. NO CONNECTION...
YOU
1. A FRIEND
2. THEIR FRIEND
3.THAT PERSON'S ACQUAINTANCE
4. THE ACQUAINTANCES'S FRIEND
5. THAT FRIEND'S CO-WORKER
6. A FAMOUS PERSON
1222
...EXCEPT THAT WE'RE ALL PEOPLE, I WON'T EVEN SAY THAT WE'RE ALL AMERICANS. HUNDREDS OF PEOPLE, FROM AS MANY AS EIGHTY DIFFERENT COUNTRIES ARE AMONG THE DEAD.
THOUSANDS ARE DEAD. AN UNTOLD NUMBER OF WOUNDED, AN EVEN GREATER NUMBER OF FAMILIES AND FRIENDS -- JUST LIKE MINE -- DEPRIVED OF THEIR LOVED ONES. ALL MADE PARTICIPANTS -- OR CASUALTIES -- IN A WAR THEY KNEW NOTHING ABOUT.
I'M CYNICAL BY NATURE. ALL OF THE SABER-RATTLING AND CHEST-THUMPING IN THE AFTERMATH MAKES ME WARY. BUT ONE THING I KNOW...
PORTLAND, OREGON
1st Lt. Phillip Staten rappels from a platform Thursday at Fort Campbell, Ky., to prepare for possible action.
MARK HUMPHREY ASSOCIATED PRESS
2001 PULITZER PRIZE WINNER FOR PUBLIC SERVICE
Justice will be done
sures nation and asks for help in war on terroris
IN GOD WE TRUST
THE PRESIDENT
Afghanistan told it must turn
...THERE'S NO POINT IN TRYING TO COUNT THE DEGREES OF SEPARATION BETWEEN MYSELF AND THE VICTIMS -- THE DEAD OR THE LIVING.
ZERO DEGREES SEPARATE US.
HAS THE WORLD CHANGED? I CAN'T SAY. BUT I HAVE.
END.

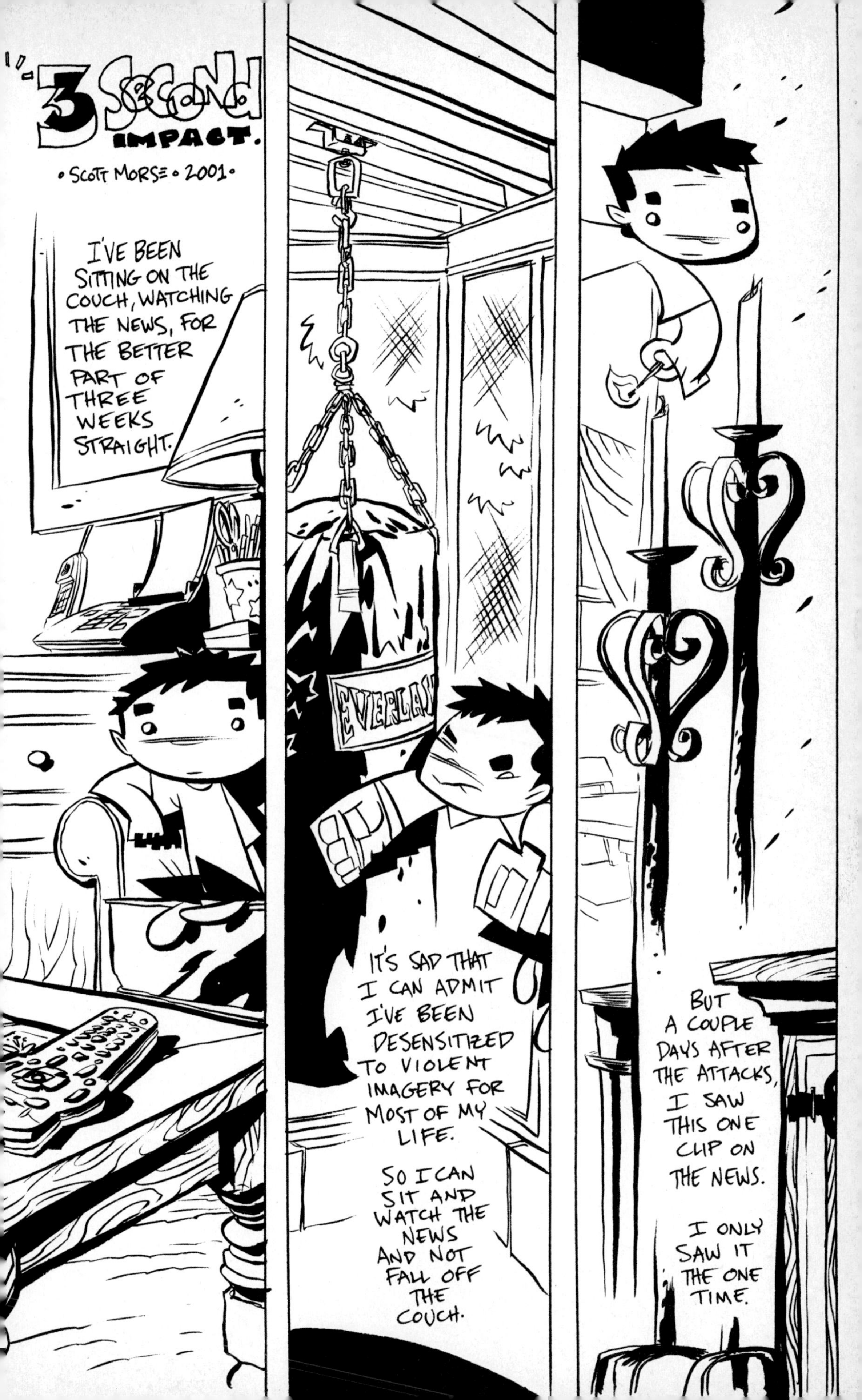
"3 SECOND IMPACT."
• SCOTT MORSE • 2001 •
I'VE BEEN SITTING ON THE COUCH, WATCHING THE NEWS, FOR THE BETTER PART OF THREE WEEKS STRAIGHT.
EVERLAST
IT'S SAD THAT I CAN ADMIT I'VE BEEN DESENSITIZED TO VIOLENT IMAGERY FOR MOST OF MY LIFE.
SO I CAN SIT AND WATCH THE NEWS AND NOT FALL OFF THE COUCH.
BUT A COUPLE DAYS AFTER THE ATTACKS, I SAW THIS ONE CLIP ON THE NEWS.
I ONLY SAW IT THE ONE TIME.

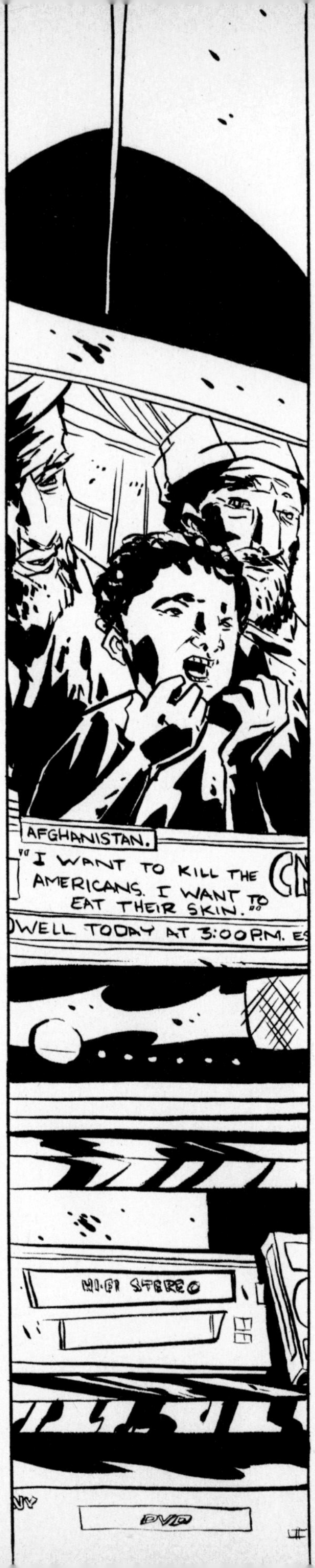
AFGHANISTAN.
"I WANT TO KILL THE AMERICANS. I WANT TO EAT THEIR SKIN."
WELL TODAY AT 3:00P.M. ES
HI-FI STEREO
DVD

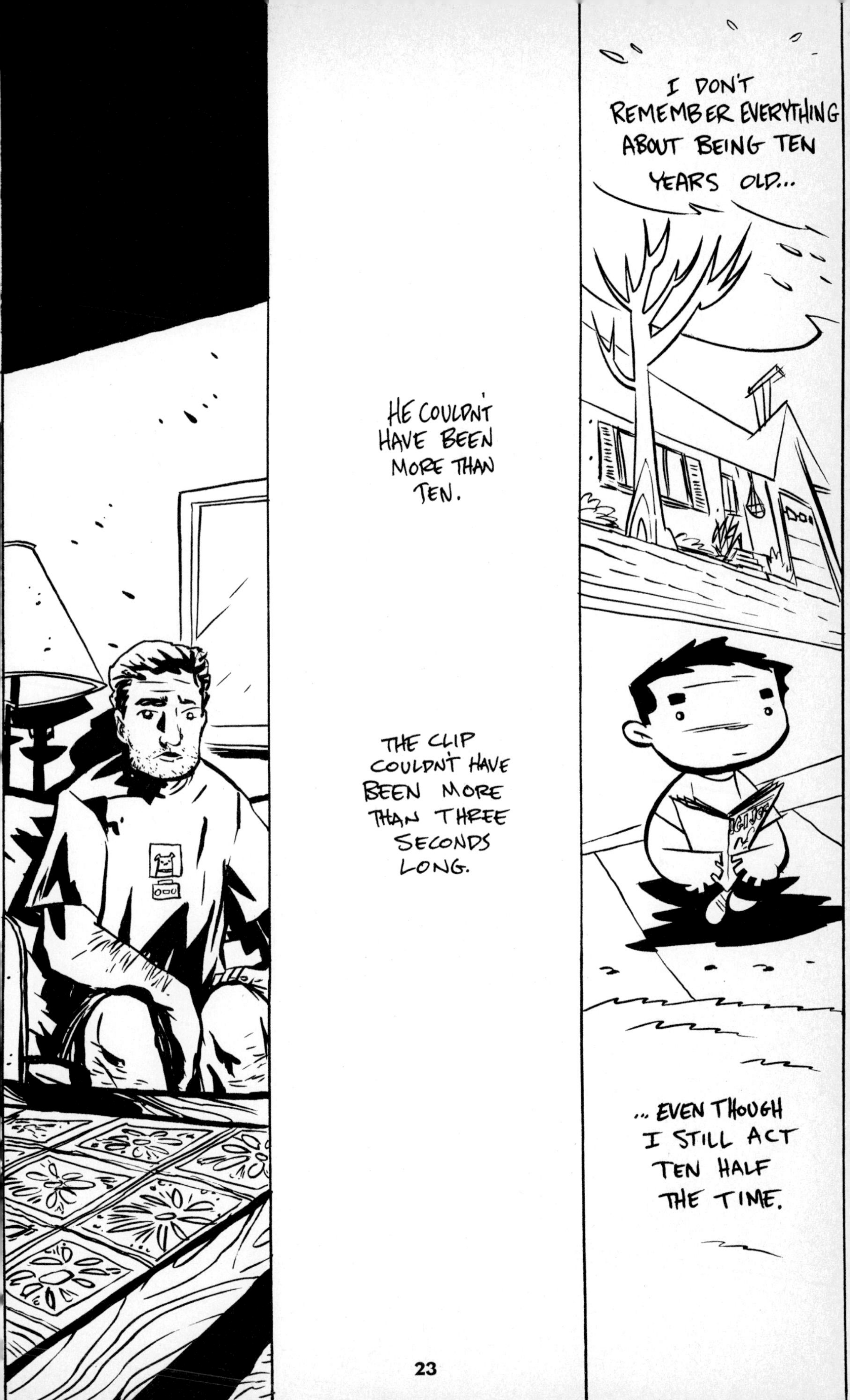
HE COULDN'T HAVE BEEN MORE THAN TEN.
THE CLIP COULDN'T HAVE BEEN MORE THAN THREE SECONDS LONG.
I DON'T REMEMBER EVERYTHING ABOUT BEING TEN YEARS OLD...
...EVEN THOUGH I STILL ACT TEN HALF THE TIME.

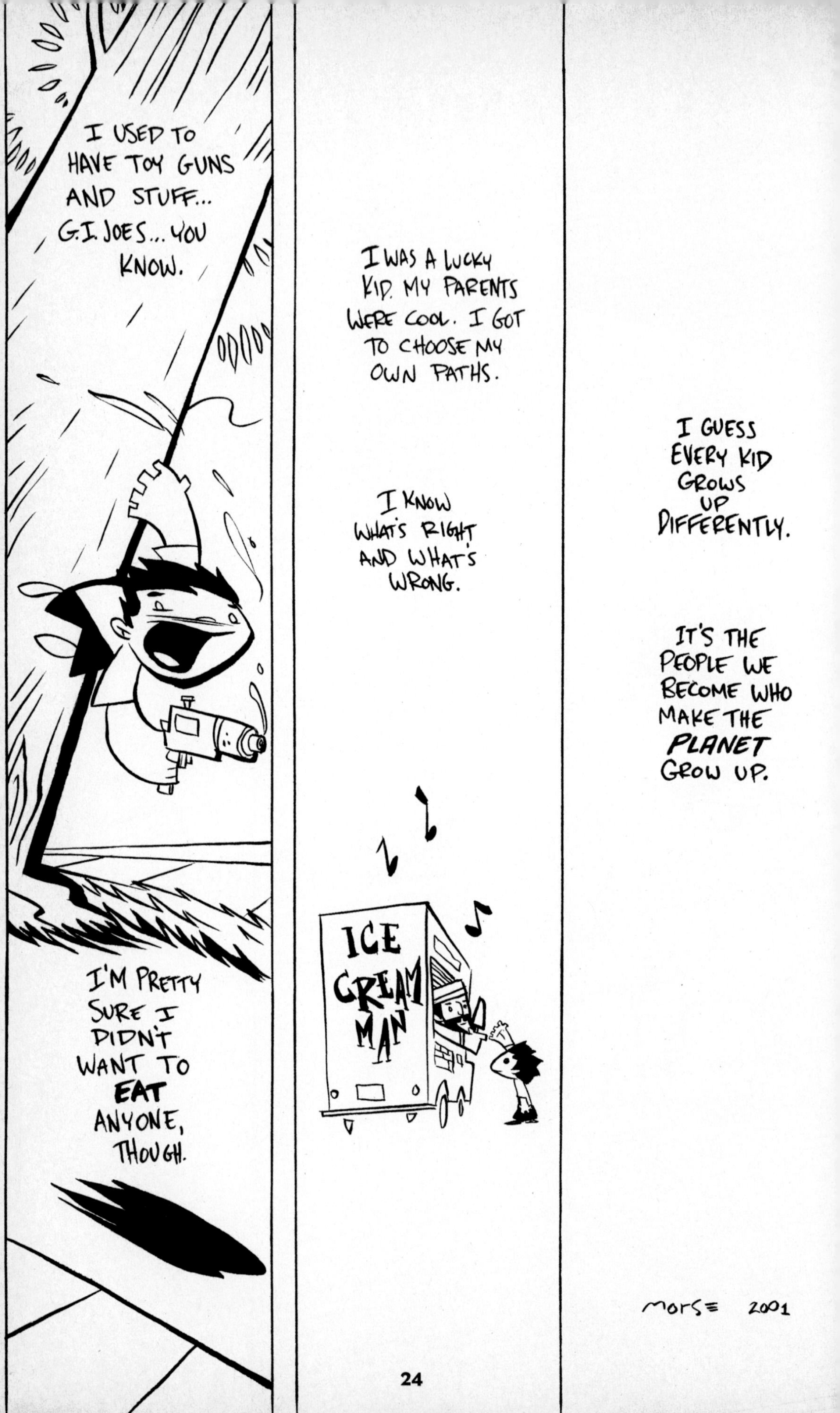
I USED TO HAVE TOY GUNS AND STUFF... G.I. JOES... YOU KNOW.
I'M PRETTY SURE I DIDN'T WANT TO EAT ANYONE, THOUGH.
I WAS A LUCKY KID. MY PARENTS WERE COOL. I GOT TO CHOOSE MY OWN PATHS.
I KNOW WHAT'S RIGHT AND WHAT'S WRONG.
ICE CREAM MAN
I GUESS EVERY KID GROWS UP DIFFERENTLY.
IT'S THE PEOPLE WE BECOME WHO MAKE THE PLANET GROW UP.
morse 2001

Phil Elliott

"After so many deaths I live and write" - George Herbert

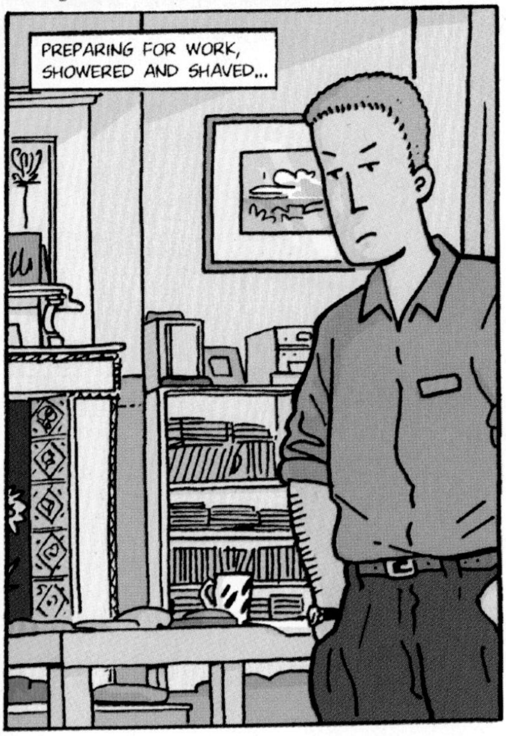
PREPARING FOR WORK,
SHOWERED AND SHAVED...

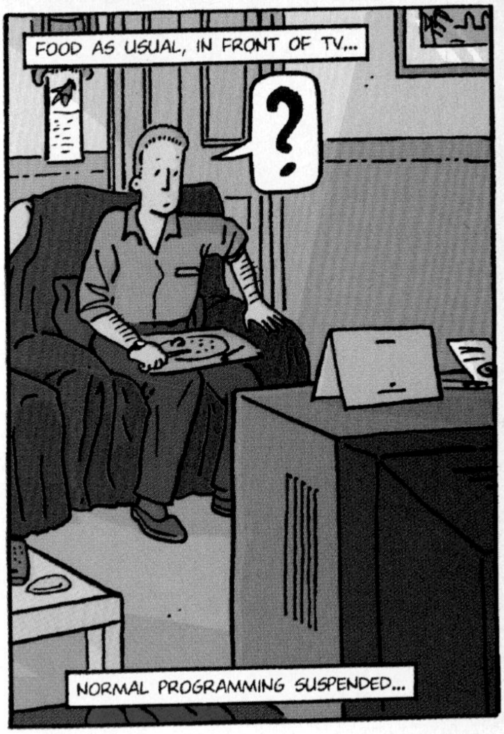
FOOD AS USUAL, IN FRONT OF TV...
?
NORMAL PROGRAMMING SUSPENDED...

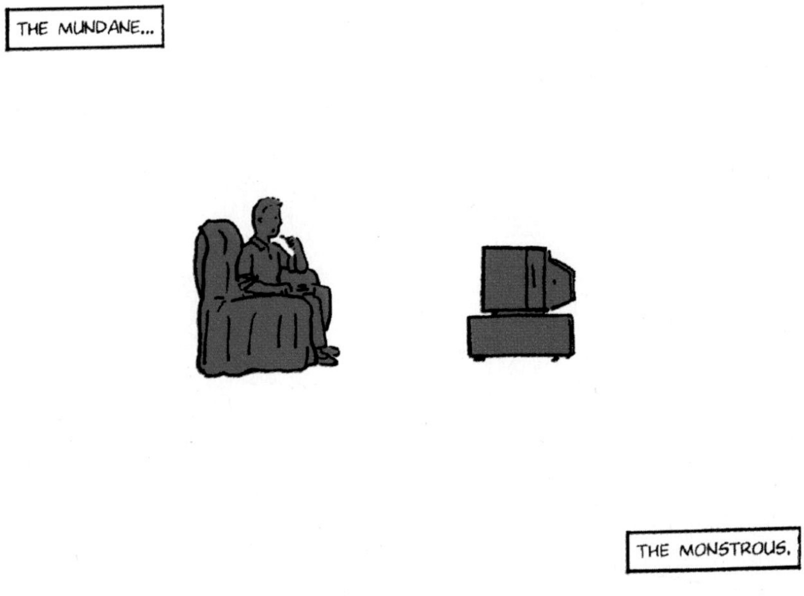
THE MUNDANE...
THE MONSTROUS.

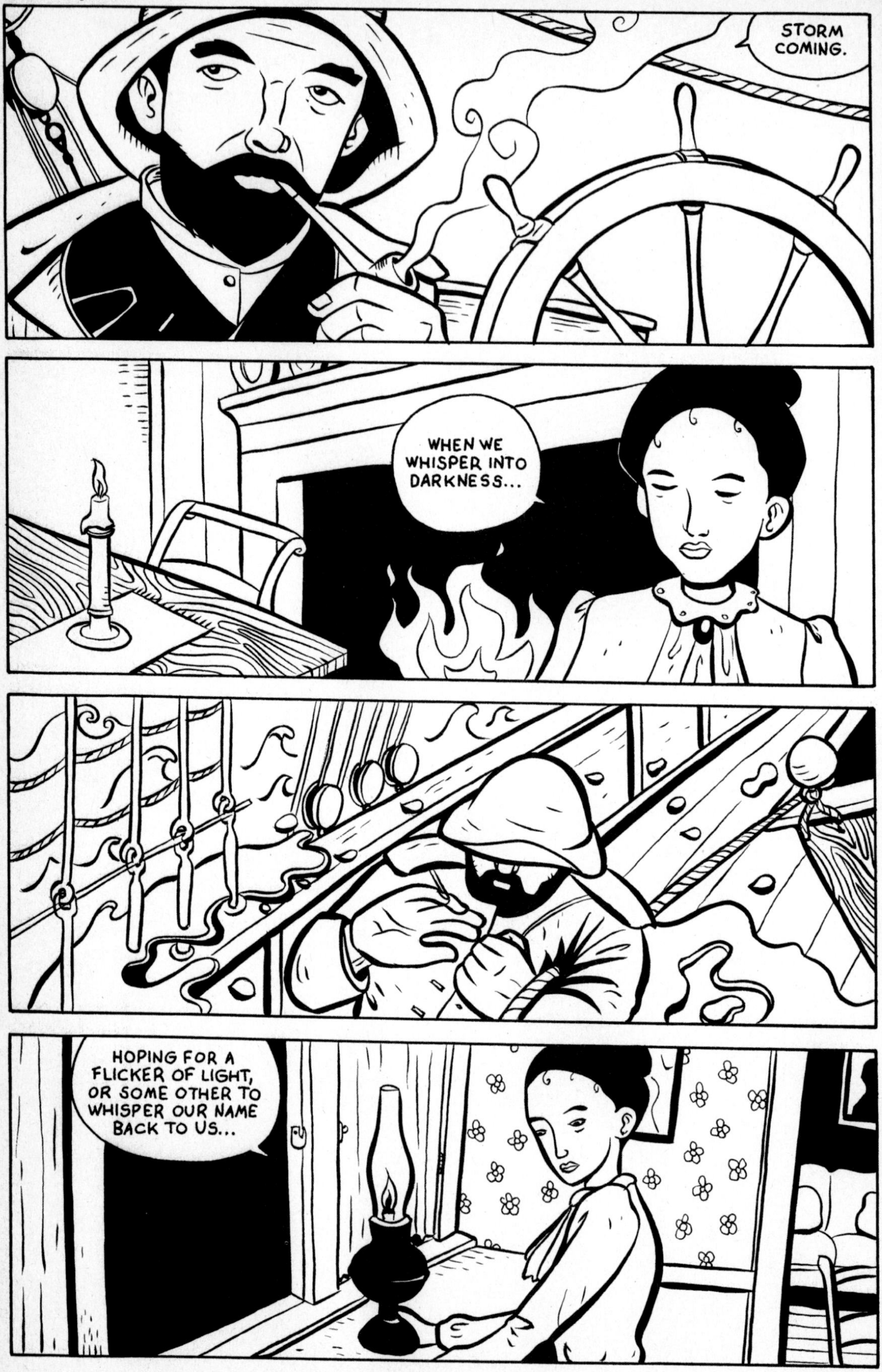
STORM COMING.
WHEN WE WHISPER INTO DARKNESS...
HOPING FOR A FLICKER OF LIGHT, OR SOME OTHER TO WHISPER OUR NAME BACK TO US...

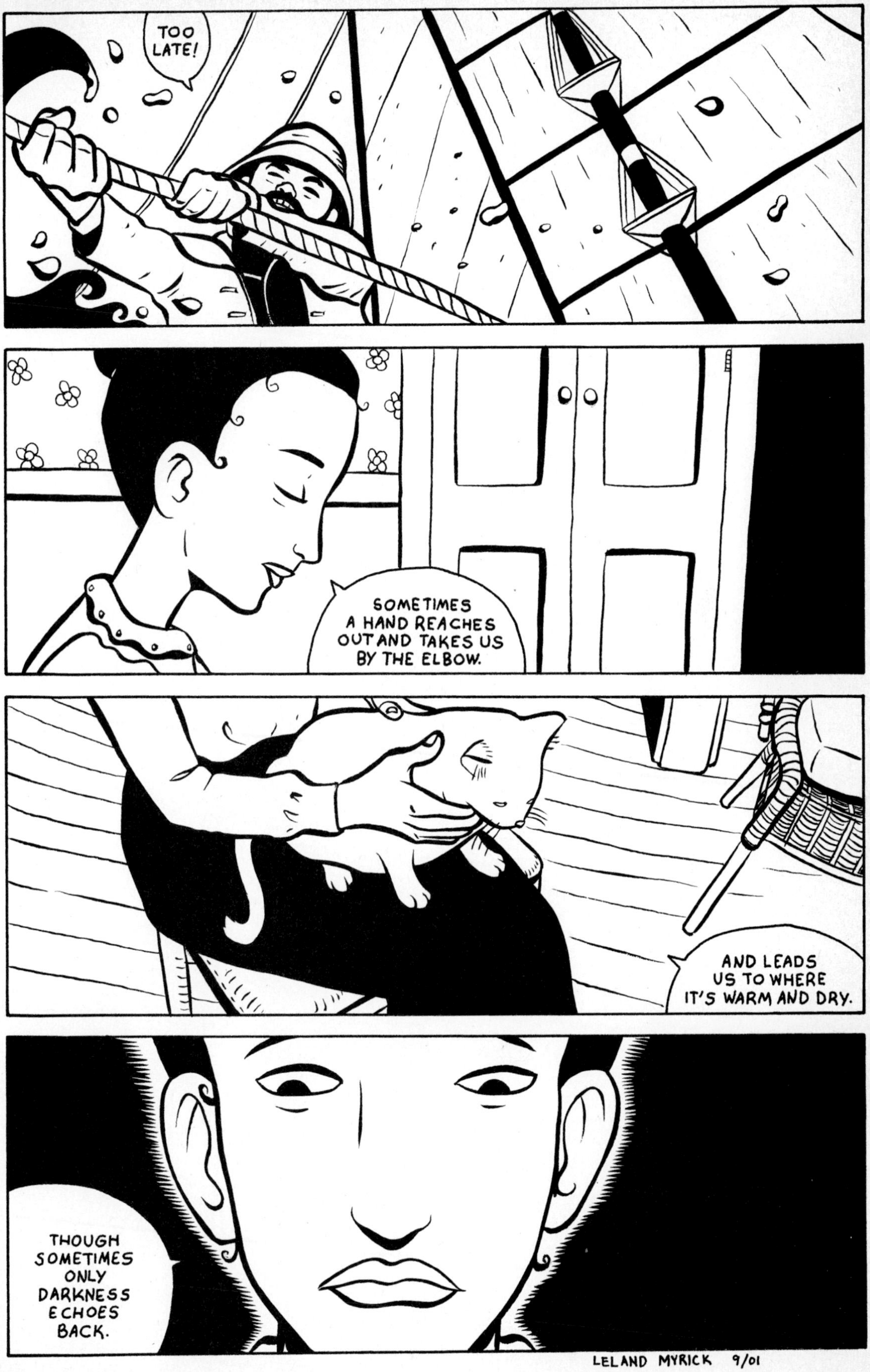
TOO LATE!
SOMETIMES A HAND REACHES OUT AND TAKES US BY THE ELBOW.
AND LEADS US TO WHERE IT'S WARM AND DRY.
THOUGH SOMETIMES ONLY DARKNESS ECHOES BACK.
LELAND MYRICK 9/01

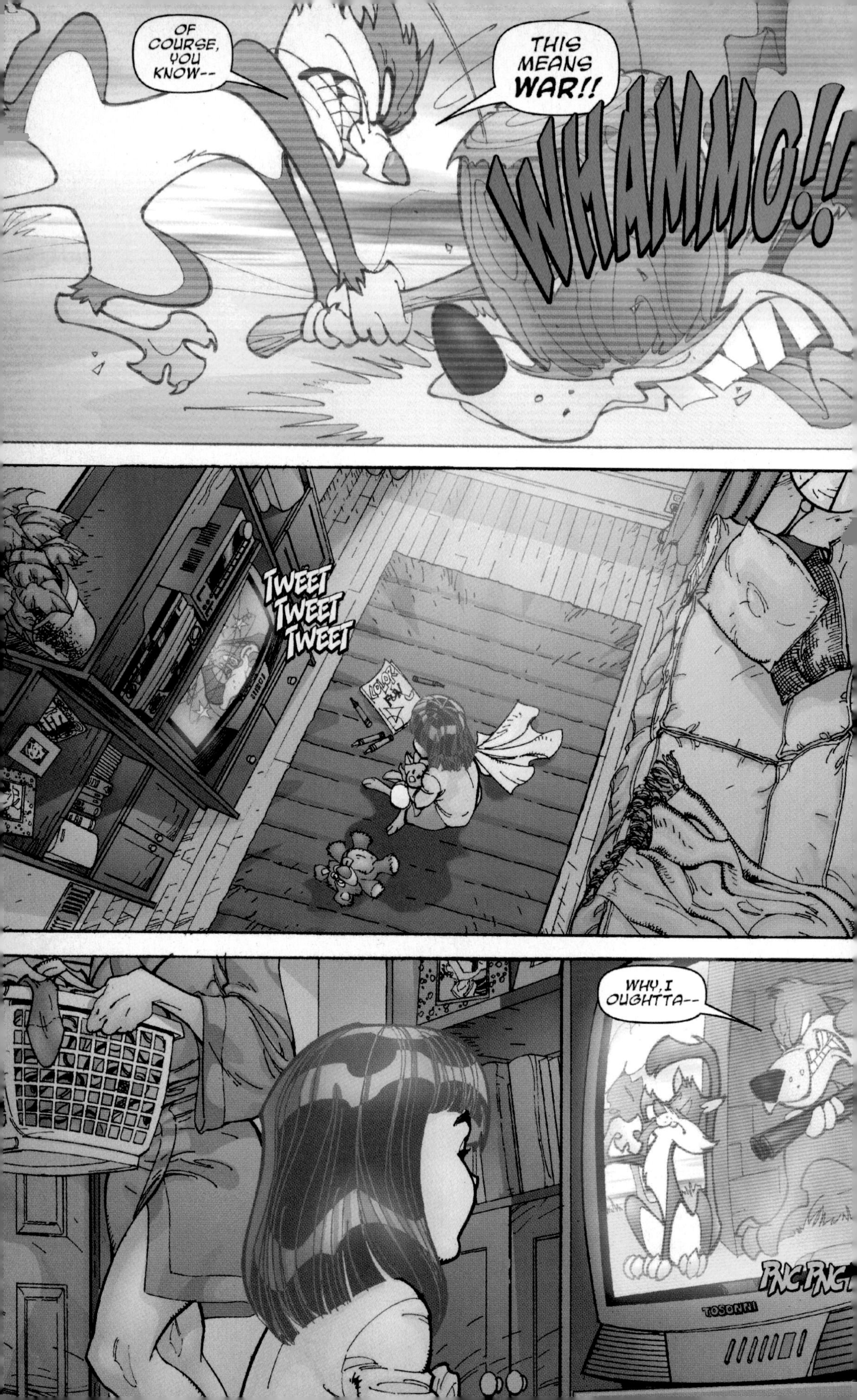
OF COURSE, YOU KNOW--
THIS MEANS WAR!!
WHAMMO!!
TWEET TWEET TWEET
WHY, I OUGHTTA--
PNC PNC
TOSONNI

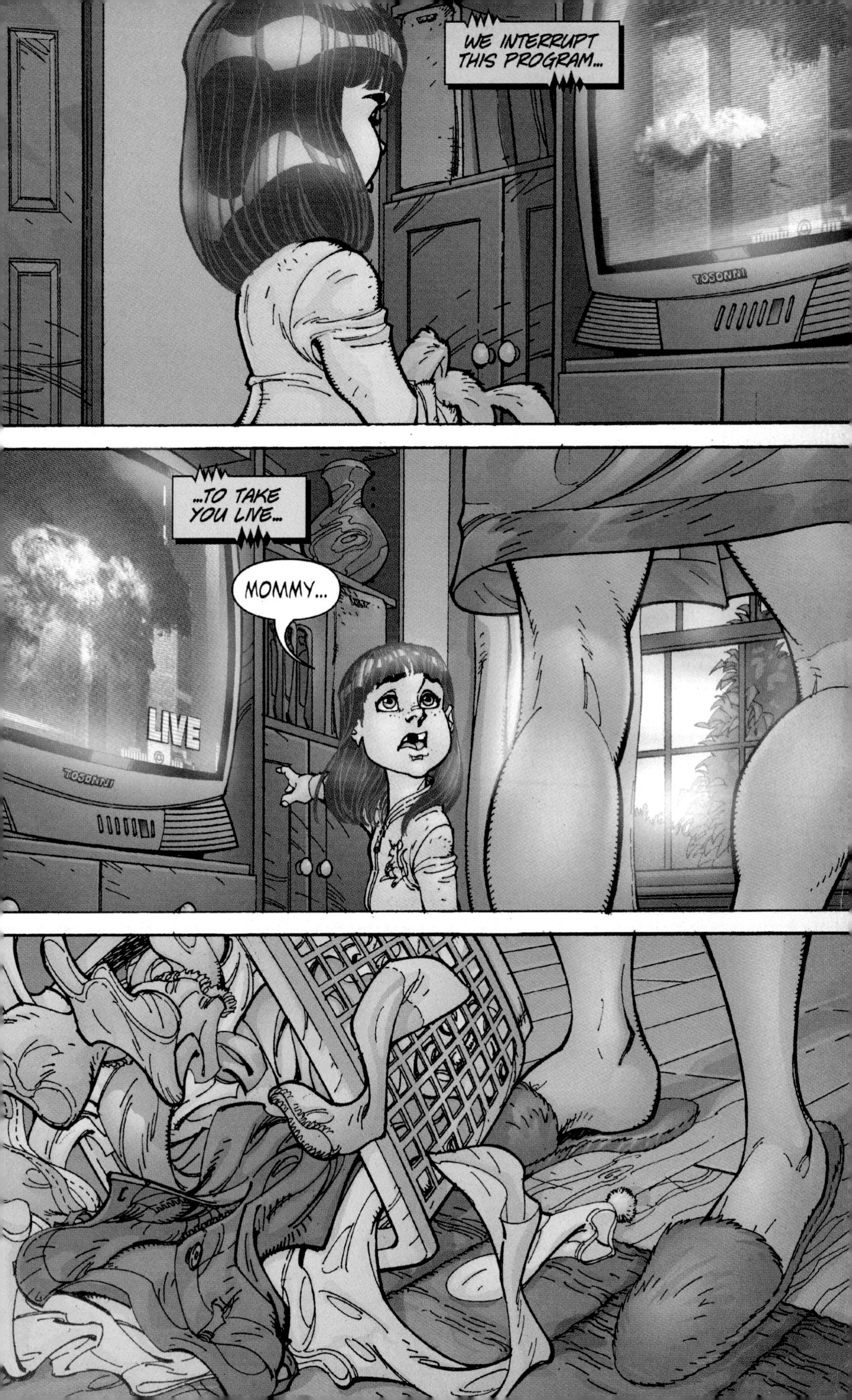
WE INTERRUPT THIS PROGRAM...
TOSONNI
...TO TAKE YOU LIVE...
MOMMY...
LIVE
TOSONNI

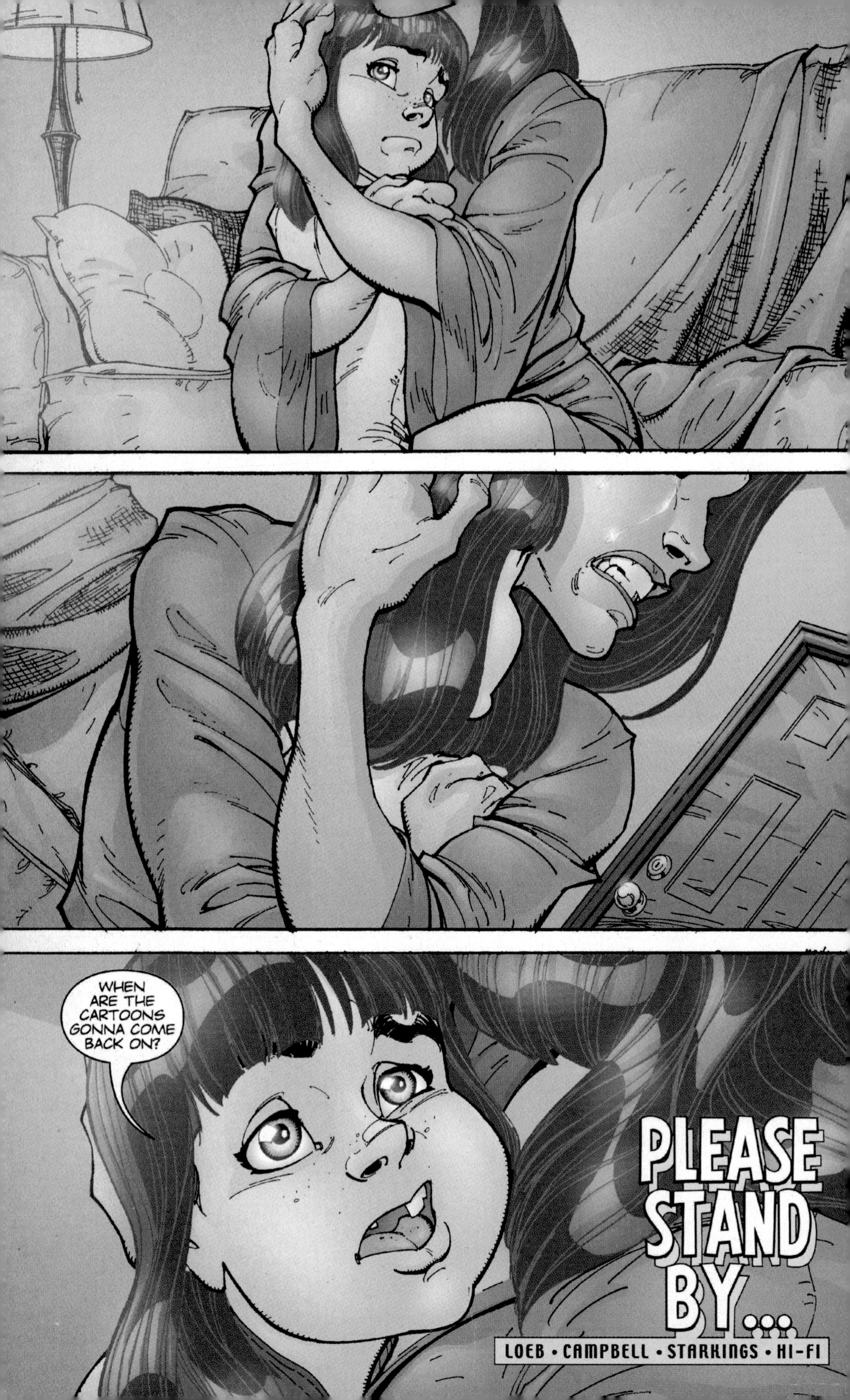
WHEN ARE THE CARTOONS GONNA COME BACK ON?
PLEASE STAND BY...
LOEB • CAMPBELL • STARKINGS • HI-FI

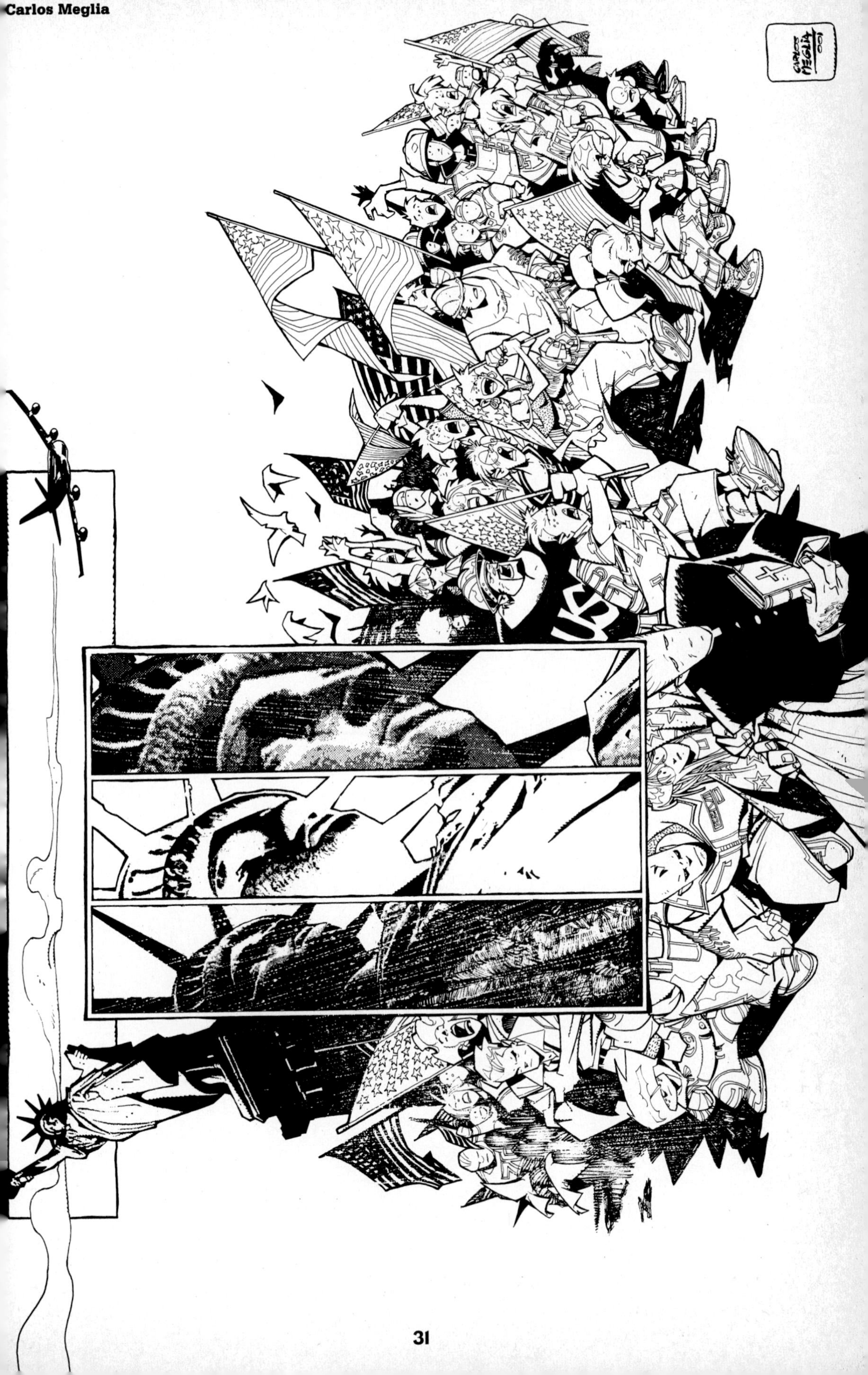
CARLOS MEGLIA

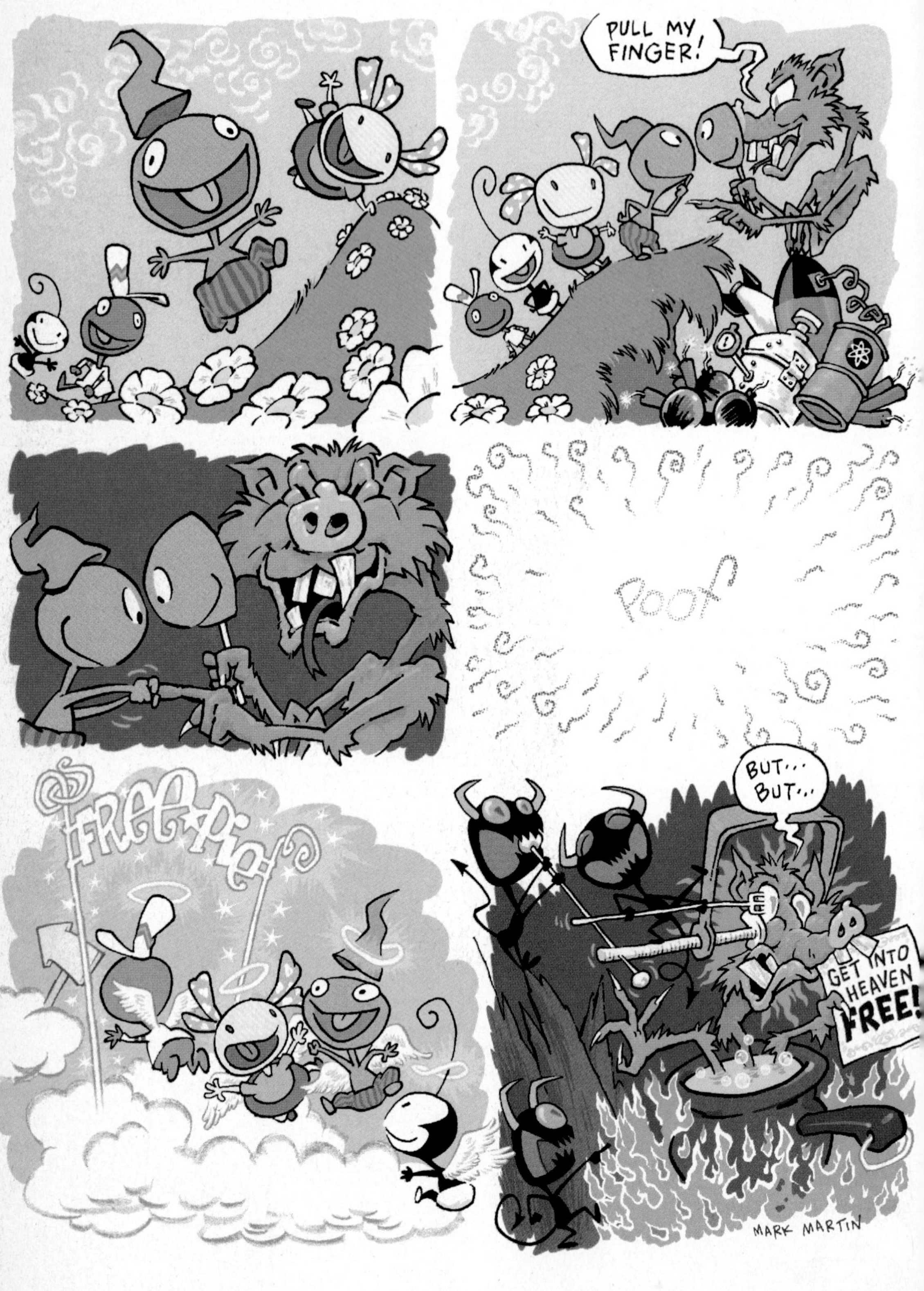
PULL MY FINGER!
POOF
FREE PIE
BUT... BUT...
GET INTO HEAVEN FREE!
MARK MARTIN

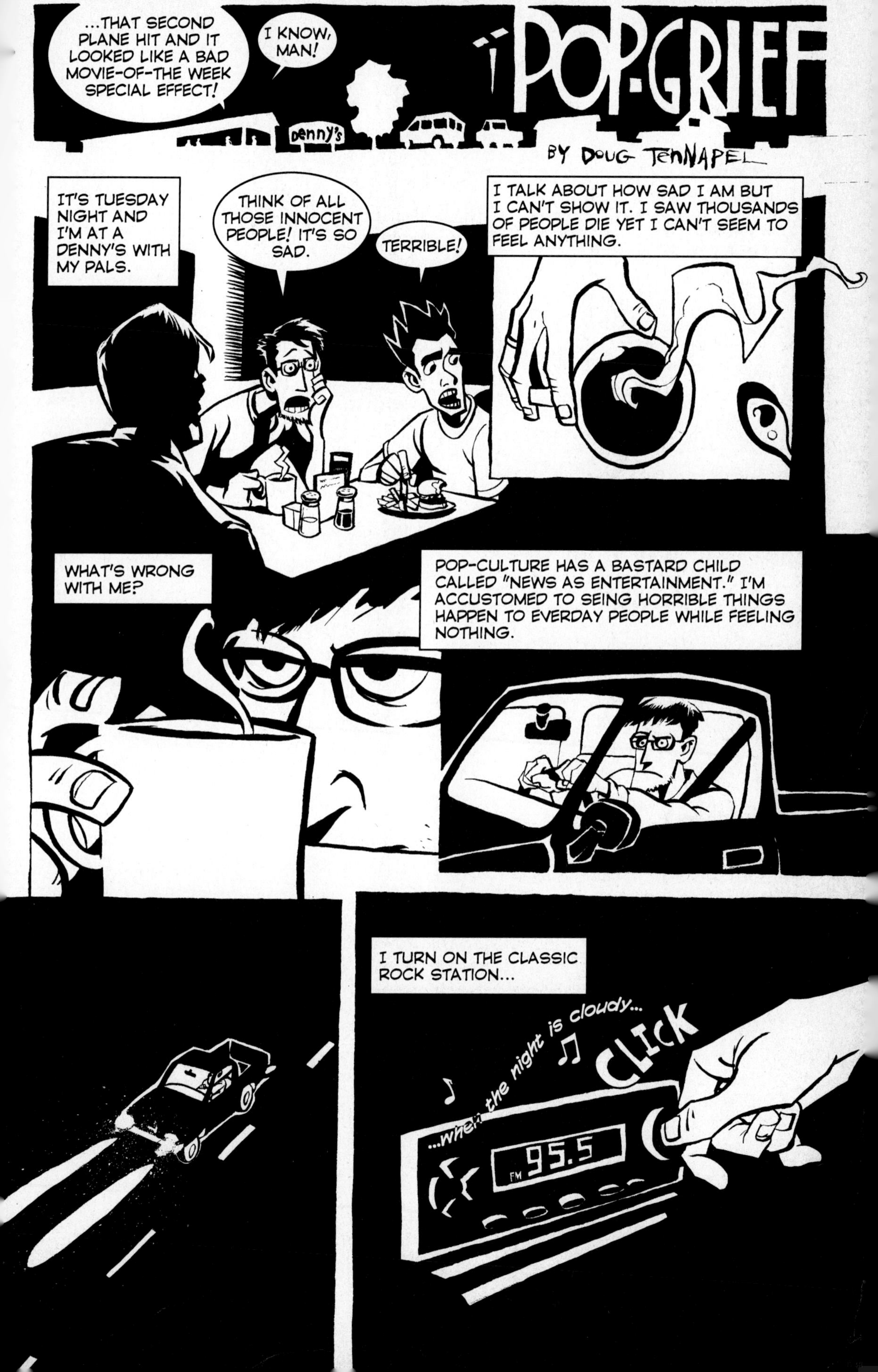

...THAT SECOND PLANE HIT AND IT LOOKED LIKE A BAD MOVIE-OF-THE WEEK SPECIAL EFFECT!
I KNOW, MAN!
POP-GRIEF
DENNY'S
BY DOUG TENNAPEL
IT'S TUESDAY NIGHT AND I'M AT A DENNY'S WITH MY PALS.
THINK OF ALL THOSE INNOCENT PEOPLE! IT'S SO SAD.
TERRIBLE!
I TALK ABOUT HOW SAD I AM BUT I CAN'T SHOW IT. I SAW THOUSANDS OF PEOPLE DIE YET I CAN'T SEEM TO FEEL ANYTHING.
WHAT'S WRONG WITH ME?
POP-CULTURE HAS A BASTARD CHILD CALLED "NEWS AS ENTERTAINMENT." I'M ACCUSTOMED TO SEING HORRIBLE THINGS HAPPEN TO EVERDAY PEOPLE WHILE FEELING NOTHING.
I TURN ON THE CLASSIC ROCK STATION...
...when the night is cloudy...
CLICK
FM 95.5

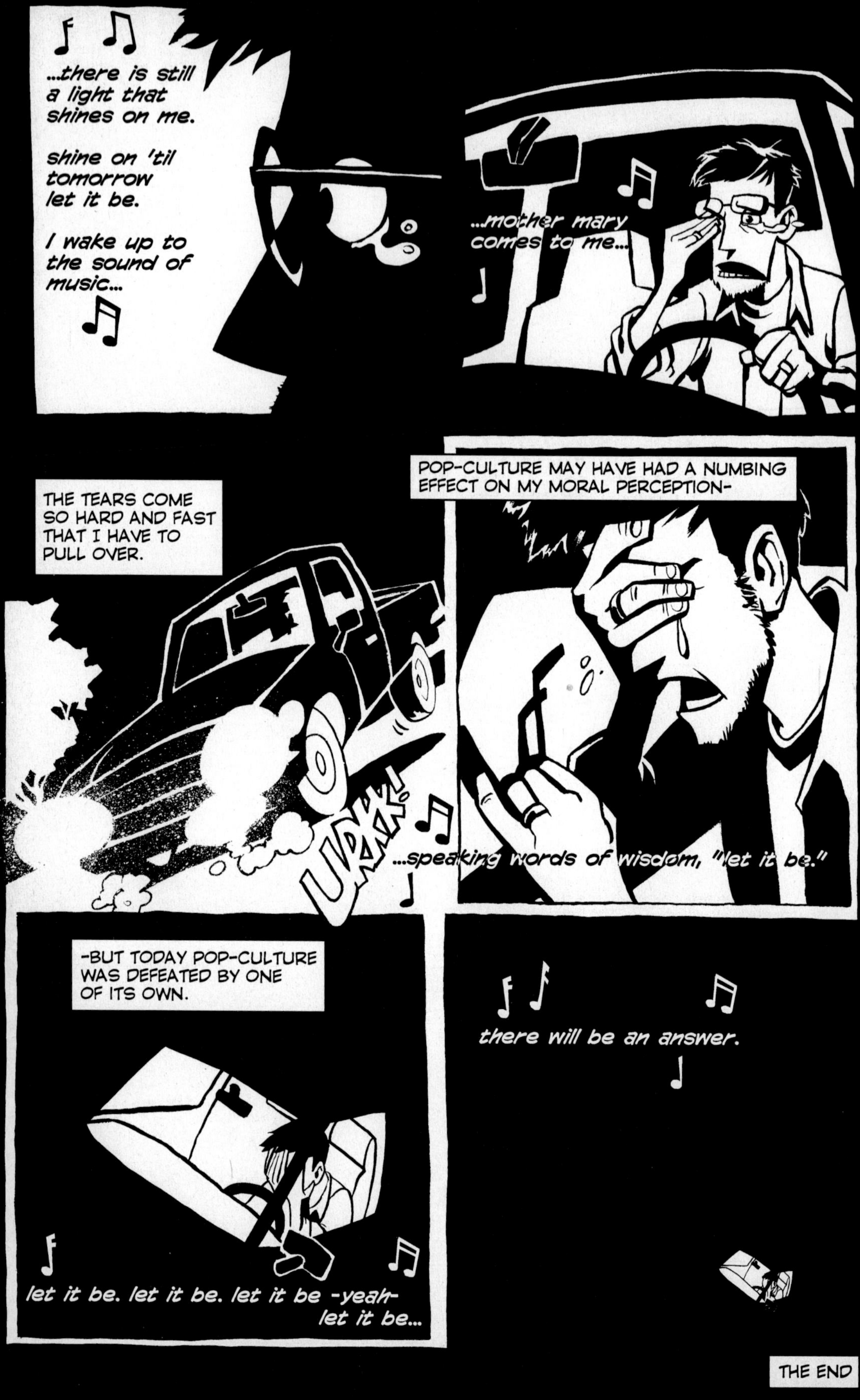

...there is still a light that shines on me.
shine on 'til tomorrow let it be.
I wake up to the sound of music...
...mother mary comes to me...
THE TEARS COME SO HARD AND FAST THAT I HAVE TO PULL OVER.
POP-CULTURE MAY HAVE HAD A NUMBING EFFECT ON MY MORAL PERCEPTION-
...speaking words of wisdom, "let it be."
-BUT TODAY POP-CULTURE WAS DEFEATED BY ONE OF ITS OWN.
let it be. let it be. let it be -yeah- let it be...
there will be an answer.
THE END

Leinil Francis Yu

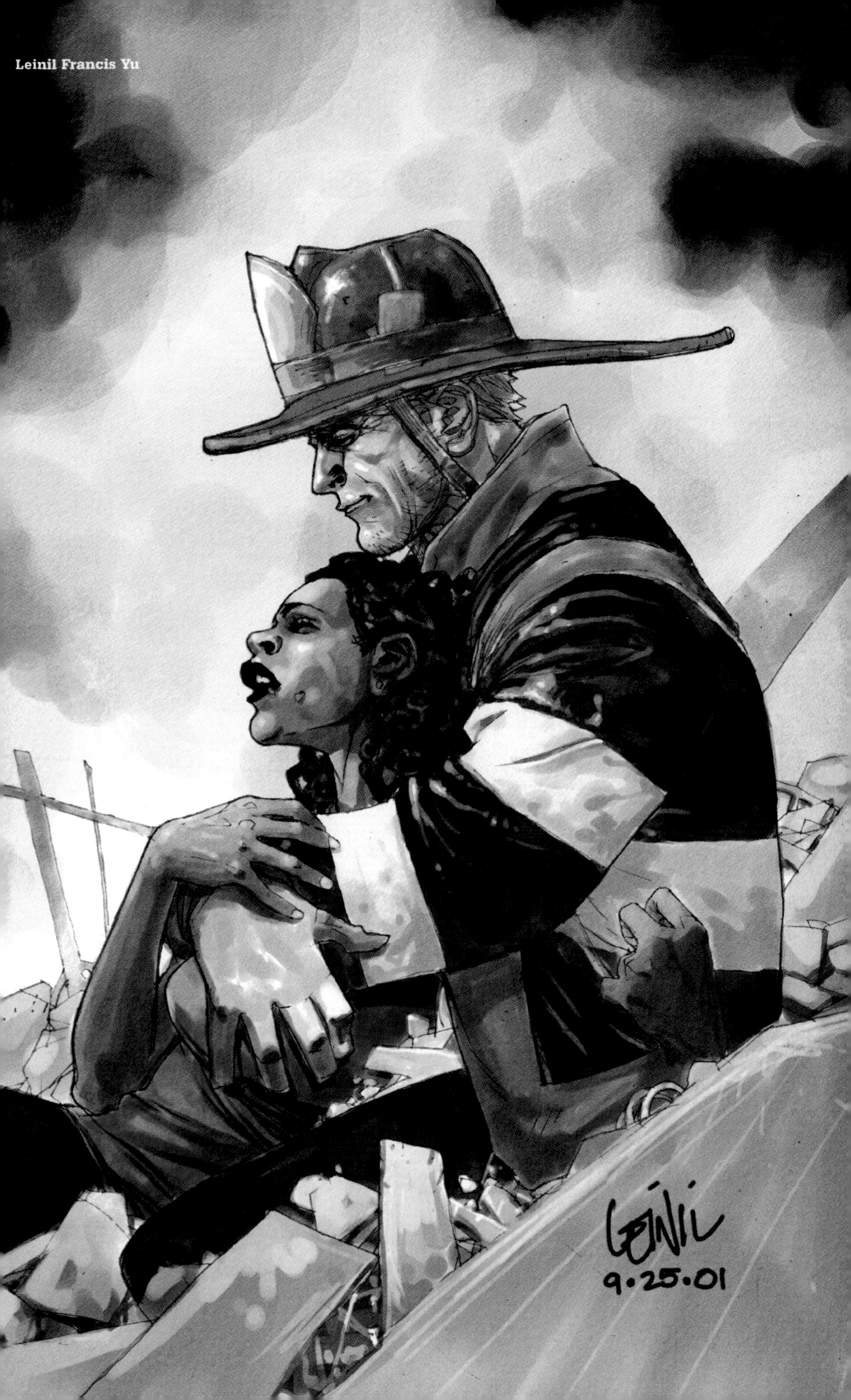
LEINIL
9.25.01

Mike Diana

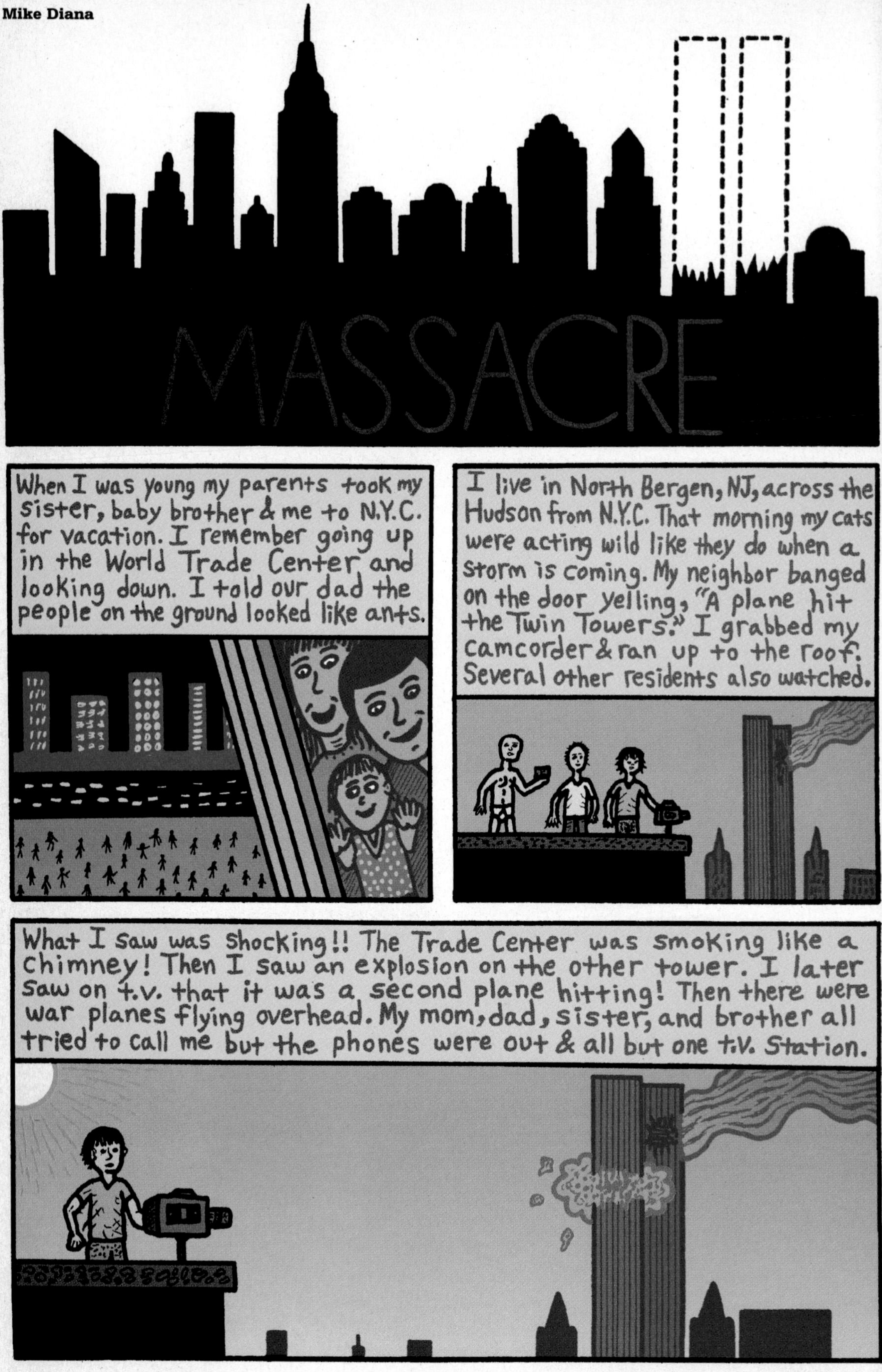
MASSACRE
When I was young my parents took my sister, baby brother & me to N.Y.C. for vacation. I remember going up in the World Trade Center and looking down. I told our dad the people on the ground looked like ants.
I live in North Bergen, NJ, across the Hudson from N.Y.C. That morning my cats were acting wild like they do when a storm is coming. My neighbor banged on the door yelling, "A plane hit the Twin Towers." I grabbed my camcorder & ran up to the roof. Several other residents also watched.
What I saw was shocking!! The Trade Center was smoking like a chimney! Then I saw an explosion on the other tower. I later saw on t.v. that it was a second plane hitting! Then there were war planes flying overhead. My mom, dad, sister, and brother all tried to call me but the phones were out & all but one t.v. station.

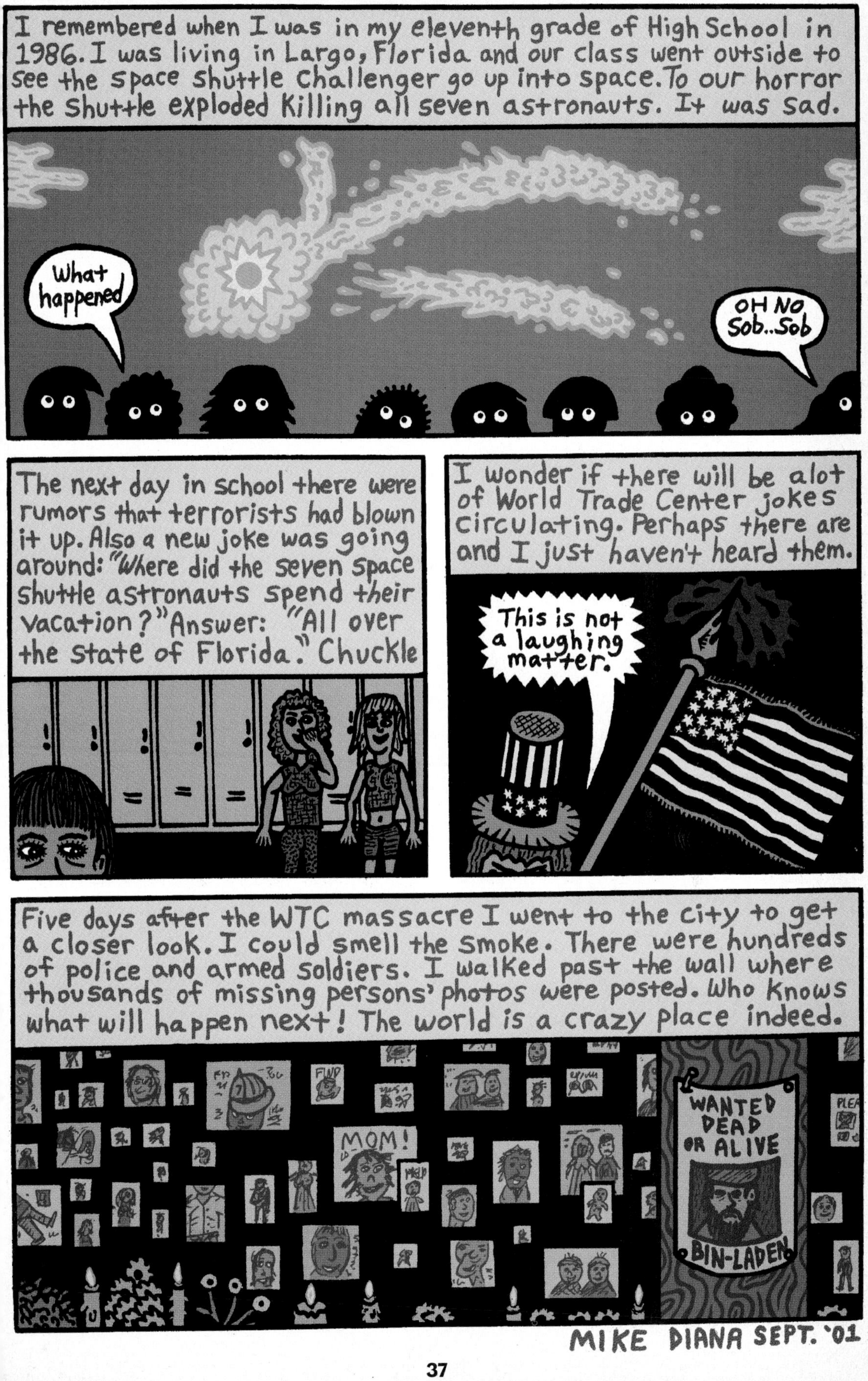
I remembered when I was in my eleventh grade of High School in 1986. I was living in Largo, Florida and our class went outside to see the space shuttle Challenger go up into space. To our horror the Shuttle exploded Killing all seven astronauts. It was sad.
What happened
OH NO Sob..Sob
The next day in school there were rumors that terrorists had blown it up. Also a new joke was going around: "Where did the seven space shuttle astronauts spend their vacation?" Answer: "All over the state of Florida." Chuckle
I wonder if there will be alot of World Trade Center jokes circulating. Perhaps there are and I just haven't heard them.
This is not a laughing matter.
Five days after the WTC massacre I went to the city to get a closer look. I could smell the smoke. There were hundreds of police and armed soldiers. I walked past the wall where thousands of missing persons' photos were posted. Who Knows what will happen next! The world is a crazy place indeed.
MOM!
WANTED DEAD OR ALIVE
BIN-LADEN
MIKE DIANA SEPT. '01

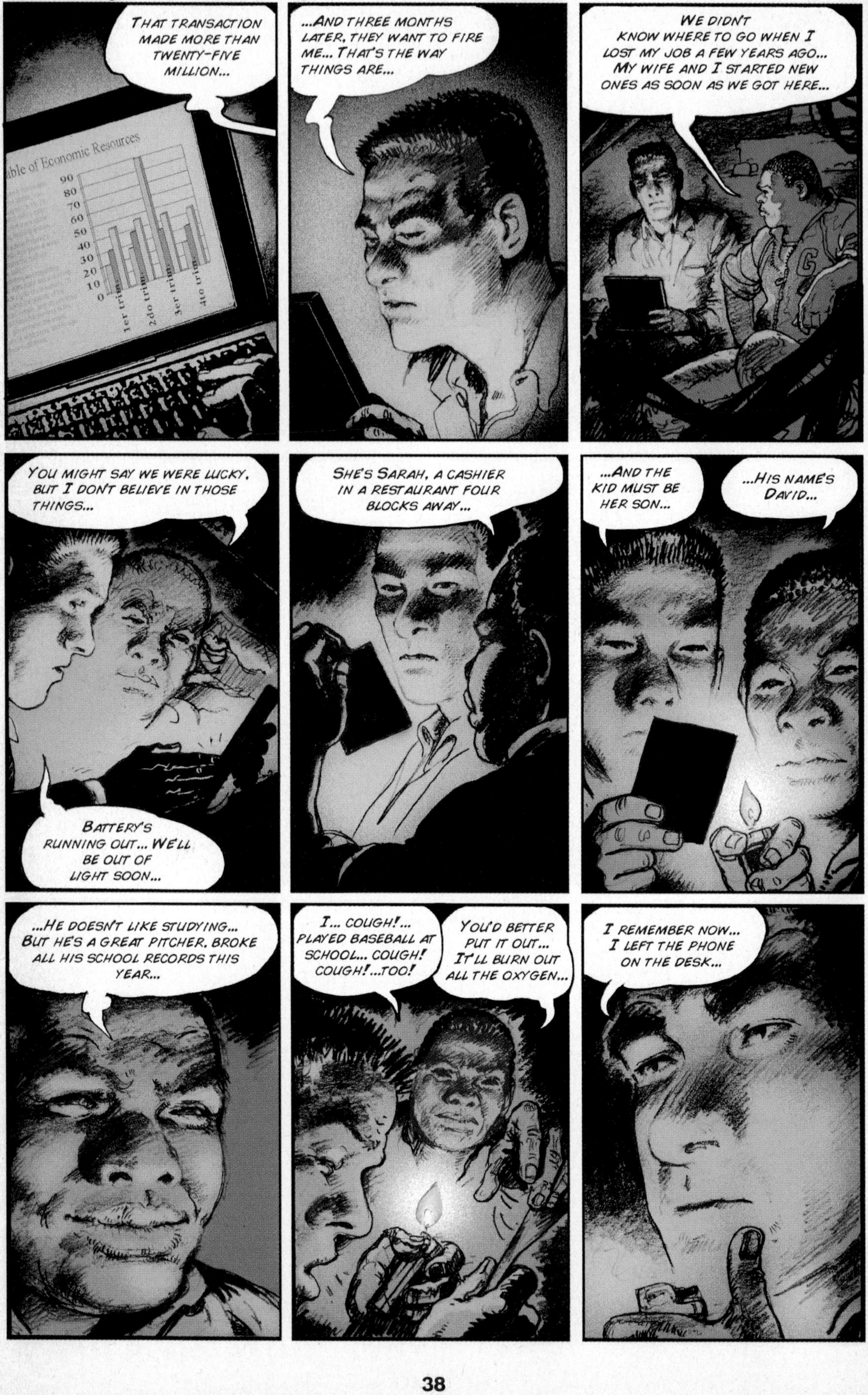
THAT TRANSACTION MADE MORE THAN TWENTY-FIVE MILLION...
...AND THREE MONTHS LATER, THEY WANT TO FIRE ME... THAT'S THE WAY THINGS ARE...
WE DIDN'T KNOW WHERE TO GO WHEN I LOST MY JOB A FEW YEARS AGO... MY WIFE AND I STARTED NEW ONES AS SOON AS WE GOT HERE...
YOU MIGHT SAY WE WERE LUCKY, BUT I DON'T BELIEVE IN THOSE THINGS...
BATTERY'S RUNNING OUT... WE'LL BE OUT OF LIGHT SOON...
SHE'S SARAH, A CASHIER IN A RESTAURANT FOUR BLOCKS AWAY...
...AND THE KID MUST BE HER SON...
...HIS NAME'S DAVID...
...HE DOESN'T LIKE STUDYING... BUT HE'S A GREAT PITCHER. BROKE ALL HIS SCHOOL RECORDS THIS YEAR...
I... COUGH!... PLAYED BASEBALL AT SCHOOL... COUGH! COUGH!...TOO!
YOU'D BETTER PUT IT OUT... IT'LL BURN OUT ALL THE OXYGEN...
I REMEMBER NOW... I LEFT THE PHONE ON THE DESK...

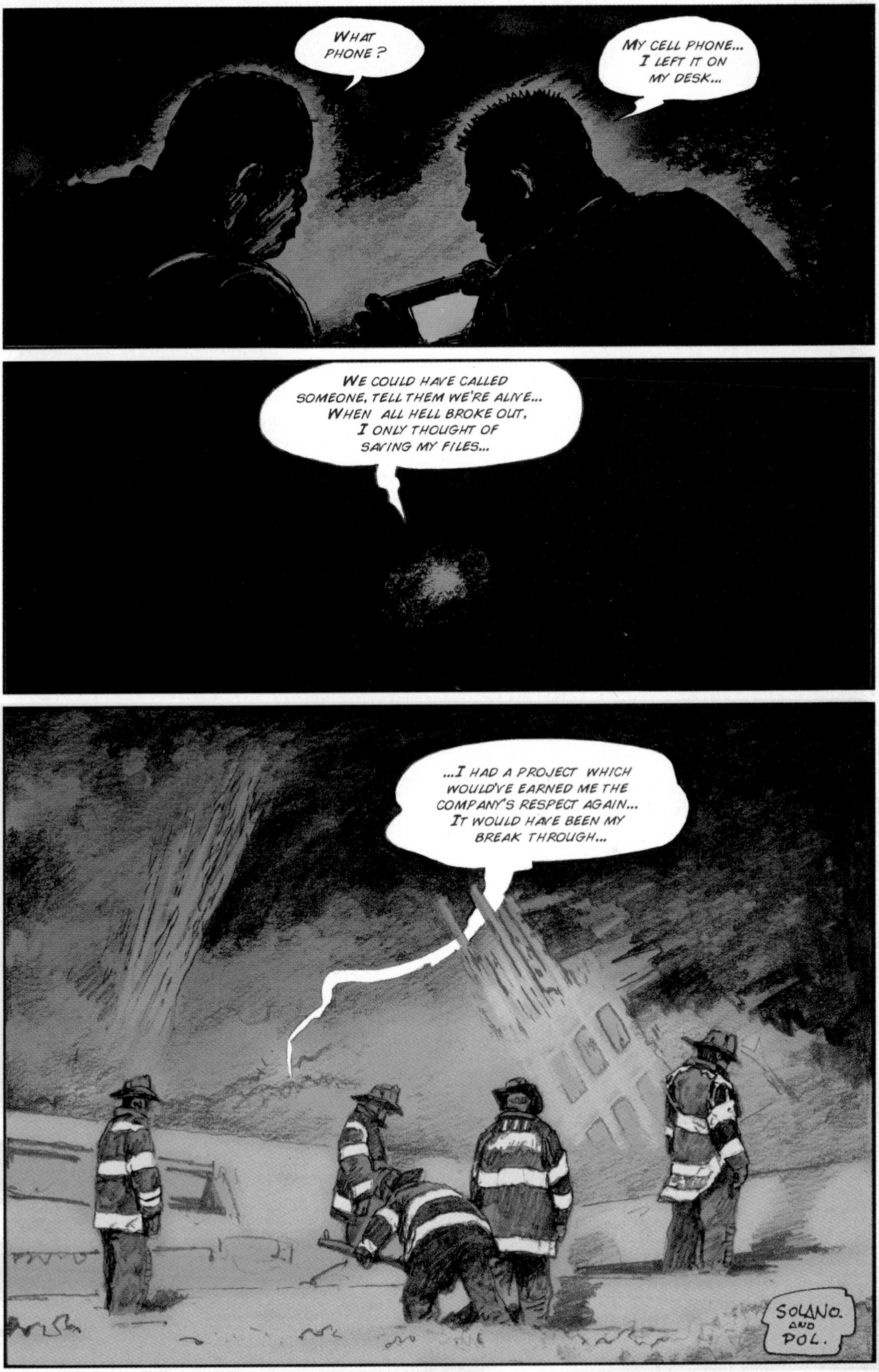
WHAT PHONE?
MY CELL PHONE... I LEFT IT ON MY DESK...
WE COULD HAVE CALLED SOMEONE, TELL THEM WE'RE ALIVE... WHEN ALL HELL BROKE OUT, I ONLY THOUGHT OF SAVING MY FILES...
...I HAD A PROJECT WHICH WOULD'VE EARNED ME THE COMPANY'S RESPECT AGAIN... IT WOULD HAVE BEEN MY BREAK THROUGH...
SOLANO. AND POL.

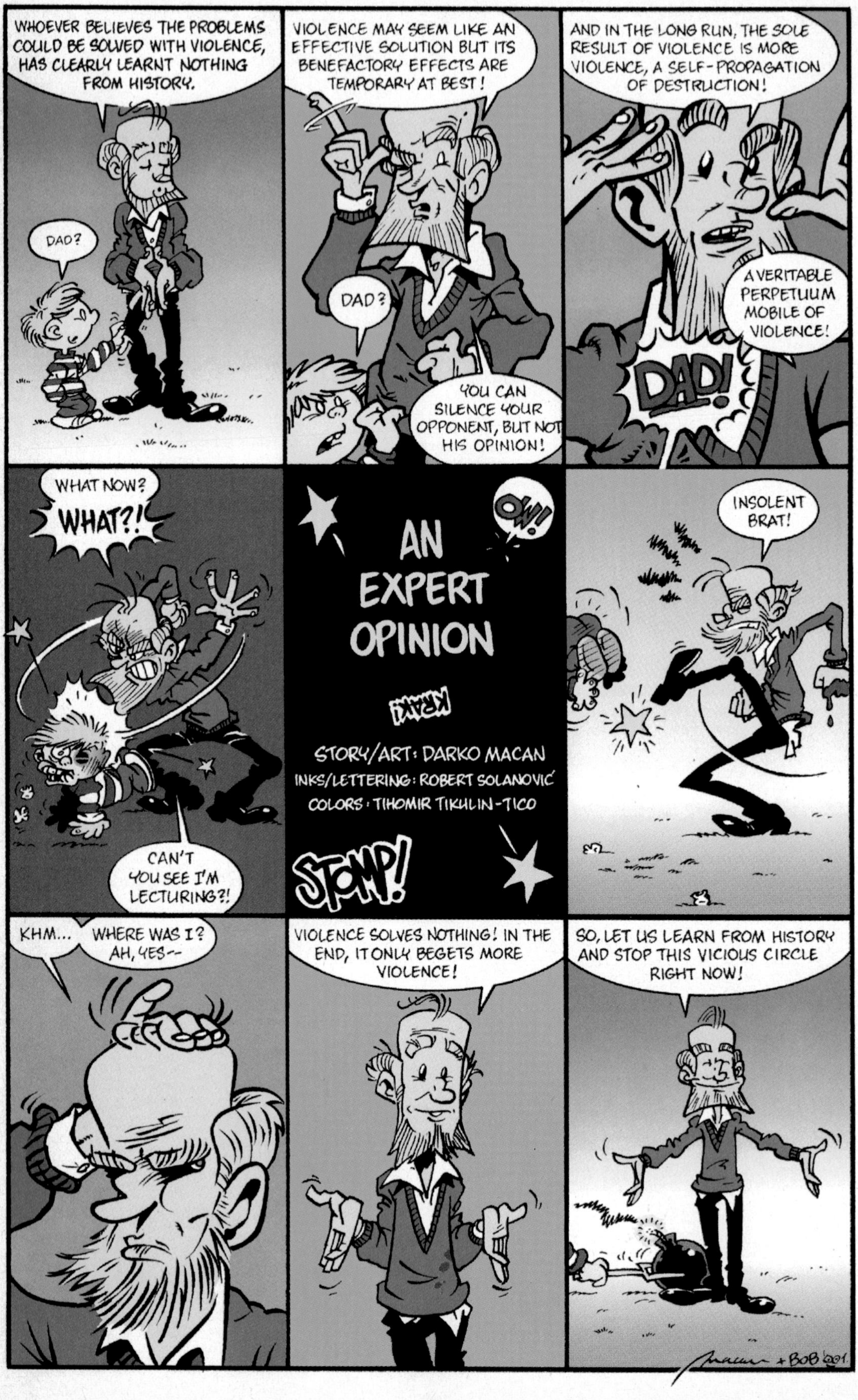
WHOEVER BELIEVES THE PROBLEMS COULD BE SOLVED WITH VIOLENCE, HAS CLEARLY LEARNT NOTHING FROM HISTORY.
DAD?
VIOLENCE MAY SEEM LIKE AN EFFECTIVE SOLUTION BUT ITS BENEFACTORY EFFECTS ARE TEMPORARY AT BEST!
DAD?
YOU CAN SILENCE YOUR OPPONENT, BUT NOT HIS OPINION!
AND IN THE LONG RUN, THE SOLE RESULT OF VIOLENCE IS MORE VIOLENCE, A SELF-PROPAGATION OF DESTRUCTION!
A VERITABLE PERPETUUM MOBILE OF VIOLENCE!
DAD!
WHAT NOW?
WHAT?!
CAN'T YOU SEE I'M LECTURING?!
OW!
AN EXPERT OPINION
KRAK!
STORY/ART: DARKO MACAN
INKS/LETTERING: ROBERT SOLANOVIĆ
COLORS: TIHOMIR TIKULIN-TICO
STOMP!
INSOLENT BRAT!
KHM...
WHERE WAS I? AH, YES--
VIOLENCE SOLVES NOTHING! IN THE END, IT ONLY BEGETS MORE VIOLENCE!
SO, LET US LEARN FROM HISTORY AND STOP THIS VICIOUS CIRCLE RIGHT NOW!

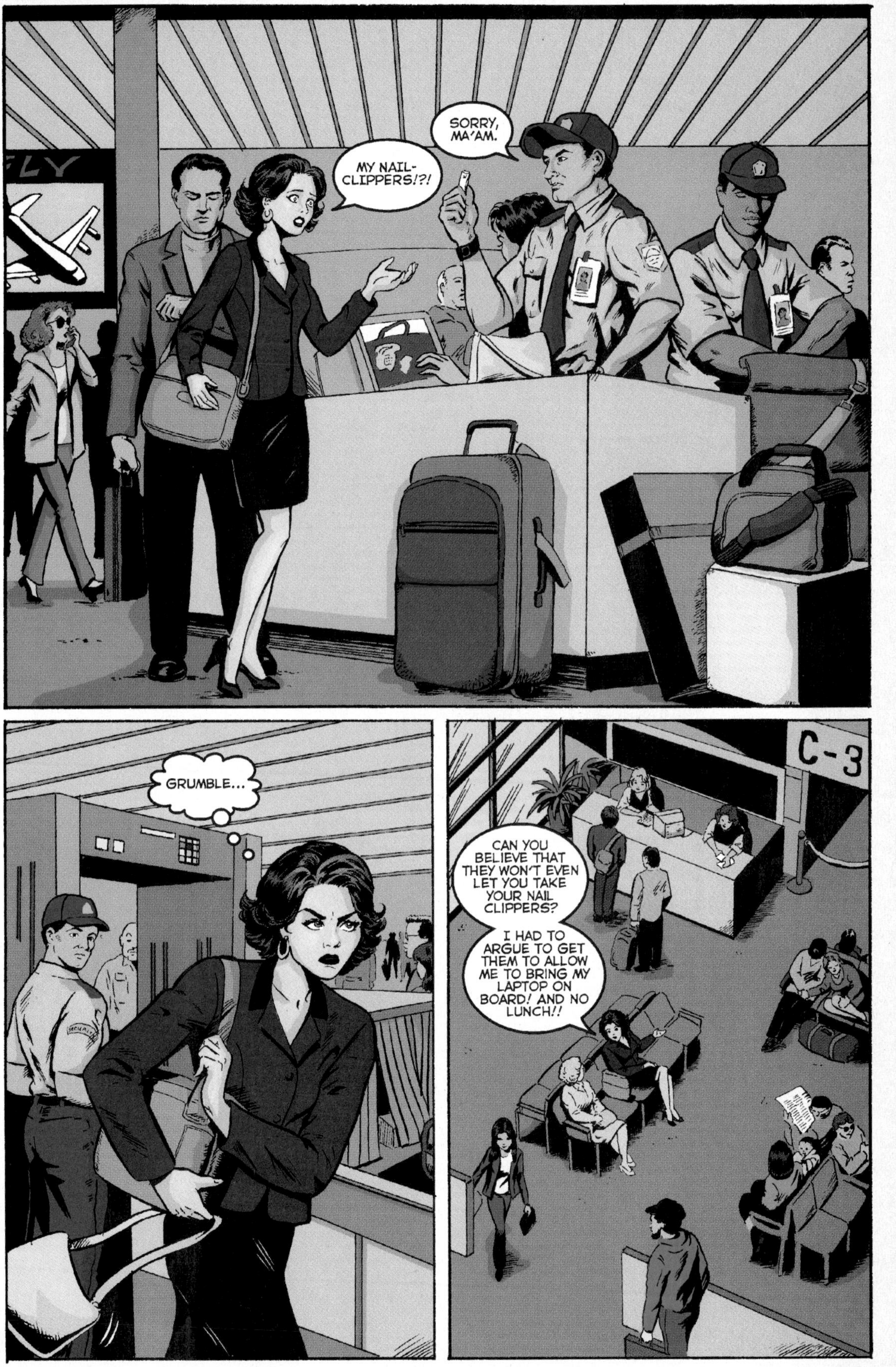
MY NAIL-CLIPPERS!?!
SORRY, MA'AM.
GRUMBLE...
CAN YOU BELIEVE THAT THEY WON'T EVEN LET YOU TAKE YOUR NAIL CLIPPERS?
I HAD TO ARGUE TO GET THEM TO ALLOW ME TO BRING MY LAPTOP ON BOARD! AND NO LUNCH!!
C-3
FLY

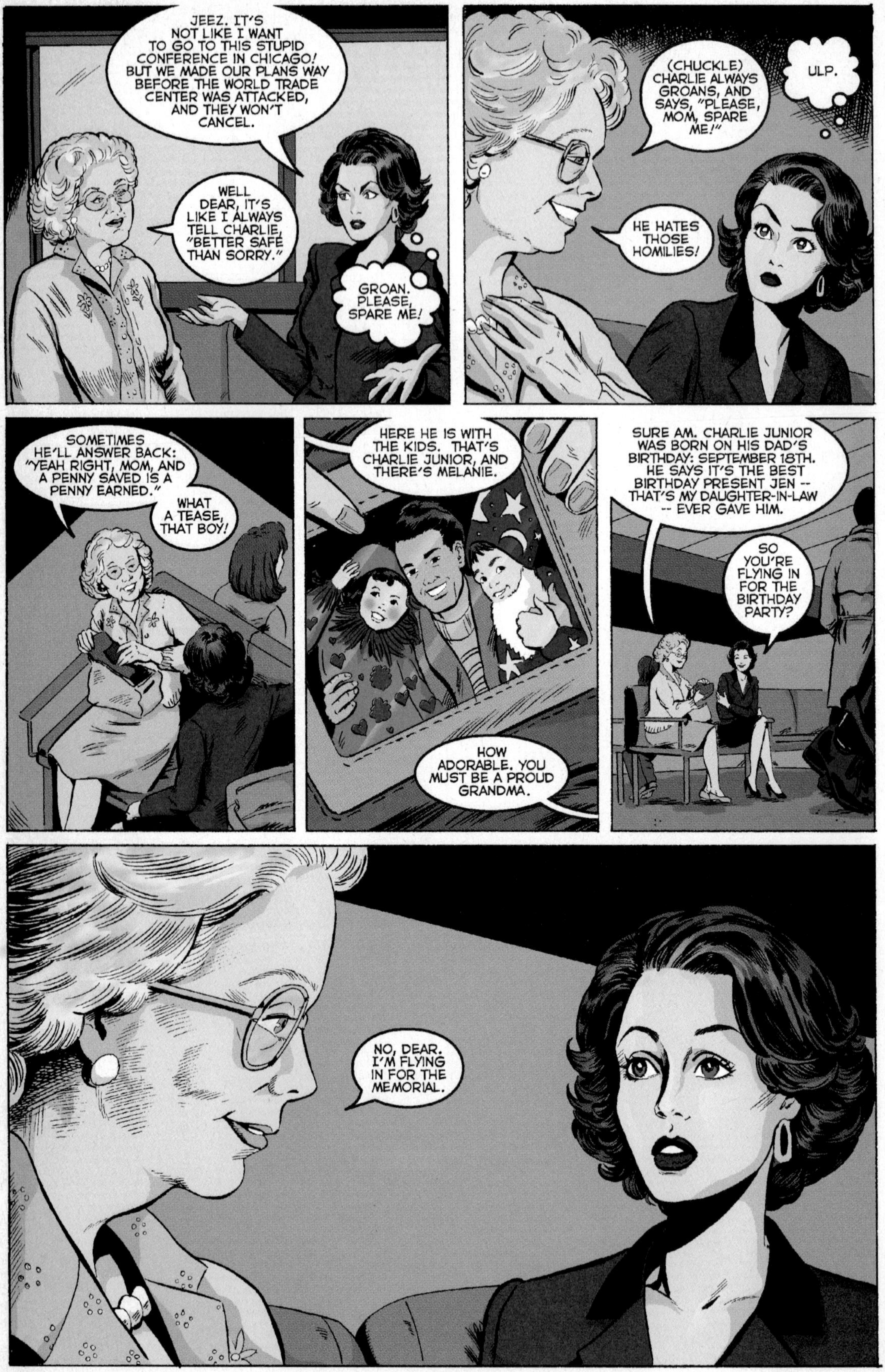
JEEZ. IT'S NOT LIKE I WANT TO GO TO THIS STUPID CONFERENCE IN CHICAGO! BUT WE MADE OUR PLANS WAY BEFORE THE WORLD TRADE CENTER WAS ATTACKED, AND THEY WON'T CANCEL.
WELL DEAR, IT'S LIKE I ALWAYS TELL CHARLIE, "BETTER SAFE THAN SORRY."
GROAN. PLEASE, SPARE ME!
(CHUCKLE) CHARLIE ALWAYS GROANS, AND SAYS, "PLEASE, MOM, SPARE ME!"
ULP.
HE HATES THOSE HOMILIES!
SOMETIMES HE'LL ANSWER BACK: "YEAH RIGHT, MOM, AND A PENNY SAVED IS A PENNY EARNED."
WHAT A TEASE, THAT BOY!
HERE HE IS WITH THE KIDS. THAT'S CHARLIE JUNIOR, AND THERE'S MELANIE.
HOW ADORABLE. YOU MUST BE A PROUD GRANDMA.
SURE AM. CHARLIE JUNIOR WAS BORN ON HIS DAD'S BIRTHDAY: SEPTEMBER 18TH. HE SAYS IT'S THE BEST BIRTHDAY PRESENT JEN -- THAT'S MY DAUGHTER-IN-LAW -- EVER GAVE HIM.
SO YOU'RE FLYING IN FOR THE BIRTHDAY PARTY?
NO, DEAR. I'M FLYING IN FOR THE MEMORIAL.

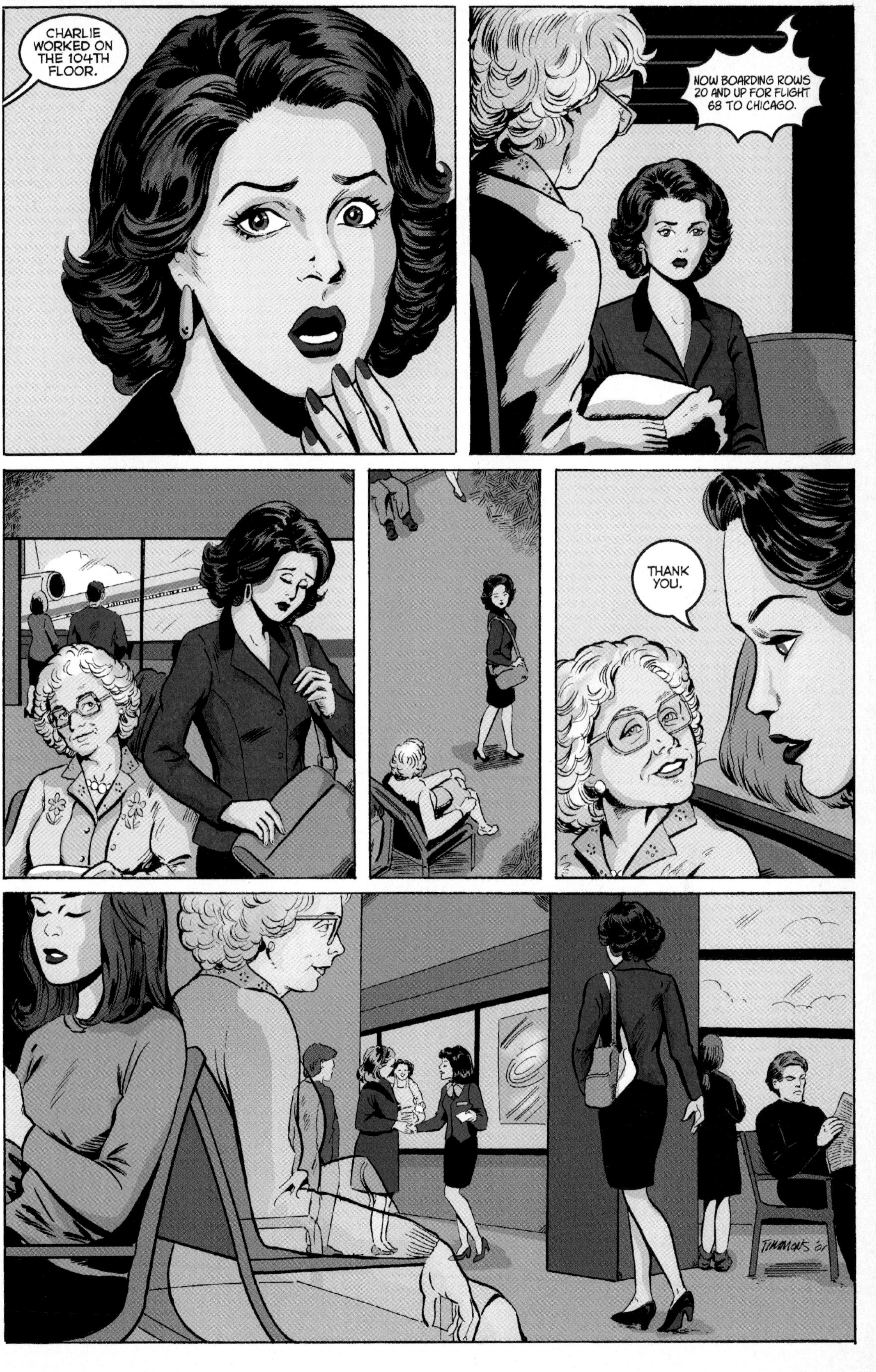
CHARLIE WORKED ON THE 104TH FLOOR.
NOW BOARDING ROWS 20 AND UP FOR FLIGHT 68 TO CHICAGO.
THANK YOU.

9/12
8:36 am
what??
end

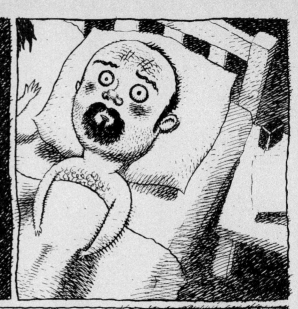

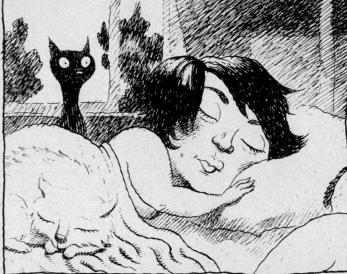

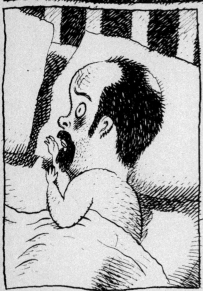

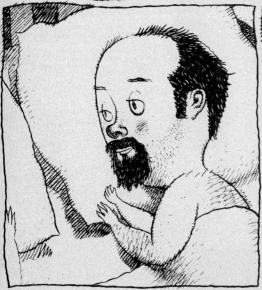

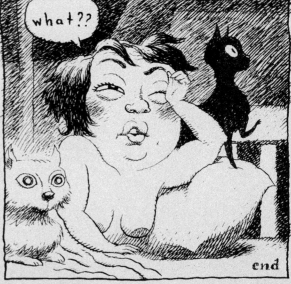

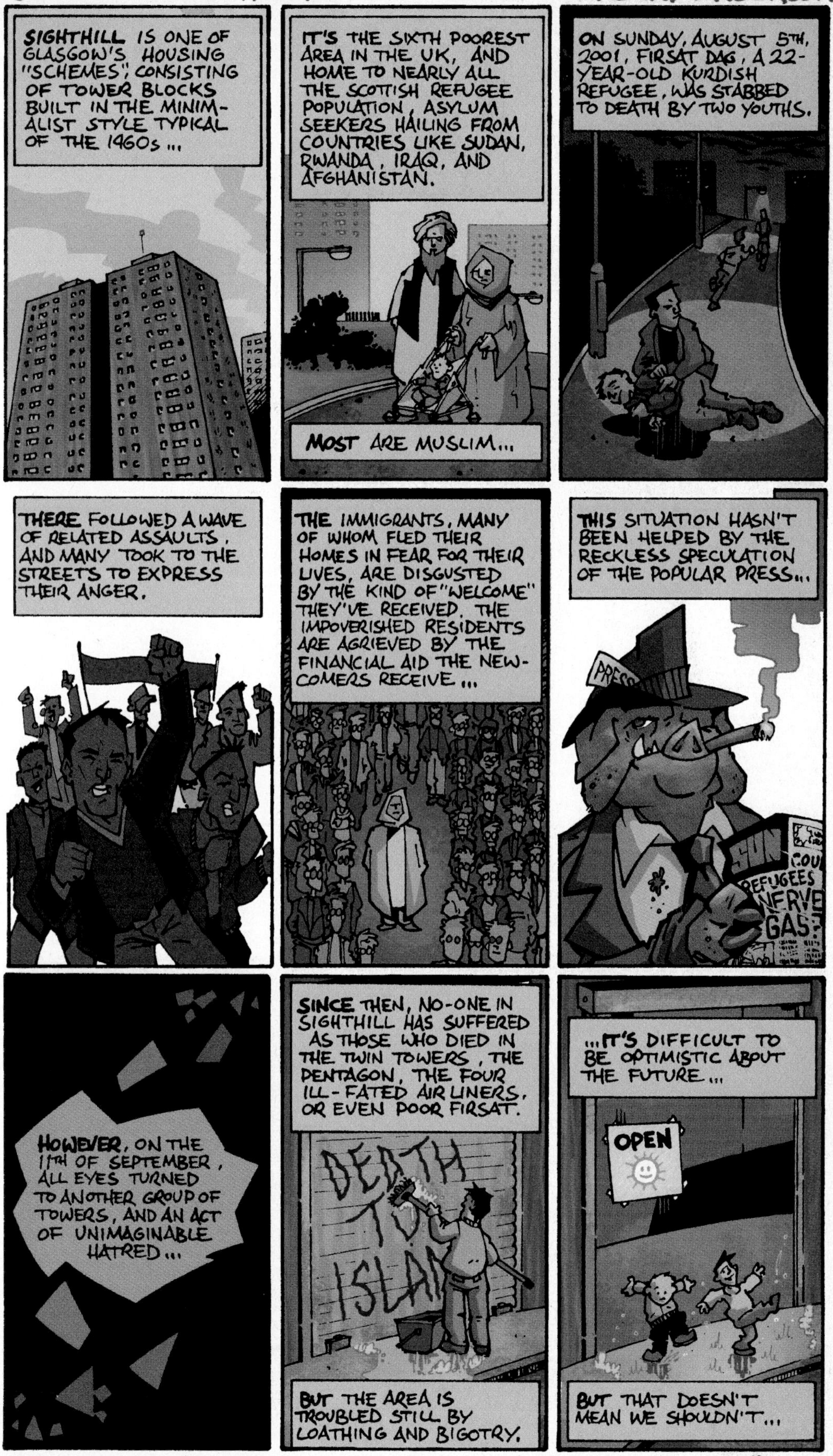
SIGHTHILL IS ONE OF GLASGOW'S HOUSING "SCHEMES", CONSISTING OF TOWER BLOCKS BUILT IN THE MINIMALIST STYLE TYPICAL OF THE 1960s...
IT'S THE SIXTH POOREST AREA IN THE UK, AND HOME TO NEARLY ALL THE SCOTTISH REFUGEE POPULATION, ASYLUM SEEKERS HAILING FROM COUNTRIES LIKE SUDAN, RWANDA, IRAQ, AND AFGHANISTAN.
MOST ARE MUSLIM...
ON SUNDAY, AUGUST 5TH, 2001, FIRSAT DAG, A 22-YEAR-OLD KURDISH REFUGEE, WAS STABBED TO DEATH BY TWO YOUTHS.
THERE FOLLOWED A WAVE OF RELATED ASSAULTS, AND MANY TOOK TO THE STREETS TO EXPRESS THEIR ANGER.
THE IMMIGRANTS, MANY OF WHOM FLED THEIR HOMES IN FEAR FOR THEIR LIVES, ARE DISGUSTED BY THE KIND OF "WELCOME" THEY'VE RECEIVED. THE IMPOVERISHED RESIDENTS ARE AGRIEVED BY THE FINANCIAL AID THE NEWCOMERS RECEIVE...
THIS SITUATION HASN'T BEEN HELPED BY THE RECKLESS SPECULATION OF THE POPULAR PRESS...
SUN
REFUGEES NERVE GAS
HOWEVER, ON THE 11TH OF SEPTEMBER, ALL EYES TURNED TO ANOTHER GROUP OF TOWERS, AND AN ACT OF UNIMAGINABLE HATRED...
SINCE THEN, NO-ONE IN SIGHTHILL HAS SUFFERED AS THOSE WHO DIED IN THE TWIN TOWERS, THE PENTAGON, THE FOUR ILL-FATED AIRLINERS, OR EVEN POOR FIRSAT.
DEATH TO ISLA
BUT THE AREA IS TROUBLED STILL BY LOATHING AND BIGOTRY.
...IT'S DIFFICULT TO BE OPTIMISTIC ABOUT THE FUTURE...
OPEN
BUT THAT DOESN'T MEAN WE SHOULDN'T...

END

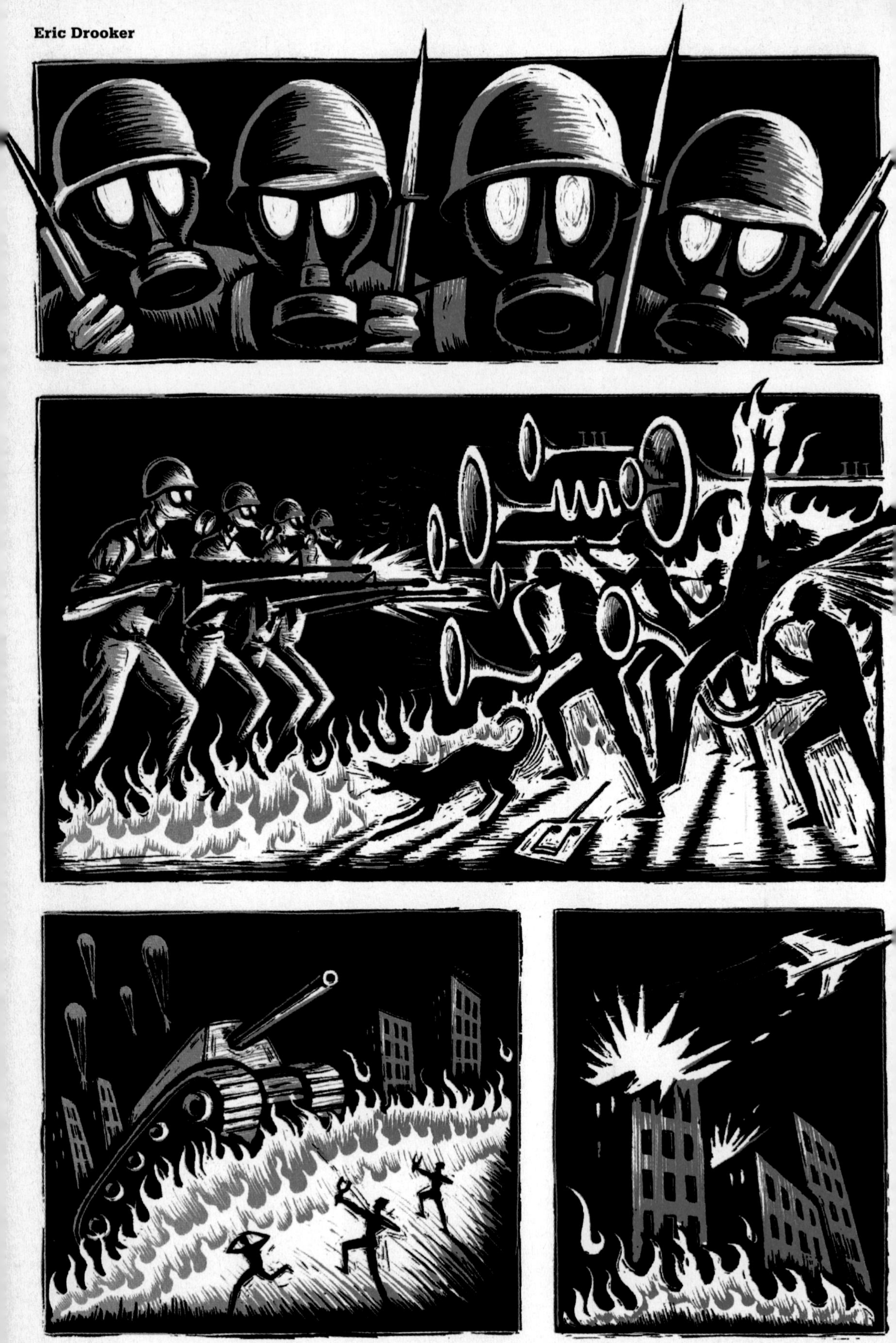

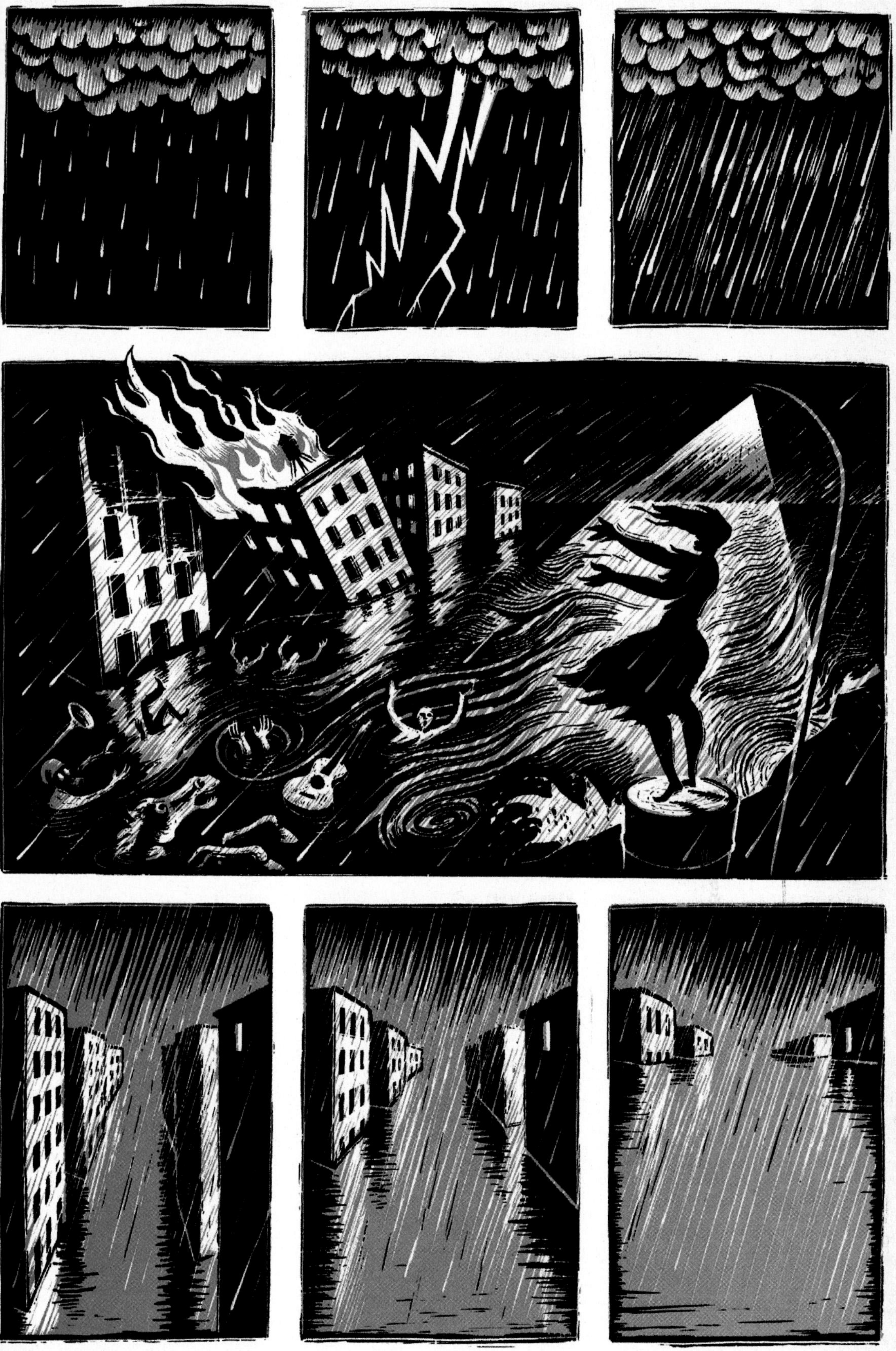

Jim Valentino

a building doesn't mean anything...

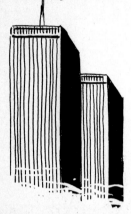

...only people do. mothers, fathers, sisters, brothers.

we sit stunned, transfixed by horror beyond comprehension.

how do you explain war to a 17 year-old who has only known peace and prosperity?

how do you explain what it really means? the suffering it causes.

what it feels like to carry a draft card.

a piece of paper in your wallet, the sword of damocles in your back pocket.

what do you say to your lover when you tell her that you must fly... and she trembles.

how do you make sense of the senseless?

what do you say to those who have lost so much?

how do you find words to make something so wrong right?

you don't.

you hurt. you cry. you try not to hate.

for in the hating you become that which you despise.

—Valentino

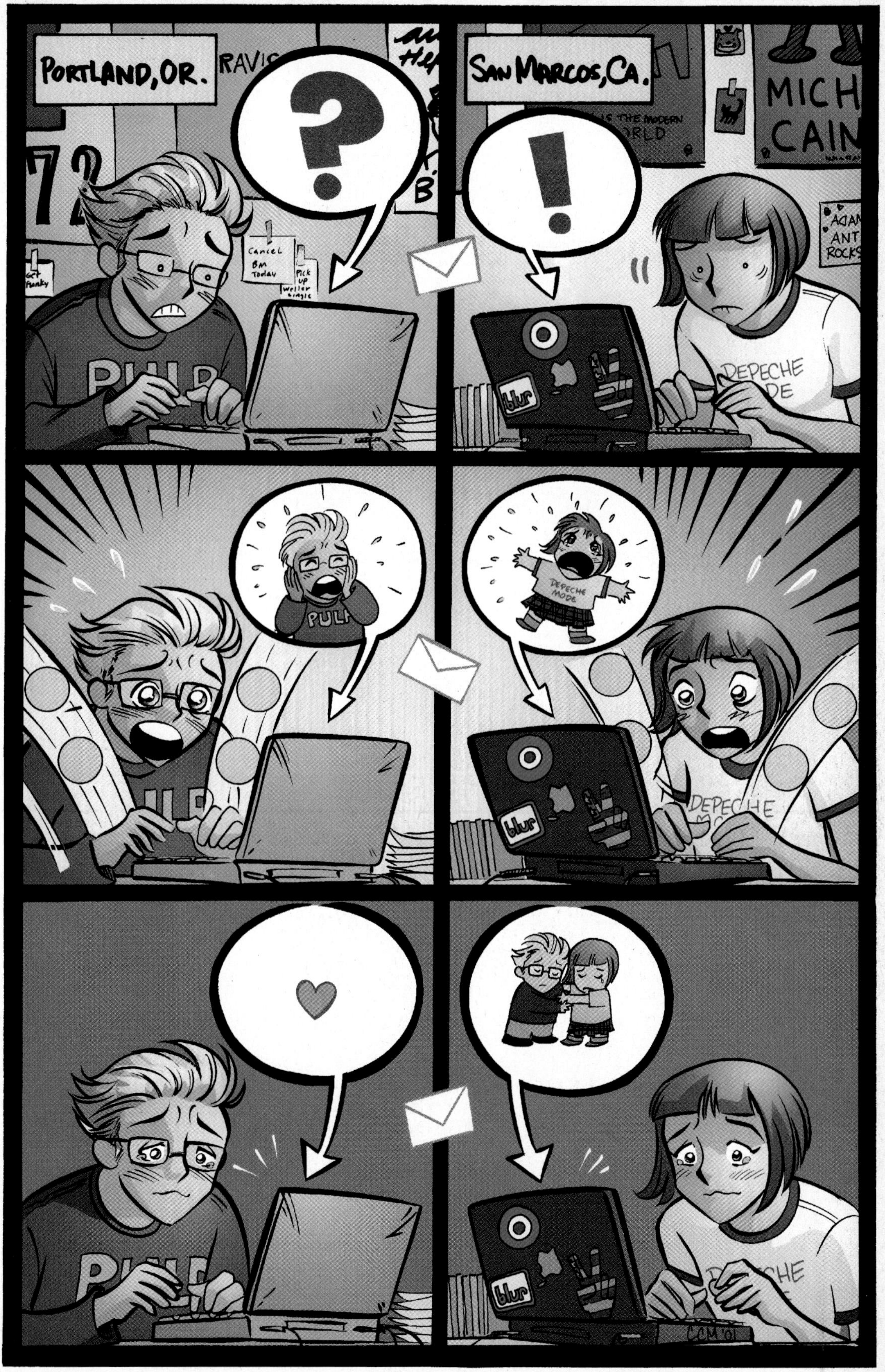
PORTLAND, OR.
?
SAN MARCOS, CA.
!

Dave McKean

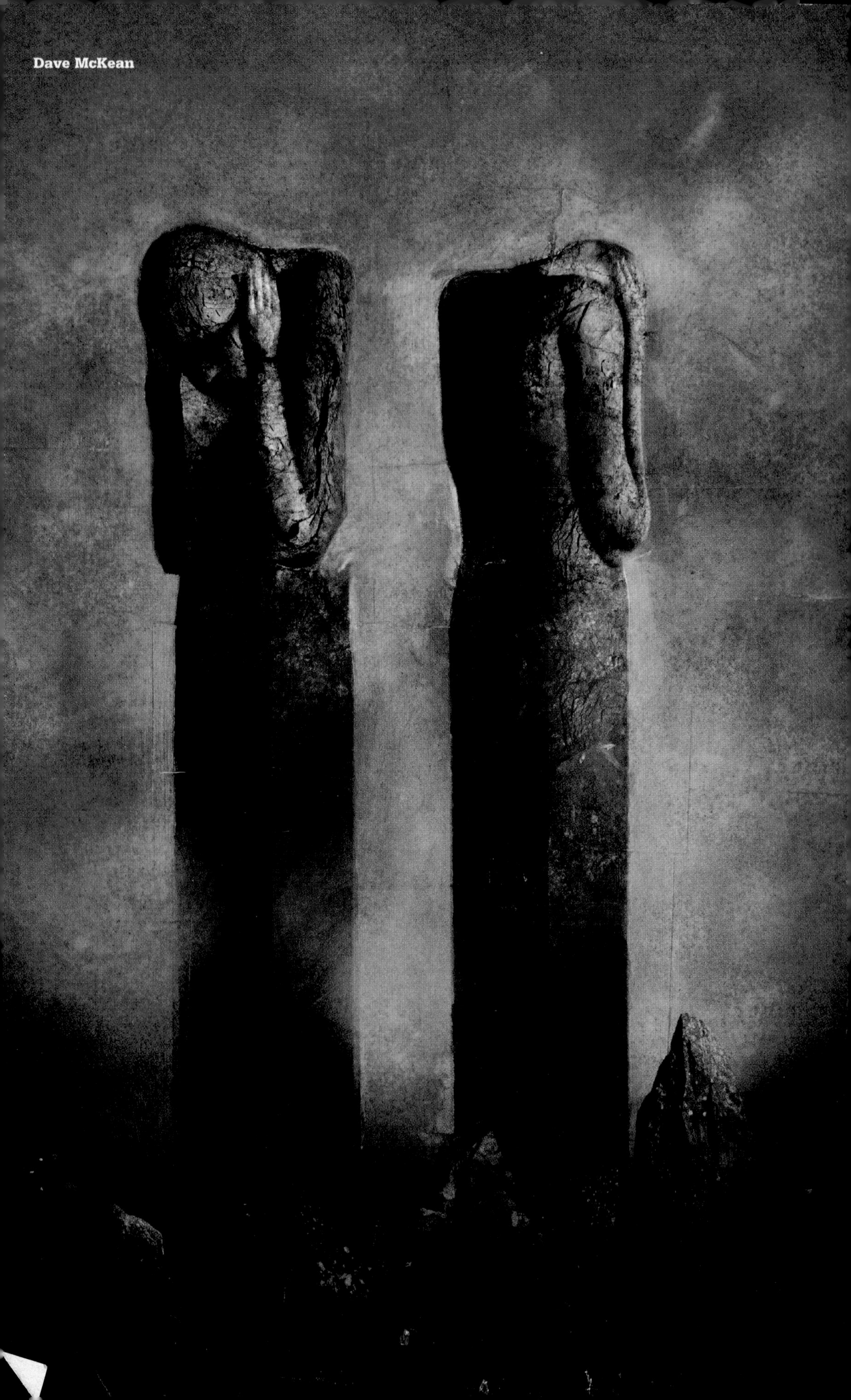

REASON

A FRED THE CLOWN CARTOON

CLOWNS' DAY OFF

©2001 ROGER LANGRIDGE

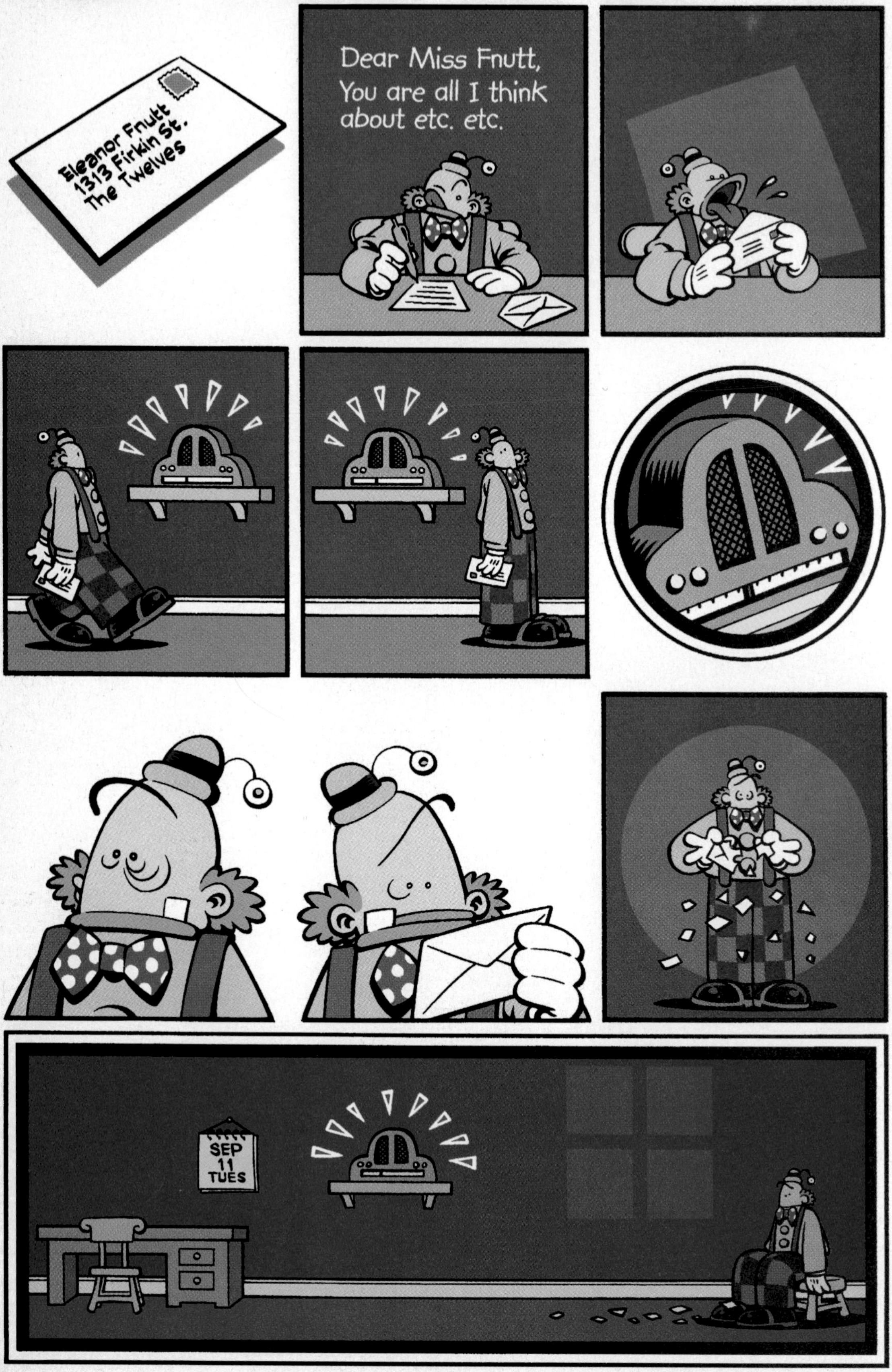

Eleanor Fnutt
1313 Firkin St.
The Twelves
Dear Miss Fnutt,
You are all I think
about etc. etc.
SEP
11
TUES

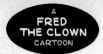

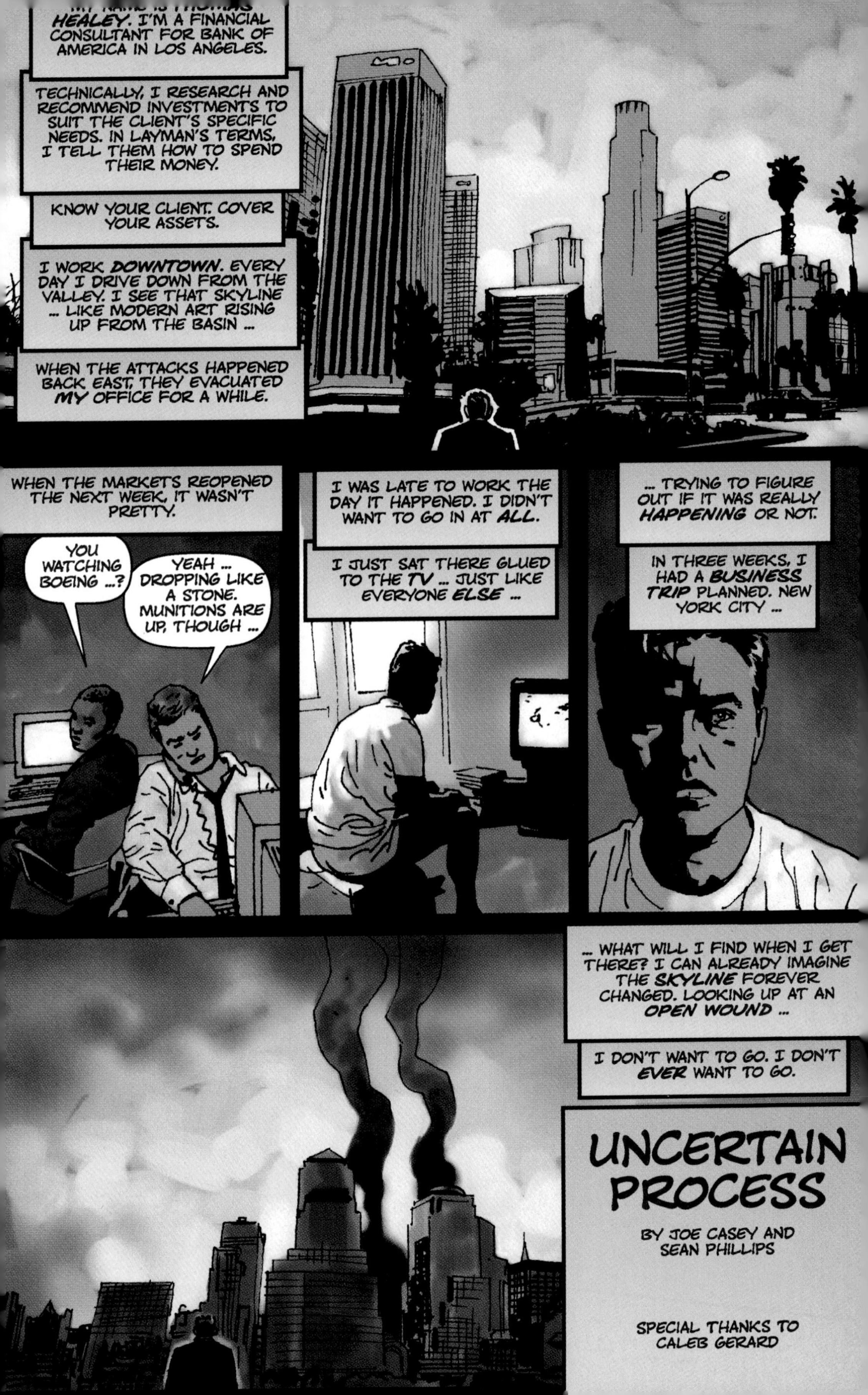
HEALEY. I'M A FINANCIAL CONSULTANT FOR BANK OF AMERICA IN LOS ANGELES.
TECHNICALLY, I RESEARCH AND RECOMMEND INVESTMENTS TO SUIT THE CLIENT'S SPECIFIC NEEDS. IN LAYMAN'S TERMS, I TELL THEM HOW TO SPEND THEIR MONEY.
KNOW YOUR CLIENT. COVER YOUR ASSETS.
I WORK *DOWNTOWN*. EVERY DAY I DRIVE DOWN FROM THE VALLEY. I SEE THAT SKYLINE ... LIKE MODERN ART RISING UP FROM THE BASIN ...
WHEN THE ATTACKS HAPPENED BACK EAST, THEY EVACUATED *MY* OFFICE FOR A WHILE.
WHEN THE MARKETS REOPENED THE NEXT WEEK, IT WASN'T PRETTY.
YOU WATCHING BOEING ...?
YEAH ... DROPPING LIKE A STONE. MUNITIONS ARE UP, THOUGH ...
I WAS LATE TO WORK THE DAY IT HAPPENED. I DIDN'T WANT TO GO IN AT *ALL*.
I JUST SAT THERE GLUED TO THE *TV* ... JUST LIKE EVERYONE *ELSE* ...
... TRYING TO FIGURE OUT IF IT WAS REALLY *HAPPENING* OR NOT.
IN THREE WEEKS, I HAD A *BUSINESS TRIP* PLANNED. NEW YORK CITY ...
... WHAT WILL I FIND WHEN I GET THERE? I CAN ALREADY IMAGINE THE *SKYLINE* FOREVER CHANGED. LOOKING UP AT AN *OPEN WOUND* ...
I DON'T WANT TO GO. I DON'T *EVER* WANT TO GO.
UNCERTAIN PROCESS
BY JOE CASEY AND SEAN PHILLIPS
SPECIAL THANKS TO CALEB GERARD

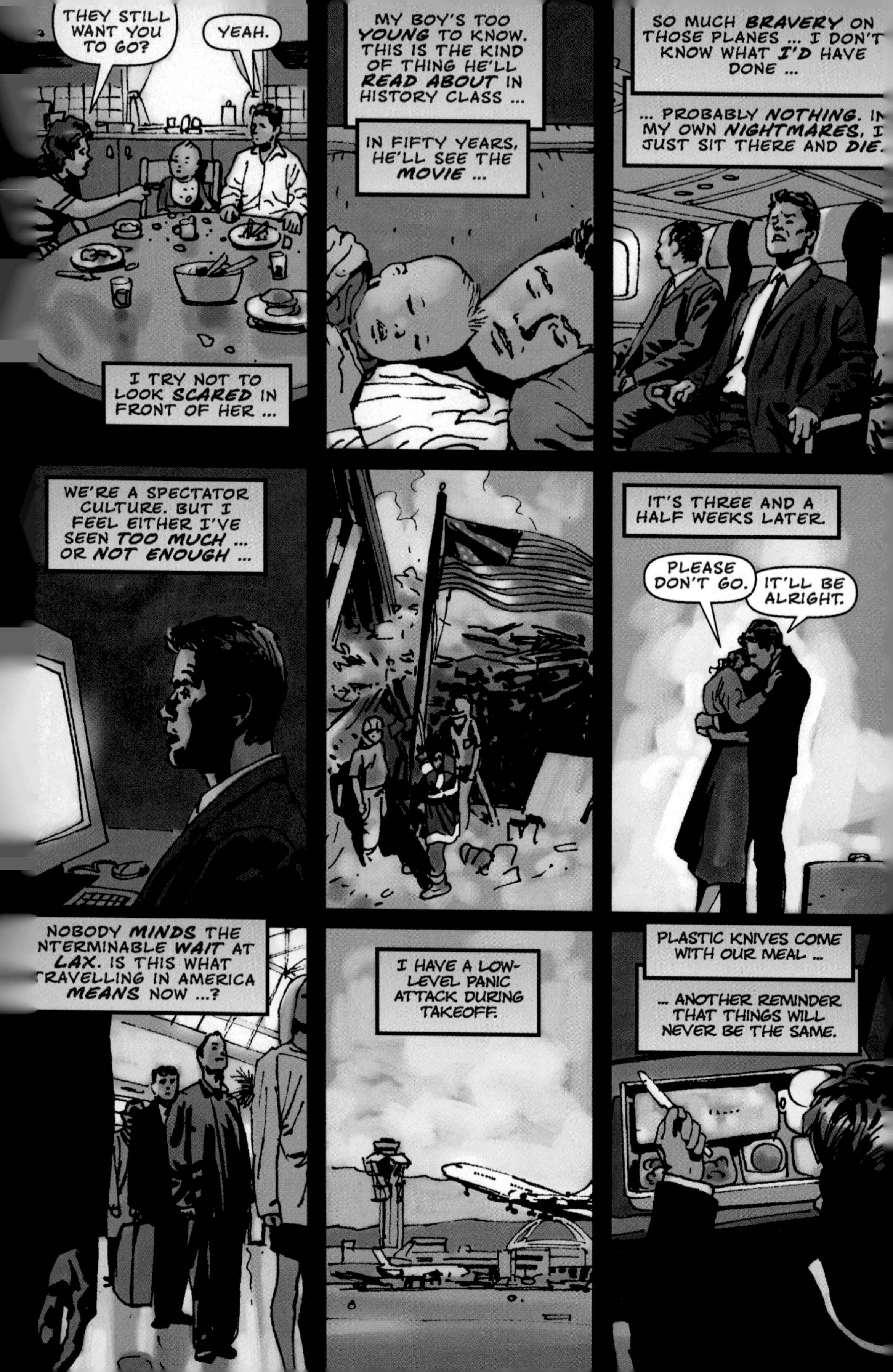
THEY STILL WANT YOU TO GO?
YEAH.
I TRY NOT TO LOOK SCARED IN FRONT OF HER ...
MY BOY'S TOO YOUNG TO KNOW. THIS IS THE KIND OF THING HE'LL READ ABOUT IN HISTORY CLASS ...
IN FIFTY YEARS, HE'LL SEE THE MOVIE ...
SO MUCH BRAVERY ON THOSE PLANES ... I DON'T KNOW WHAT I'D HAVE DONE ...
... PROBABLY NOTHING. IN MY OWN NIGHTMARES, I JUST SIT THERE AND DIE.
WE'RE A SPECTATOR CULTURE. BUT I FEEL EITHER I'VE SEEN TOO MUCH ... OR NOT ENOUGH ...
IT'S THREE AND A HALF WEEKS LATER.
PLEASE DON'T GO.
IT'LL BE ALRIGHT.
NOBODY MINDS THE INTERMINABLE WAIT AT LAX. IS THIS WHAT TRAVELLING IN AMERICA MEANS NOW ...?
I HAVE A LOW-LEVEL PANIC ATTACK DURING TAKEOFF.
PLASTIC KNIVES COME WITH OUR MEAL ...
... ANOTHER REMINDER THAT THINGS WILL NEVER BE THE SAME.

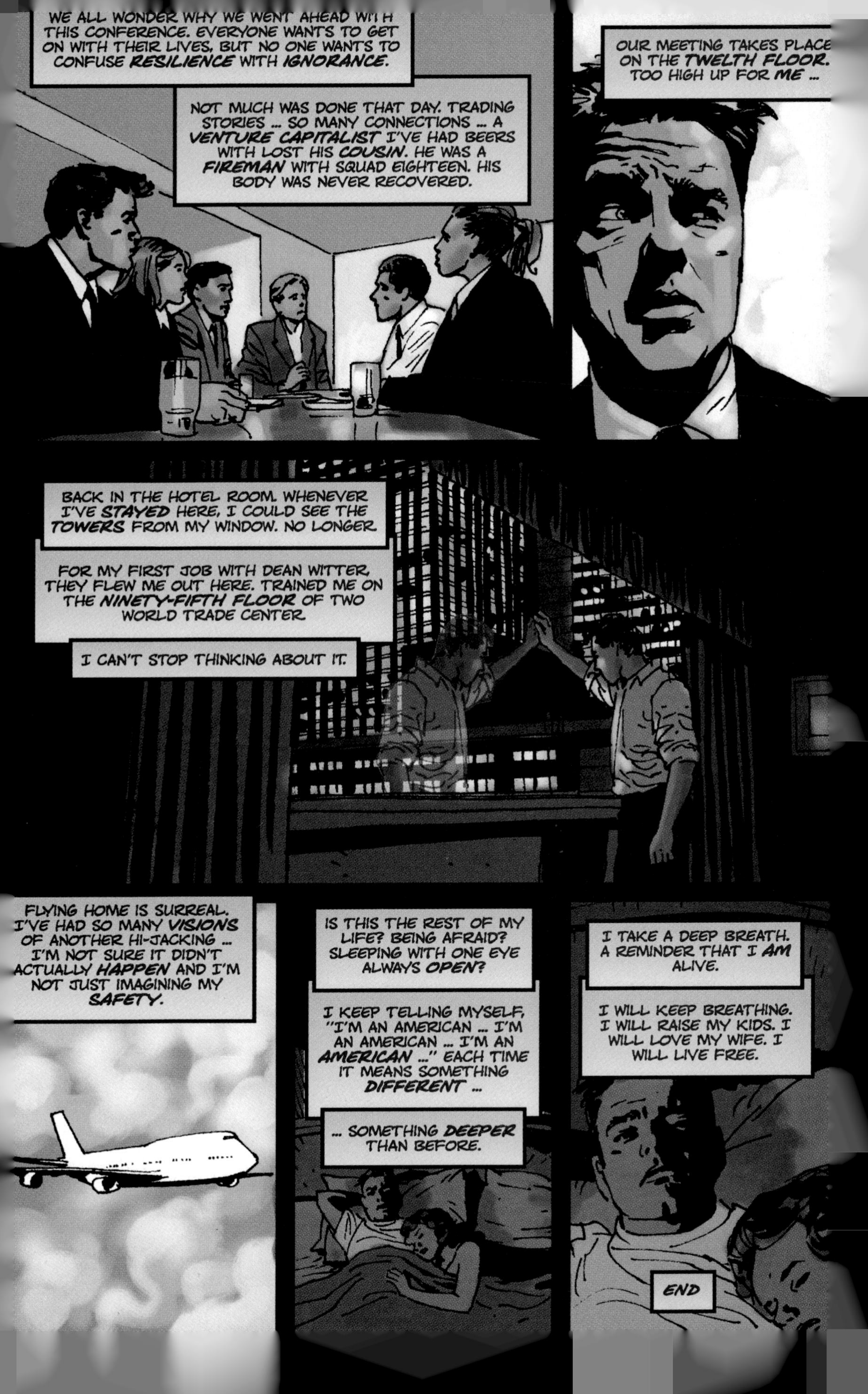

WE ALL WONDER WHY WE WENT AHEAD WITH THIS CONFERENCE. EVERYONE WANTS TO GET ON WITH THEIR LIVES, BUT NO ONE WANTS TO CONFUSE *RESILIENCE* WITH *IGNORANCE*.
NOT MUCH WAS DONE THAT DAY. TRADING STORIES ... SO MANY CONNECTIONS ... A *VENTURE CAPITALIST* I'VE HAD BEERS WITH LOST HIS *COUSIN*. HE WAS A *FIREMAN* WITH SQUAD EIGHTEEN. HIS BODY WAS NEVER RECOVERED.
OUR MEETING TAKES PLACE ON THE *TWELTH FLOOR*. TOO HIGH UP FOR *ME* ...
BACK IN THE HOTEL ROOM. WHENEVER I'VE *STAYED* HERE, I COULD SEE THE *TOWERS* FROM MY WINDOW. NO LONGER.
FOR MY FIRST JOB WITH DEAN WITTER, THEY FLEW ME OUT HERE. TRAINED ME ON THE *NINETY-FIFTH FLOOR* OF TWO WORLD TRADE CENTER.
I CAN'T STOP THINKING ABOUT IT.
FLYING HOME IS SURREAL. I'VE HAD SO MANY *VISIONS* OF ANOTHER HI-JACKING ... I'M NOT SURE IT DIDN'T ACTUALLY *HAPPEN* AND I'M NOT JUST IMAGINING MY *SAFETY*.
IS THIS THE REST OF MY LIFE? BEING AFRAID? SLEEPING WITH ONE EYE ALWAYS *OPEN*?
I KEEP TELLING MYSELF, "I'M AN AMERICAN ... I'M AN AMERICAN ... I'M AN *AMERICAN* ..." EACH TIME IT MEANS SOMETHING *DIFFERENT* ...
... SOMETHING *DEEPER* THAN BEFORE.
I TAKE A DEEP BREATH. A REMINDER THAT I *AM* ALIVE.
I WILL KEEP BREATHING. I WILL RAISE MY KIDS. I WILL LOVE MY WIFE. I WILL LIVE FREE.
END

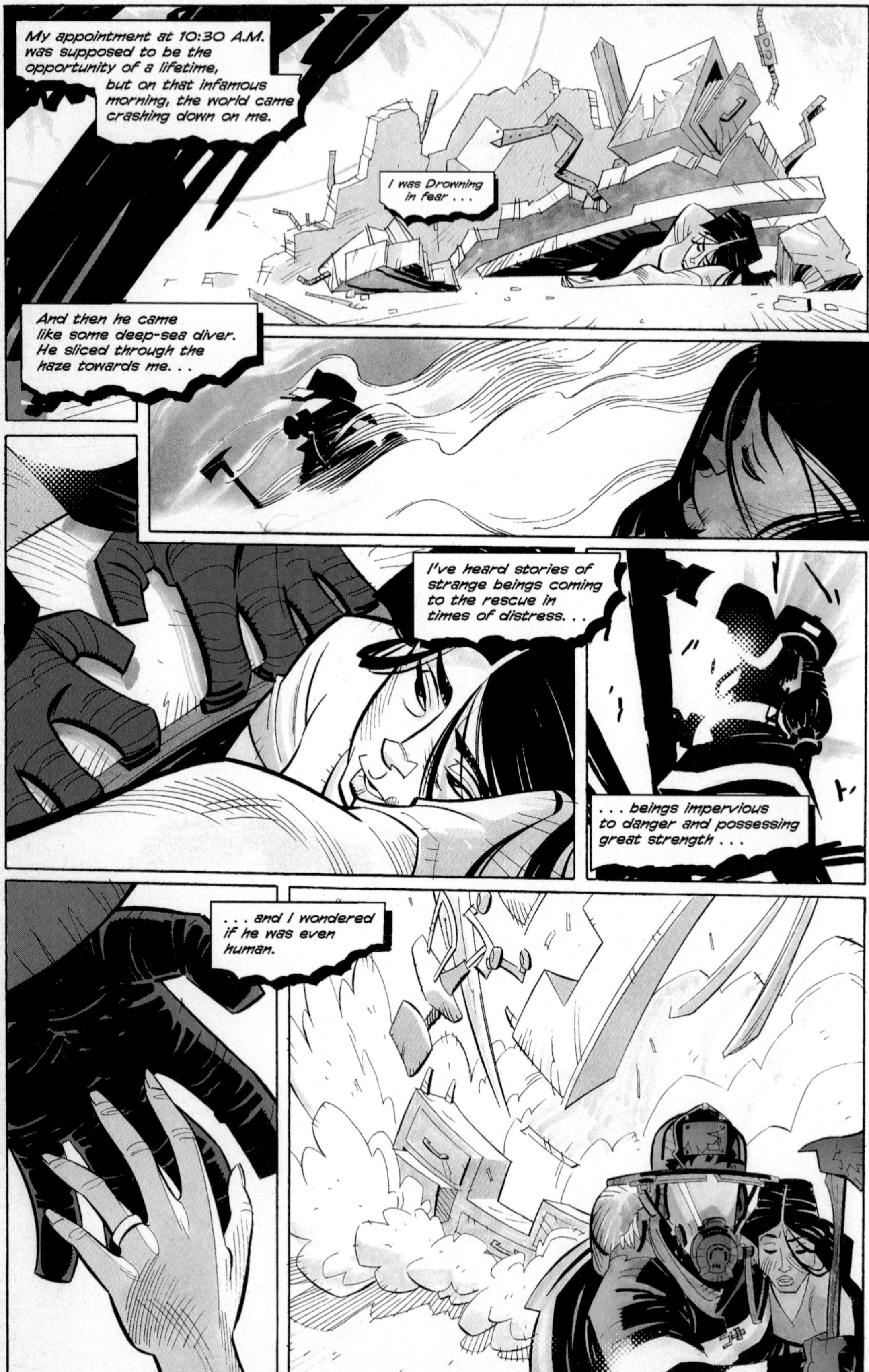
My appointment at 10:30 A.M. was supposed to be the opportunity of a lifetime,
but on that infamous morning, the world came crashing down on me.
I was Drowning in fear . . .
And then he came like some deep-sea diver. He sliced through the haze towards me. . .
I've heard stories of strange beings coming to the rescue in times of distress. . .
. . . beings impervious to danger and possessing great strength . . .
. . . and I wondered if he was even human.

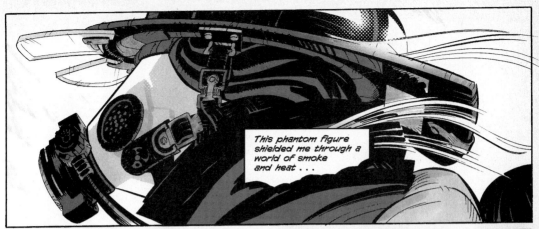

This phantom figure shielded me through a world of smoke and heat . . .

. . . and delivered me into safe hands.

I descended into heaven below. . .

. . . as he turned back for the hell above.

He gave one last glance at me . . .

. . . and I saw his eyes ablaze with life.

He was just an ordinary person.

Like me, he was just keeping his appointments.

in honor of Michael Baksh

END

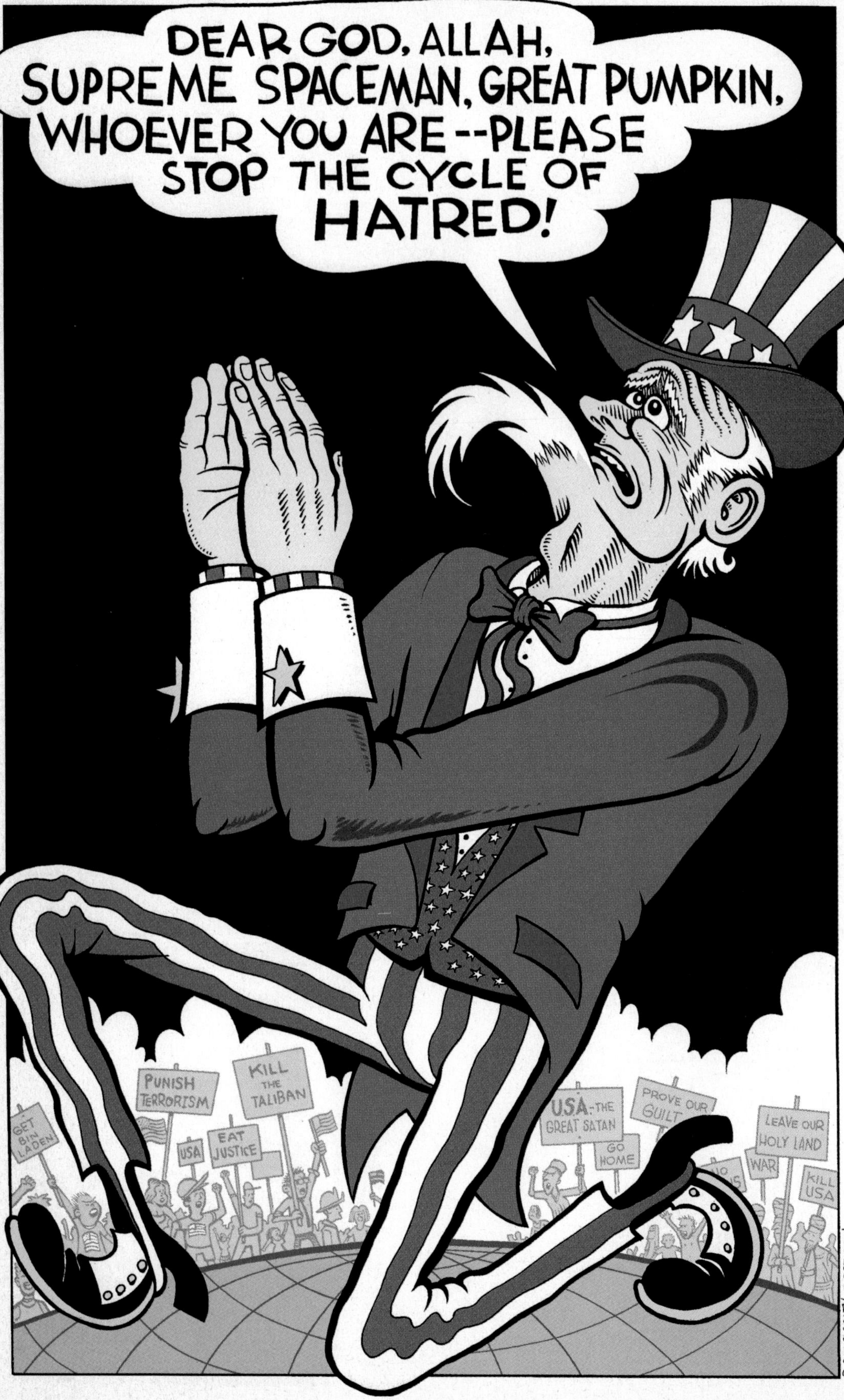
DEAR GOD, ALLAH, SUPREME SPACEMAN, GREAT PUMPKIN, WHOEVER YOU ARE --PLEASE STOP THE CYCLE OF HATRED!
GET BIN LADEN
PUNISH TERRORISM
USA
EAT JUSTICE
KILL THE TALIBAN
U.S.A.-THE GREAT SATAN
GO HOME
PROVE OUR GUILT
WAR
LEAVE OUR HOLY LAND
KILL USA
P. MORIARITY SEPT, 2001

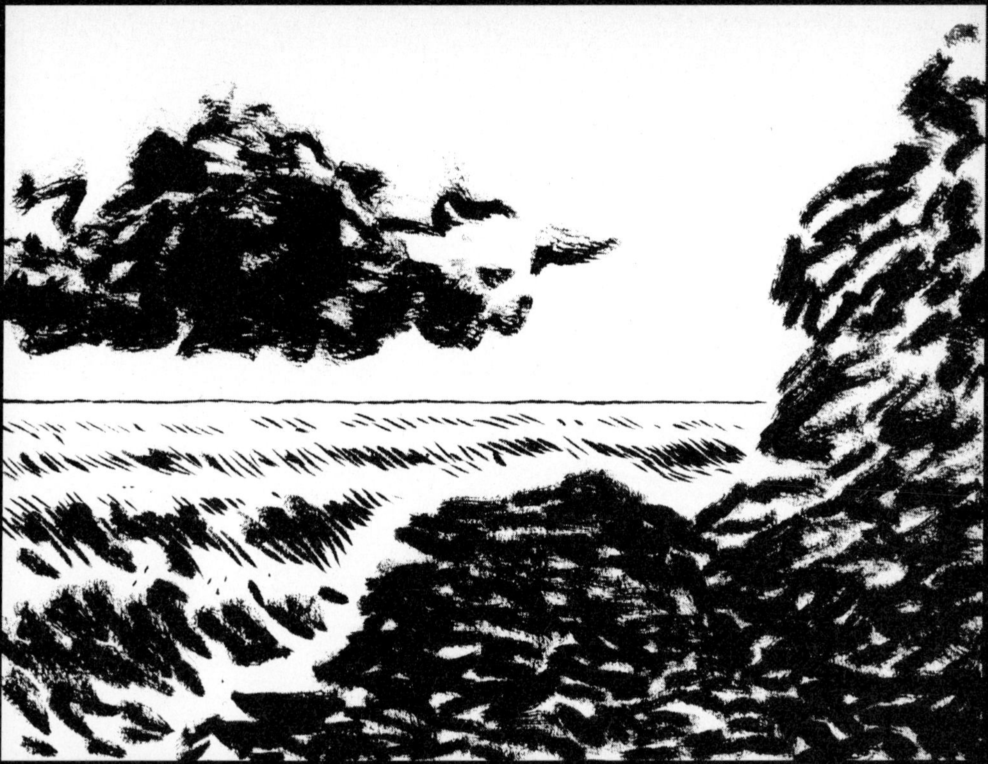

I'm climbing around the rocks as the tide comes in.

Somewhere up ahead are my wife and child. She's a better climber than I am, but our son is only six and these rocks are getting pretty steep.

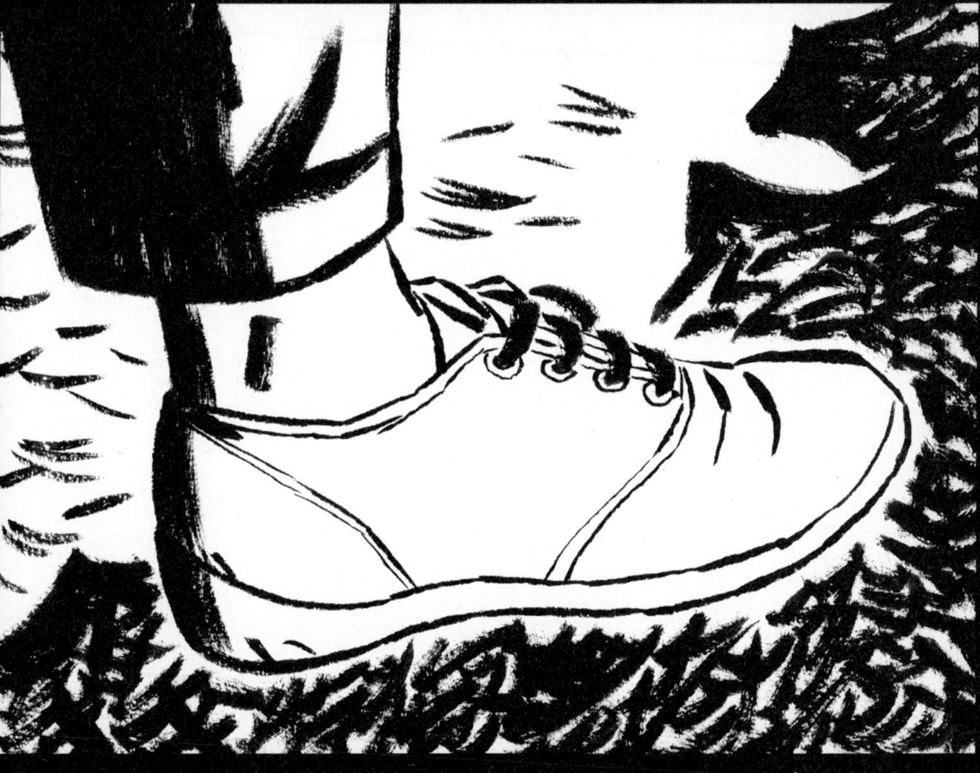

I haven't seen them in a while - maybe they went up to the road already? Or maybe they're around the next corner, playing in a sheltered bay...

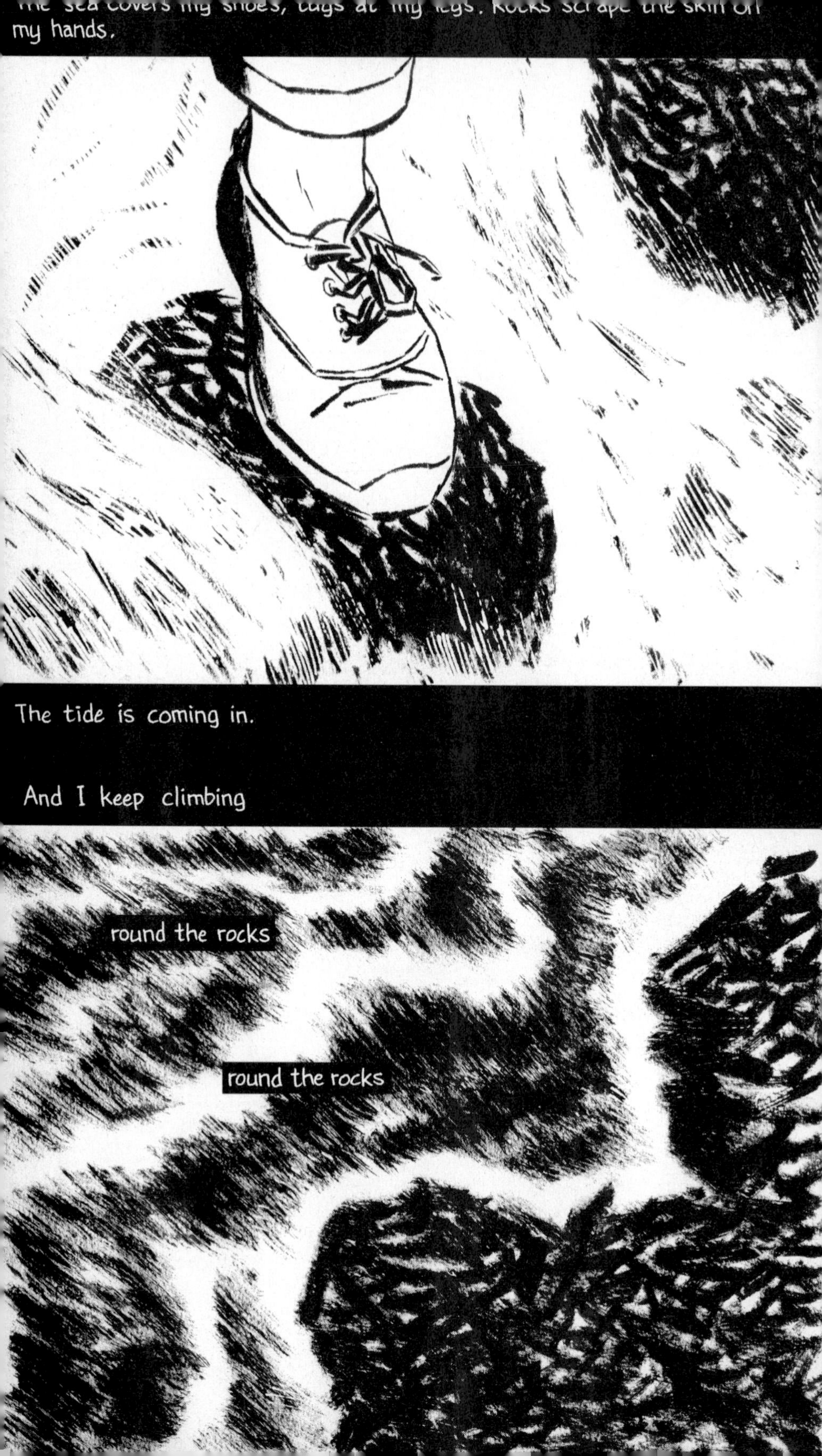
The sea covers my shoes, tugs at my legs. Rocks scrape the skin off my hands.
The tide is coming in.
And I keep climbing
round the rocks
round the rocks

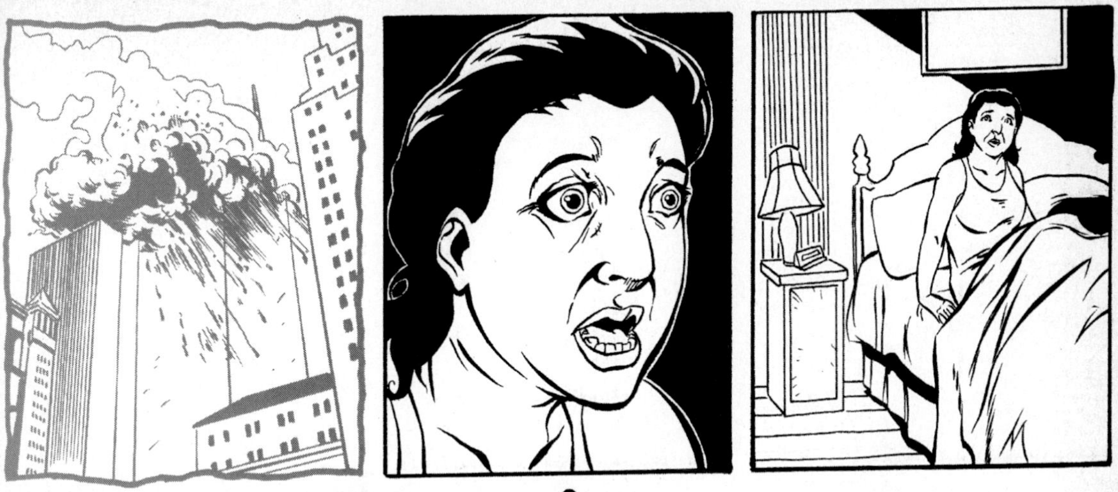

Sunday Mourning

Story: Antony Johnston
Art: Mike Norton

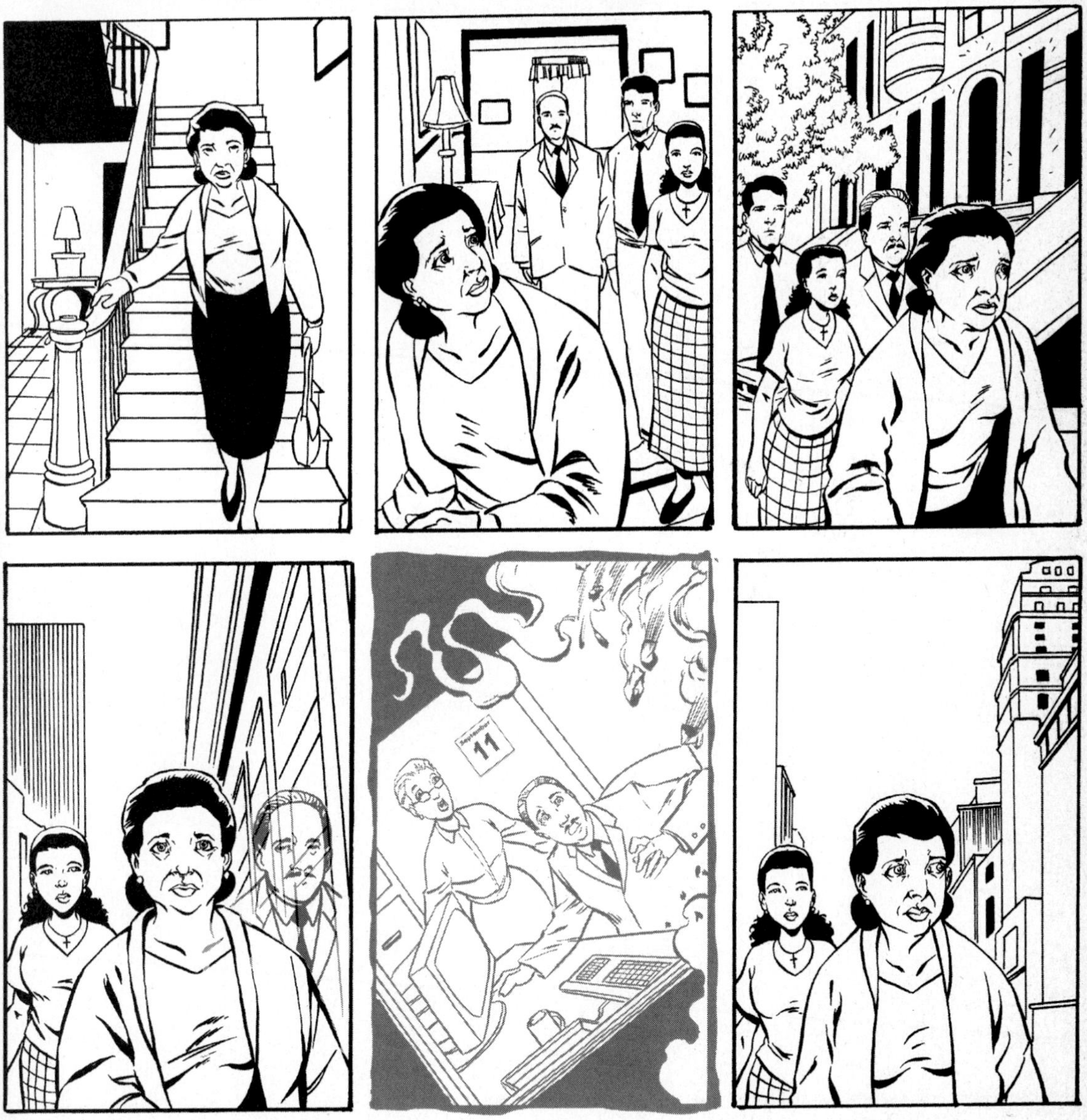

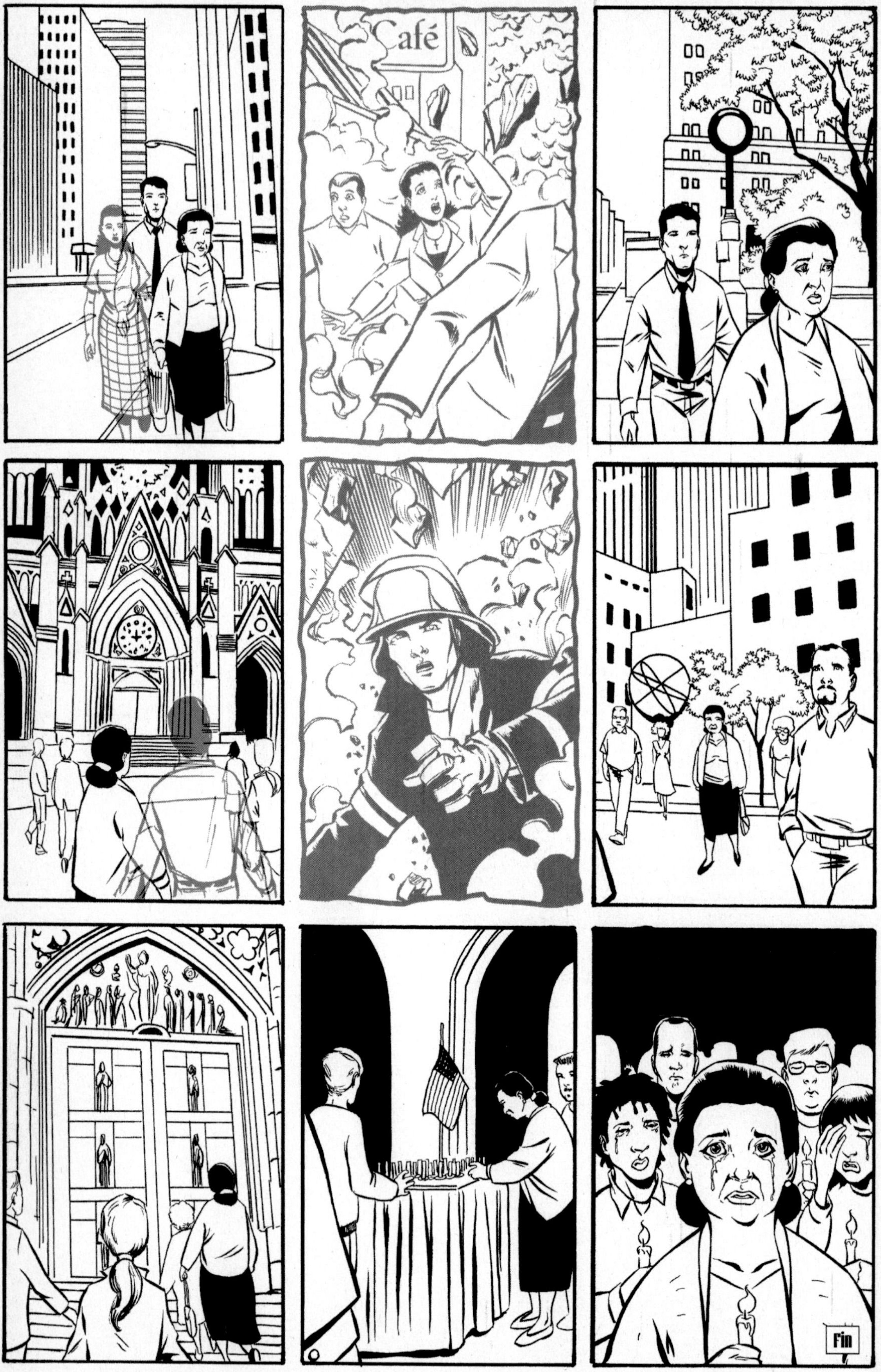
Café
Fin

IT DOESN'T SEEM POSSIBLE, BUT FALLING WATER CARVES MOUNTAINS INTO SAND.

THE MOUNTAIN HAS NEVER RISEN THAT WILL NOT SOMEDAY VANISH...

...LEAVING ONLY SAND.

I WASN'T ON A MOUNTAIN ON SEPT. 11, 2001. I WAS IN AN OFFICE BUILDING IN CHAMPAIGN, ILLINOIS.

THE MOUNTAINS ARE FAR FROM ME NOW.

BUT I HAVE NOT FORGOTTEN WHAT THE MOUNTAINS TAUGHT ME.

AS MOUNTAINS CRUMBLE INTO SAND...

...THE VERY WATER THAT DESTROYS THEM WASHES THE SAND TO THE SEA...

...WHERE IT WILL ONE DAY BECOME MOUNTAINS AGAIN.

THE WATER THAT DESTROYS THEM...

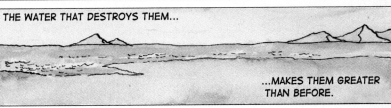

...MAKES THEM GREATER THAN BEFORE.

NOTHING IS MADE THAT CANNOT BE CHANGED...

BUT NOTHING THAT EXISTS CAN EVER CEASE TO BE.

IT ONLY CHANGES, AND RISES AGAIN.

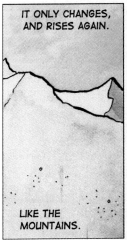

LIKE THE MOUNTAINS.

Script + Art — Layla Lawlor

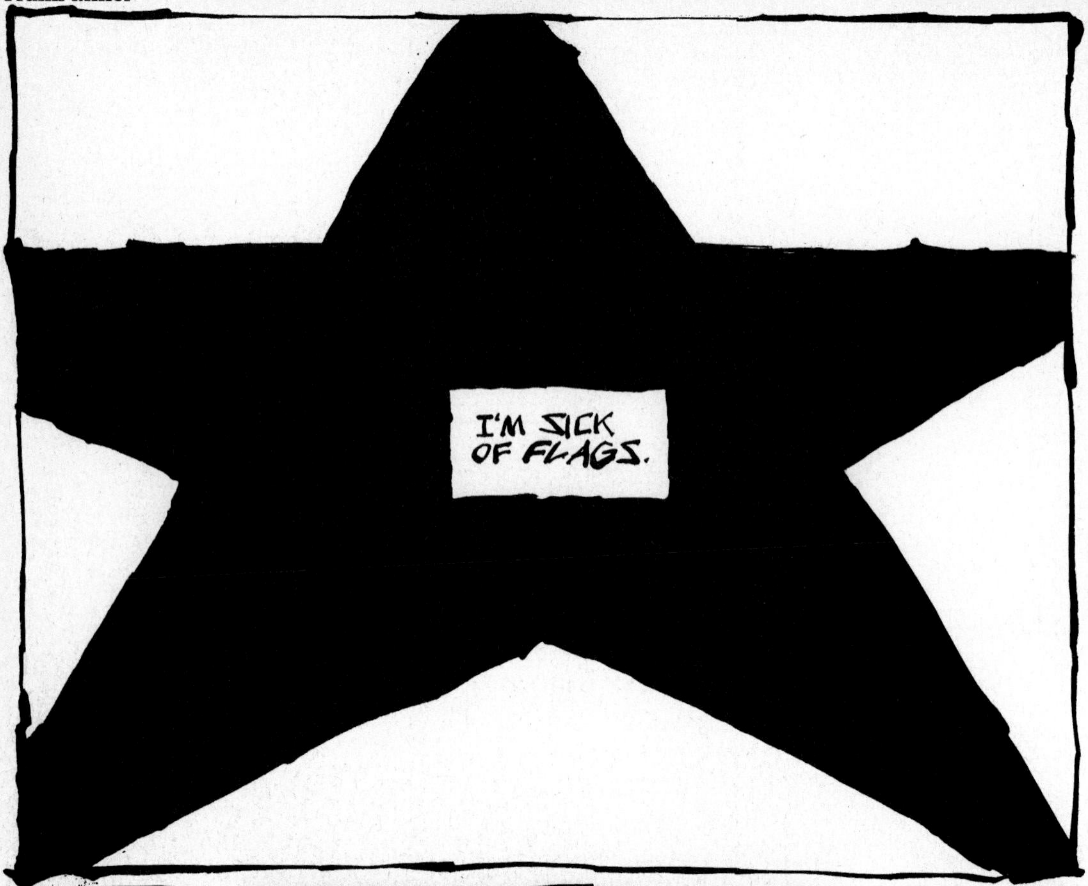
I'M SICK
OF FLAGS.

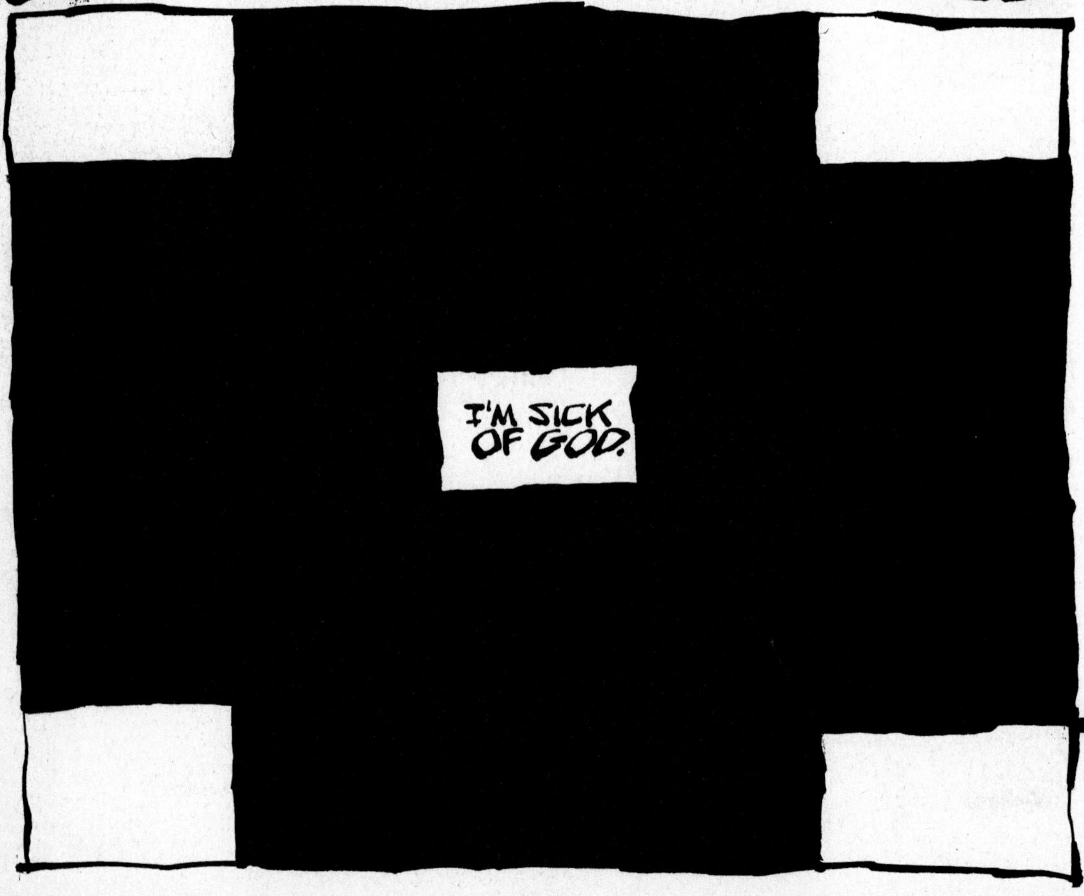
I'M SICK
OF GOD.

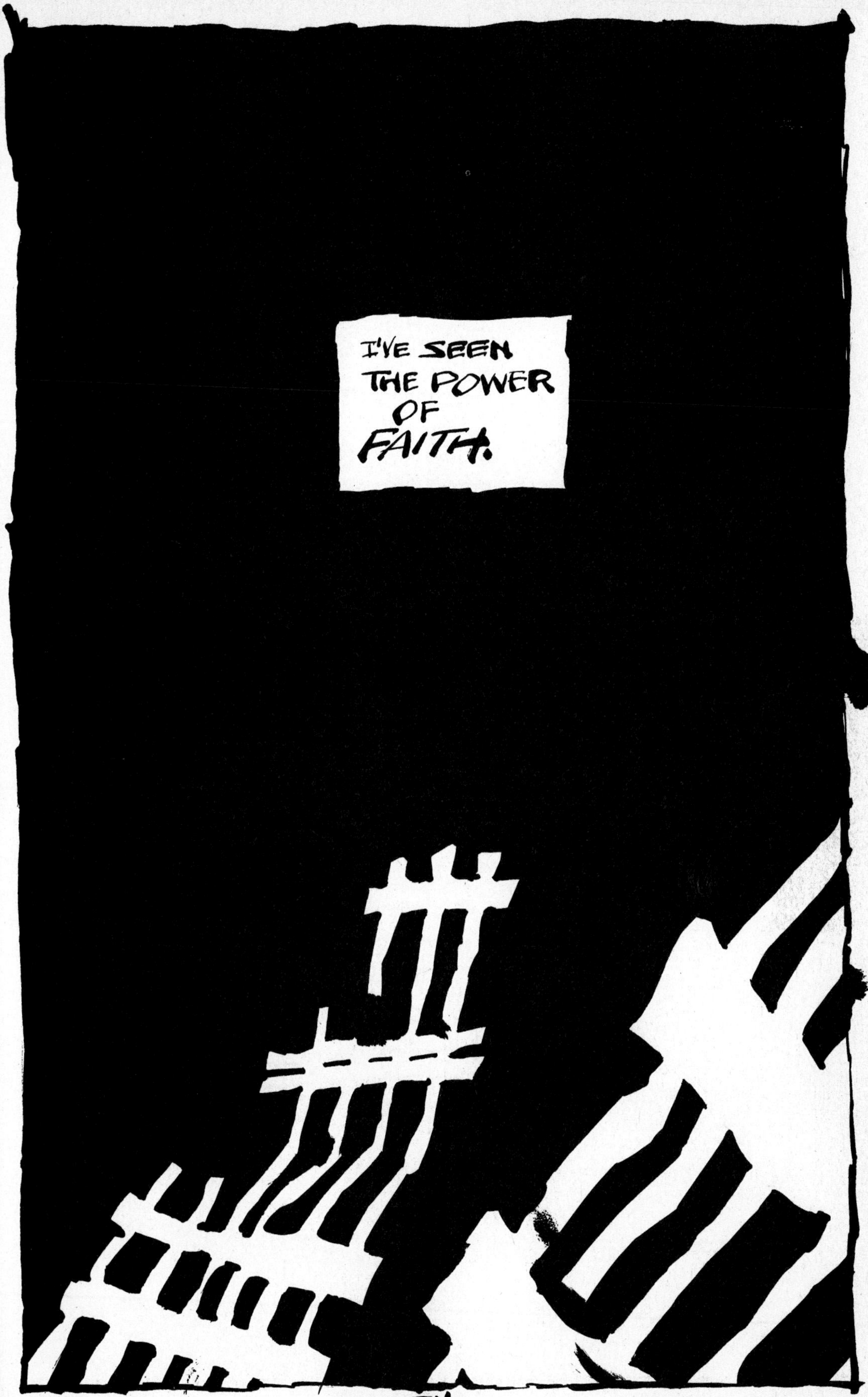
I'VE SEEN THE POWER OF FAITH.

FM

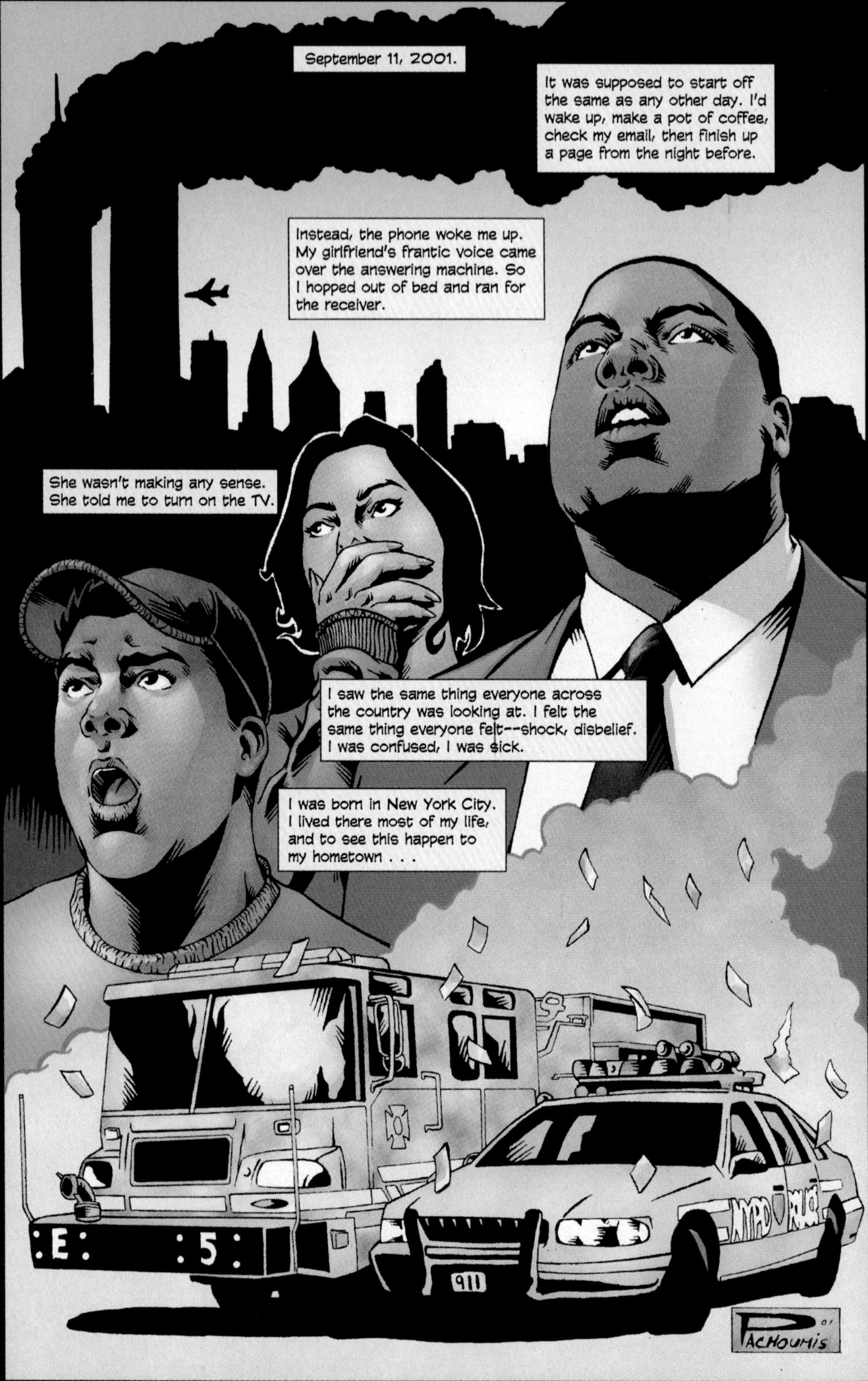
September 11, 2001.
It was supposed to start off the same as any other day. I'd wake up, make a pot of coffee, check my email, then finish up a page from the night before.
Instead, the phone woke me up. My girlfriend's frantic voice came over the answering machine. So I hopped out of bed and ran for the receiver.
She wasn't making any sense. She told me to turn on the TV.
I saw the same thing everyone across the country was looking at. I felt the same thing everyone felt--shock, disbelief. I was confused, I was sick.
I was born in New York City. I lived there most of my life, and to see this happen to my hometown . . .
E
5
911
NYPD
POLICE
PACHOUMIS '01

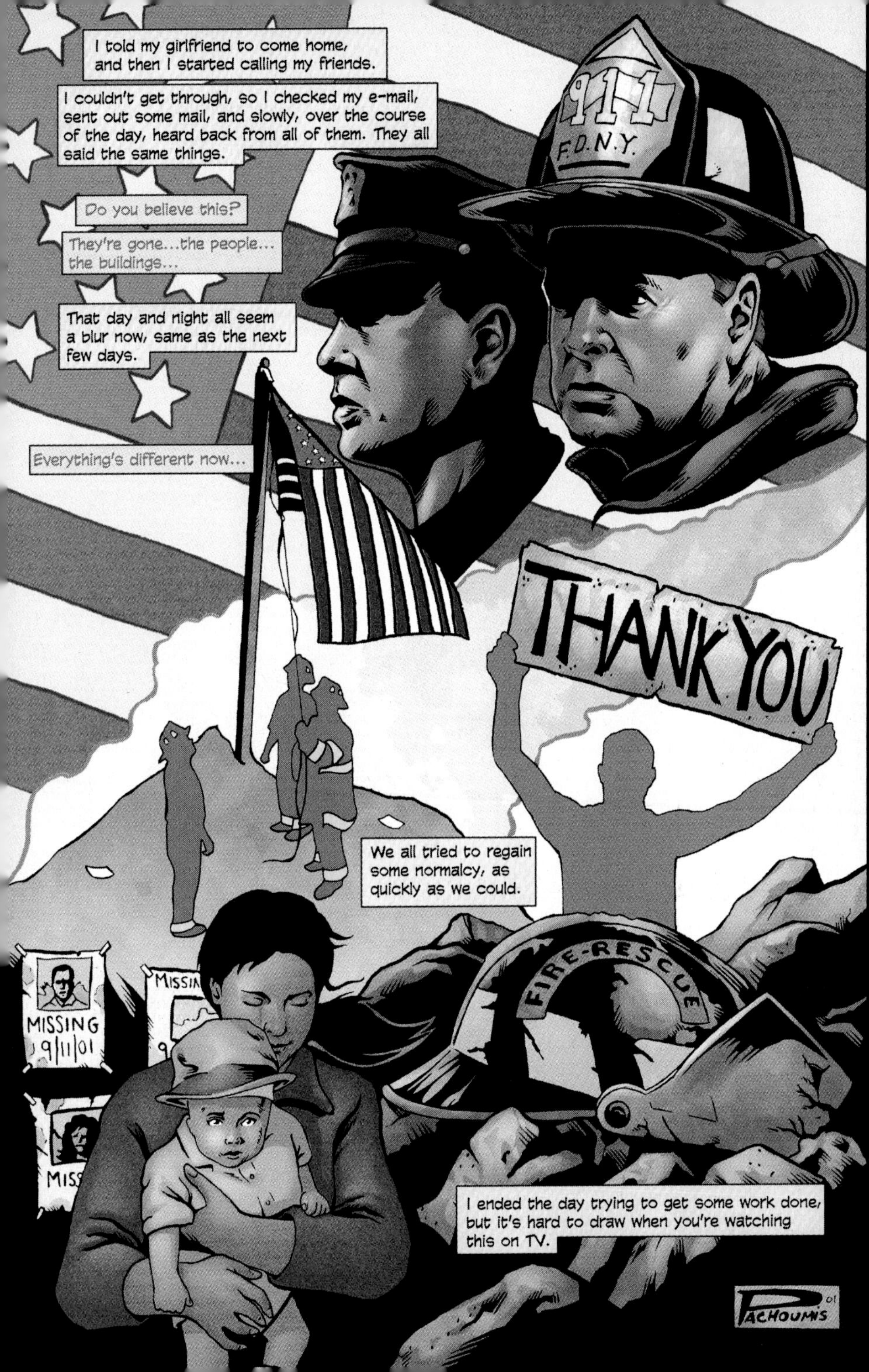

I told my girlfriend to come home, and then I started calling my friends.
I couldn't get through, so I checked my e-mail, sent out some mail, and slowly, over the course of the day, heard back from all of them. They all said the same things.
Do you believe this?
They're gone...the people... the buildings...
That day and night all seem a blur now, same as the next few days.
911 F.D.N.Y.
Everything's different now...
THANK YOU
We all tried to regain some normalcy, as quickly as we could.
MISSING 9/11/01
FIRE-RESCUE
I ended the day trying to get some work done, but it's hard to draw when you're watching this on TV.
PACHOUMIS '01

THE PATRIOT

by JP Leon

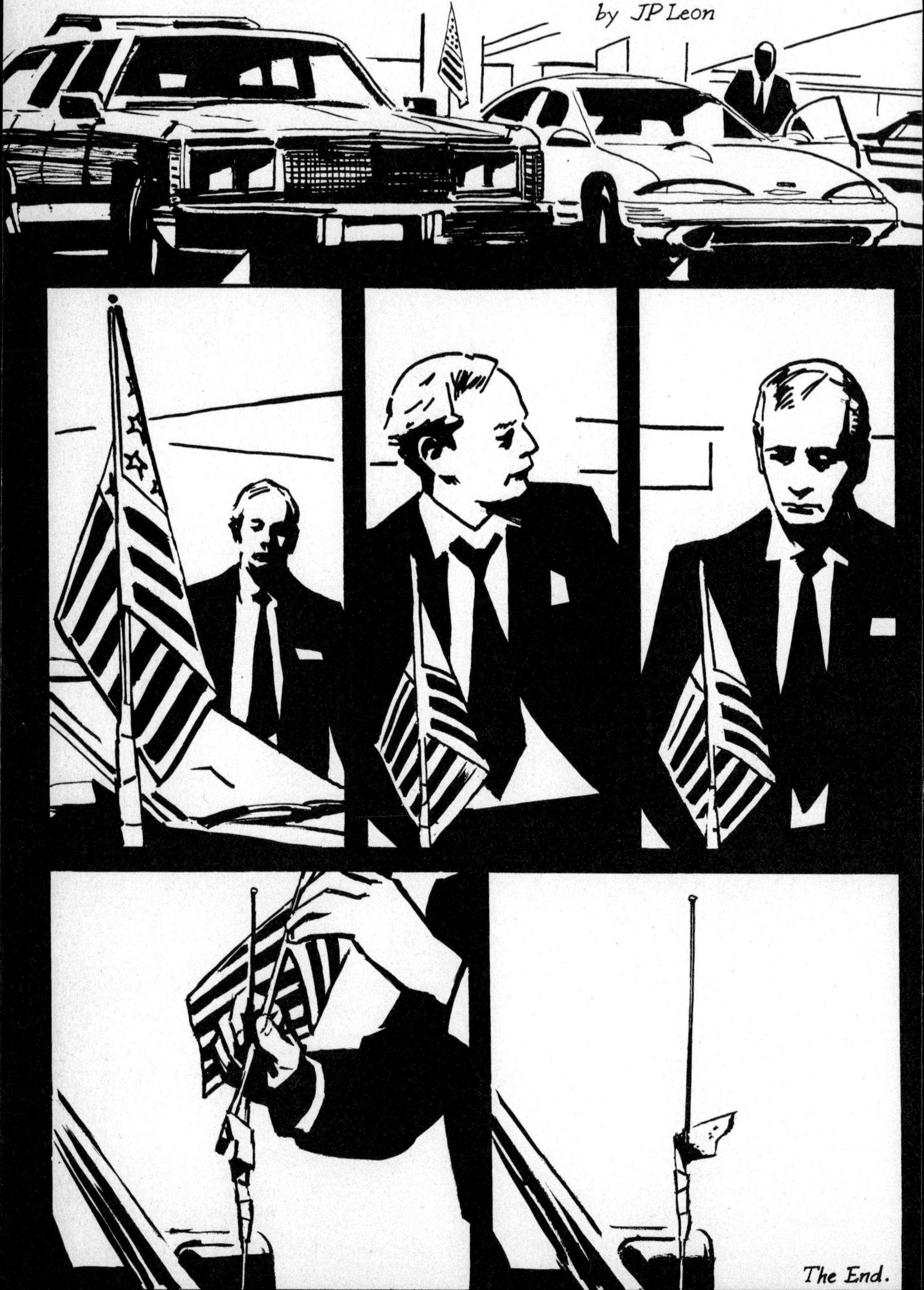
The End.

WHAT'S IMPORTANT

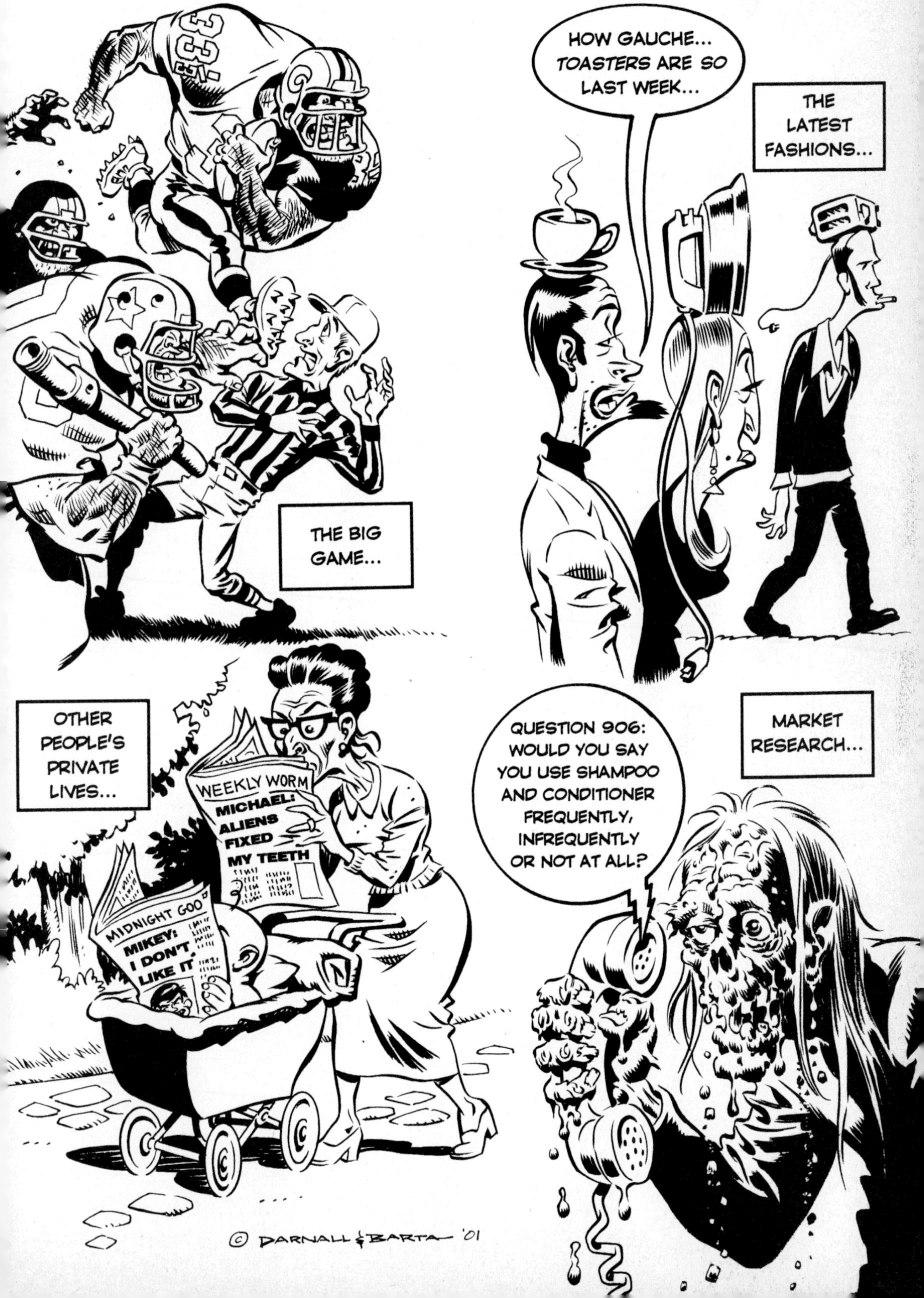
THE BIG GAME...
THE LATEST FASHIONS...
HOW GAUCHE... *TOASTERS* ARE SO LAST WEEK...
OTHER PEOPLE'S PRIVATE LIVES...
WEEKLY WORM
MICHAEL: ALIENS FIXED MY TEETH
MIDNIGHT GOO
MIKEY: I DON'T LIKE IT
MARKET RESEARCH...
QUESTION 906: WOULD YOU SAY YOU USE SHAMPOO AND CONDITIONER FREQUENTLY, INFREQUENTLY OR NOT AT ALL?
© DARNALL & BARTA '01

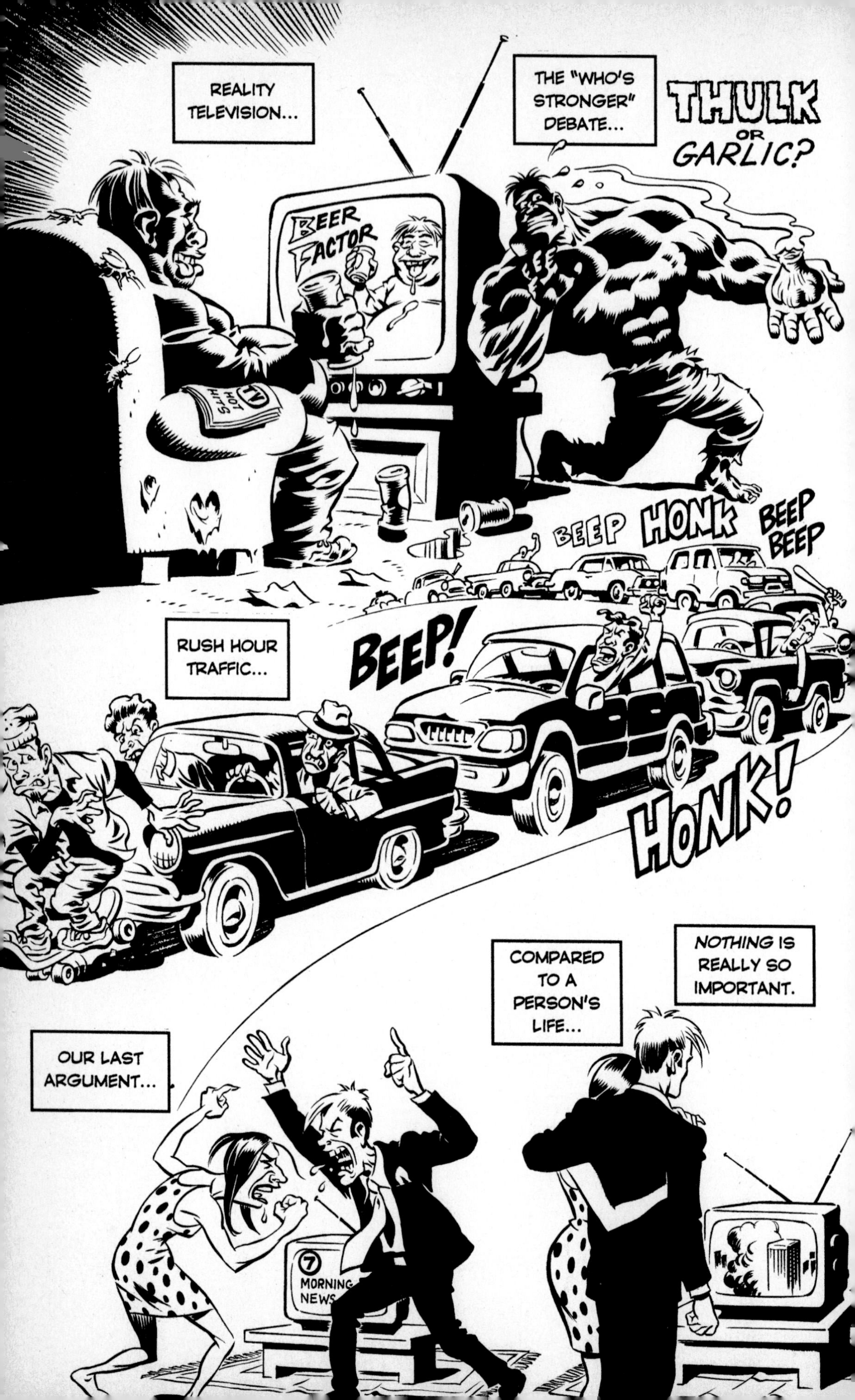
REALITY TELEVISION...
BEER FACTOR
TV HOT HITS
THE "WHO'S STRONGER" DEBATE...
THULK OR GARLIC?
BEEP
HONK
BEEP BEEP
RUSH HOUR TRAFFIC...
BEEP!
HONK!
OUR LAST ARGUMENT...
7 MORNING NEWS
COMPARED TO A PERSON'S LIFE...
NOTHING IS REALLY SO IMPORTANT.

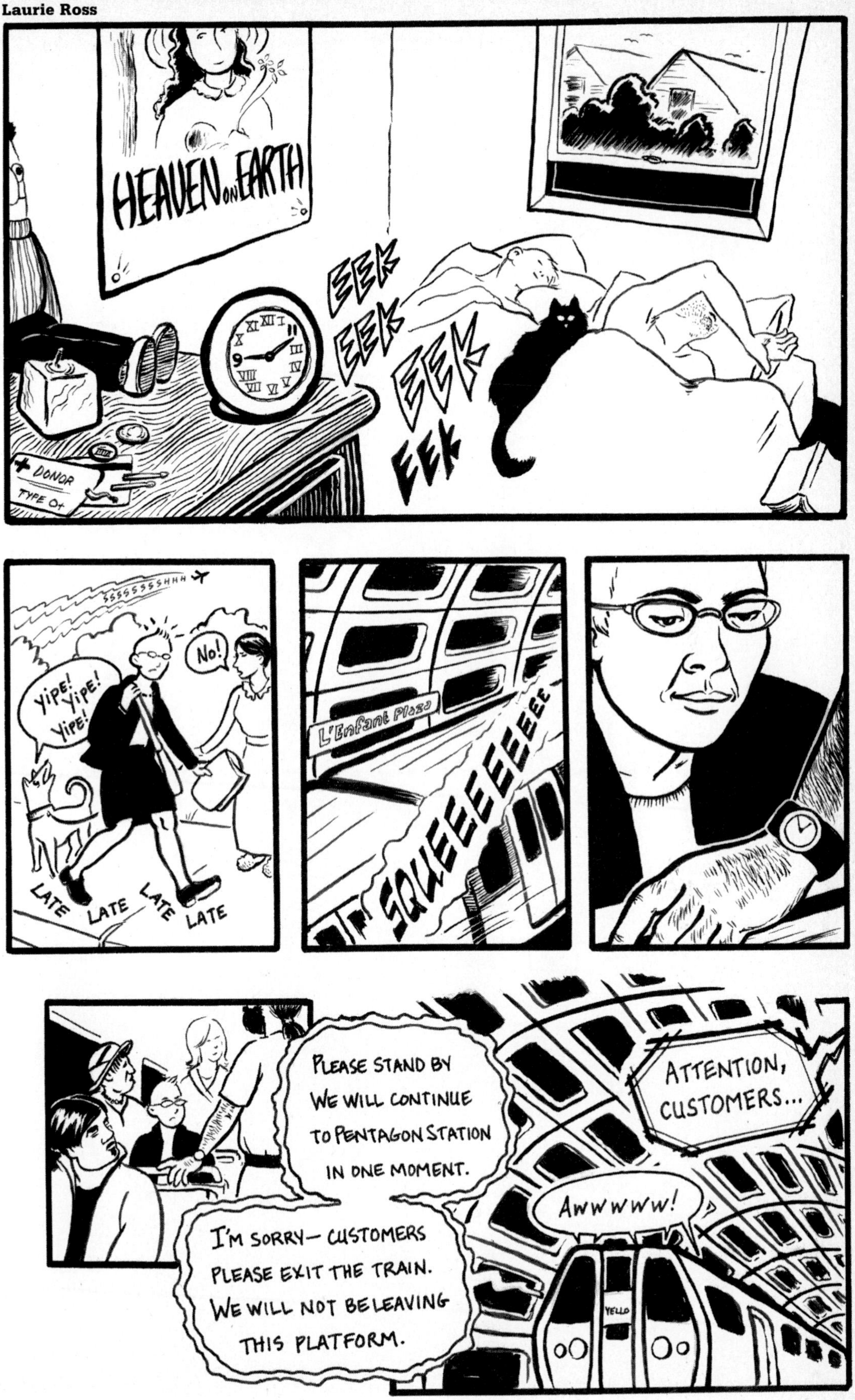
HEAVEN ON EARTH
+ DONOR
TYPE O+
EEK EEK EEK EEK
SSSSSSSSHHH
Yipe! Yipe! Yipe!
No!
LATE LATE LATE LATE
L'Enfant Plaza
SQUEEEEEEEEEEE
PLEASE STAND BY WE WILL CONTINUE TO PENTAGON STATION IN ONE MOMENT.
ATTENTION, CUSTOMERS...
AWWWWW!
I'M SORRY— CUSTOMERS PLEASE EXIT THE TRAIN. WE WILL NOT BE LEAVING THIS PLATFORM.
YELLO

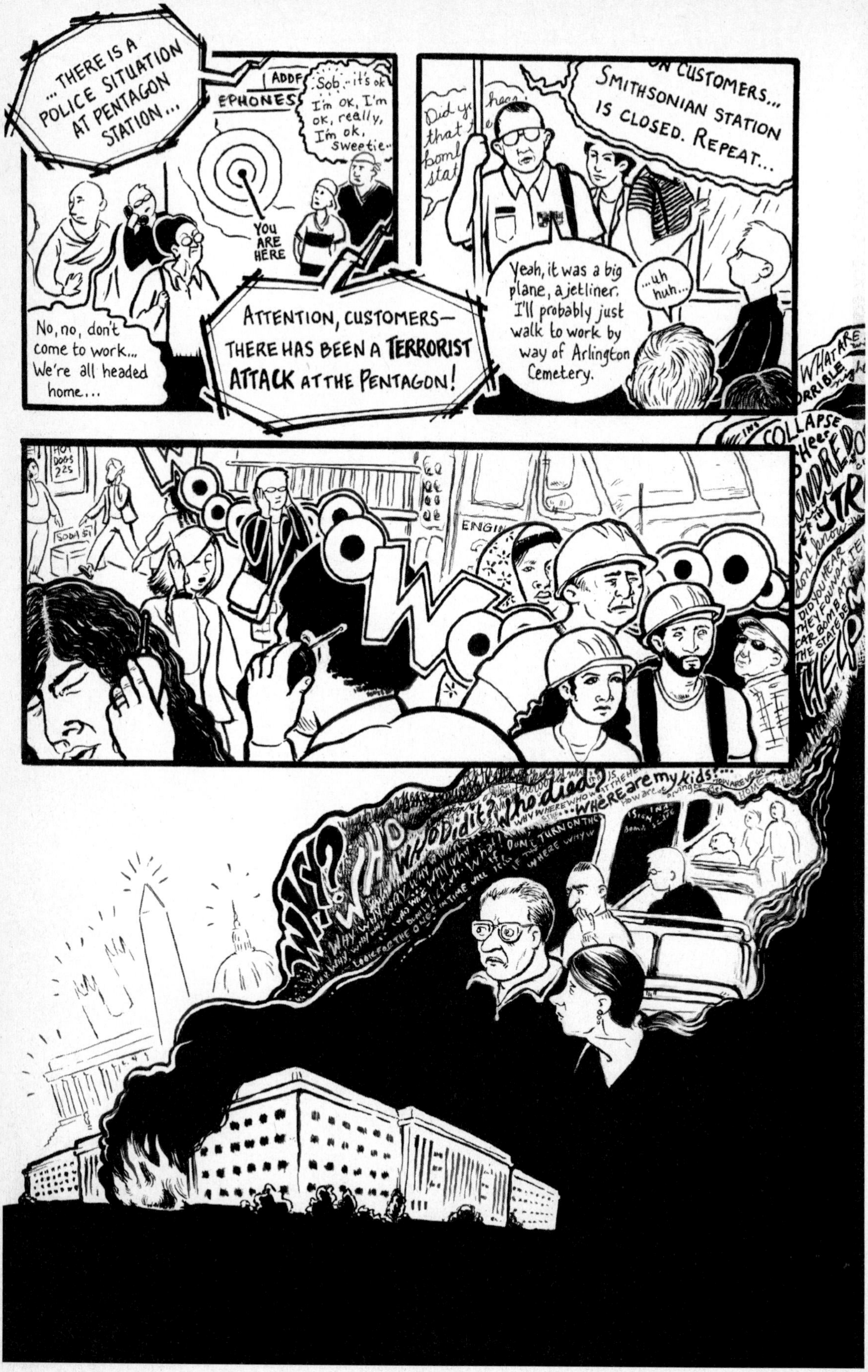
... THERE IS A POLICE SITUATION AT PENTAGON STATION...
ADDF
EPHONES
Sob... it's ok I'm ok, I'm ok, really, I'm ok, sweetie...
YOU ARE HERE
No, no, don't come to work... We're all headed home...
ATTENTION, CUSTOMERS— THERE HAS BEEN A TERRORIST ATTACK AT THE PENTAGON!
CUSTOMERS... SMITHSONIAN STATION IS CLOSED. REPEAT...
Yeah, it was a big plane, a jetliner. I'll probably just walk to work by way of Arlington Cemetery.
...uh huh...
WHAT ARE
ORRIBLE
COLLAPSE
DID YOU HEAR THEY FOUND A CAR BOMB AT THE STATE DE
HOT DOGS 2.25
SODA $1
ENGIN
WHY? WHO WHO DID IT? Who died?
WHERE are my kids?...
DON'T TURN ON THE
LOOK FOR THE ONES
WHERE WHY
HOME

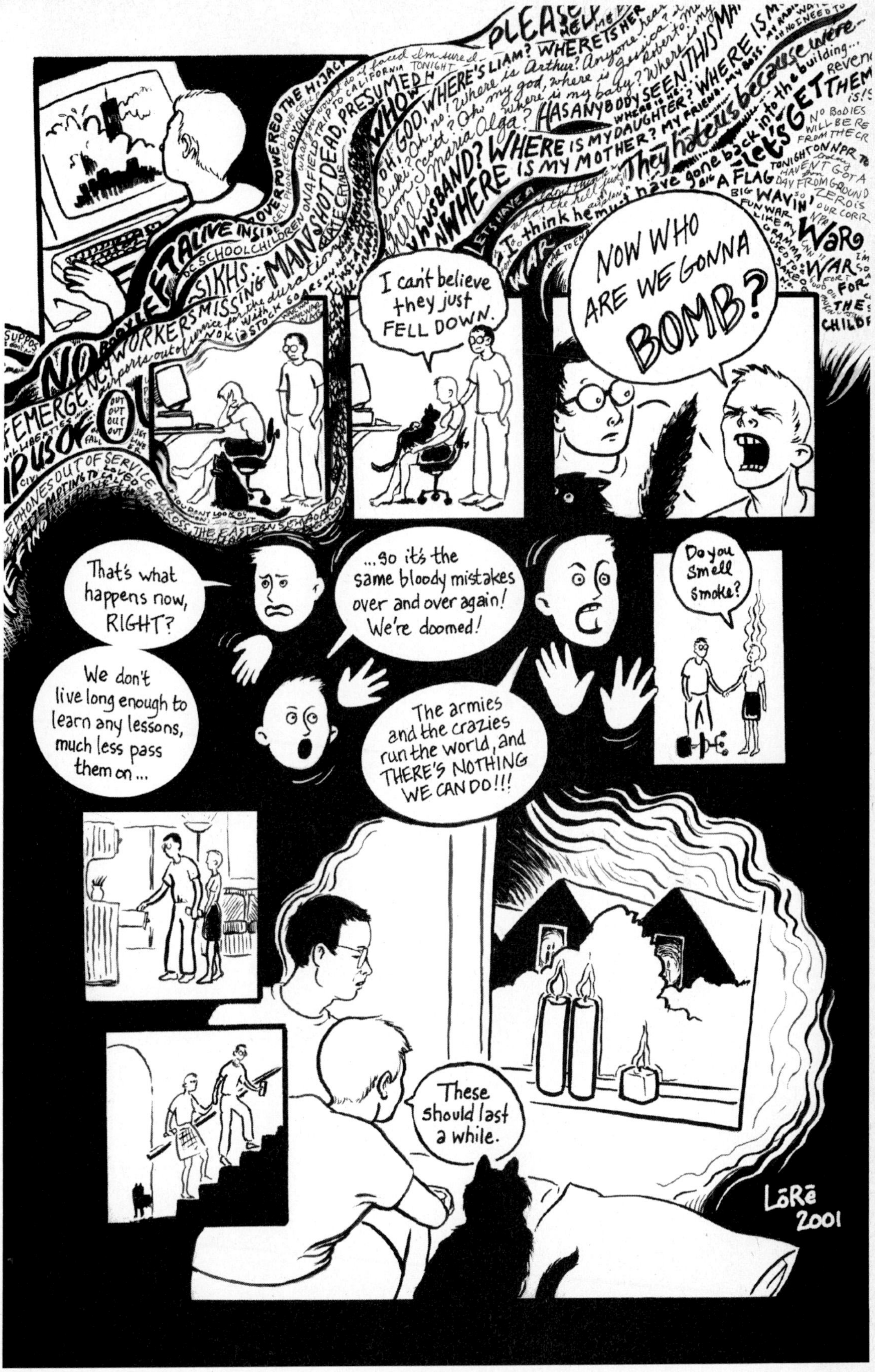
I can't believe they just FELL DOWN.
NOW WHO ARE WE GONNA BOMB?
That's what happens now, RIGHT?
...so it's the same bloody mistakes over and over again! We're doomed!
Do you smell smoke?
We don't live long enough to learn any lessons, much less pass them on...
The armies and the crazies run the world, and THERE'S NOTHING WE CAN DO!!!
These should last a while.
LōRē 2001

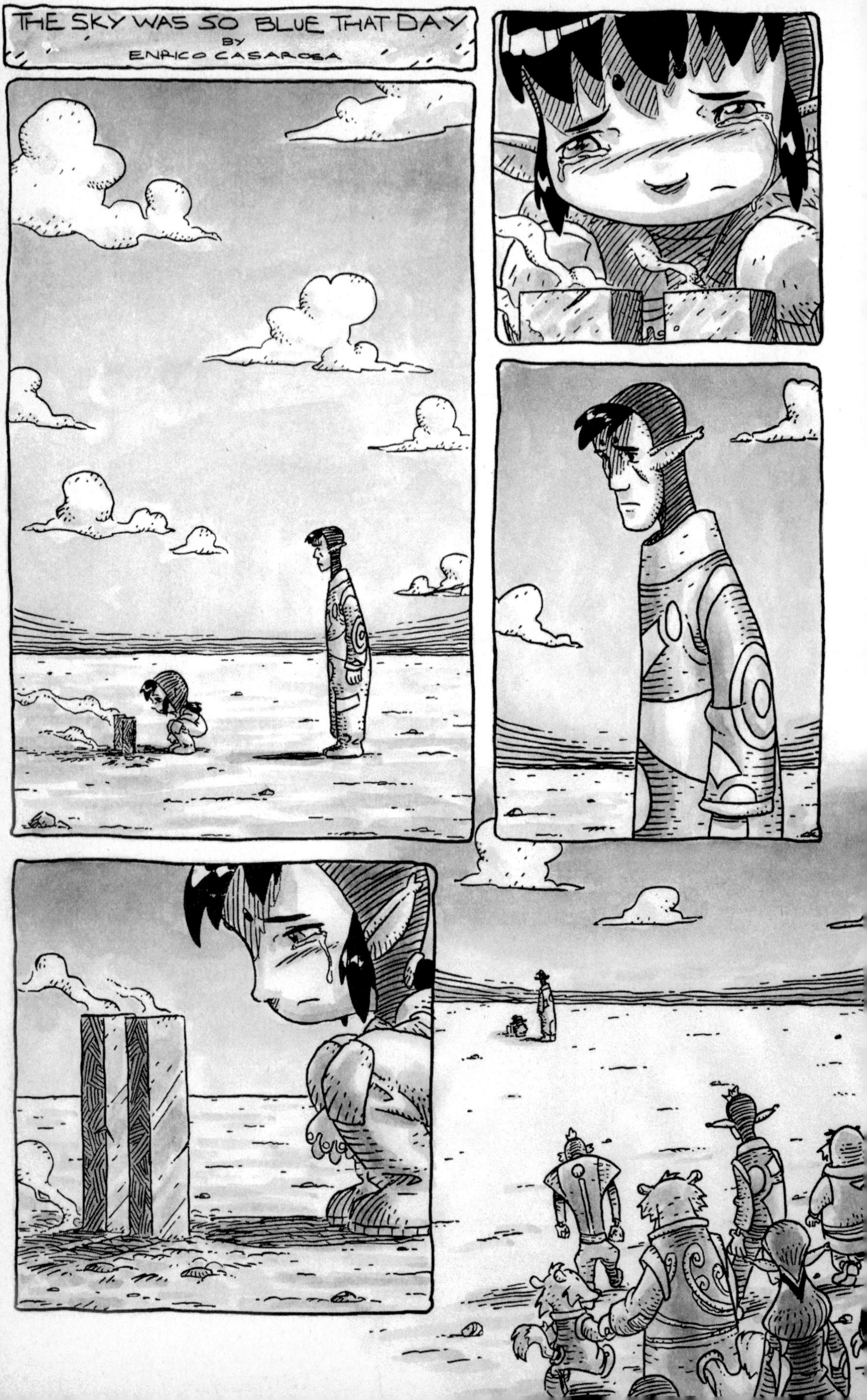
THE SKY WAS SO BLUE THAT DAY
BY
ENRICO CASAROSA

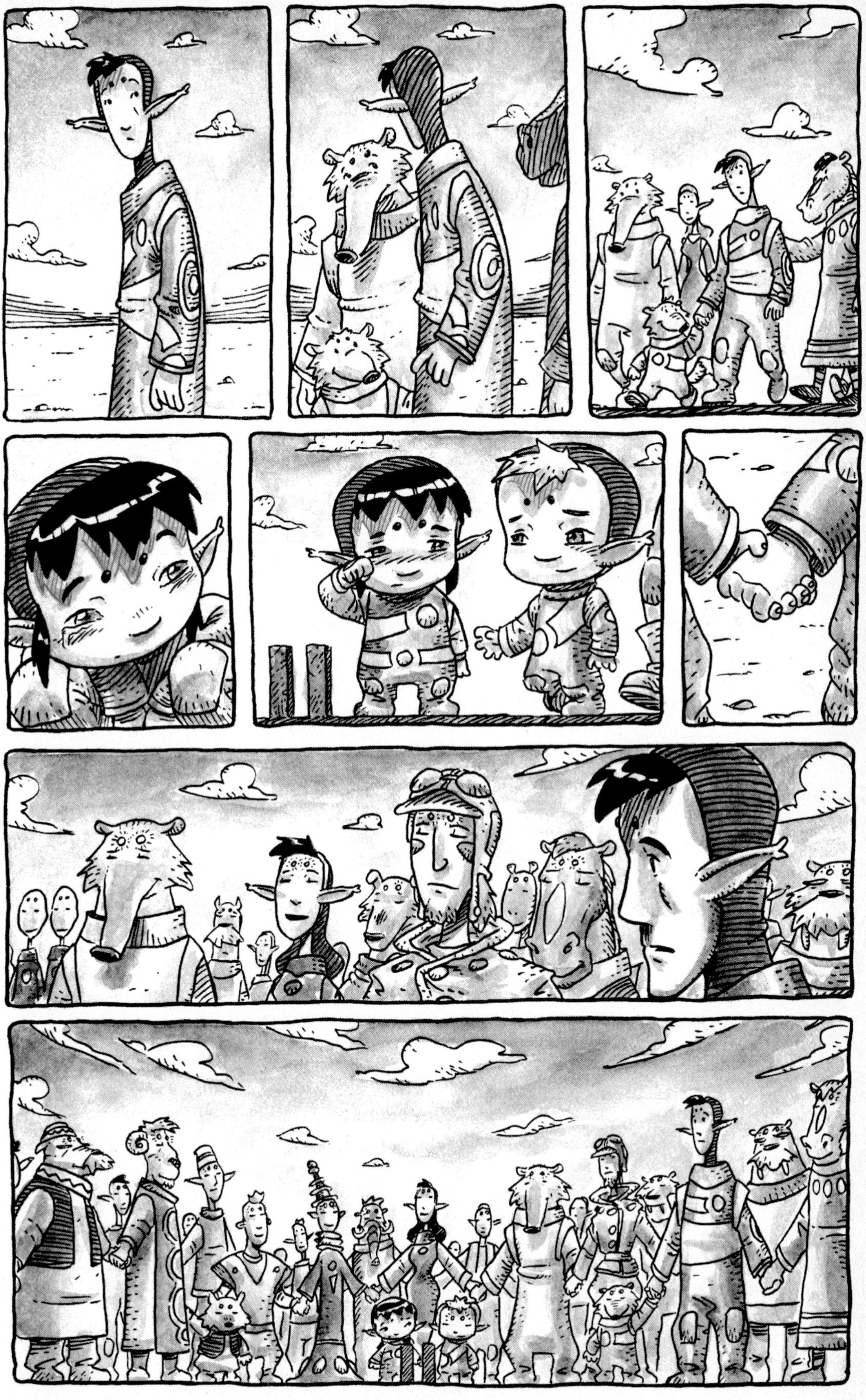

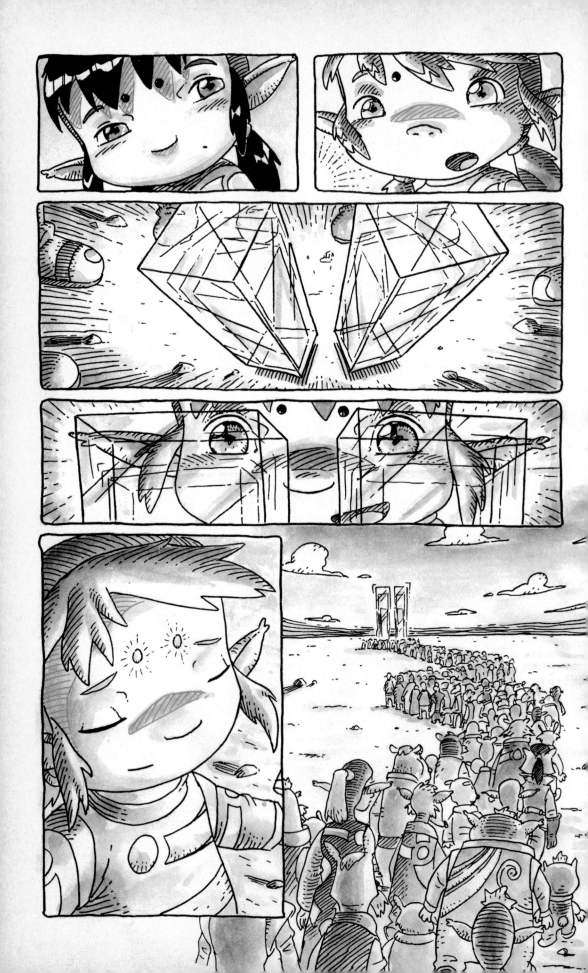

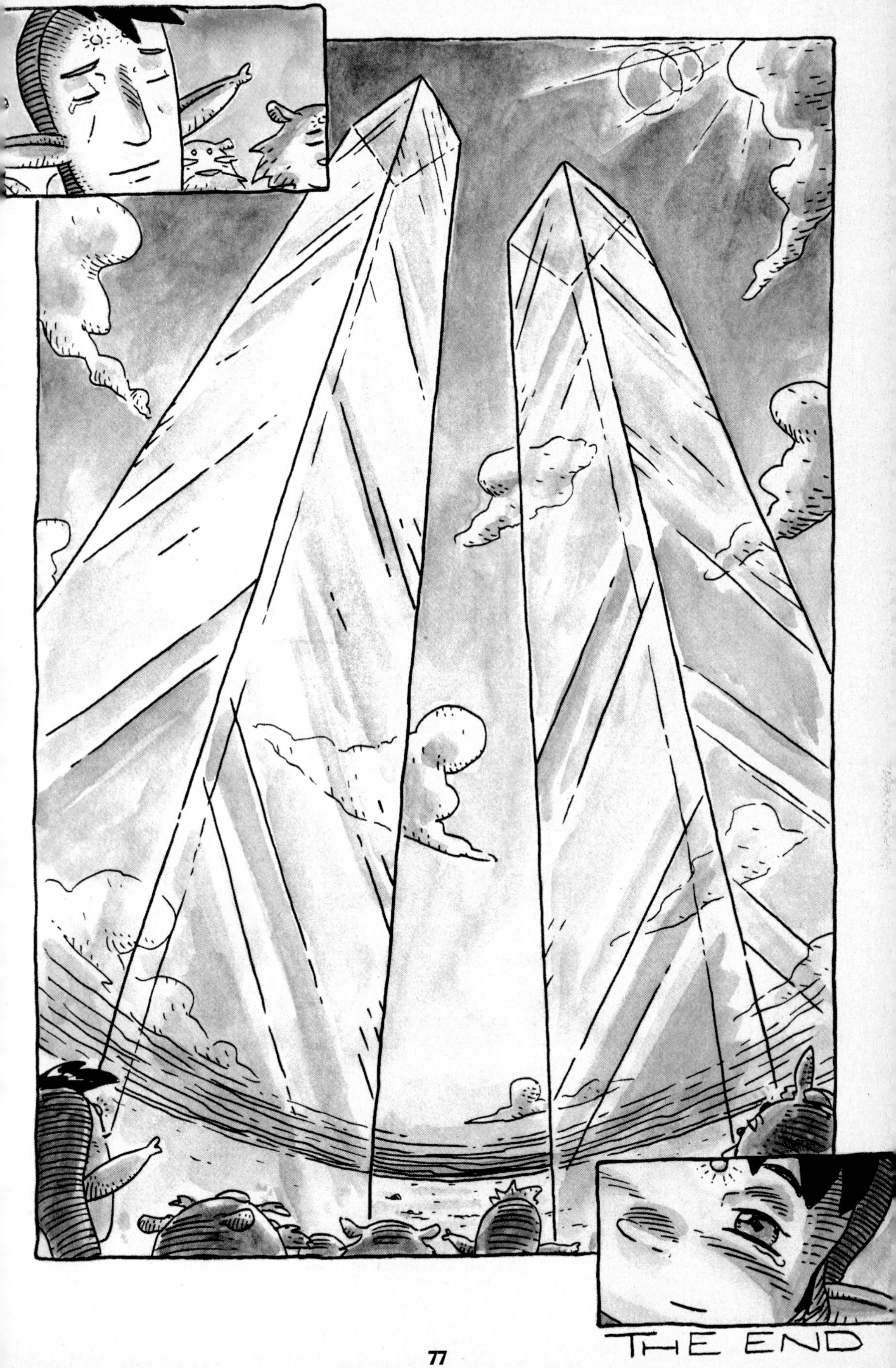
THE END

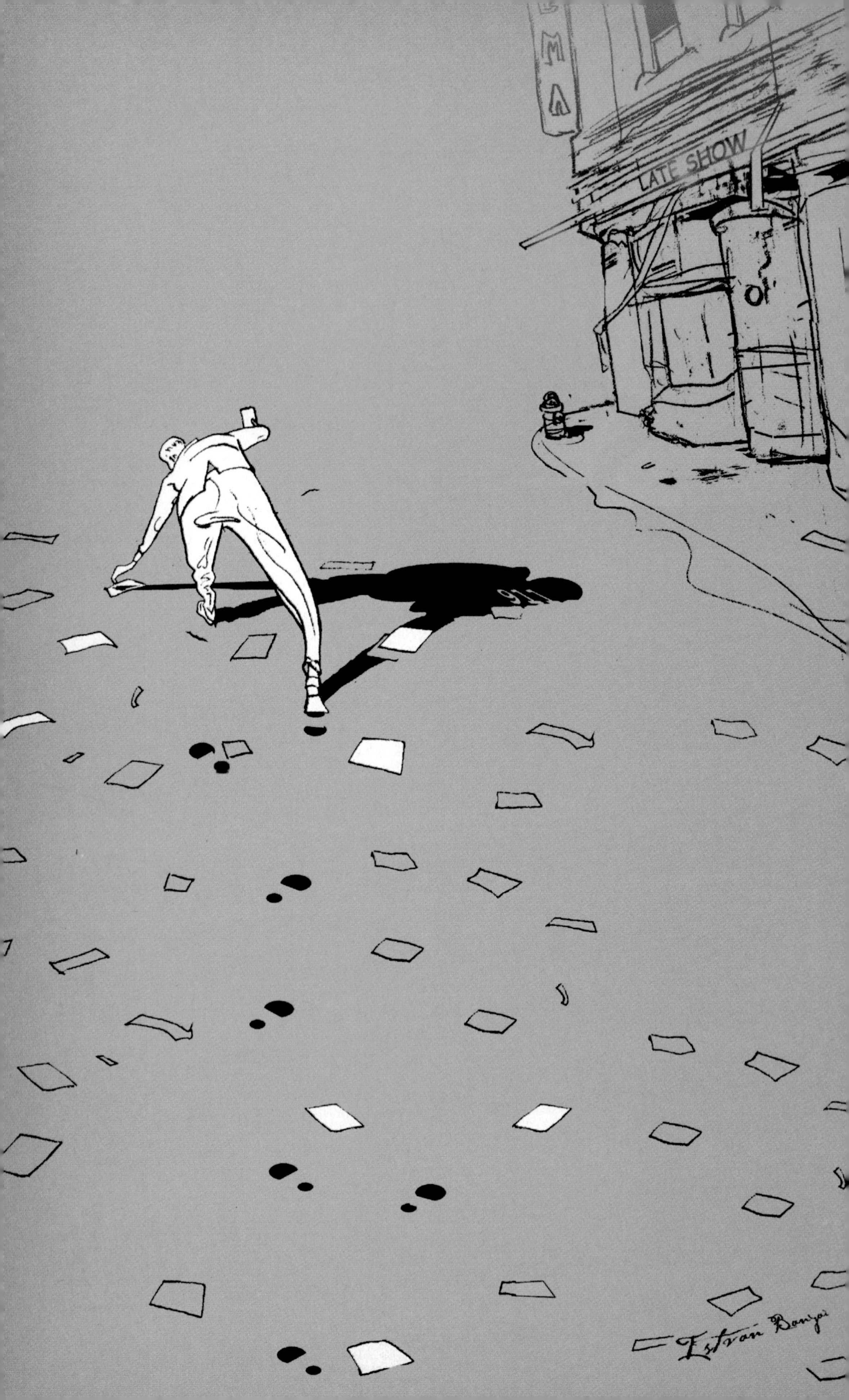
LATE SHOW
Istvan Banyai

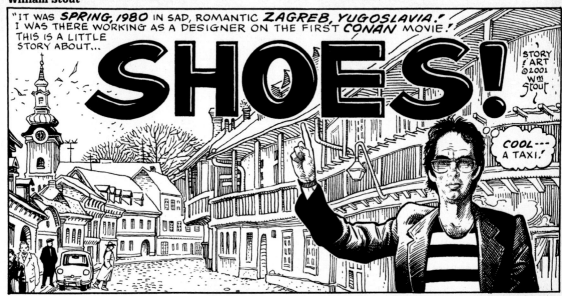

"IT WAS *SPRING, 1980* IN SAD, ROMANTIC *ZAGREB, YUGOSLAVIA!* I WAS THERE WORKING AS A DESIGNER ON THE FIRST *CONAN* MOVIE! THIS IS A LITTLE STORY ABOUT...

SHOES!

STORY & ART © 2001 WM STOUT

COOL--- A TAXI!

"I WAS STILL ADJUSTING TO THE TIME CHANGE AND HAD *OVERSLEPT!* I NEEDED A CAB RIDE TO WORK..."

WHERE YOU GO?

JADRAN FILM STUDIO!

"I WATCHED THE ATTRACTIVE ARCHITECTURE AND CITIZENS OF MY NEW, TEMPORARY HOME CITY WITH FASCINATION AND PLEASURE THROUGH THE CAR'S WINDOWS.

YOU *AMERICAN?*

YEAH.

BUSTED! IT WAS MY LOOK OR MY ACCENT--- *OR BOTH!*"

AT END OF WAR* I WAS SMALL BOY...

*WORLD WAR TWO

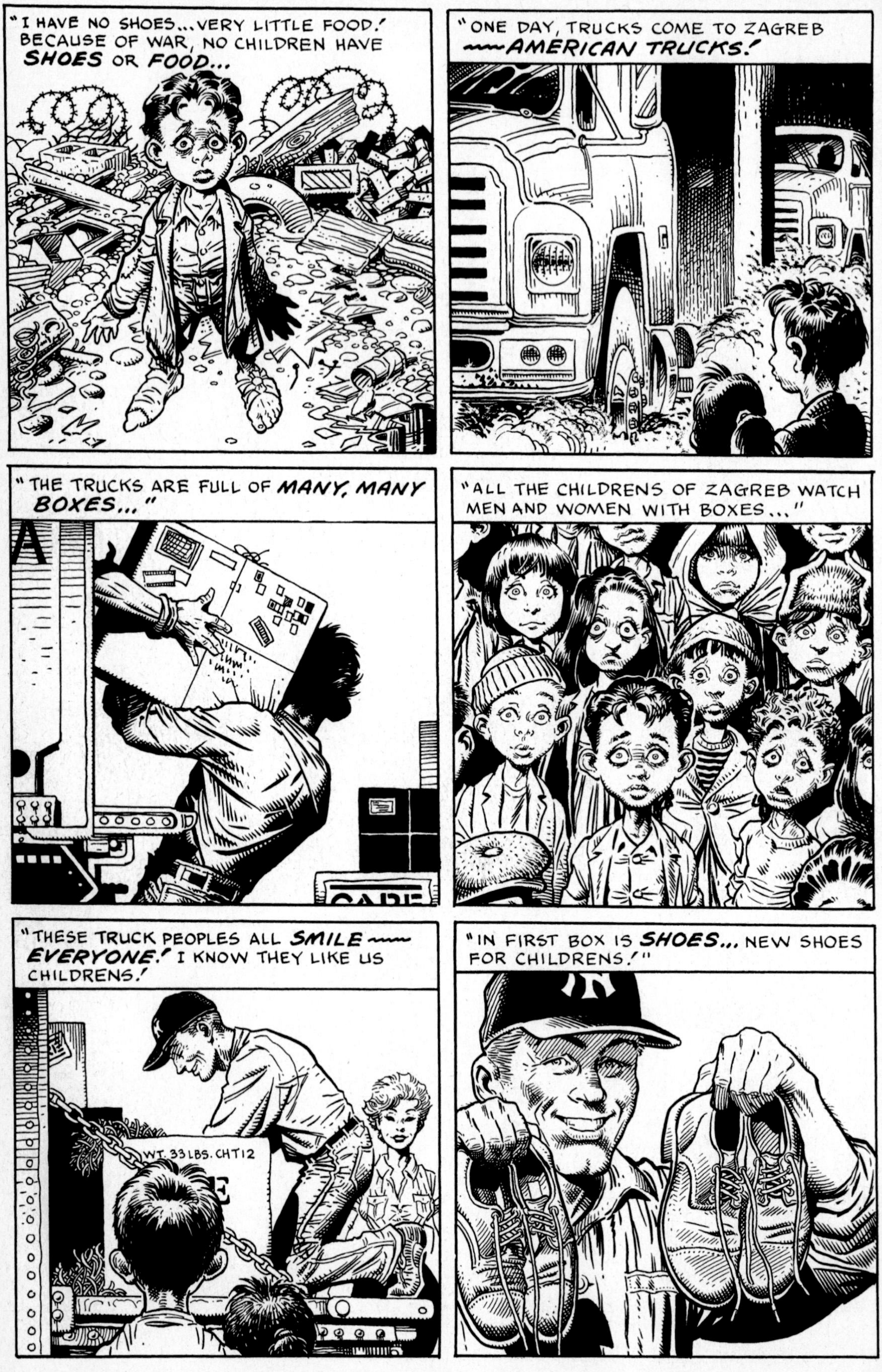
"I HAVE NO SHOES... VERY LITTLE FOOD! BECAUSE OF WAR, NO CHILDREN HAVE SHOES OR FOOD...
"ONE DAY, TRUCKS COME TO ZAGREB — AMERICAN TRUCKS!
"THE TRUCKS ARE FULL OF MANY, MANY BOXES..."
"ALL THE CHILDRENS OF ZAGREB WATCH MEN AND WOMEN WITH BOXES..."
"THESE TRUCK PEOPLES ALL SMILE — EVERYONE! I KNOW THEY LIKE US CHILDRENS!
WT. 33 LBS. CHT12
"IN FIRST BOX IS SHOES... NEW SHOES FOR CHILDRENS!"

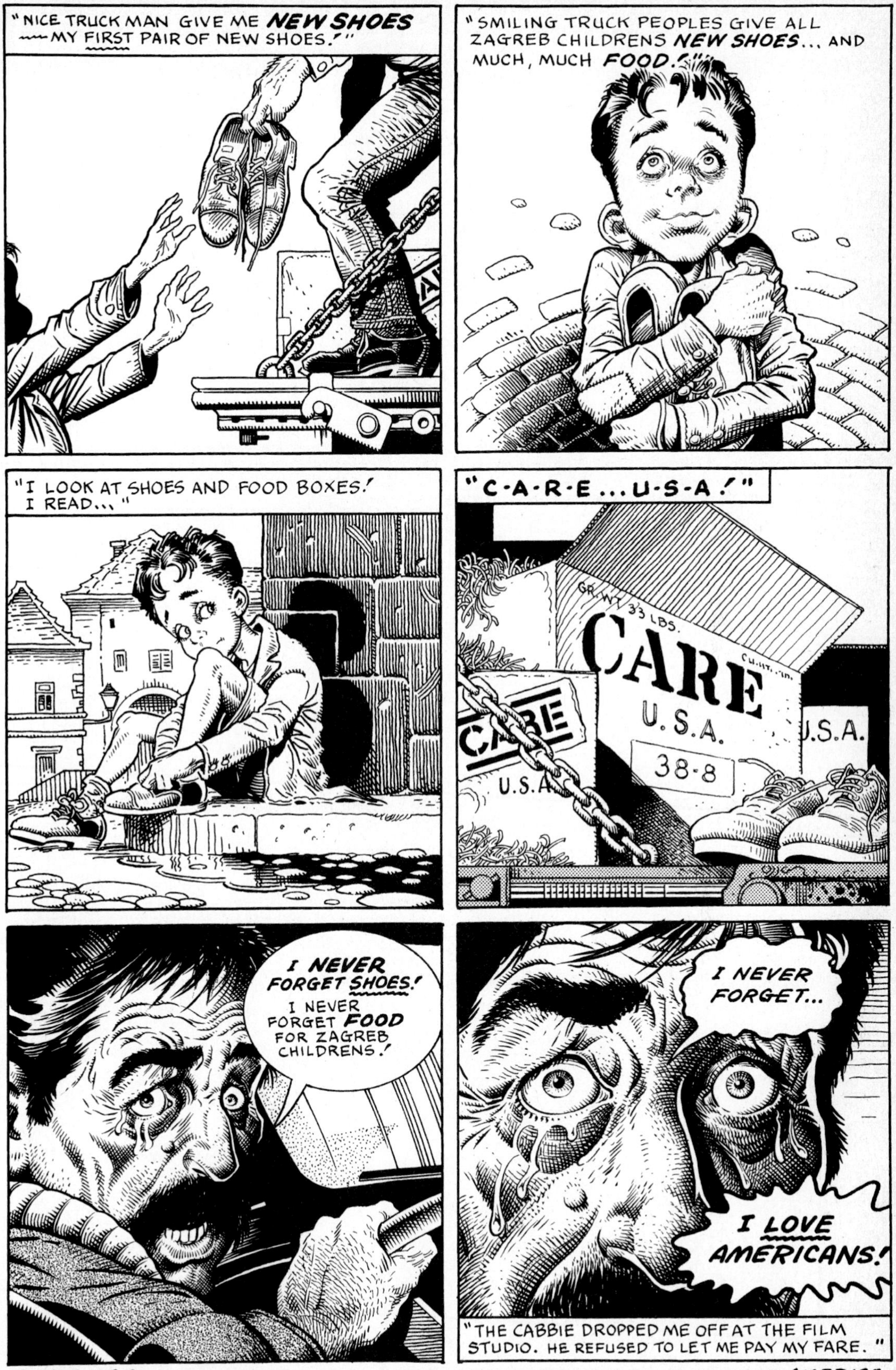
"NICE TRUCK MAN GIVE ME NEW SHOES
— MY FIRST PAIR OF NEW SHOES!"
"SMILING TRUCK PEOPLES GIVE ALL ZAGREB CHILDRENS NEW SHOES... AND MUCH, MUCH FOOD!"
"I LOOK AT SHOES AND FOOD BOXES! I READ..."
"C-A-R-E...U-S-A!"
GR WT 33 LBS.
CARE
U.S.A.
38-8
CARE
U.S.A
U.S.A.
I NEVER FORGET SHOES!
I NEVER FORGET FOOD FOR ZAGREB CHILDRENS!
I NEVER FORGET...
I LOVE AMERICANS!
"THE CABBIE DROPPED ME OFF AT THE FILM STUDIO. HE REFUSED TO LET ME PAY MY FARE."

CARE USA IS STILL IN EXISTENCE, BRINGING RELIEF AND THE BEST FACE AND SPIRIT OF **AMERICA** TO PEOPLE IN NEED AROUND THE WORLD! PLEASE VISIT THEIR WEBSITE: **WWW.CARE.ORG**

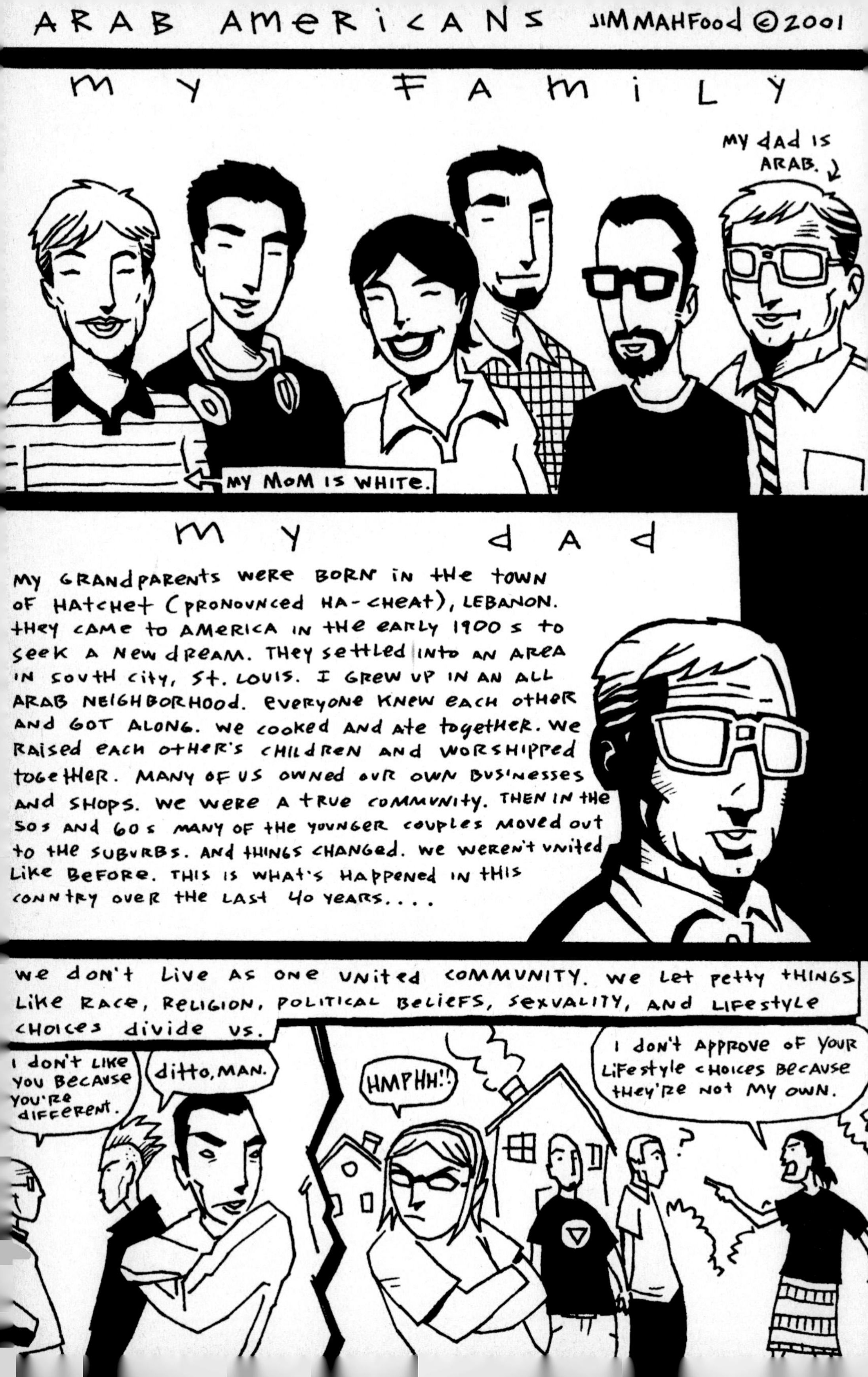
ARAB AMERICANS
JIMMAHFood ©2001
MY FAMILY
MY DAD IS ARAB.
MY MOM IS WHITE.
MY DAD
MY GRANDPARENTS WERE BORN IN THE TOWN OF HATCHET (PRONOUNCED HA-CHEAT), LEBANON. THEY CAME TO AMERICA IN THE EARLY 1900S TO SEEK A NEW DREAM. THEY SETTLED INTO AN AREA IN SOUTH CITY, ST. LOUIS. I GREW UP IN AN ALL ARAB NEIGHBORHOOD. EVERYONE KNEW EACH OTHER AND GOT ALONG. WE COOKED AND ATE TOGETHER. WE RAISED EACH OTHER'S CHILDREN AND WORSHIPPED TOGETHER. MANY OF US OWNED OUR OWN BUSINESSES AND SHOPS. WE WERE A TRUE COMMUNITY. THEN IN THE 50S AND 60S MANY OF THE YOUNGER COUPLES MOVED OUT TO THE SUBURBS. AND THINGS CHANGED. WE WEREN'T UNITED LIKE BEFORE. THIS IS WHAT'S HAPPENED IN THIS CONNTRY OVER THE LAST 40 YEARS....
WE DON'T LIVE AS ONE UNITED COMMUNITY. WE LET PETTY THINGS LIKE RACE, RELIGION, POLITICAL BELIEFS, SEXUALITY, AND LIFESTYLE CHOICES DIVIDE US.
I DON'T LIKE YOU BECAUSE YOU'RE DIFFERENT.
DITTO, MAN.
HMPHH!
I DON'T APPROVE OF YOUR LIFESTYLE CHOICES BECAUSE THEY'RE NOT MY OWN.
?

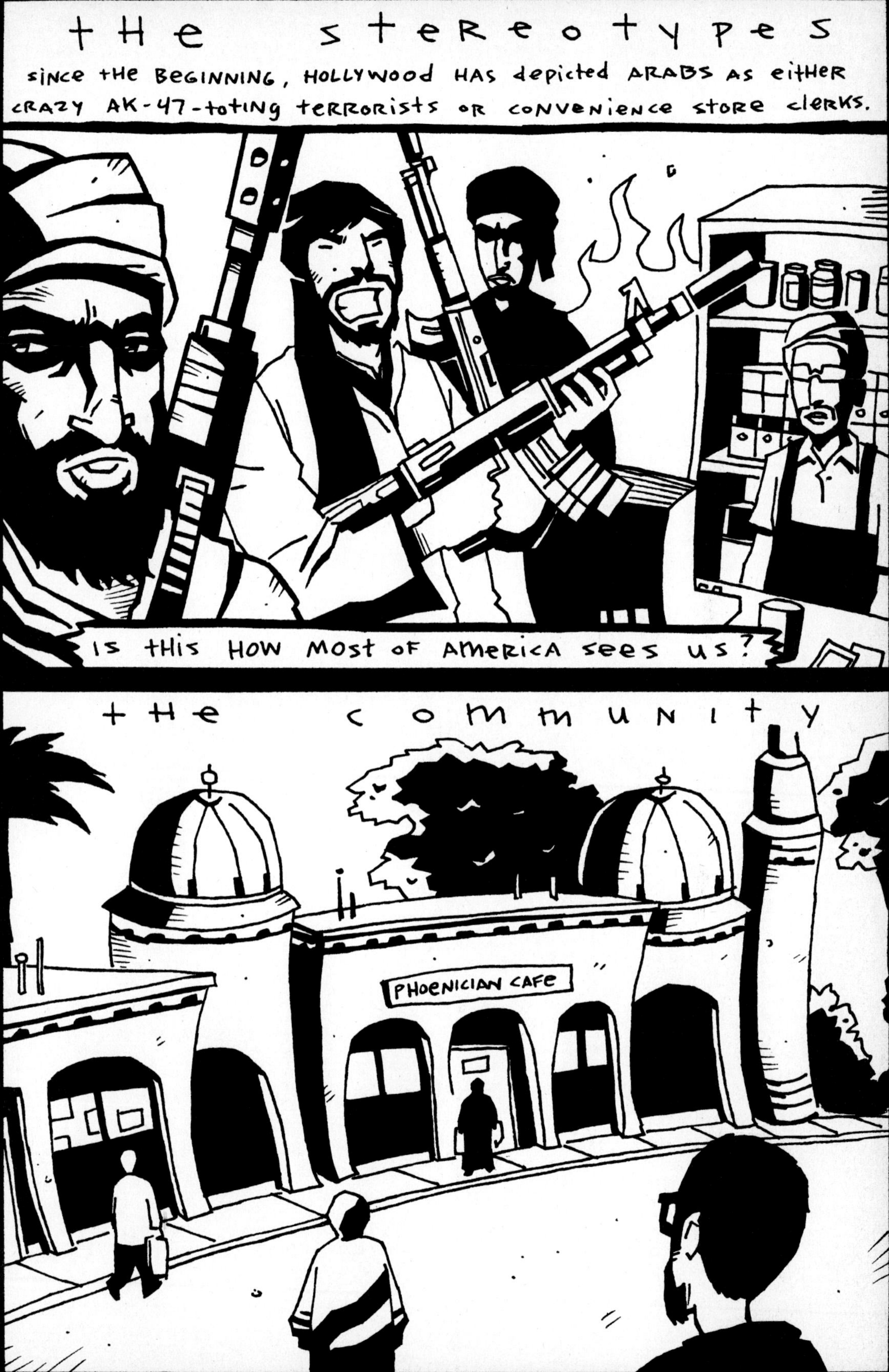
the stereotypes
since the beginning, hollywood has depicted arabs as either crazy AK-47-toting terrorists or convenience store clerks.
is this how most of america sees us?
the community
PHOENICIAN CAFE

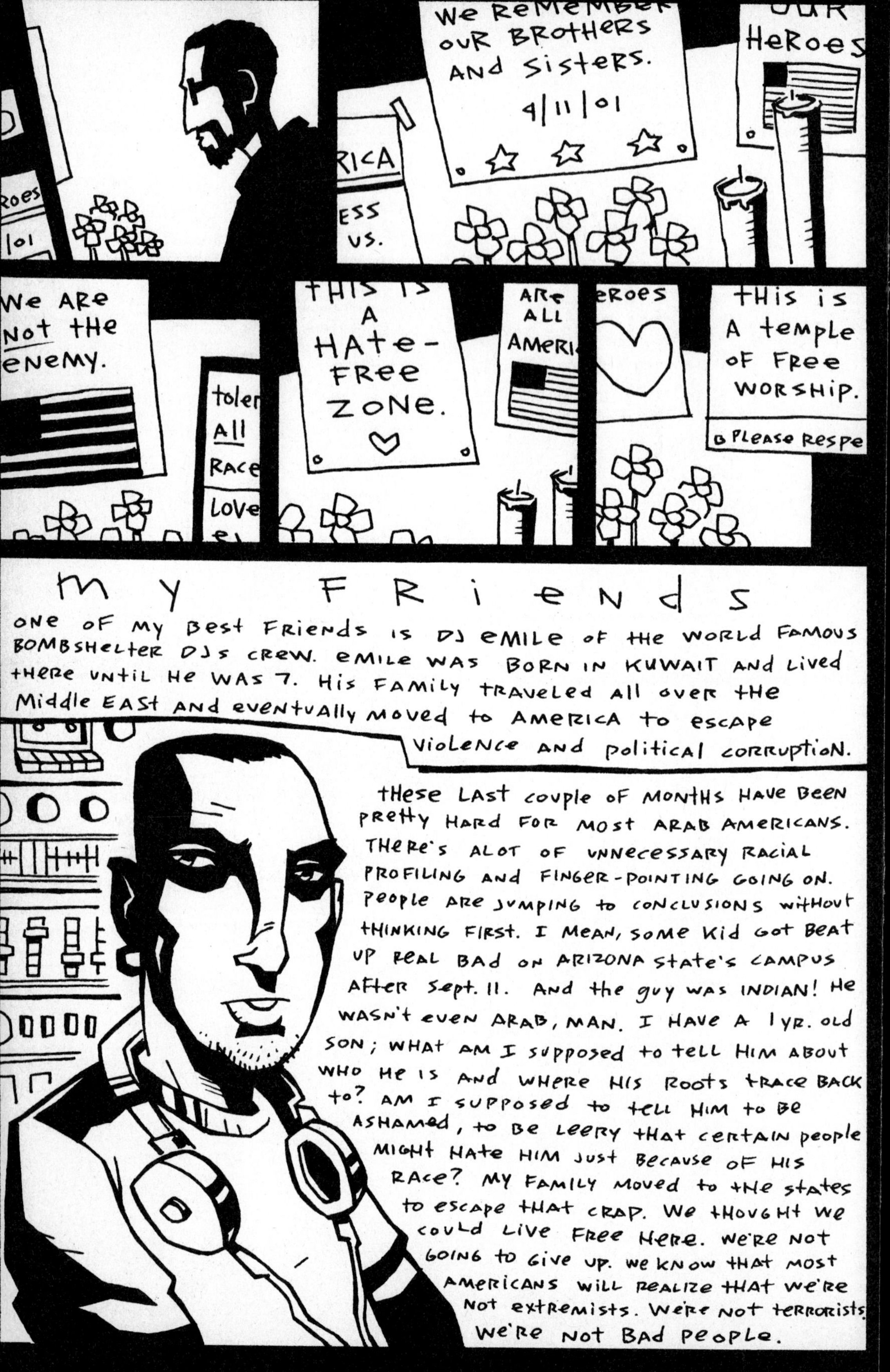

We Remember our Brothers and Sisters.
9/11/01
Heroes
ESS US.
We are not the enemy.
This is a Hate-Free zone.
Are All Ameri
eroes
This is a temple of Free worship.
Please Respe
toler
All
Race
Love
My Friends
One of my best friends is DJ Emile of the world famous Bombshelter DJs crew. Emile was born in Kuwait and lived there until he was 7. His family traveled all over the Middle East and eventually moved to America to escape violence and political corruption.
These last couple of months have been pretty hard for most Arab Americans. There's alot of unnecessary racial profiling and finger-pointing going on. People are jumping to conclusions without thinking first. I mean, some kid got beat up real bad on Arizona State's campus after Sept. 11. And the guy was Indian! He wasn't even Arab, man. I have a 1yr. old son; what am I supposed to tell him about who he is and where his roots trace back to? Am I supposed to tell him to be ashamed, to be leery that certain people might hate him just because of his race? My family moved to the states to escape that crap. We thought we could live free here. We're not going to give up. We know that most Americans will realize that we're not extremists. We're not terrorists. We're not bad people.

MY FRIEND BASSEL WAS BORN AND RAISED IN LEBANON. HE MOVED TO THE STATES SO THAT HE COULD OWN HIS OWN BUSINESS AND START A FAMILY. BASSEL OWNS AND OPERATES A VERY SUCESSFUL MIDDLE EASTERN RESTAURANT IN TEMPE, AZ.

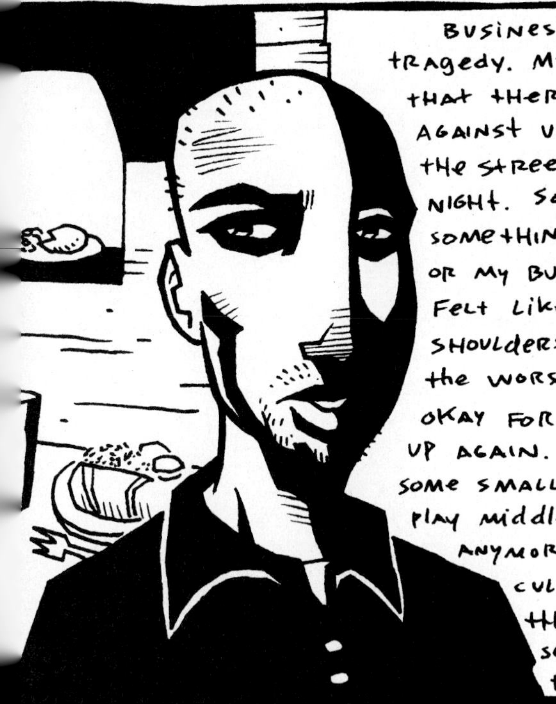

BUSINESS SLOWED DOWN AFTER THE SEPT. 11TH TRAGEDY. MY EMPLOYEES AND I WERE WORRIED THAT THERE MIGHT BE SOME SORT OF BACKLASH AGAINST US. ANOTHER ARABIC RESTAURANT DOWN THE STREET HAD ITS WINDOWS SHOT OUT ONE NIGHT. SO I WAS PARANOID FOR AWHILE THAT SOMETHING MIGHT HAPPEN TO ONE OF MY WORKERS, OR MY BUSINESS, OR EVEN MYSELF. WE ALL FELT LIKE WE WERE LOOKING OVER OUR SHOULDERS ALOT. LIKE WE WERE EXPECTING THE WORST TO HAPPEN. BUT THINGS HAVE BEEN OKAY FOR THE MOST PART. BUSINESS HAS PICKED UP AGAIN. UNFORTUNATELY, WE'VE HAD TO MAKE SOME SMALL CHANGES HERE AND THERE. I DON'T PLAY MIDDLE EASTERN MUSIC IN THE RESTAURANT ANYMORE. IT'S NOT THAT I'M ASHAMED OF MY CULTURE OR ANYTHING. IT JUST SEEMS THAT MOST PEOPLE ARE STILL OVERLY SENSITIVE TO THINGS LIKE THAT. HOPEFULLY, THAT WILL CHANGE IN TIME...

THE FUTURE

"IF YOU LIVE IN FEAR AND PARANOIA, IF YOU DON'T LIVE YOUR LIFE LIKE YOU NORMALLY WOULD, THEN THE TERRORISTS HAVE WON". WE'VE ALL HEARD THAT SAYING A MILLION TIMES SINCE THE ATTACK. IT DEFINITELY HAS SOME VALIDITY TO IT. BUT TERRORISTS OR NOT, I THINK THE BOTTOM LINE IS THIS: WE STILL HAVE ALOT OF UNITING TO DO IN THIS COUNTRY. WE STILL HAVE ALOT OF OBSTACLES TO OVERCOME WITH EACH OTHER. AS AMERICANS I THINK WE HAVE TO ASK OURSELVES WHAT WE'RE GOING TO DO ABOUT THE PROBLEM.

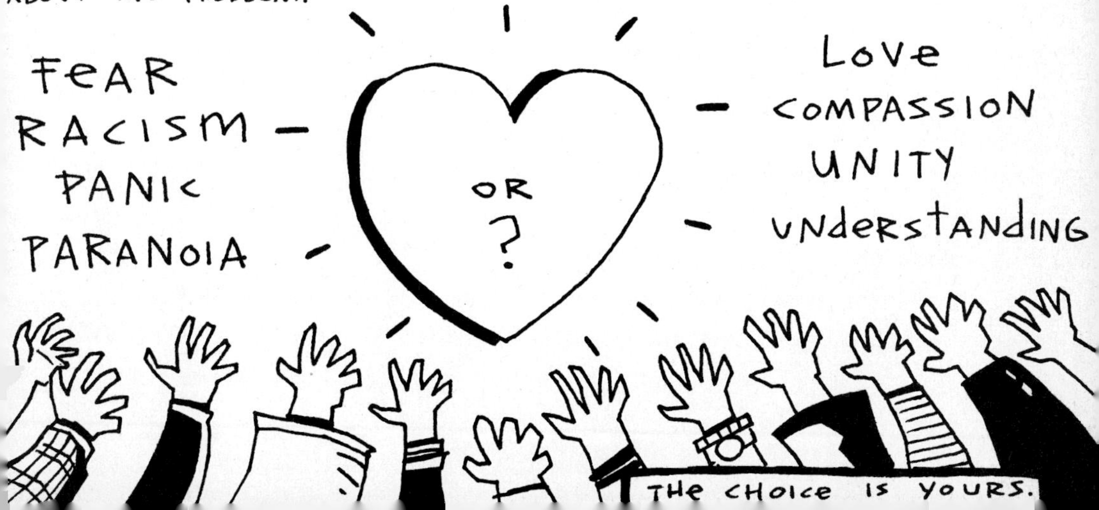
FEAR
RACISM
PANIC
PARANOIA
OR
?
LOVE
COMPASSION
UNITY
UNDERSTANDING

THE CHOICE IS YOURS.

John Snyder

A VIEW FROM D.C.

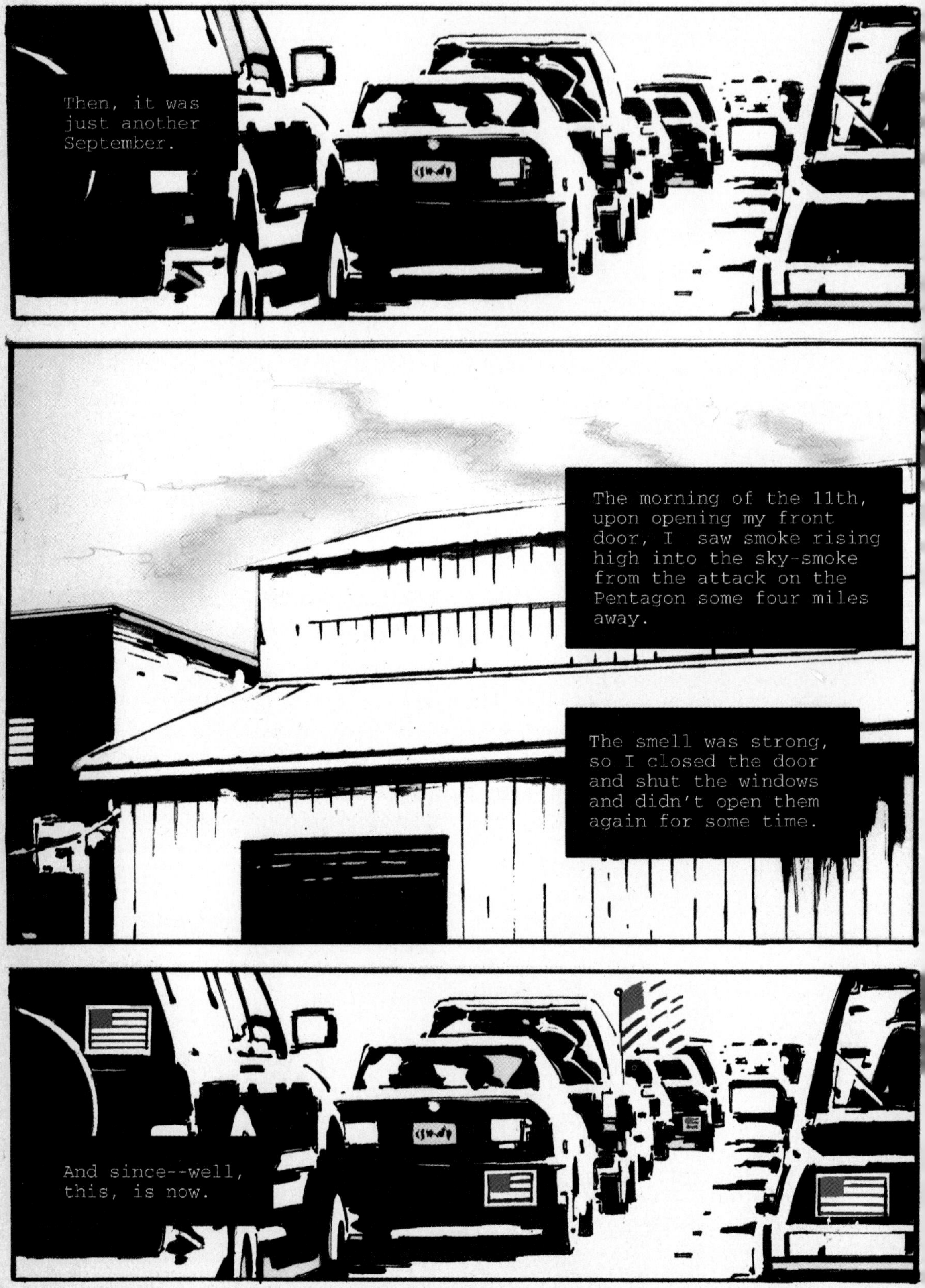

Then, it was just another September.
The morning of the 11th, upon opening my front door, I saw smoke rising high into the sky-smoke from the attack on the Pentagon some four miles away.
The smell was strong, so I closed the door and shut the windows and didn't open them again for some time.
And since--well, this, is now.

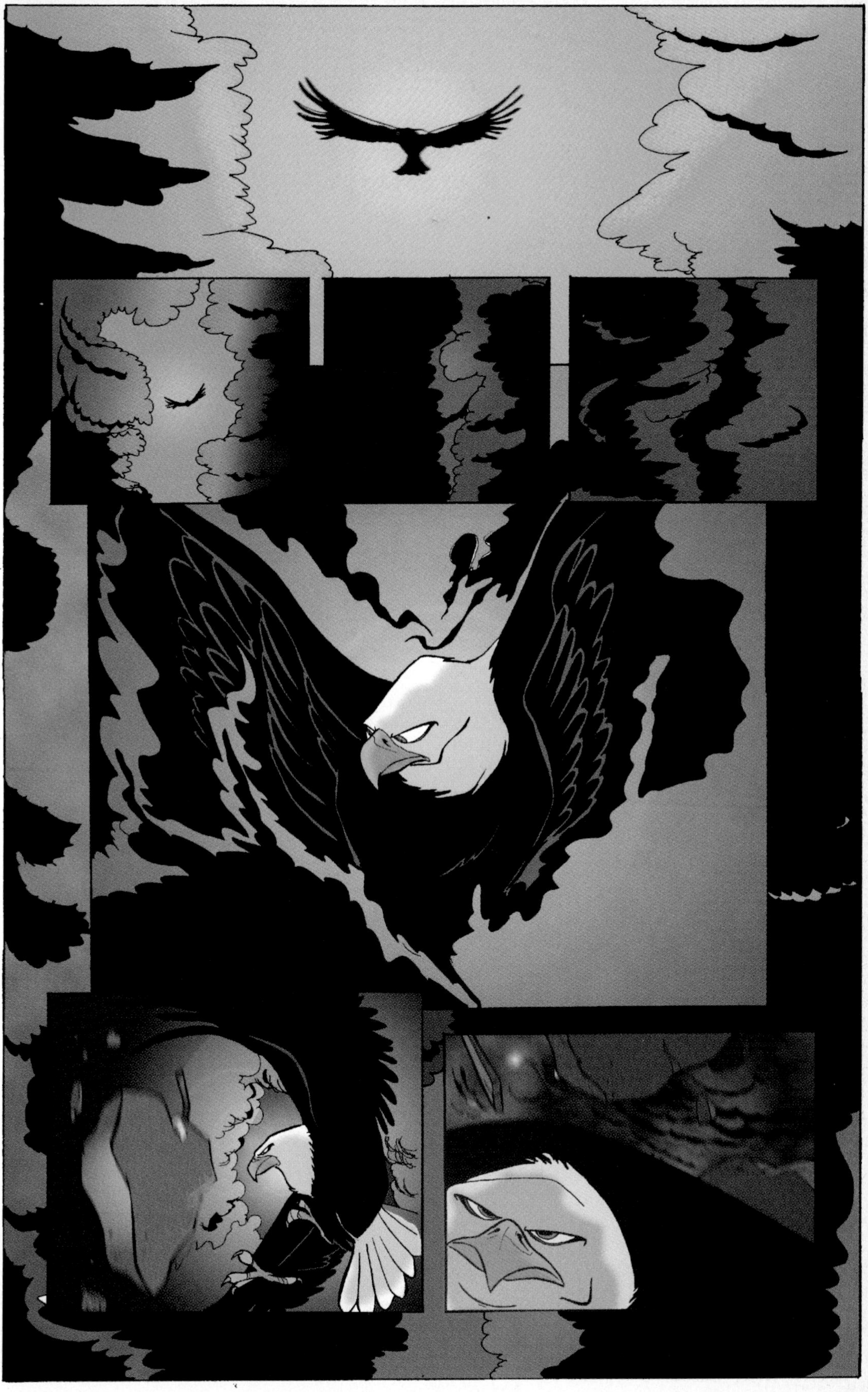

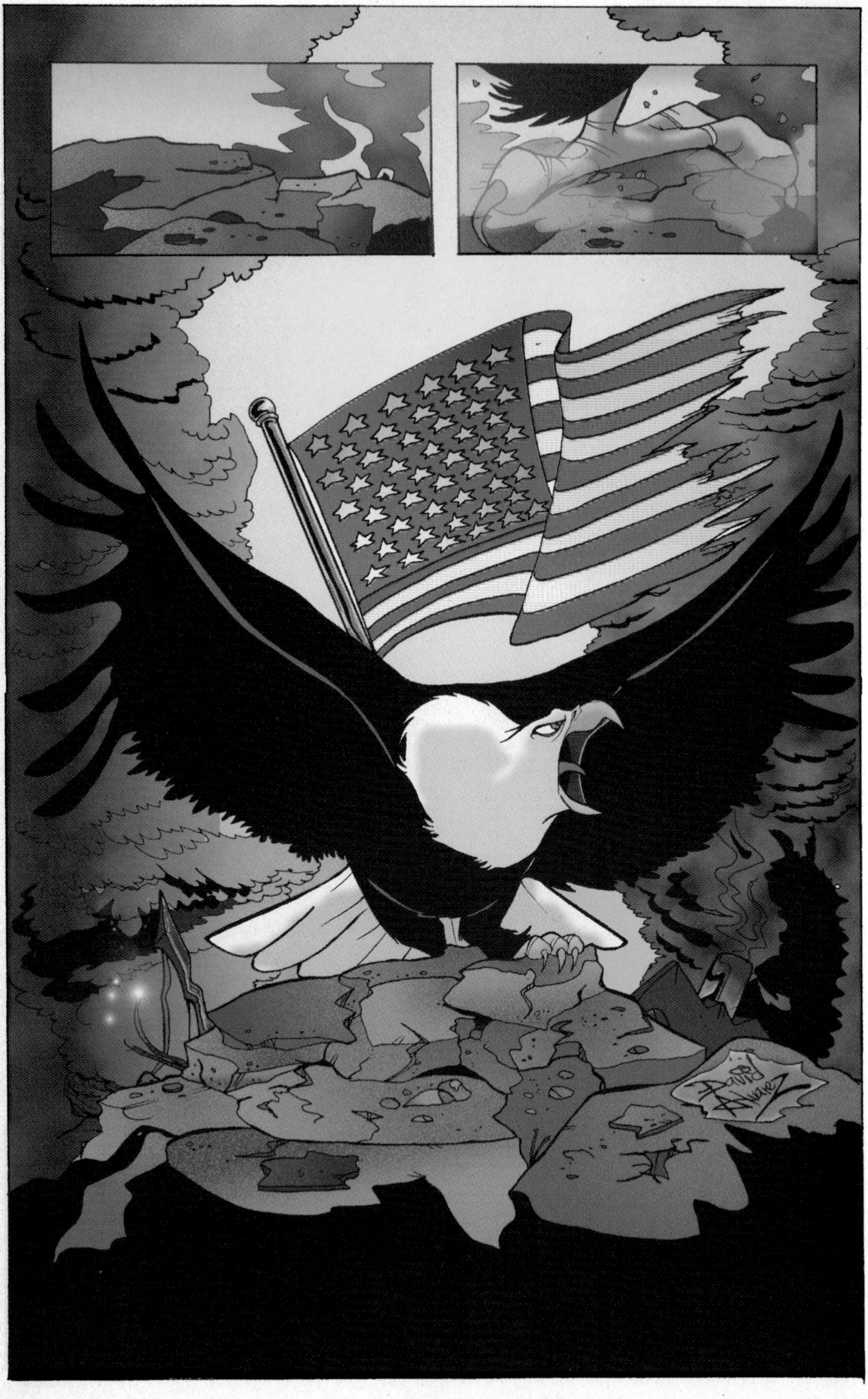

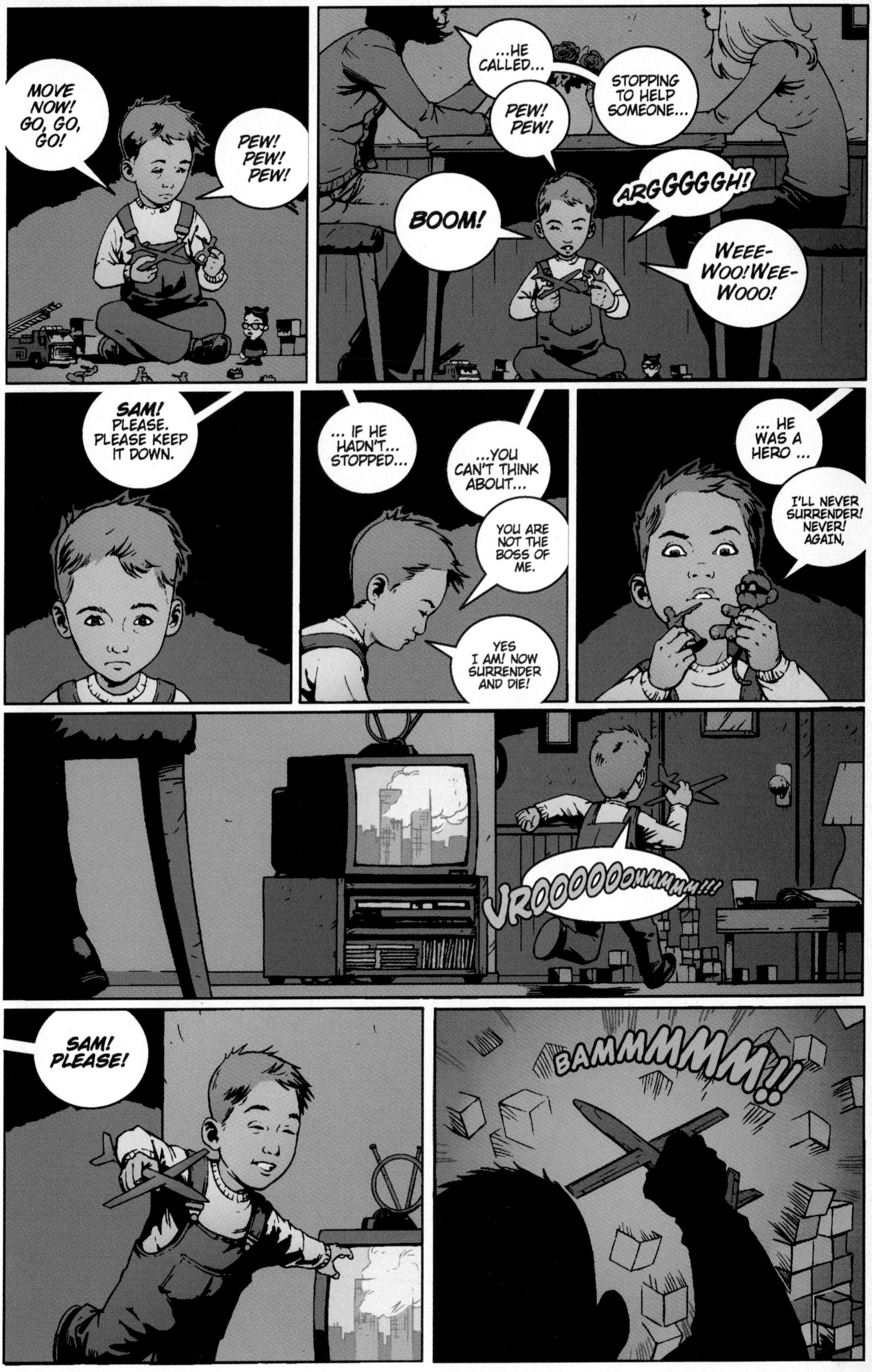
MOVE NOW! GO, GO, GO!
PEW! PEW! PEW!
...HE CALLED...
STOPPING TO HELP SOMEONE...
PEW! PEW!
ARGGGGGH!
BOOM!
WEEE-WOO! WEE-WOOO!
SAM! PLEASE. PLEASE KEEP IT DOWN.
... IF HE HADN'T... STOPPED...
...YOU CAN'T THINK ABOUT...
YOU ARE NOT THE BOSS OF ME.
YES I AM! NOW SURRENDER AND DIE!
... HE WAS A HERO ...
I'LL NEVER SURRENDER! NEVER! AGAIN,
VROOOOOOmmmmm!!!
SAM! PLEASE!
BAMMMMMM!!

WeeWoo-WeeWoo-Weeeeeee

COME ON. PUT AWAY YOUR TOYS, HONEY. IT'S TIME TO GO TO SCHOOL

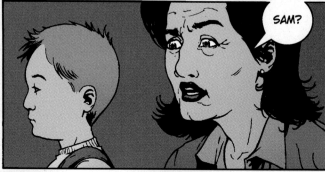

SAM?

I'M NOT GOING UNTIL DAD COMES HOME. I TOLD YOU.

OH... HONEY. WE TALKED ABOUT THIS. DAD...

HE CAN'T COME HOME. NOT ...EVER.

COME HERE, SWEETIE. IT'S OKAY...

BOOM! BOOM!

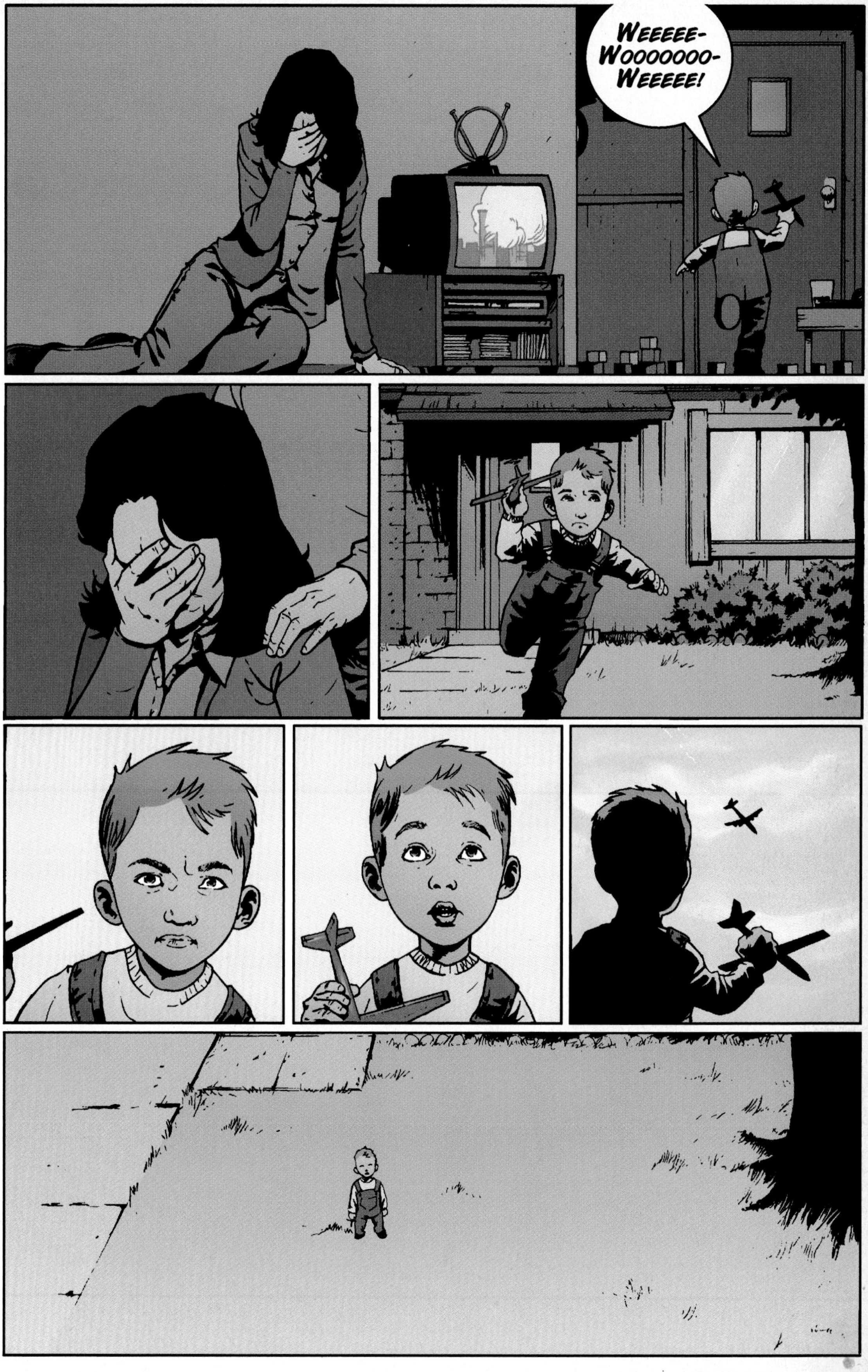
WEEEEE-WOOOOOOO-WEEEEE!

R. Sikoryak

ALL TRUE

NEW YORK REPORT

NO FUN

LATE SEPTEMBER EDITION

UNBELIEVABLE *A Tuesday in September*

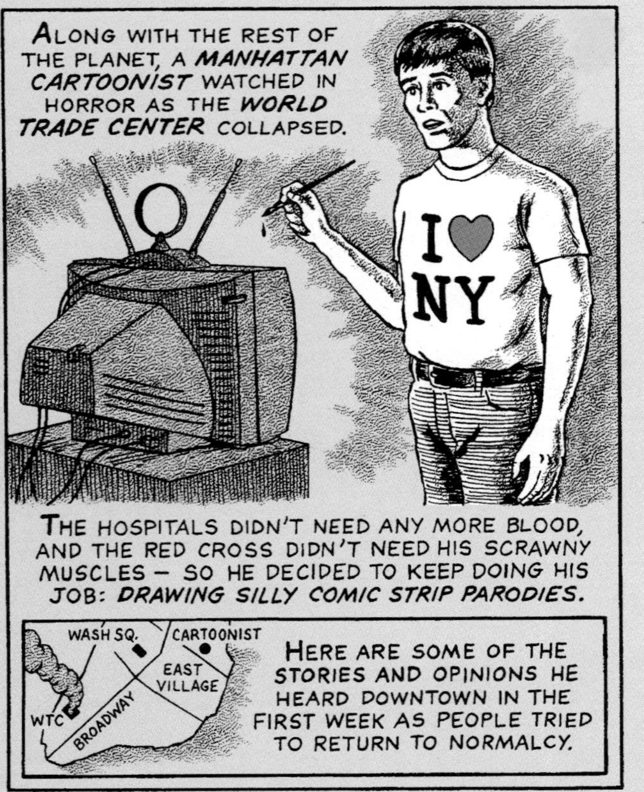

ALONG WITH THE REST OF THE PLANET, A MANHATTAN CARTOONIST WATCHED IN HORROR AS THE WORLD TRADE CENTER COLLAPSED.
I ♥ NY
THE HOSPITALS DIDN'T NEED ANY MORE BLOOD, AND THE RED CROSS DIDN'T NEED HIS SCRAWNY MUSCLES — SO HE DECIDED TO KEEP DOING HIS JOB: DRAWING SILLY COMIC STRIP PARODIES.
WASH SQ.
CARTOONIST
EAST VILLAGE
WTC
BROADWAY
HERE ARE SOME OF THE STORIES AND OPINIONS HE HEARD DOWNTOWN IN THE FIRST WEEK AS PEOPLE TRIED TO RETURN TO NORMALCY.

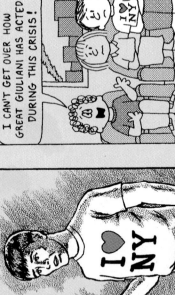

ANTIPATHY *A talk with friends in the East Village*

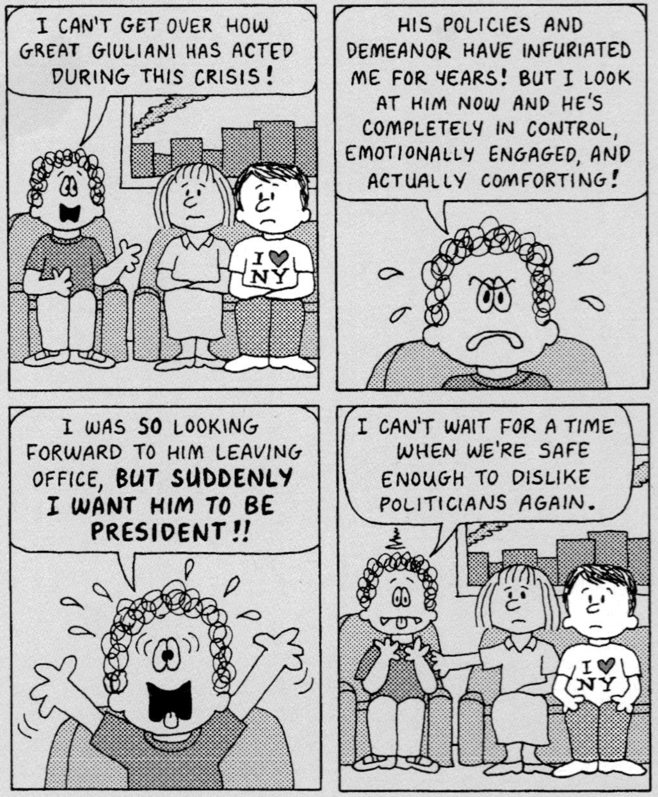

I CAN'T GET OVER HOW GREAT GIULIANI HAS ACTED DURING THIS CRISIS!
I ♥ NY
HIS POLICIES AND DEMEANOR HAVE INFURIATED ME FOR YEARS! BUT I LOOK AT HIM NOW AND HE'S COMPLETELY IN CONTROL, EMOTIONALLY ENGAGED, AND ACTUALLY COMFORTING!
I WAS SO LOOKING FORWARD TO HIM LEAVING OFFICE, BUT SUDDENLY I WANT HIM TO BE PRESIDENT!!
I CAN'T WAIT FOR A TIME WHEN WE'RE SAFE ENOUGH TO DISLIKE POLITICIANS AGAIN.
I ♥ NY

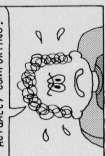

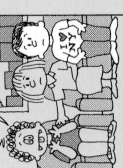

ADVICE

DEAR President Bush: What's going on? Can you believe this? How can we ever understand it?

Why has this occurred? Who would do it? How did it happen? Is there any way to explain it? What brought us to this point?

How can this be prevented? Could we have seen it coming? What does this mean? What are we supposed to do now? Is there any proper response? How can we find it?

How can we go on? Where will it all end? What am I saying? Will somebody please help?

--Puzzled in NYC

To Puzzled: Thank you for emailing President Bush. Your ideas and comments are very important to him. If your message is about the September 11 terrorist attack on the United States, please go to www.whitehouse.gov to learn more about the American response and relief efforts. Unfortunately, because of the large volume of email received, the President cannot personally respond to each message. However, the White House staff considers and reports citizen ideas and concerns. Your interest in the work of President Bush and his administration is appreciated.

Write the President at
president@Whitehouse.GOV

BEST AND WORST *A late-night gathering at Washington Square Park*

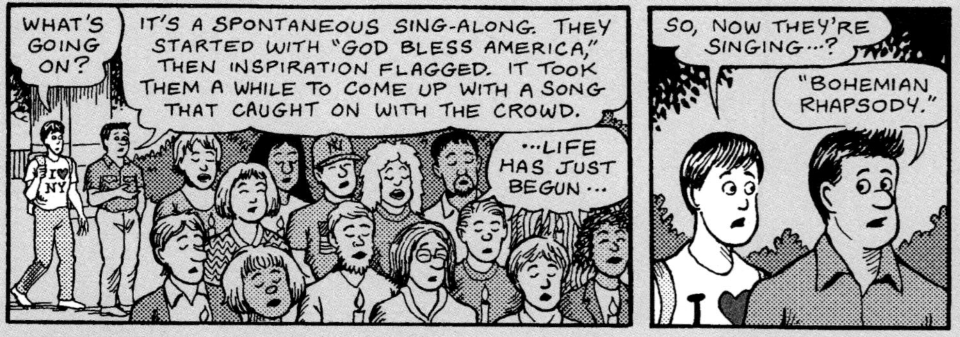
WHAT'S GOING ON?
IT'S A SPONTANEOUS SING-ALONG. THEY STARTED WITH "GOD BLESS AMERICA," THEN INSPIRATION FLAGGED. IT TOOK THEM A WHILE TO COME UP WITH A SONG THAT CAUGHT ON WITH THE CROWD.
...LIFE HAS JUST BEGUN...
SO, NOW THEY'RE SINGING...?
"BOHEMIAN RHAPSODY."
THE ROCK SONG? BY QUEEN?
YEAH. MOST EVERYONE HERE KNOWS THE WORDS. NOW I'M READY TO GO HOME.

JOE CAN-DO *A lunch with his parents, visiting from New Jersey*

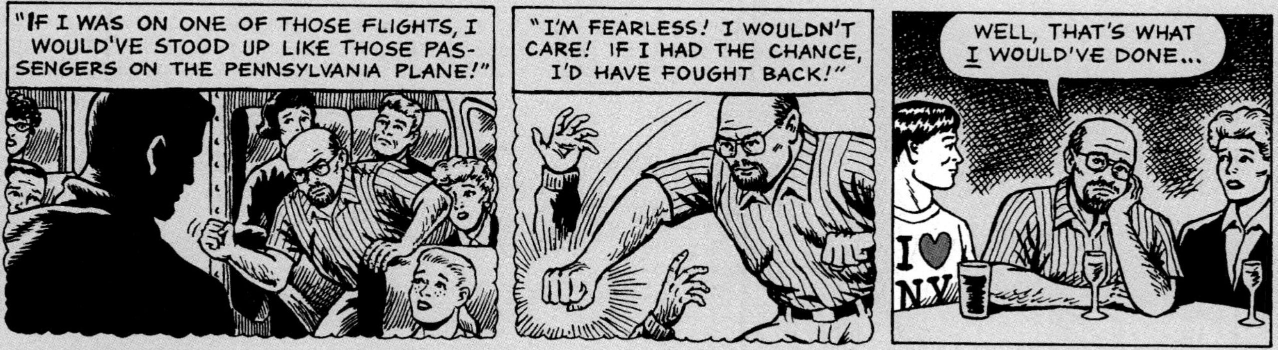
"IF I WAS ON ONE OF THOSE FLIGHTS, I WOULD'VE STOOD UP LIKE THOSE PASSENGERS ON THE PENNSYLVANIA PLANE!"
"I'M FEARLESS! I WOULDN'T CARE! IF I HAD THE CHANCE, I'D HAVE FOUGHT BACK!"
WELL, THAT'S WHAT I WOULD'VE DONE...

INSIGNIFICANTS *A walk around town with his wife*

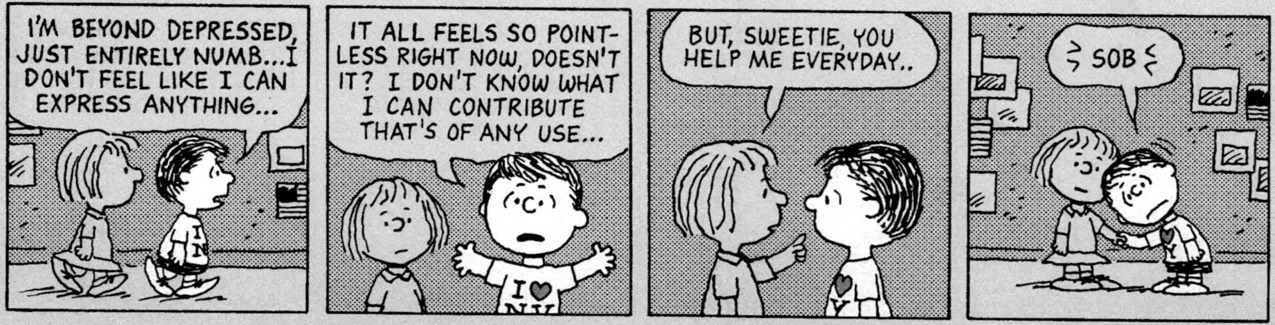
I'M BEYOND DEPRESSED, JUST ENTIRELY NUMB...I DON'T FEEL LIKE I CAN EXPRESS ANYTHING...
IT ALL FEELS SO POINTLESS RIGHT NOW, DOESN'T IT? I DON'T KNOW WHAT I CAN CONTRIBUTE THAT'S OF ANY USE...
BUT, SWEETIE, YOU HELP ME EVERYDAY..
SOB

WORD SEARCH

Can you find the words in the puzzle below that express your feelings?

T	R	L	V	F	J	P	Y	R	J	T	D	M	L
J	T	X	D	M	K	J	P	F	L	C	T	P	X
L	S	G	X	S	B	H	L	C	P	H	M	H	F
G	H	T	S	P	L	M	K	D	B	R	C	G	R
P	K	K	R	K	P	W	J	W	V	L	Z	F	J
D	S	M	P	J	R	N	S	R	G	H	W	V	M
J	J	B	W	H	B	T	Z	V	X	P	P	C	B
D	L	V	Z	G	F	G	D	D	W	M	K	S	N
Z	F	Z	P	S	A	D	R	T	Q	V	H	Z	M
N	L	R	J	V	Q	D	M	H	S	H	W	X	W
K	W	T	H	B	Y	C	Y	N	D	L	R	N	S
L	M	P	F	T	Z	B	T	M	Z	V	K	K	X
W	D	G	R	M	G	H	N	K	X	P	T	C	R
D	Q	K	W	D	V	X	V	F	G	J	M	L	P

Answer: probably not.

CITY QUIZ

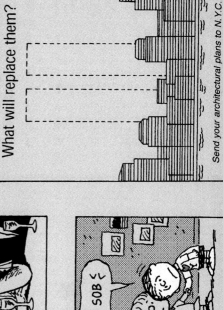

What will replace them?

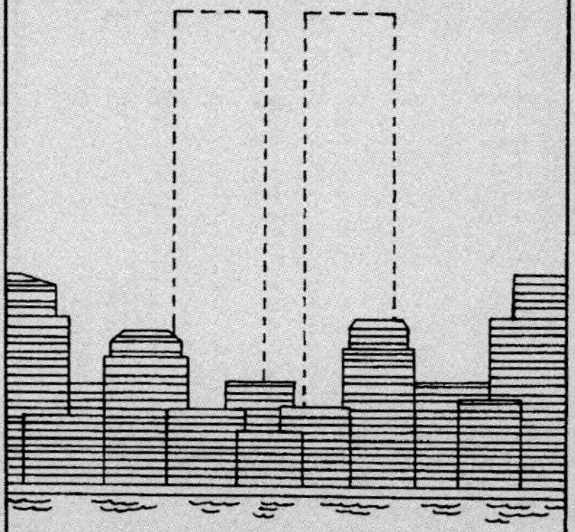

Send your architectural plans to N.Y.C.

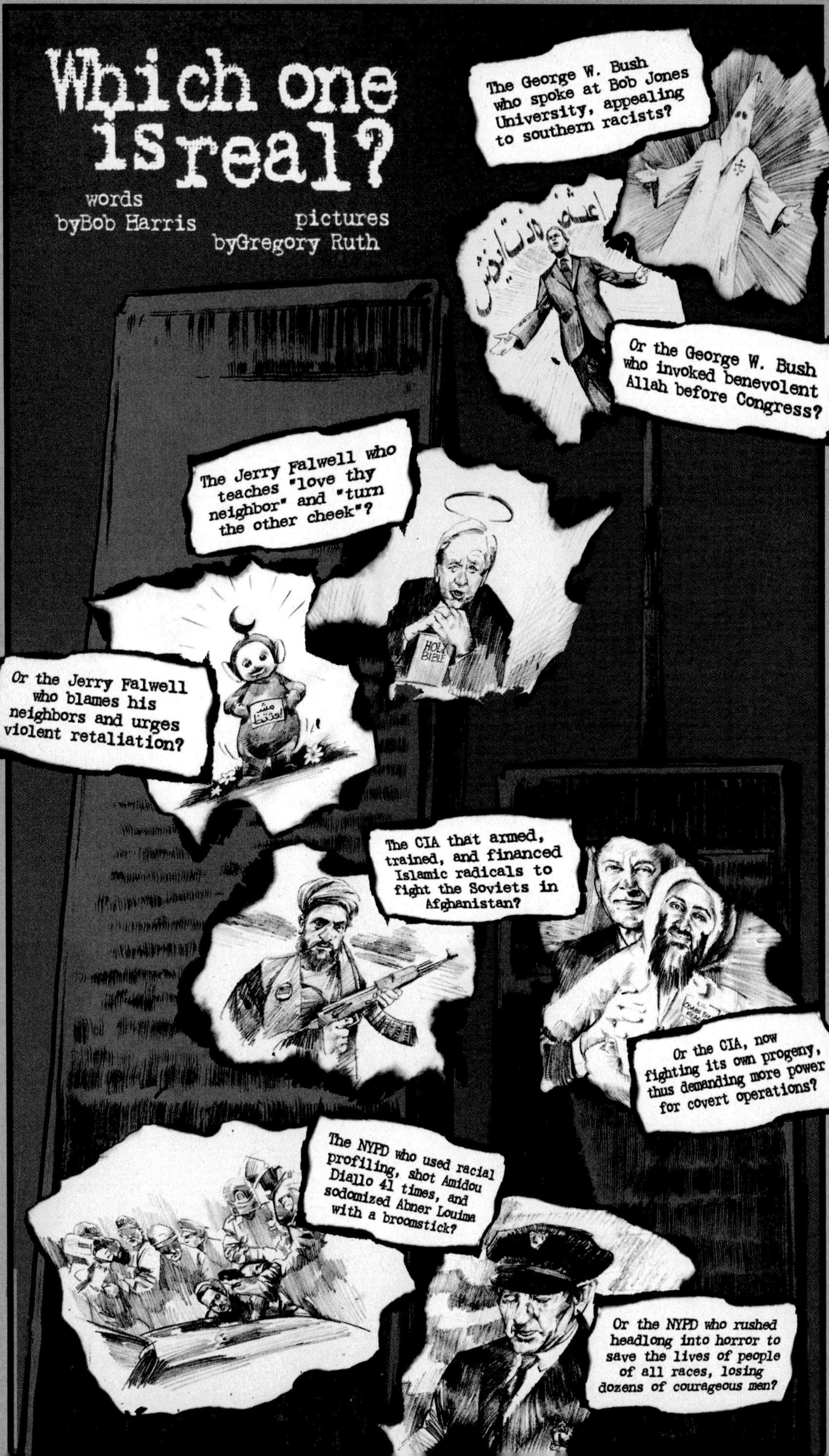
Which one is real?
words byBob Harris
pictures byGregory Ruth
The George W. Bush who spoke at Bob Jones University, appealing to southern racists?
Or the George W. Bush who invoked benevolent Allah before Congress?
The Jerry Falwell who teaches "love thy neighbor" and "turn the other cheek"?
HOLY BIBLE
Or the Jerry Falwell who blames his neighbors and urges violent retaliation?
The CIA that armed, trained, and financed Islamic radicals to fight the Soviets in Afghanistan?
Or the CIA, now fighting its own progeny, thus demanding more power for covert operations?
The NYPD who used racial profiling, shot Amidou Diallo 41 times, and sodomized Abner Louima with a broomstick?
Or the NYPD who rushed headlong into horror to save the lives of people of all races, losing dozens of courageous men?

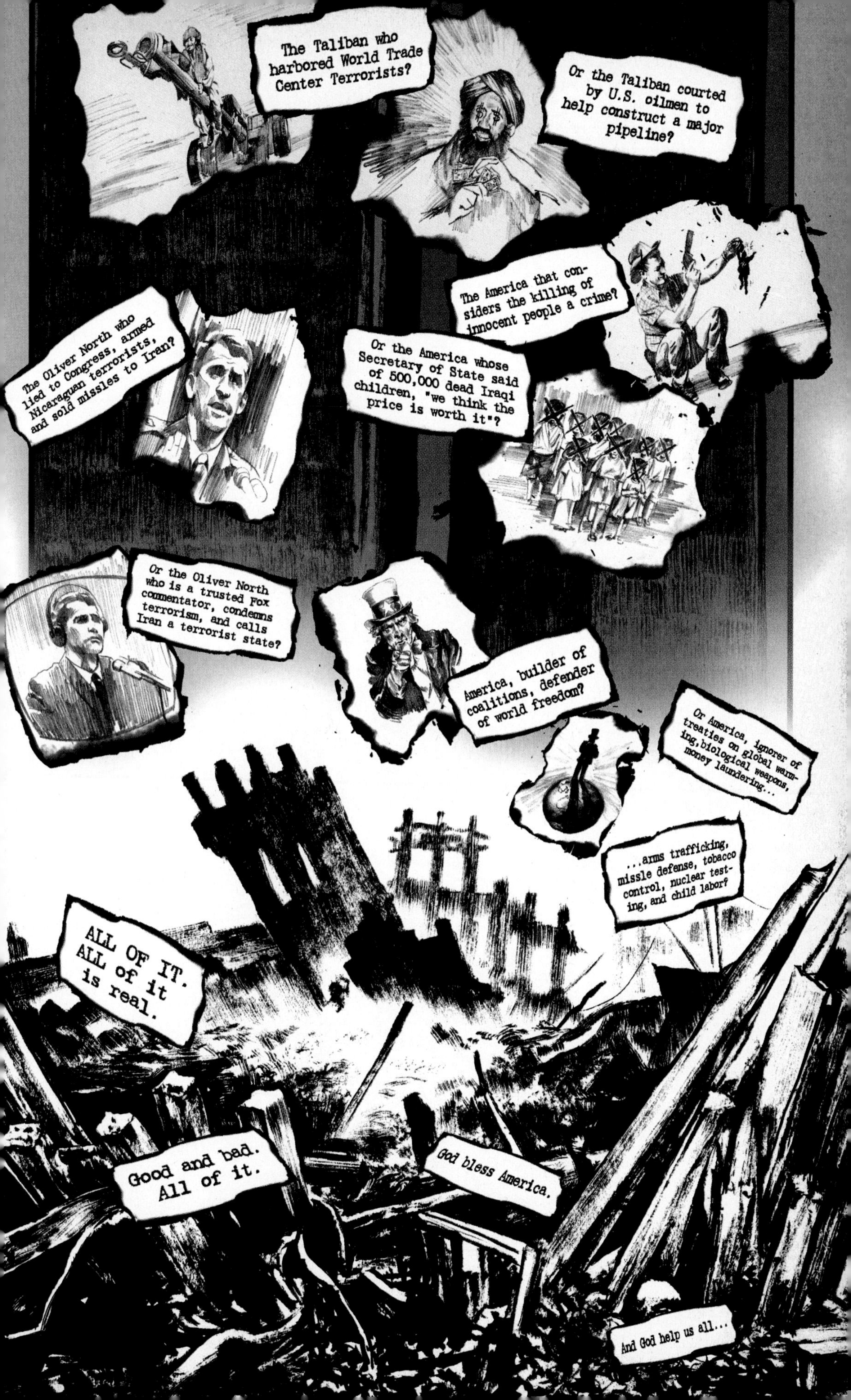

The Taliban who harbored World Trade Center Terrorists?
Or the Taliban courted by U.S. oilmen to help construct a major pipeline?
The Oliver North who lied to Congress, armed Nicaraguan terrorists, and sold missles to Iran?
The America that considers the killing of innocent people a crime?
Or the America whose Secretary of State said of 500,000 dead Iraqi children, "we think the price is worth it"?
Or the Oliver North who is a trusted Fox commentator, condemns terrorism, and calls Iran a terrorist state?
America, builder of coalitions, defender of world freedom?
Or America, ignorer of treaties on global warming, biological weapons, money laundering...
...arms trafficking, missle defense, tobacco control, nuclear testing, and child labor?
ALL OF IT. ALL of it is real.
Good and bad. All of it.
God bless America.
And God help us all...

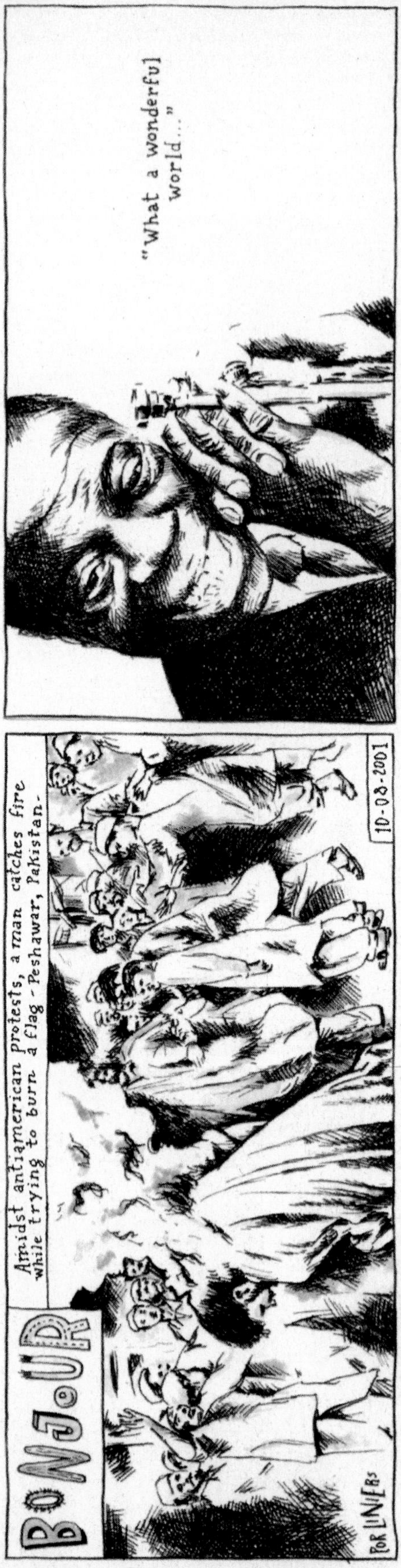
BONJOUR
POR LINIERS
Amidst antiamerican protests, a man catches fire while trying to burn a flag - Peshawar, Pakistan-
10-08-2001
"What a wonderful world..."

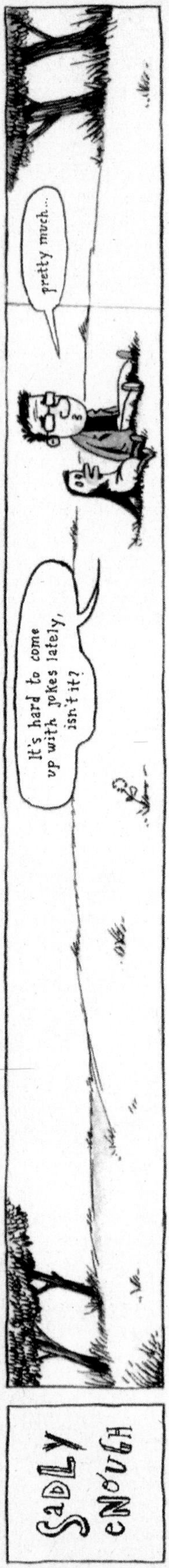
SADLY ENOUGH
It's hard to come up with jokes lately, isn't it?
pretty much...

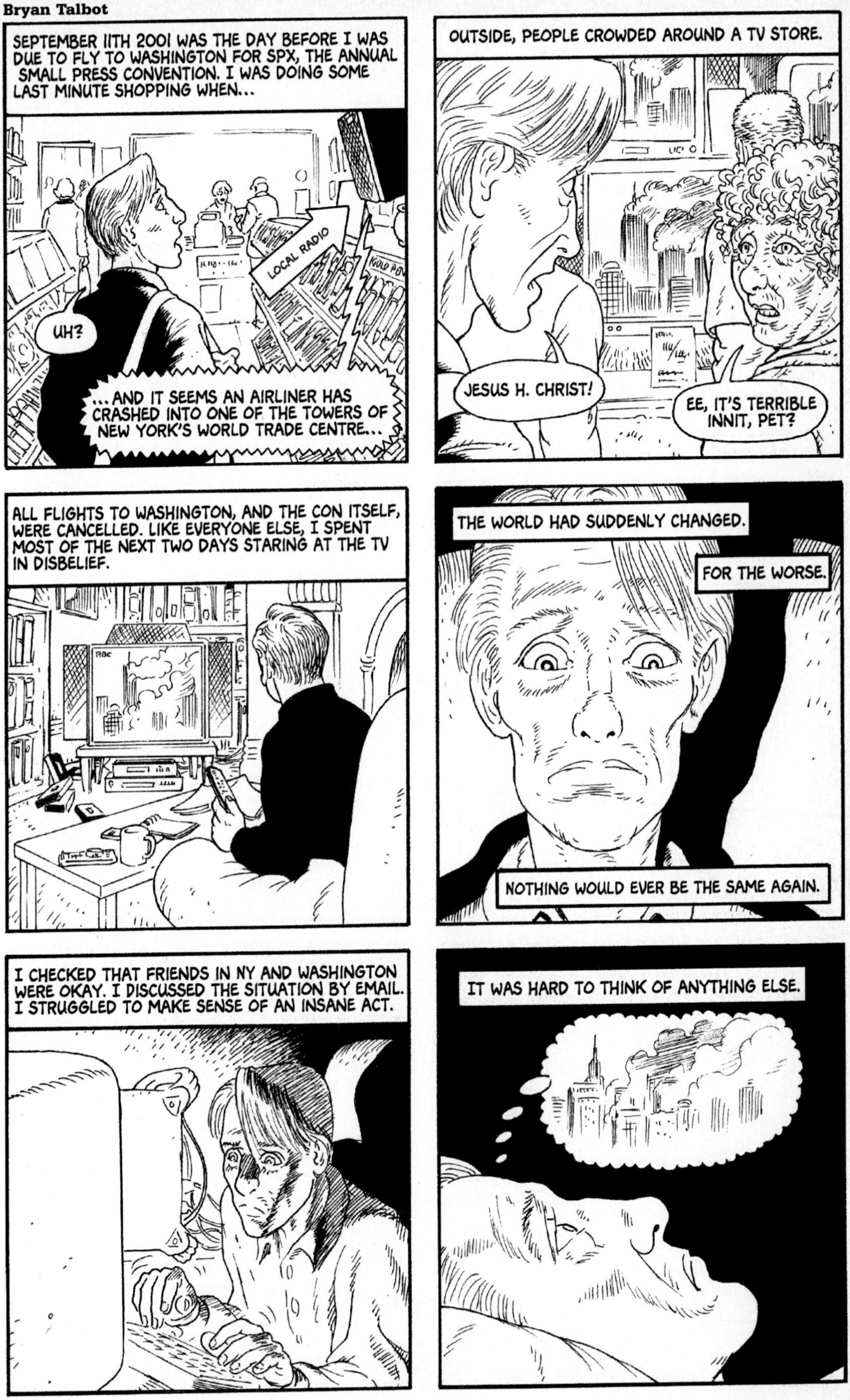
SEPTEMBER 11TH 2001 WAS THE DAY BEFORE I WAS DUE TO FLY TO WASHINGTON FOR SPX, THE ANNUAL SMALL PRESS CONVENTION. I WAS DOING SOME LAST MINUTE SHOPPING WHEN...
LOCAL RADIO
UH?
...AND IT SEEMS AN AIRLINER HAS CRASHED INTO ONE OF THE TOWERS OF NEW YORK'S WORLD TRADE CENTRE...
OUTSIDE, PEOPLE CROWDED AROUND A TV STORE.
JESUS H. CHRIST!
EE, IT'S TERRIBLE INNIT, PET?
ALL FLIGHTS TO WASHINGTON, AND THE CON ITSELF, WERE CANCELLED. LIKE EVERYONE ELSE, I SPENT MOST OF THE NEXT TWO DAYS STARING AT THE TV IN DISBELIEF.
BBC
THE WORLD HAD SUDDENLY CHANGED.
FOR THE WORSE.
NOTHING WOULD EVER BE THE SAME AGAIN.
I CHECKED THAT FRIENDS IN NY AND WASHINGTON WERE OKAY. I DISCUSSED THE SITUATION BY EMAIL. I STRUGGLED TO MAKE SENSE OF AN INSANE ACT.
IT WAS HARD TO THINK OF ANYTHING ELSE.

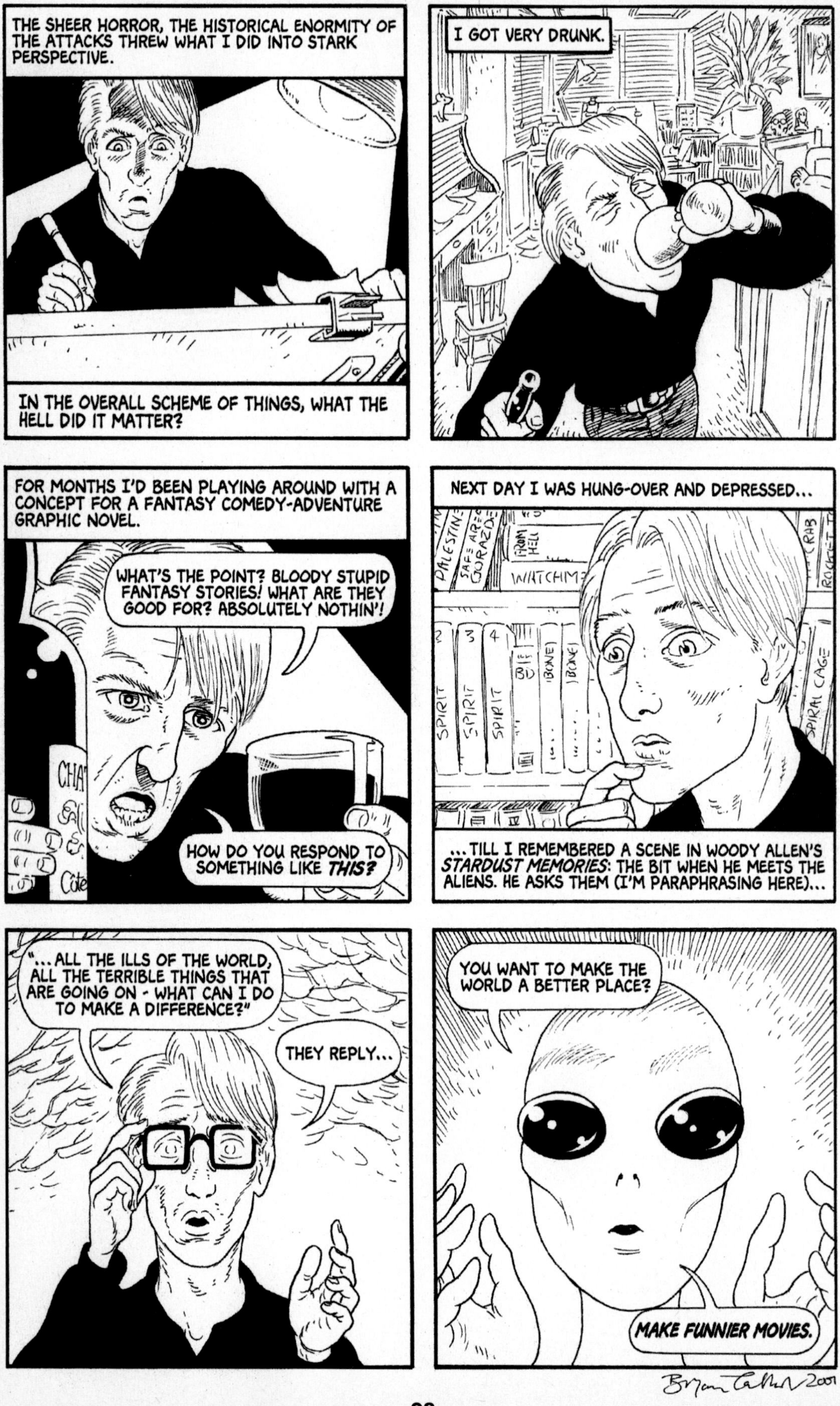
THE SHEER HORROR, THE HISTORICAL ENORMITY OF THE ATTACKS THREW WHAT I DID INTO STARK PERSPECTIVE.
IN THE OVERALL SCHEME OF THINGS, WHAT THE HELL DID IT MATTER?
I GOT VERY DRUNK.
FOR MONTHS I'D BEEN PLAYING AROUND WITH A CONCEPT FOR A FANTASY COMEDY-ADVENTURE GRAPHIC NOVEL.
WHAT'S THE POINT? BLOODY STUPID FANTASY STORIES! WHAT ARE THEY GOOD FOR? ABSOLUTELY NOTHIN'!
HOW DO YOU RESPOND TO SOMETHING LIKE *THIS?*
NEXT DAY I WAS HUNG-OVER AND DEPRESSED...
...TILL I REMEMBERED A SCENE IN WOODY ALLEN'S *STARDUST MEMORIES*: THE BIT WHEN HE MEETS THE ALIENS. HE ASKS THEM (I'M PARAPHRASING HERE)...
"...ALL THE ILLS OF THE WORLD, ALL THE TERRIBLE THINGS THAT ARE GOING ON - WHAT CAN I DO TO MAKE A DIFFERENCE?"
THEY REPLY...
YOU WANT TO MAKE THE WORLD A BETTER PLACE?
MAKE FUNNIER MOVIES.

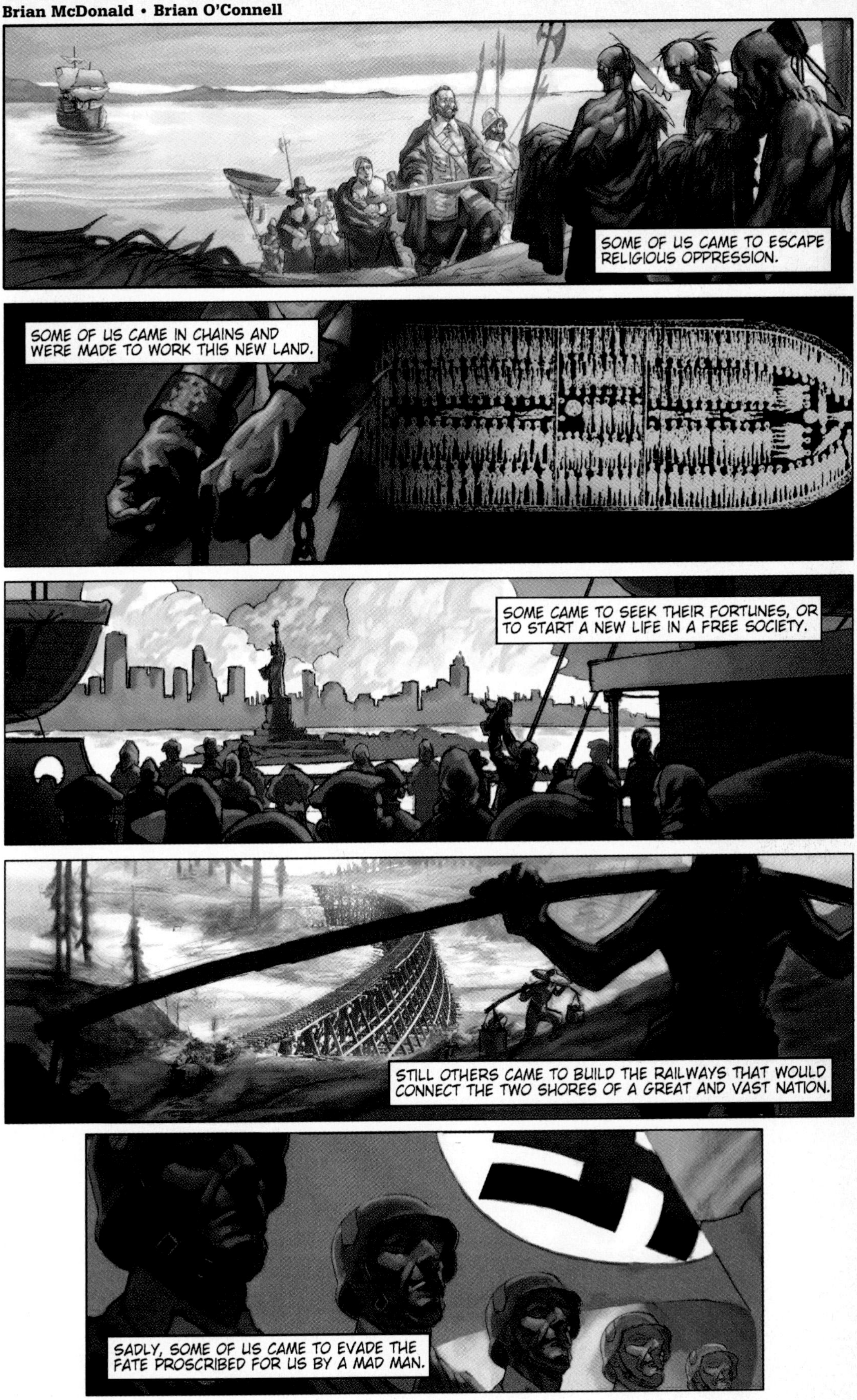
SOME OF US CAME TO ESCAPE RELIGIOUS OPPRESSION.
SOME OF US CAME IN CHAINS AND WERE MADE TO WORK THIS NEW LAND.
SOME CAME TO SEEK THEIR FORTUNES, OR TO START A NEW LIFE IN A FREE SOCIETY.
STILL OTHERS CAME TO BUILD THE RAILWAYS THAT WOULD CONNECT THE TWO SHORES OF A GREAT AND VAST NATION.
SADLY, SOME OF US CAME TO EVADE THE FATE PROSCRIBED FOR US BY A MAD MAN.

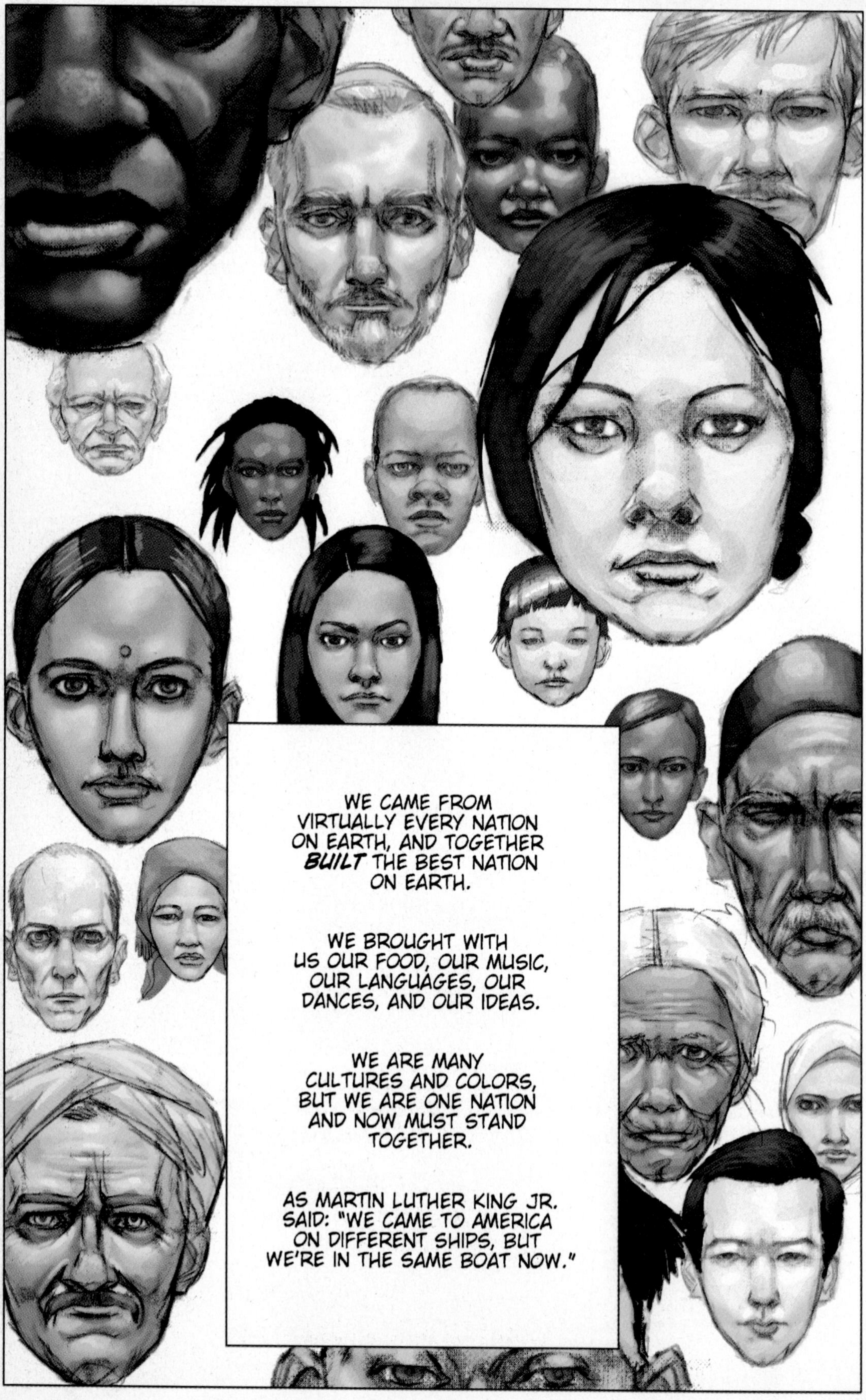
WE CAME FROM VIRTUALLY EVERY NATION ON EARTH, AND TOGETHER *BUILT* THE BEST NATION ON EARTH.
WE BROUGHT WITH US OUR FOOD, OUR MUSIC, OUR LANGUAGES, OUR DANCES, AND OUR IDEAS.
WE ARE MANY CULTURES AND COLORS, BUT WE ARE ONE NATION AND NOW MUST STAND TOGETHER.
AS MARTIN LUTHER KING JR. SAID: "WE CAME TO AMERICA ON DIFFERENT SHIPS, BUT WE'RE IN THE SAME BOAT NOW."

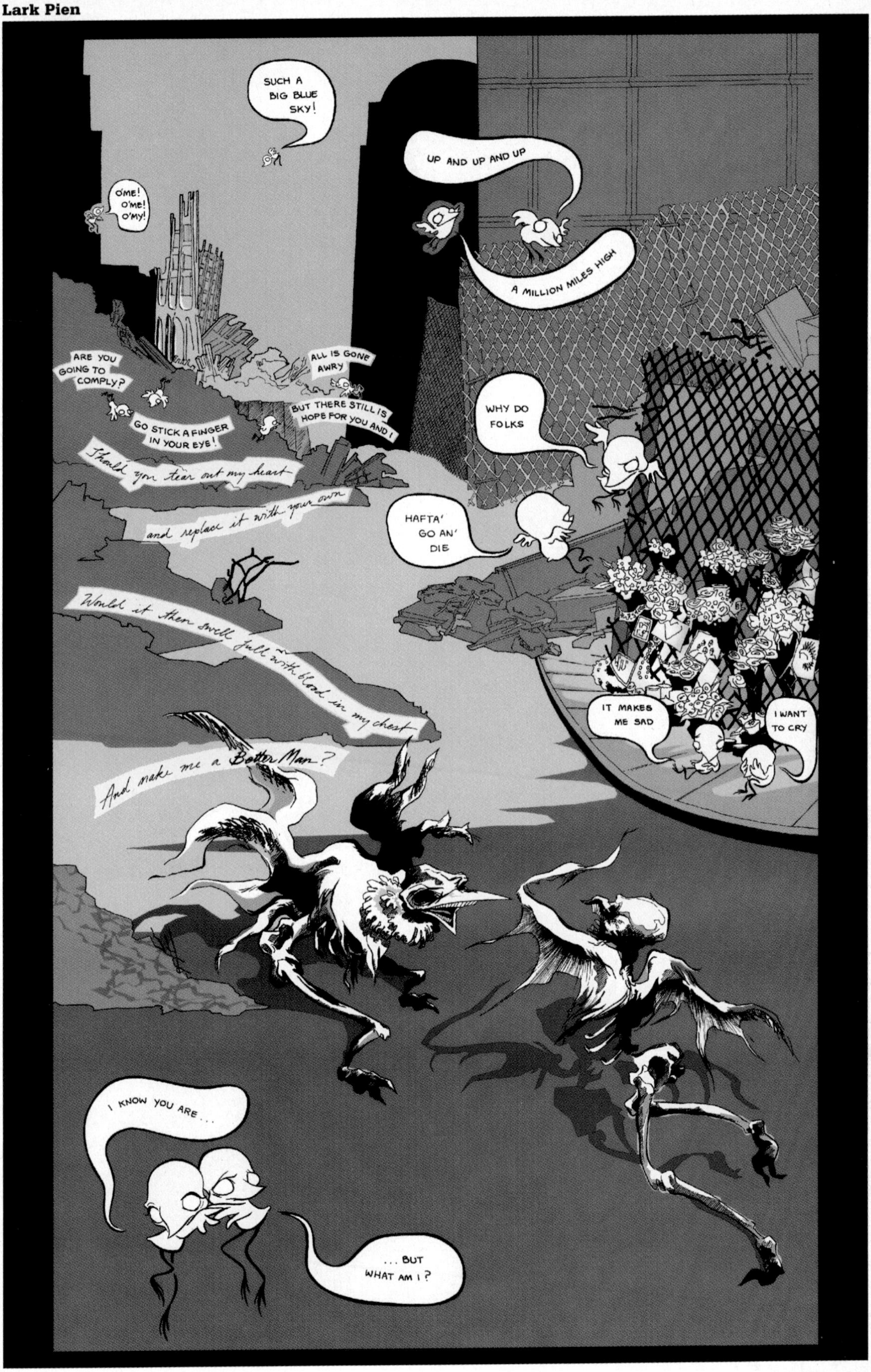
SUCH A BIG BLUE SKY!
O'ME! O'ME! O'MY!
UP AND UP AND UP
A MILLION MILES HIGH
ARE YOU GOING TO COMPLY?
GO STICK A FINGER IN YOUR EYE!
ALL IS GONE AWRY
BUT THERE STILL IS HOPE FOR YOU AND I
WHY DO FOLKS
HAFTA' GO AN' DIE
Should you tear out my heart
and replace it with your own
Would it then swell full with blood in my chest
And make me a Better Man?
IT MAKES ME SAD
I WANT TO CRY
I KNOW YOU ARE...
...BUT WHAT AM I?

As I grew older and accumulated memories,
I came to feel more keenly about the
disappearances of people and landmarks.
Especially troubling to me was the callous removal
of buildings. I felt that, somehow, they had
a kind of soul.

I know now that these structures, barnacled with
laughter and stained by tears, are more than lifeless
edifices. It cannot be that having been part
of life, they did not somehow absorb the radiation
from human interaction.

And I wonder what is left behind when a
building is torn down.

FLORIDA, 1987

Peter Kuper

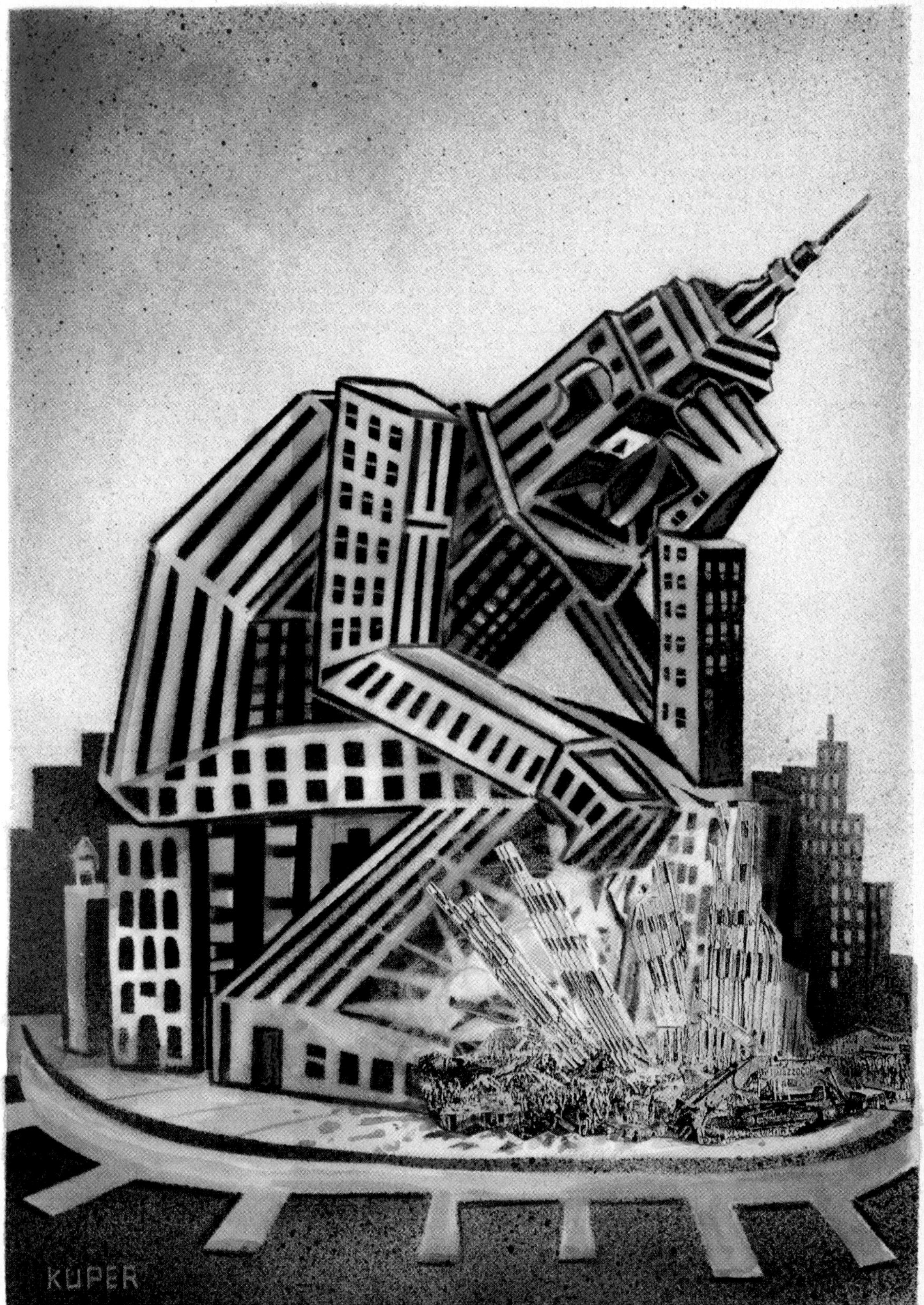
KUPER

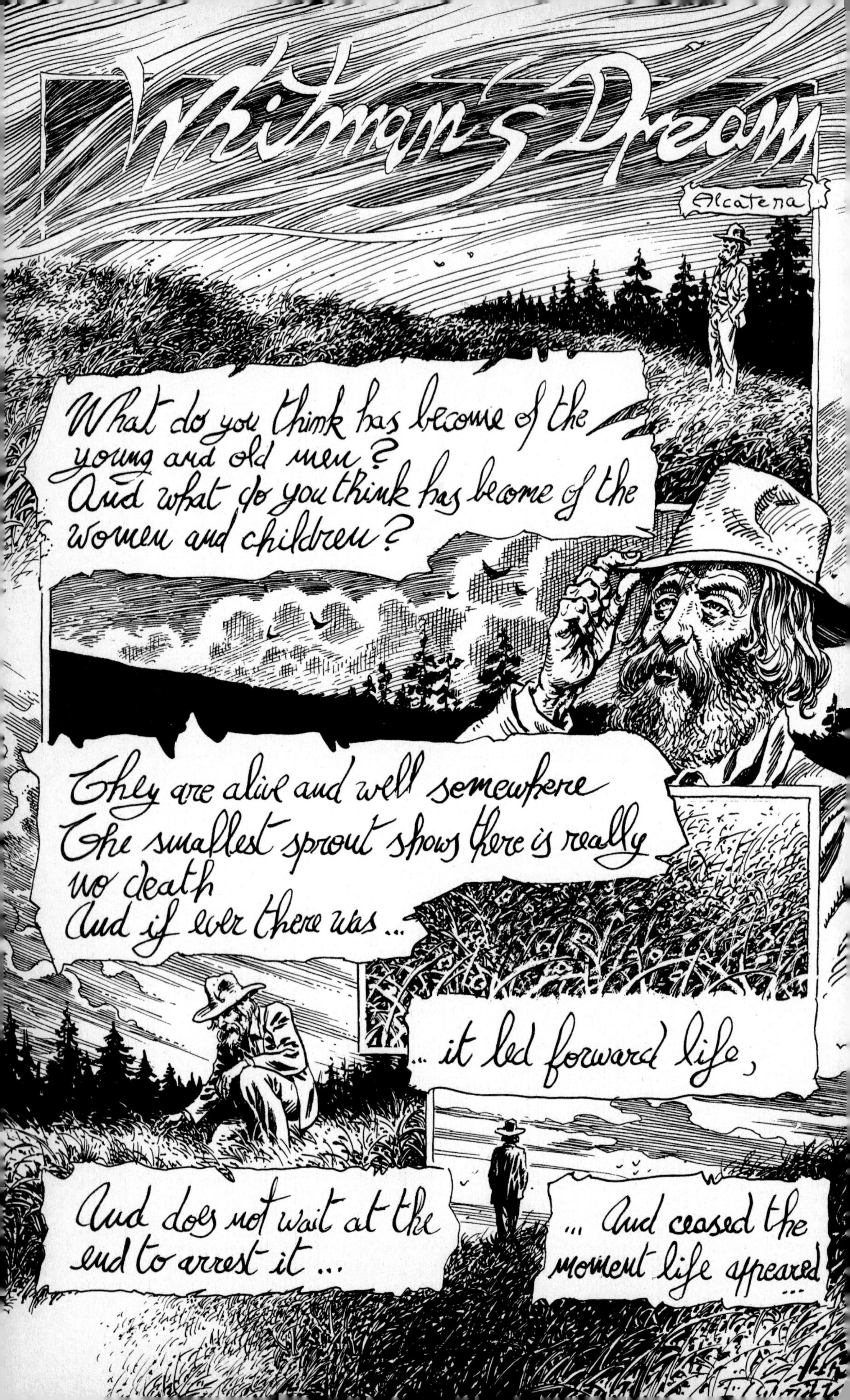
Whitman's Dream
Alcatena
What do you think has become of the young and old men?
And what do you think has become of the women and children?
They are alive and well somewhere
The smallest sprout shows there is really no death
And if ever there was ...
... it led forward life,
And does not wait at the end to arrest it ...
... And ceased the moment life appeared ...

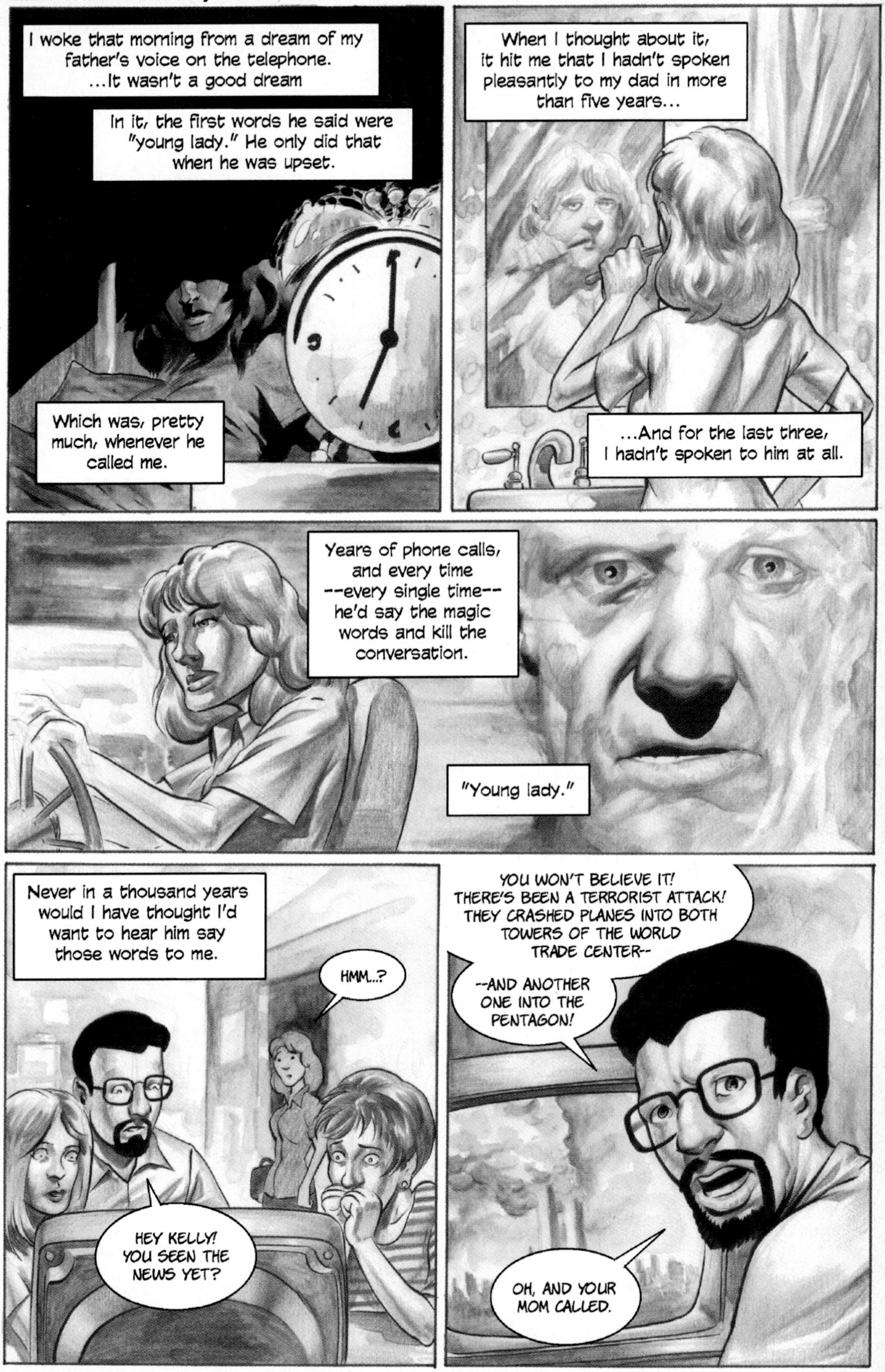
I woke that morning from a dream of my father's voice on the telephone. ...It wasn't a good dream
In it, the first words he said were "young lady." He only did that when he was upset.
Which was, pretty much, whenever he called me.
When I thought about it, it hit me that I hadn't spoken pleasantly to my dad in more than five years...
...And for the last three, I hadn't spoken to him at all.
Years of phone calls, and every time --every single time-- he'd say the magic words and kill the conversation.
"Young lady."
Never in a thousand years would I have thought I'd want to hear him say those words to me.
HMM...?
HEY KELLY! YOU SEEN THE NEWS YET?
YOU WON'T BELIEVE IT! THERE'S BEEN A TERRORIST ATTACK! THEY CRASHED PLANES INTO BOTH TOWERS OF THE WORLD TRADE CENTER--
--AND ANOTHER ONE INTO THE PENTAGON!
OH, AND YOUR MOM CALLED.

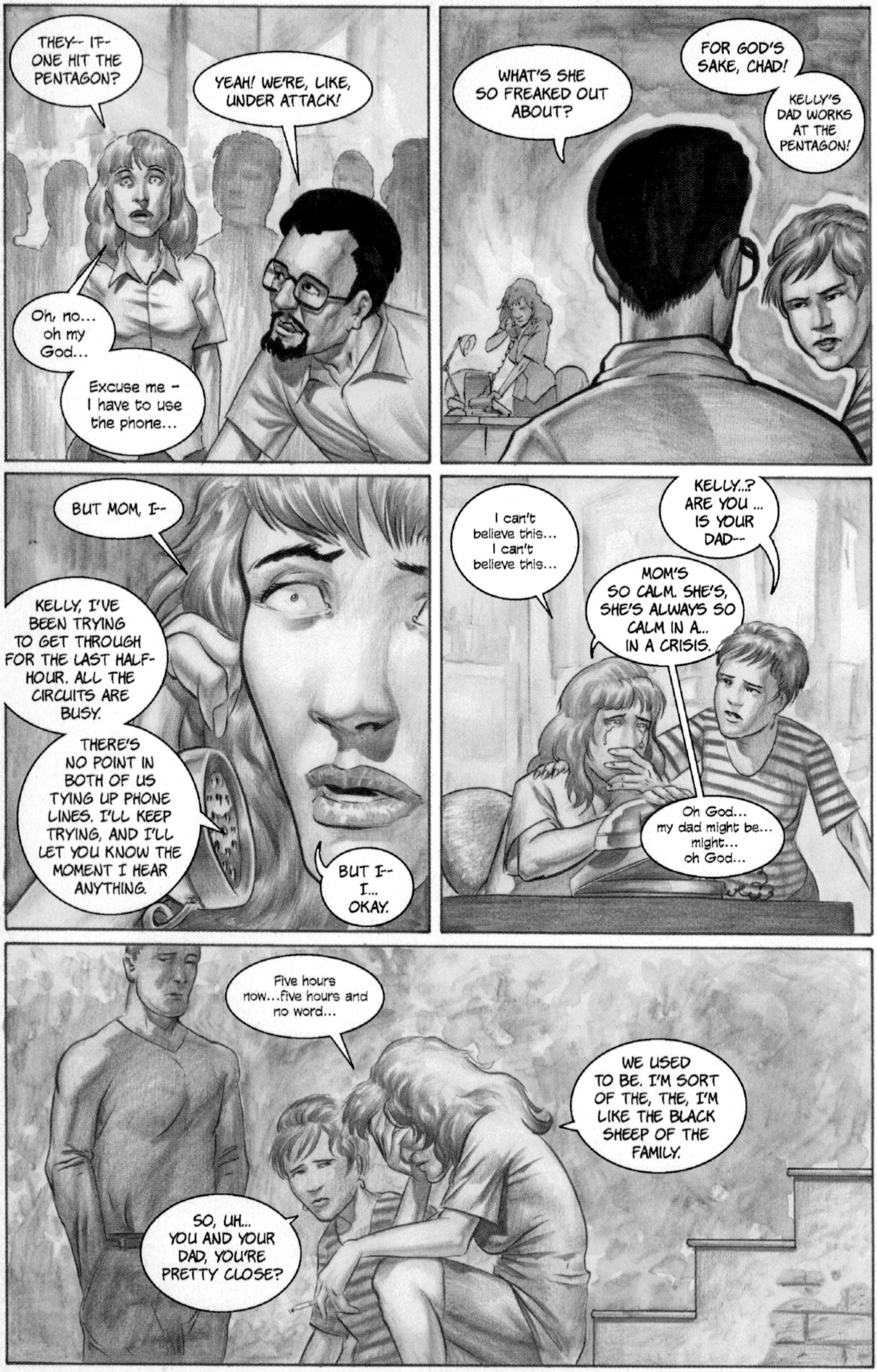
THEY-- IT-- ONE HIT THE PENTAGON?
YEAH! WE'RE, LIKE, UNDER ATTACK!
Oh, no... oh my God...
Excuse me - I have to use the phone...
WHAT'S SHE SO FREAKED OUT ABOUT?
FOR GOD'S SAKE, CHAD!
KELLY'S DAD WORKS AT THE PENTAGON!
BUT MOM, I--
KELLY, I'VE BEEN TRYING TO GET THROUGH FOR THE LAST HALF-HOUR. ALL THE CIRCUITS ARE BUSY.
THERE'S NO POINT IN BOTH OF US TYING UP PHONE LINES. I'LL KEEP TRYING, AND I'LL LET YOU KNOW THE MOMENT I HEAR ANYTHING.
BUT I-- I... OKAY.
I can't believe this... I can't believe this...
KELLY...? ARE YOU ... IS YOUR DAD--
MOM'S SO CALM. SHE'S, SHE'S ALWAYS SO CALM IN A... IN A CRISIS.
Oh God... my dad might be... might... oh God...
Five hours now...five hours and no word...
SO, UH... YOU AND YOUR DAD, YOU'RE PRETTY CLOSE?
WE USED TO BE. I'M SORT OF THE, THE, I'M LIKE THE BLACK SHEEP OF THE FAMILY.

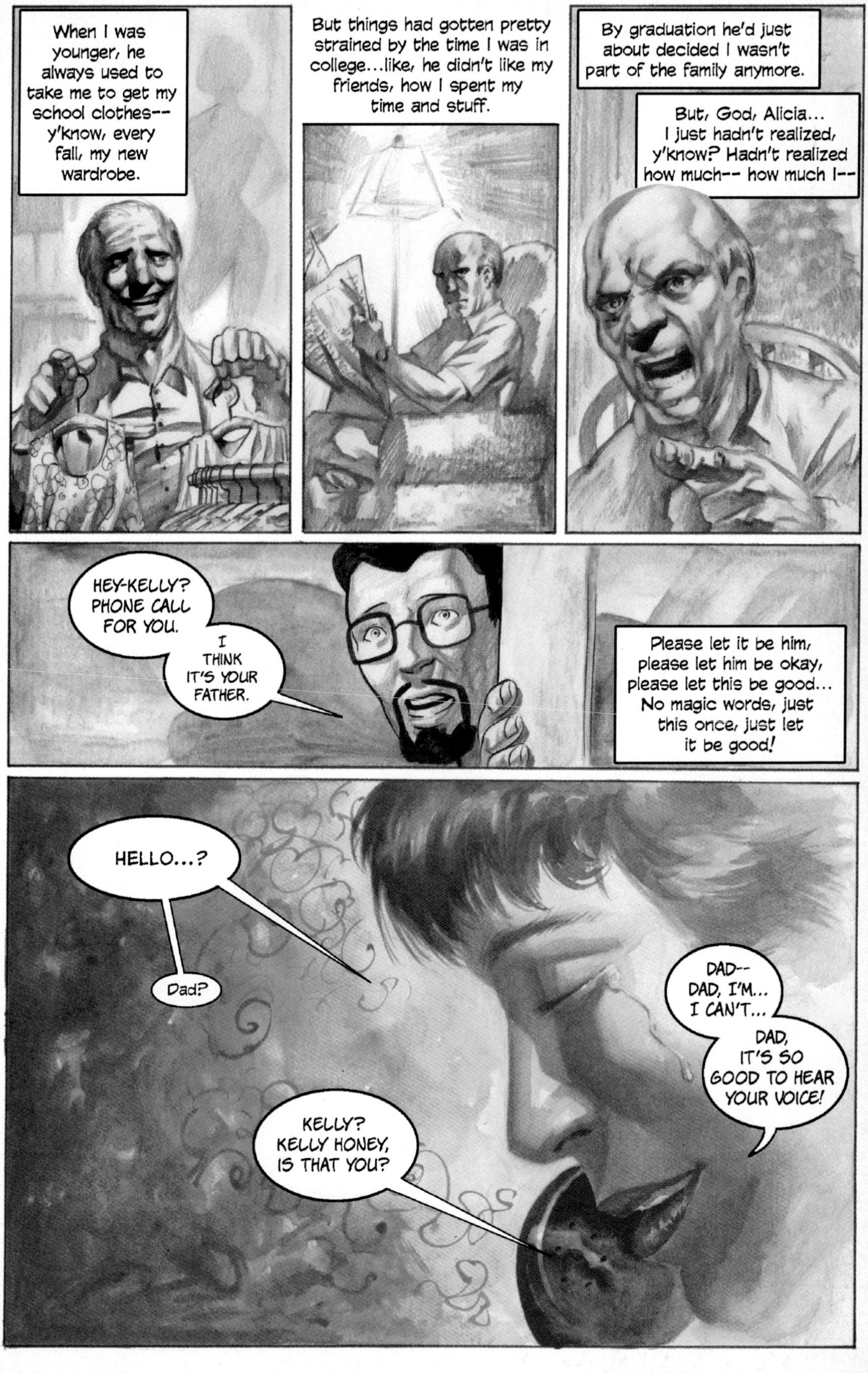

When I was younger, he always used to take me to get my school clothes-- y'know, every fall, my new wardrobe.
But things had gotten pretty strained by the time I was in college...like, he didn't like my friends, how I spent my time and stuff.
By graduation he'd just about decided I wasn't part of the family anymore.
But, God, Alicia... I just hadn't realized, y'know? Hadn't realized how much-- how much I--
HEY-KELLY? PHONE CALL FOR YOU.
I THINK IT'S YOUR FATHER.
Please let it be him, please let him be okay, please let this be good... No magic words, just this once, just let it be good!
HELLO...?
Dad?
DAD-- DAD, I'M... I CAN'T...
DAD, IT'S SO GOOD TO HEAR YOUR VOICE!
KELLY? KELLY HONEY, IS THAT YOU?

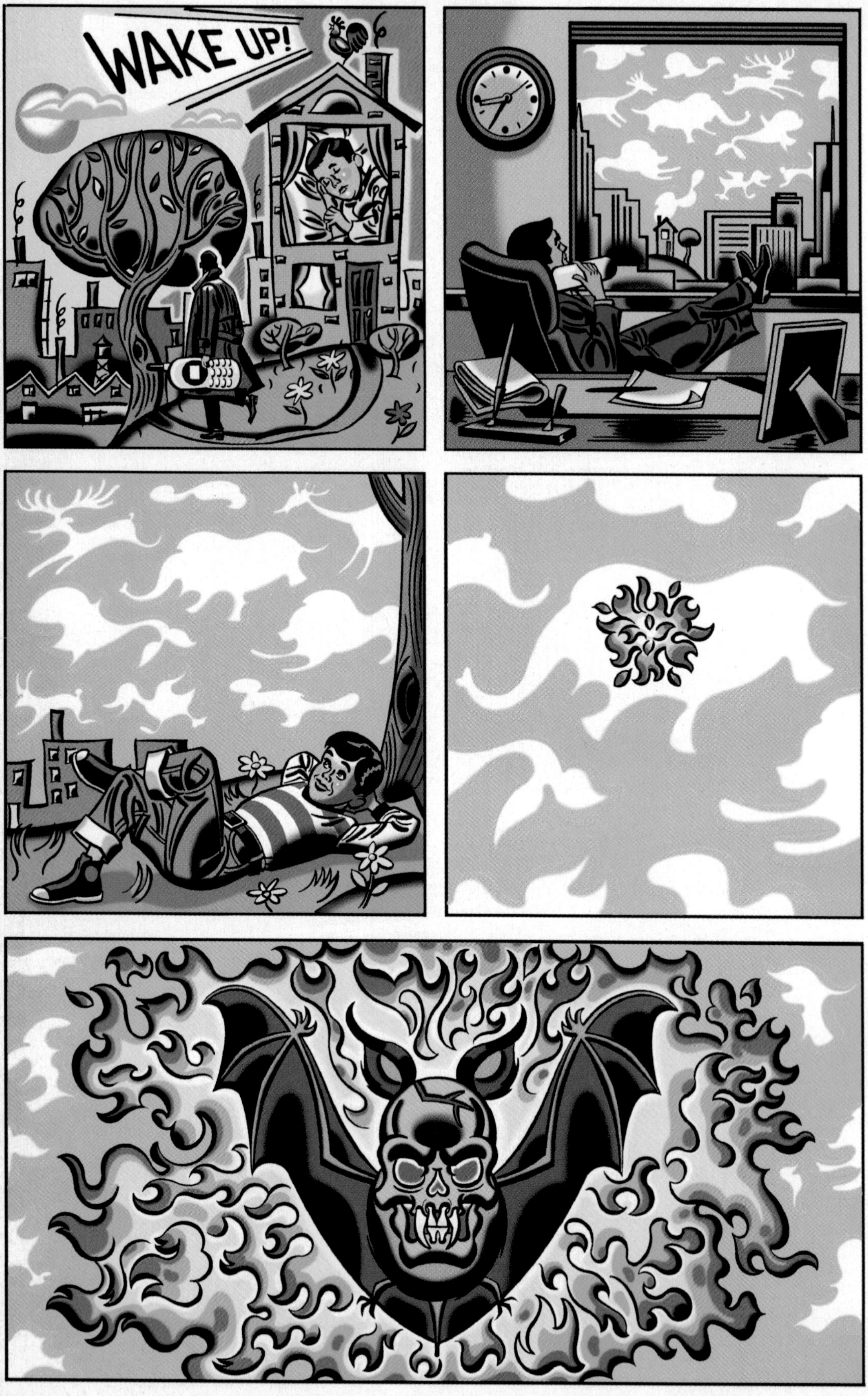
WAKE UP!

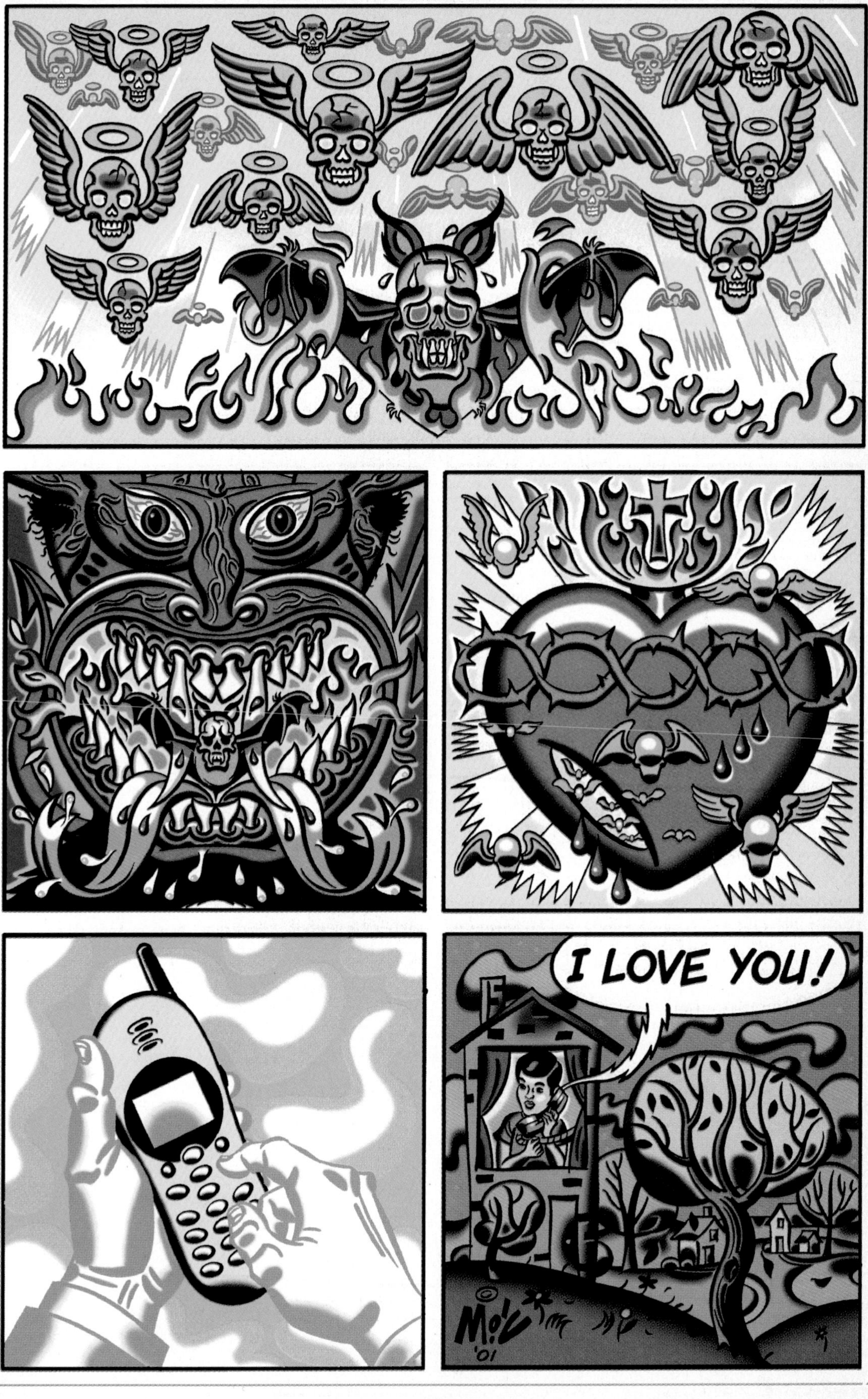
I LOVE YOU!
MOV
'01

when they sound that last all clear

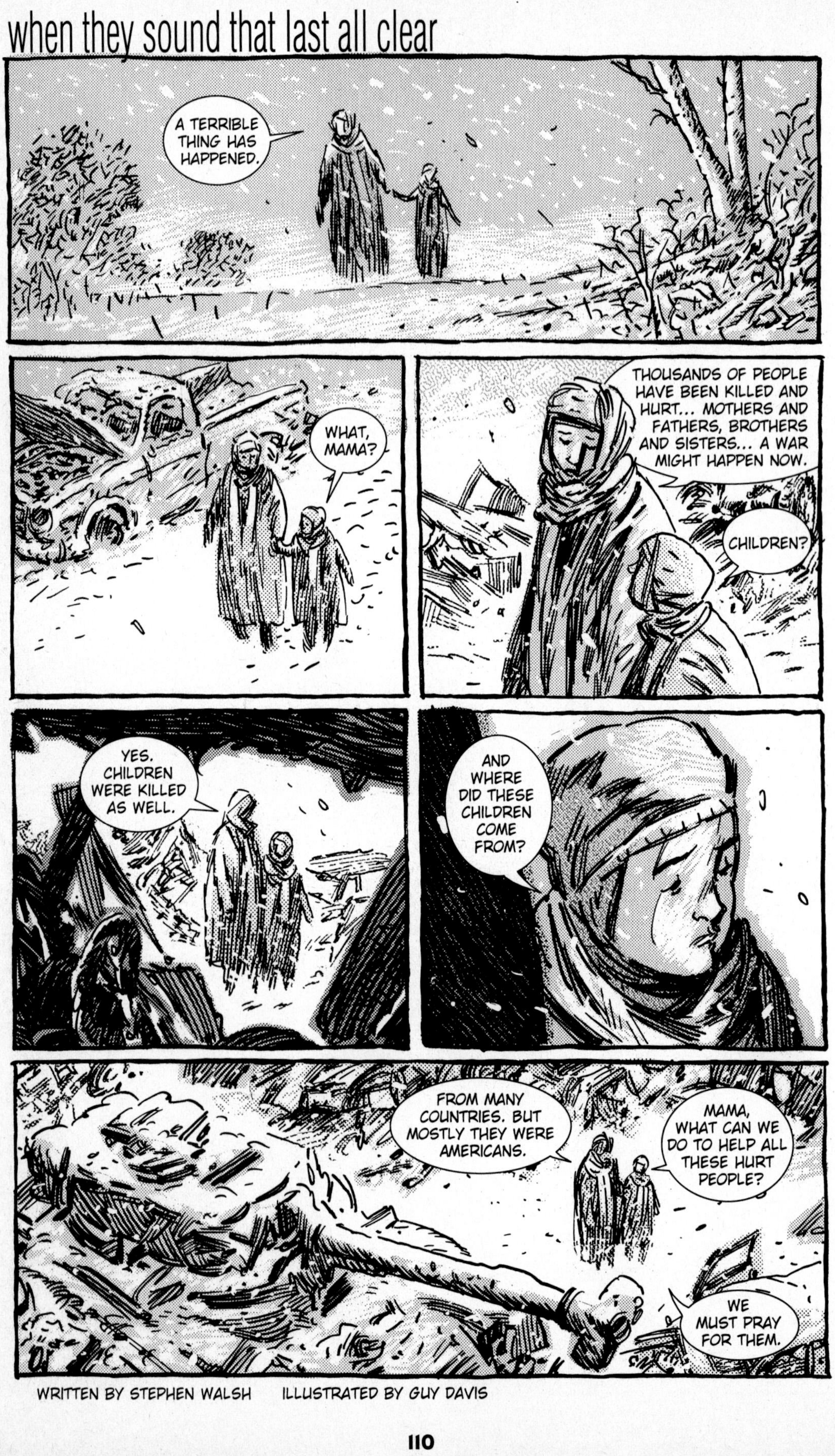
A TERRIBLE THING HAS HAPPENED.
WHAT, MAMA?
THOUSANDS OF PEOPLE HAVE BEEN KILLED AND HURT... MOTHERS AND FATHERS, BROTHERS AND SISTERS... A WAR MIGHT HAPPEN NOW.
CHILDREN?
YES. CHILDREN WERE KILLED AS WELL.
AND WHERE DID THESE CHILDREN COME FROM?
FROM MANY COUNTRIES. BUT MOSTLY THEY WERE AMERICANS.
MAMA, WHAT CAN WE DO TO HELP ALL THESE HURT PEOPLE?
WE MUST PRAY FOR THEM.

WRITTEN BY STEPHEN WALSH ILLUSTRATED BY GUY DAVIS

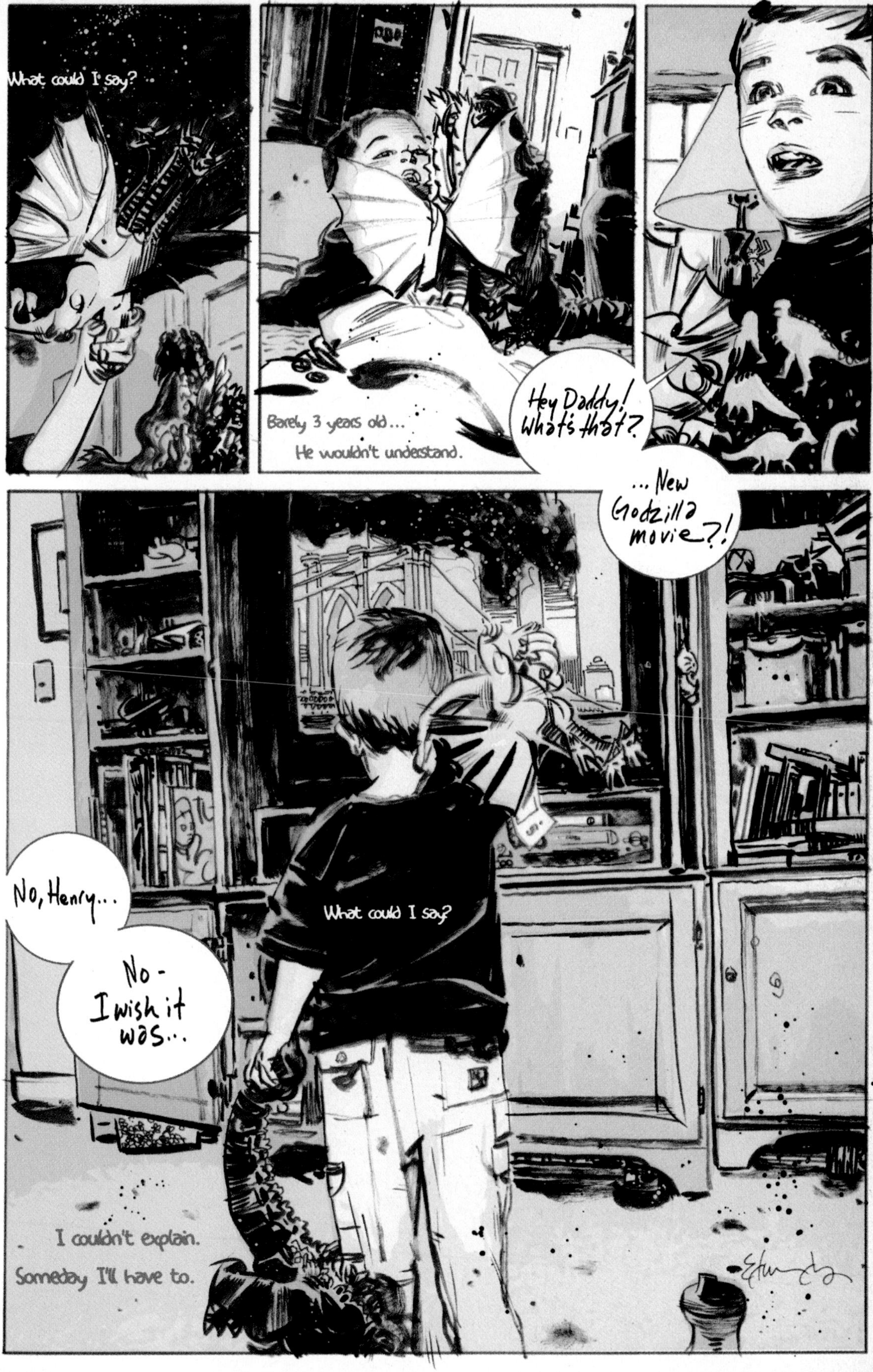
What could I say?
Barely 3 years old...
He wouldn't understand.
Hey Daddy! What's that?
... New Godzilla movie?!
No, Henry...
No - I wish it was...
What could I say?
I couldn't explain.
Someday I'll have to.

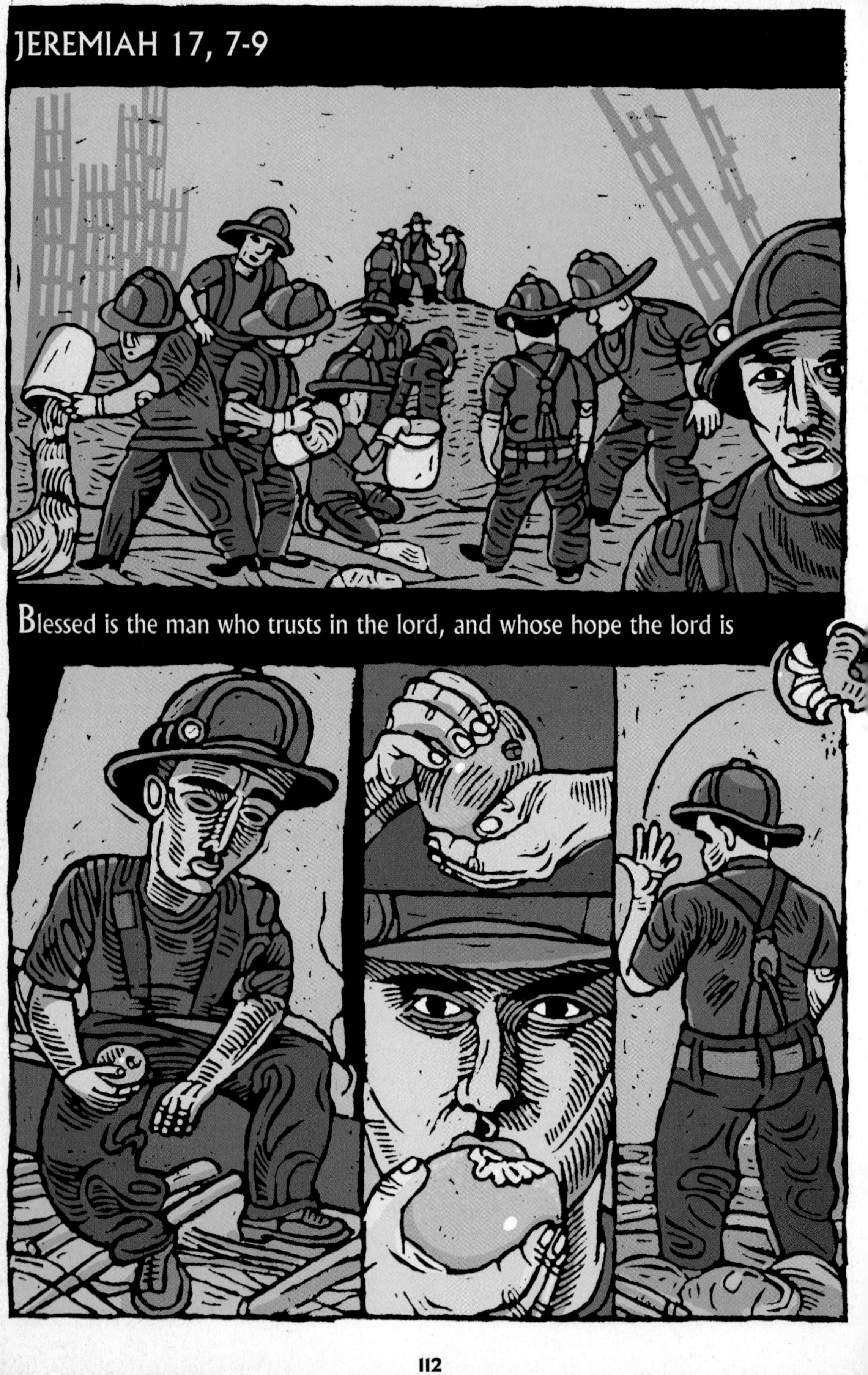
JEREMIAH 17, 7-9
Blessed is the man who trusts in the lord, and whose hope the lord is

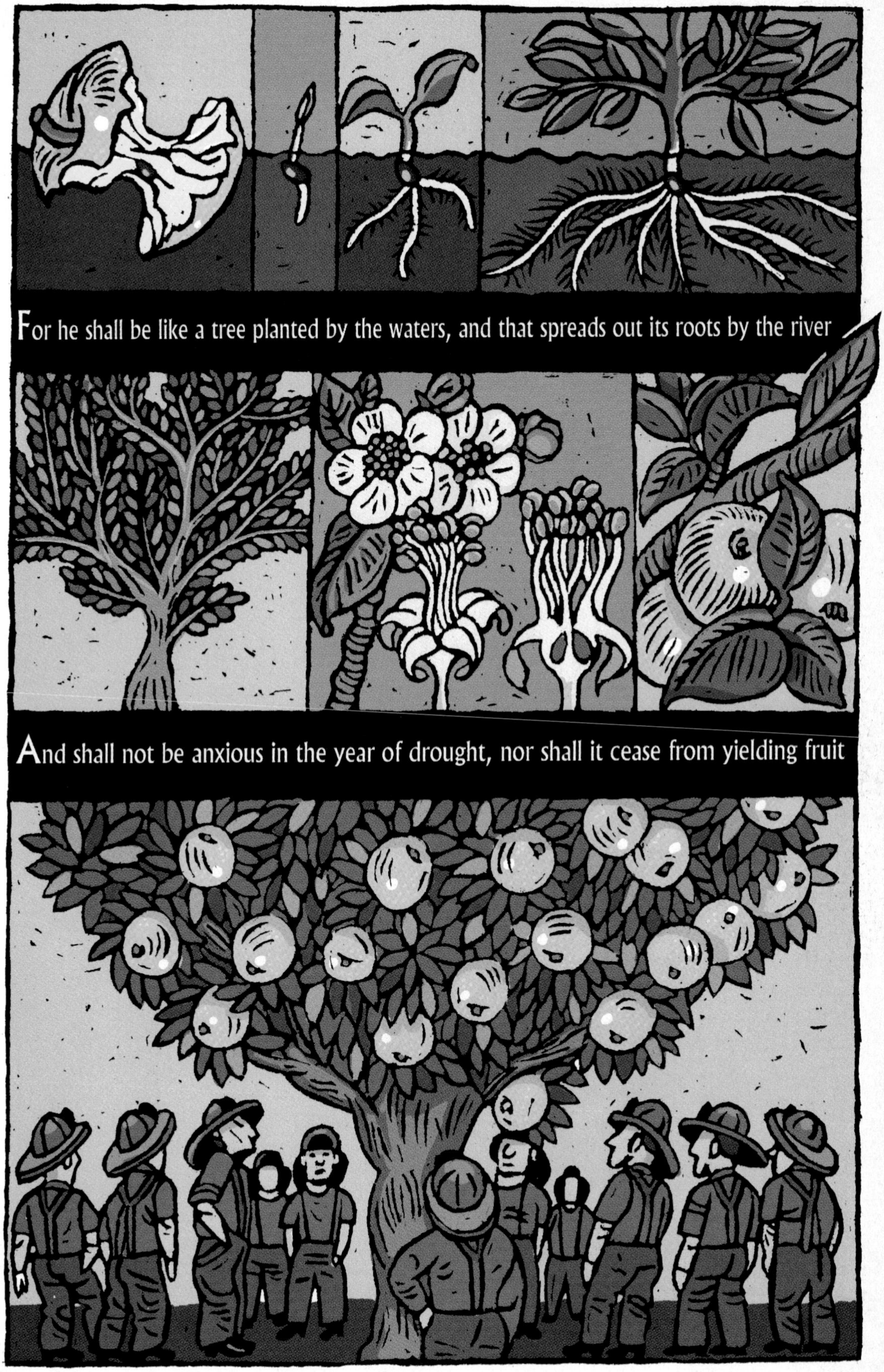
For he shall be like a tree planted by the waters, and that spreads out its roots by the river
And shall not be anxious in the year of drought, nor shall it cease from yielding fruit

Aaron Renier

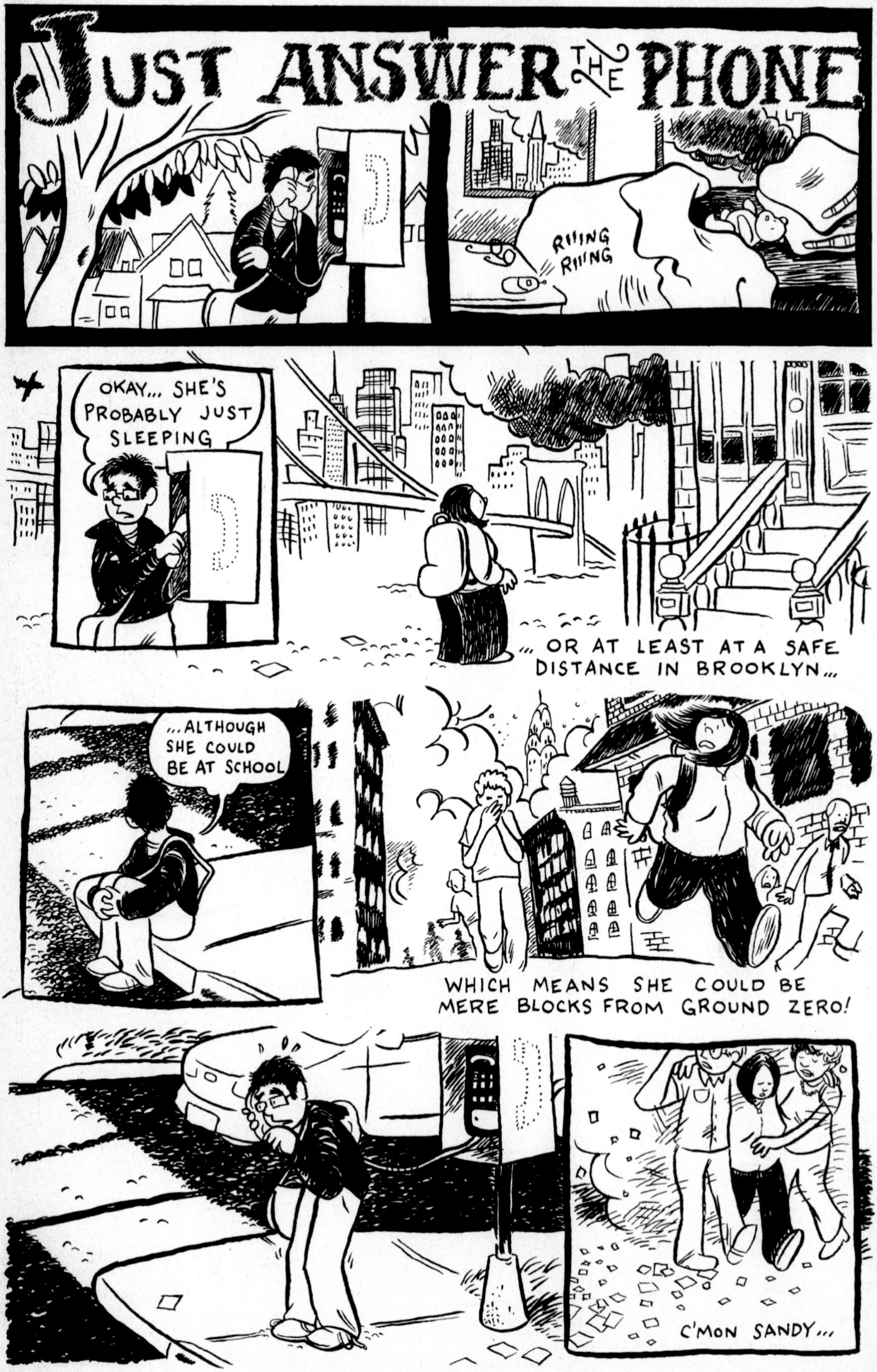
JUST ANSWER THE PHONE
RIIING RIIING
OKAY... SHE'S PROBABLY JUST SLEEPING
... OR AT LEAST AT A SAFE DISTANCE IN BROOKLYN...
...ALTHOUGH SHE COULD BE AT SCHOOL
WHICH MEANS SHE COULD BE MERE BLOCKS FROM GROUND ZERO!
C'MON SANDY...

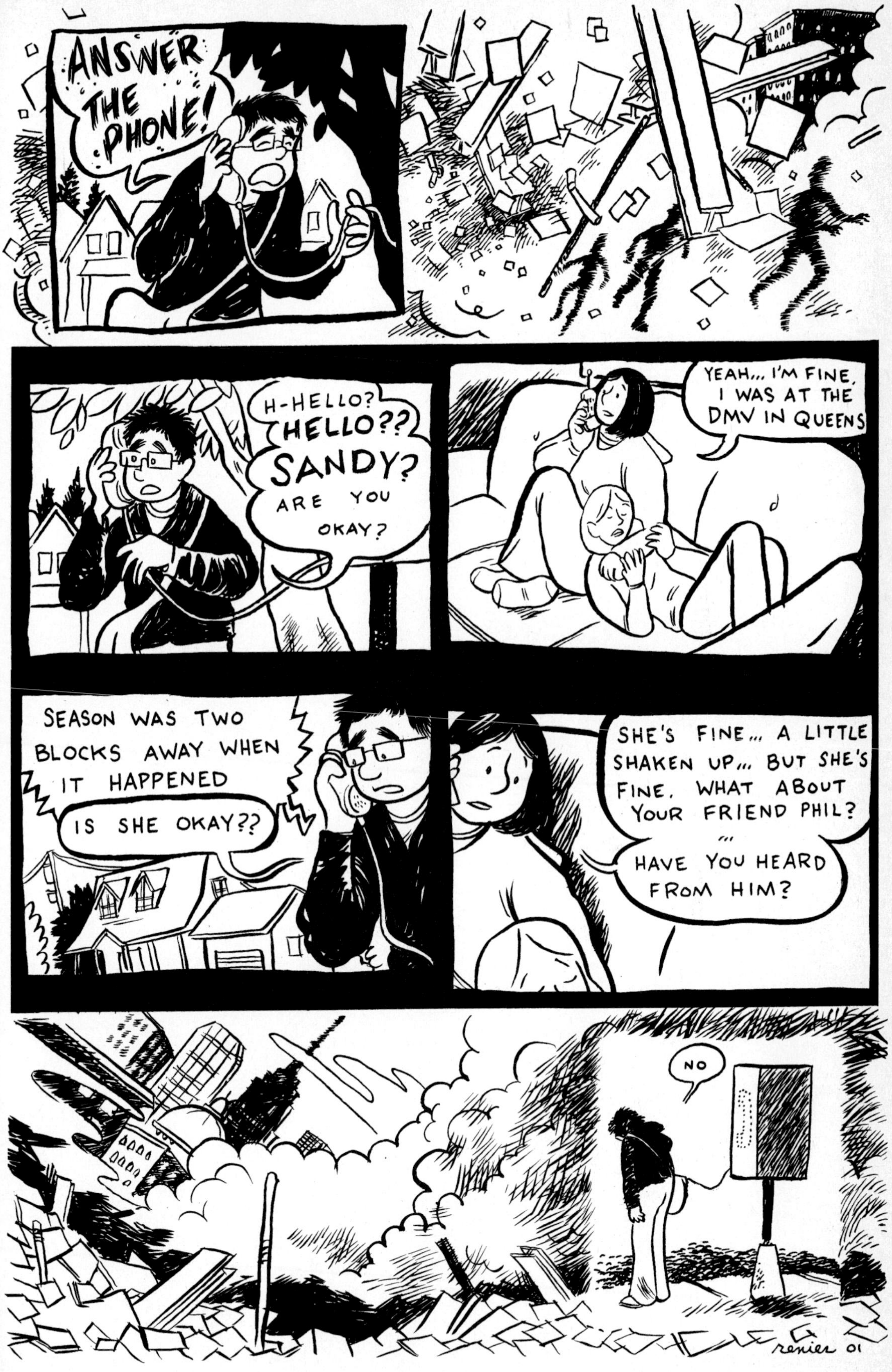
ANSWER THE PHONE!
H-HELLO? HELLO?? SANDY? ARE YOU OKAY?
YEAH... I'M FINE, I WAS AT THE DMV IN QUEENS
SEASON WAS TWO BLOCKS AWAY WHEN IT HAPPENED
IS SHE OKAY??
SHE'S FINE... A LITTLE SHAKEN UP... BUT SHE'S FINE. WHAT ABOUT YOUR FRIEND PHIL?
... HAVE YOU HEARD FROM HIM?
NO
renier 01

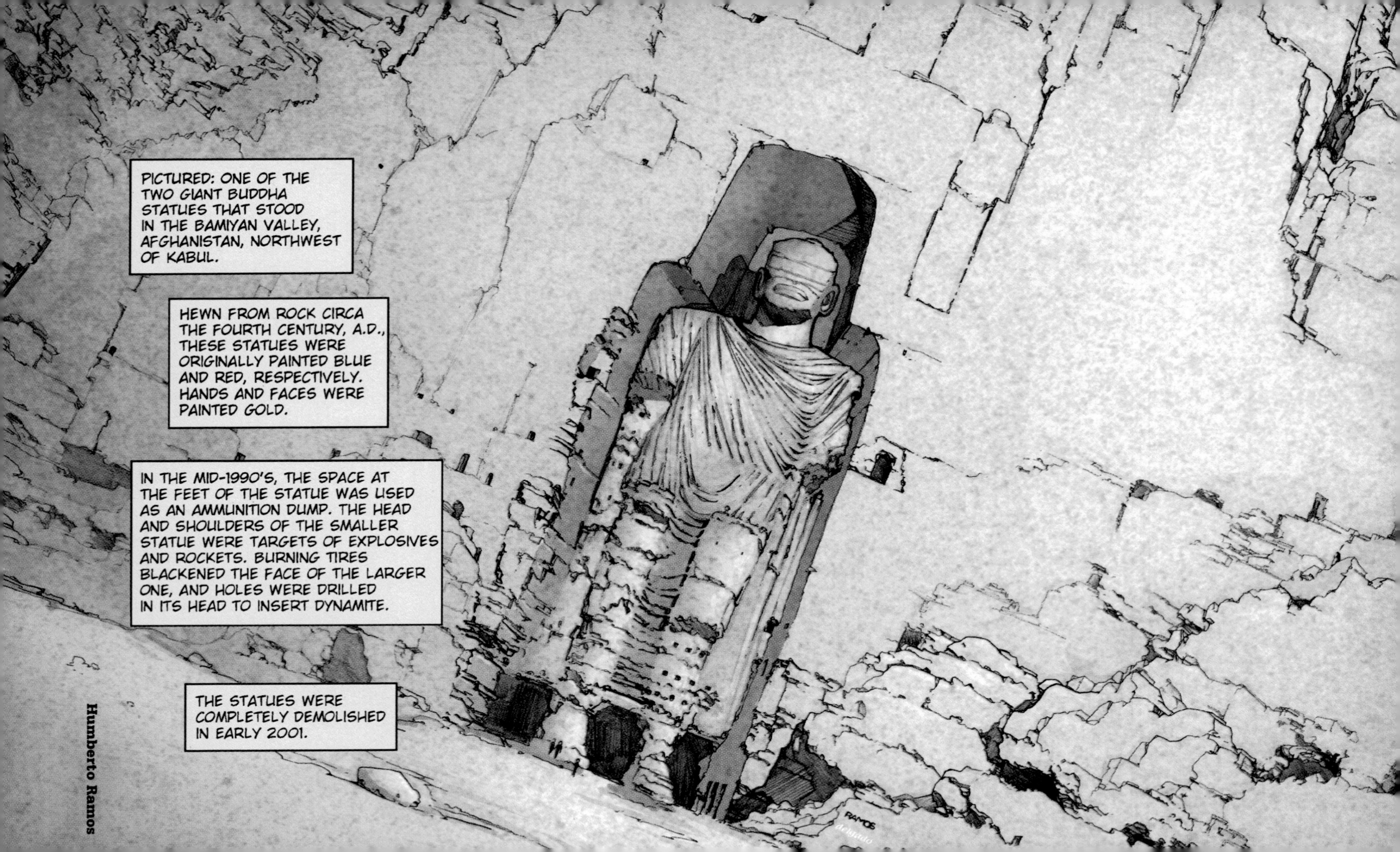
PICTURED: ONE OF THE TWO GIANT BUDDHA STATUES THAT STOOD IN THE BAMIYAN VALLEY, AFGHANISTAN, NORTHWEST OF KABUL.
HEWN FROM ROCK CIRCA THE FOURTH CENTURY, A.D., THESE STATUES WERE ORIGINALLY PAINTED BLUE AND RED, RESPECTIVELY. HANDS AND FACES WERE PAINTED GOLD.
IN THE MID-1990'S, THE SPACE AT THE FEET OF THE STATUE WAS USED AS AN AMMUNITION DUMP. THE HEAD AND SHOULDERS OF THE SMALLER STATUE WERE TARGETS OF EXPLOSIVES AND ROCKETS. BURNING TIRES BLACKENED THE FACE OF THE LARGER ONE, AND HOLES WERE DRILLED IN ITS HEAD TO INSERT DYNAMITE.
THE STATUES WERE COMPLETELY DEMOLISHED IN EARLY 2001.
RAMOS

Humberto Ramos

LOS ANGELES
SEPTEMBER 10, 2001
MONDAY NIGHT

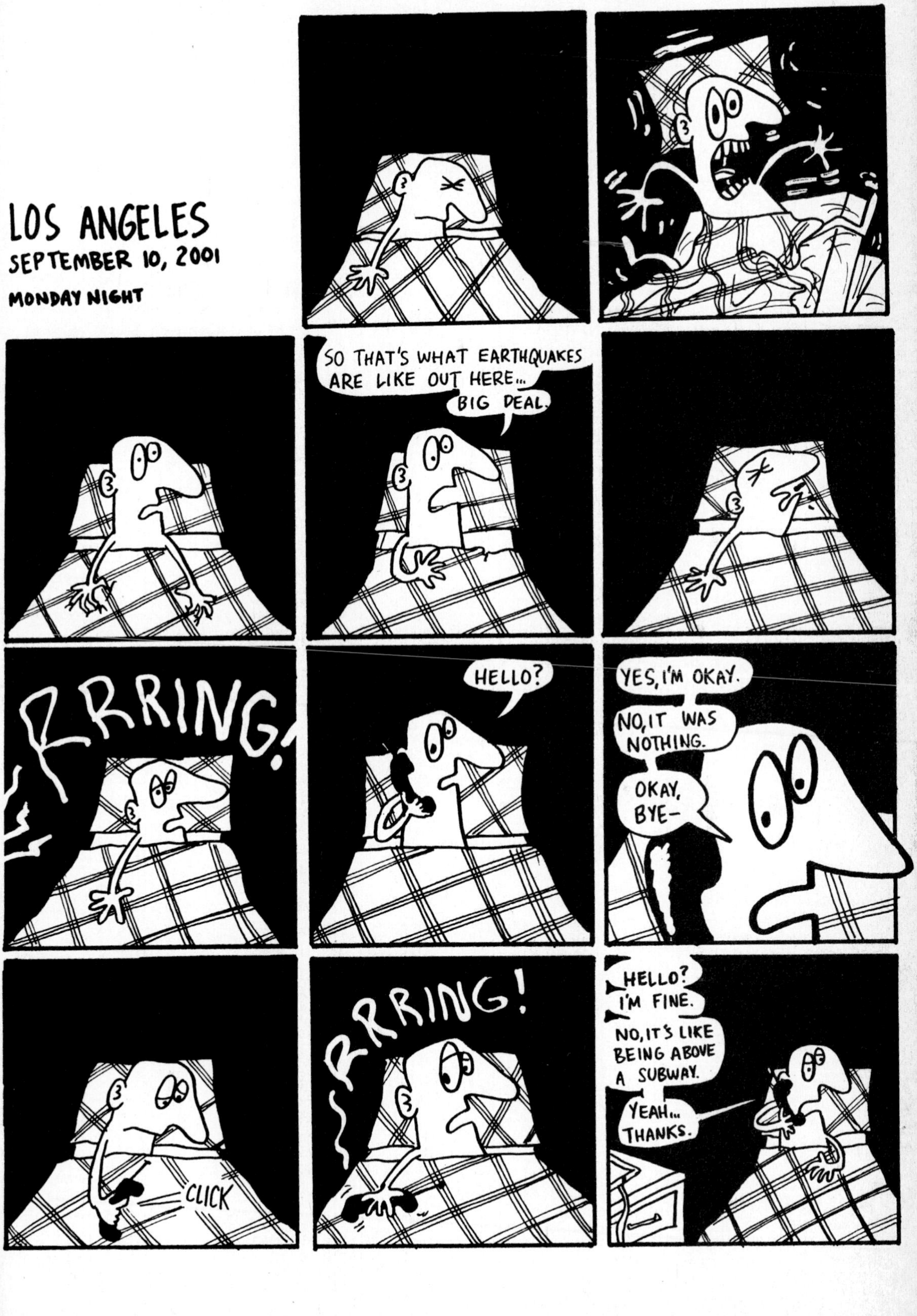
SO THAT'S WHAT EARTHQUAKES ARE LIKE OUT HERE...
BIG DEAL.
RRRING!
HELLO?
YES, I'M OKAY.
NO, IT WAS NOTHING.
OKAY, BYE-
CLICK
RRRING!
HELLO? I'M FINE.
NO, IT'S LIKE BEING ABOVE A SUBWAY.
YEAH... THANKS.

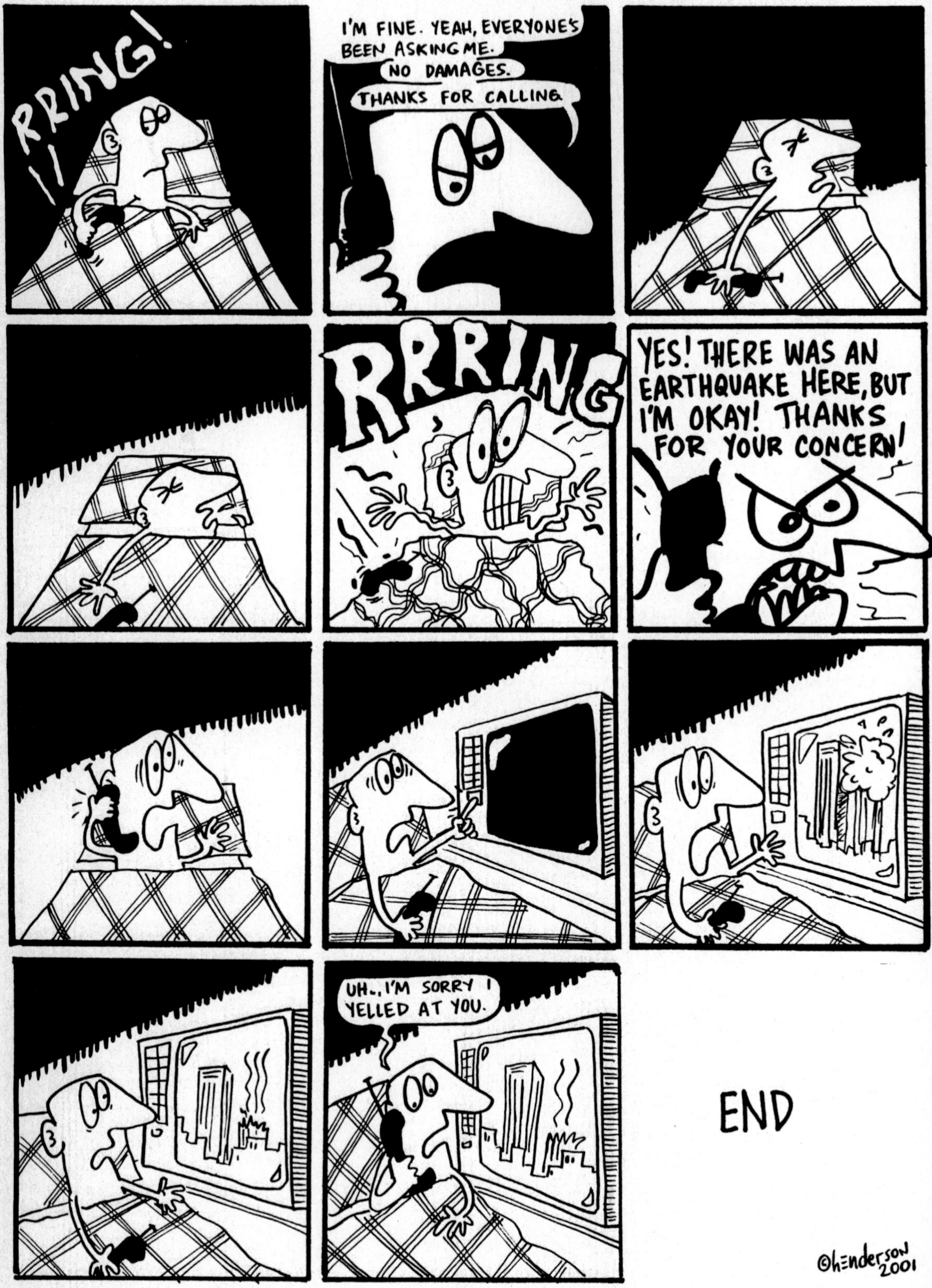
RRING!!
I'M FINE. YEAH, EVERYONE'S BEEN ASKING ME.
NO DAMAGES.
THANKS FOR CALLING
RRRING
YES! THERE WAS AN EARTHQUAKE HERE, BUT I'M OKAY! THANKS FOR YOUR CONCERN!
UH.. I'M SORRY I YELLED AT YOU.
END
©henderson 2001

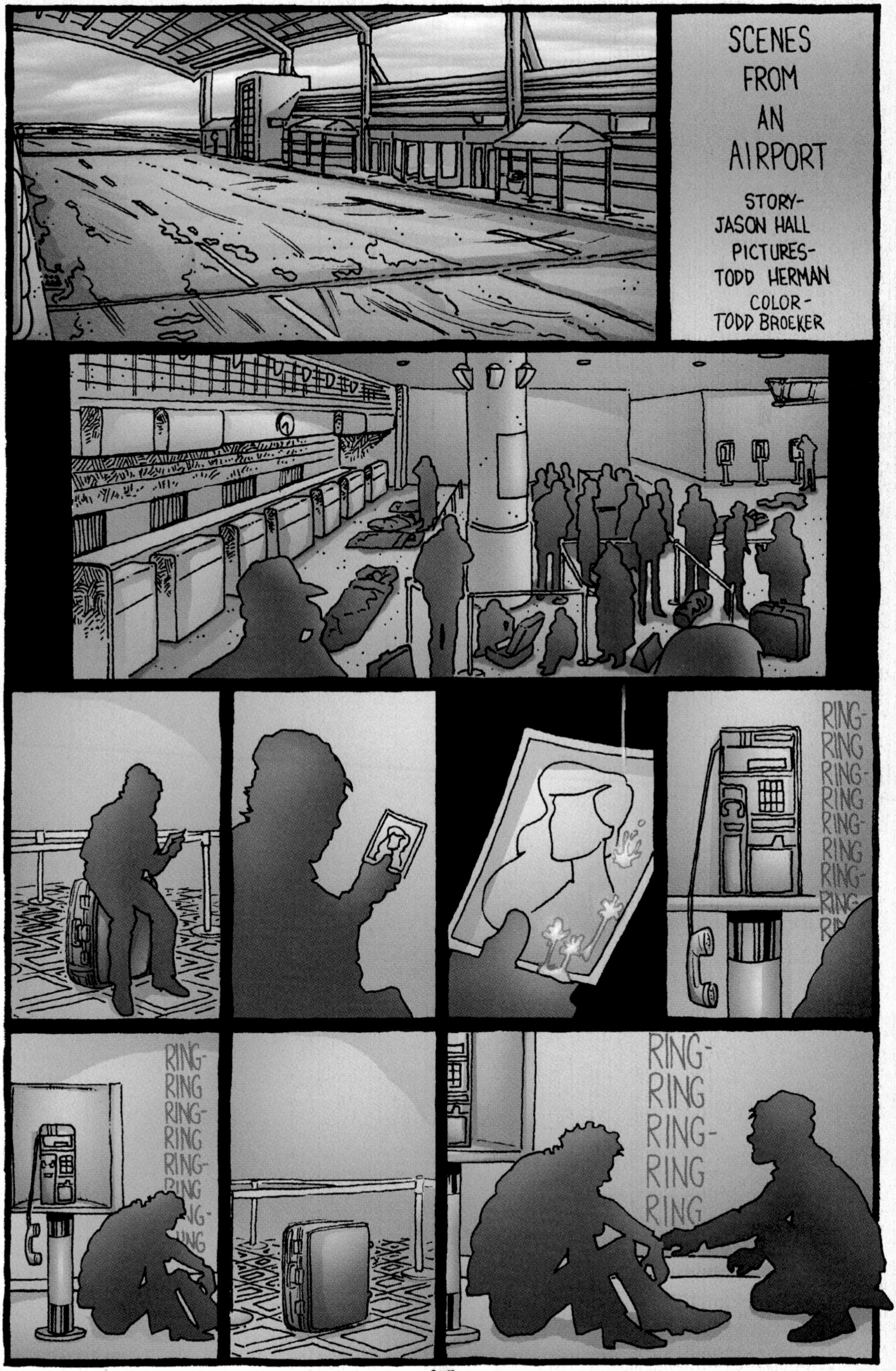
SCENES FROM AN AIRPORT
STORY- JASON HALL
PICTURES- TODD HERMAN
COLOR- TODD BROEKER
RING-
RING
RING-
RING
RING-
RING
RING-
RING-
RING
RING-
RING
RING-
RING-
RING
RING-
RING
RING

ONE

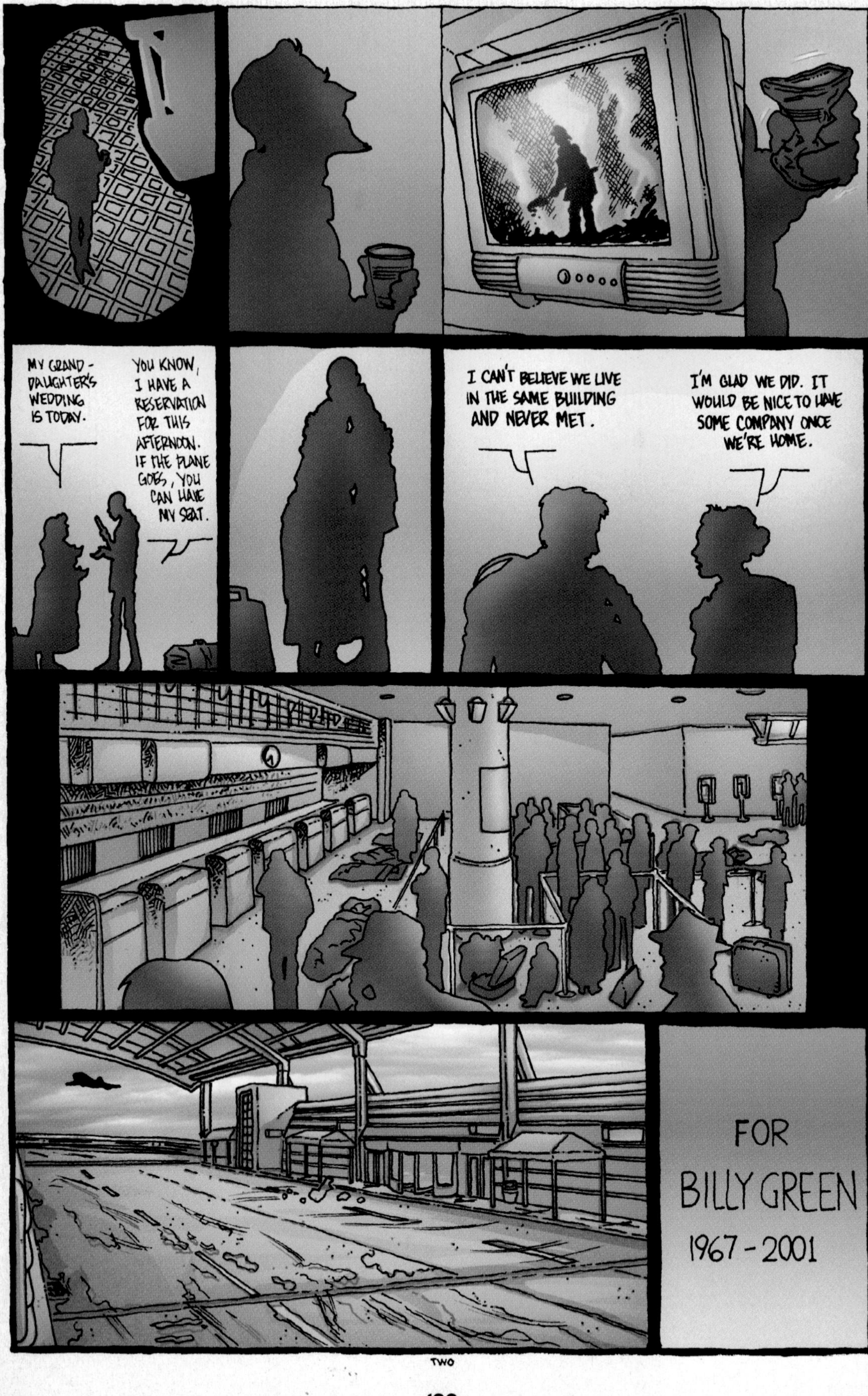
MY GRAND-DAUGHTER'S WEDDING IS TODAY.
YOU KNOW, I HAVE A RESERVATION FOR THIS AFTERNOON. IF THE PLANE GOES, YOU CAN HAVE MY SEAT.
I CAN'T BELIEVE WE LIVE IN THE SAME BUILDING AND NEVER MET.
I'M GLAD WE DID. IT WOULD BE NICE TO HAVE SOME COMPANY ONCE WE'RE HOME.
FOR BILLY GREEN 1967 - 2001

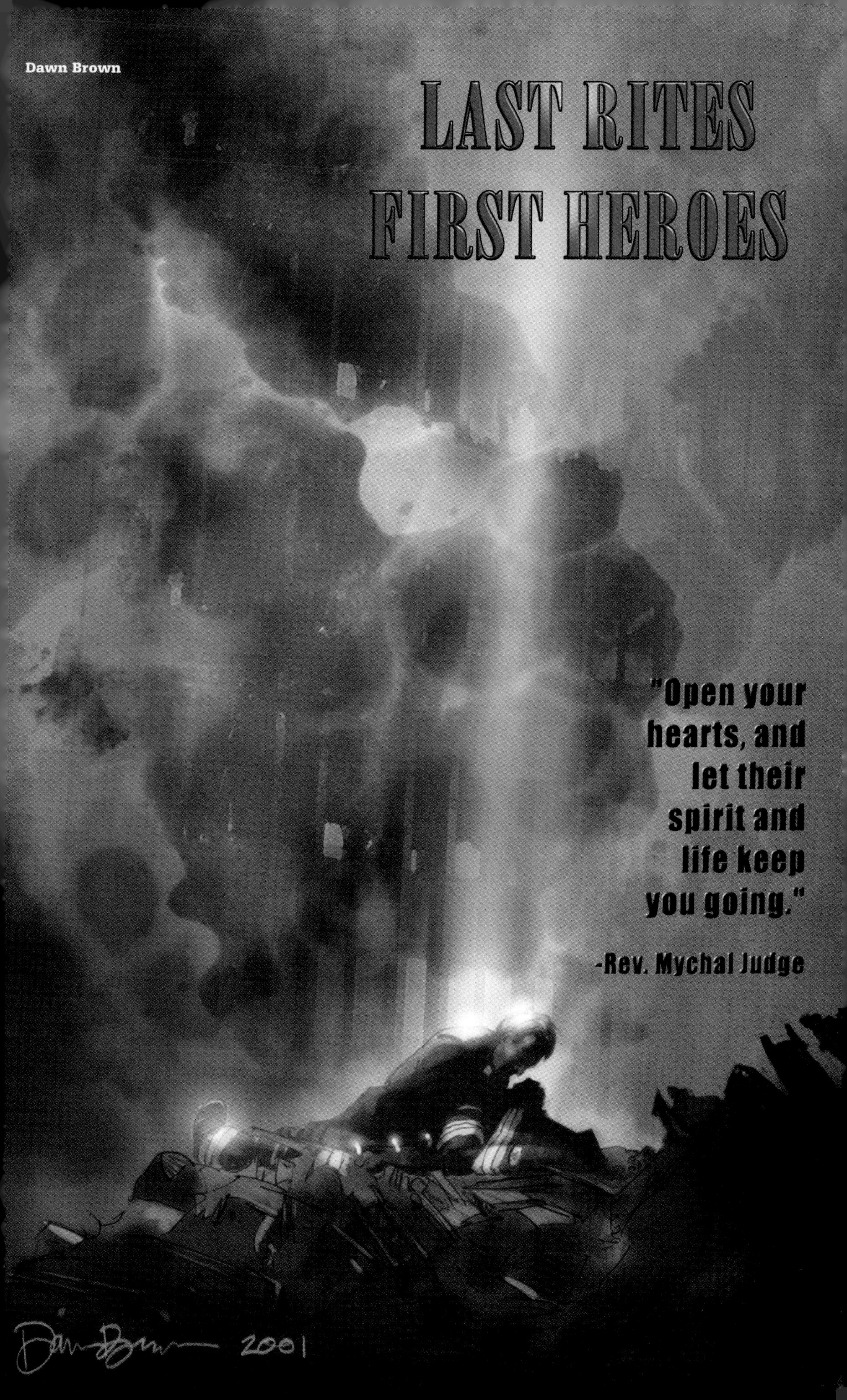
Dawn Brown
LAST RITES
FIRST HEROES
"Open your hearts, and let their spirit and life keep you going."
-Rev. Mychal Judge
Dawn Brown 2001

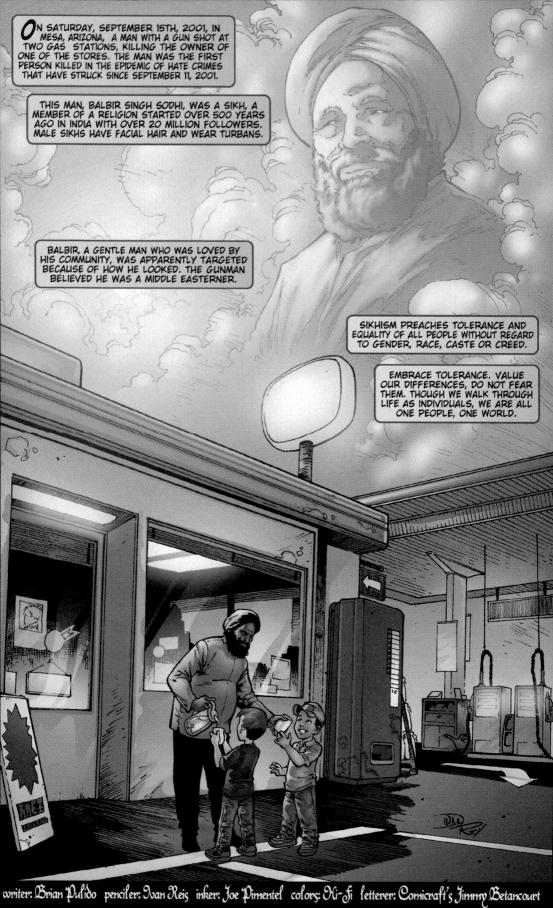

ON SATURDAY, SEPTEMBER 15TH, 2001, IN MESA, ARIZONA, A MAN WITH A GUN SHOT AT TWO GAS STATIONS, KILLING THE OWNER OF ONE OF THE STORES. THE MAN WAS THE FIRST PERSON KILLED IN THE EPIDEMIC OF HATE CRIMES THAT HAVE STRUCK SINCE SEPTEMBER 11, 2001.

THIS MAN, BALBIR SINGH SODHI, WAS A SIKH, A MEMBER OF A RELIGION STARTED OVER 500 YEARS AGO IN INDIA WITH OVER 20 MILLION FOLLOWERS. MALE SIKHS HAVE FACIAL HAIR AND WEAR TURBANS.

BALBIR, A GENTLE MAN WHO WAS LOVED BY HIS COMMUNITY, WAS APPARENTLY TARGETED BECAUSE OF HOW HE LOOKED. THE GUNMAN BELIEVED HE WAS A MIDDLE EASTERNER.

SIKHISM PREACHES TOLERANCE AND EQUALITY OF ALL PEOPLE WITHOUT REGARD TO GENDER, RACE, CASTE OR CREED.

EMBRACE TOLERANCE. VALUE OUR DIFFERENCES, DO NOT FEAR THEM. THOUGH WE WALK THROUGH LIFE AS INDIVIDUALS, WE ARE ALL ONE PEOPLE, ONE WORLD.

writer: Brian Pulido   penciler: Ivan Reis   inker: Joe Pimentel   colors: Hi-Fi   letterer: Comicraft's Jimmy Betancourt

Fabian Nicieza • Cliff Richards

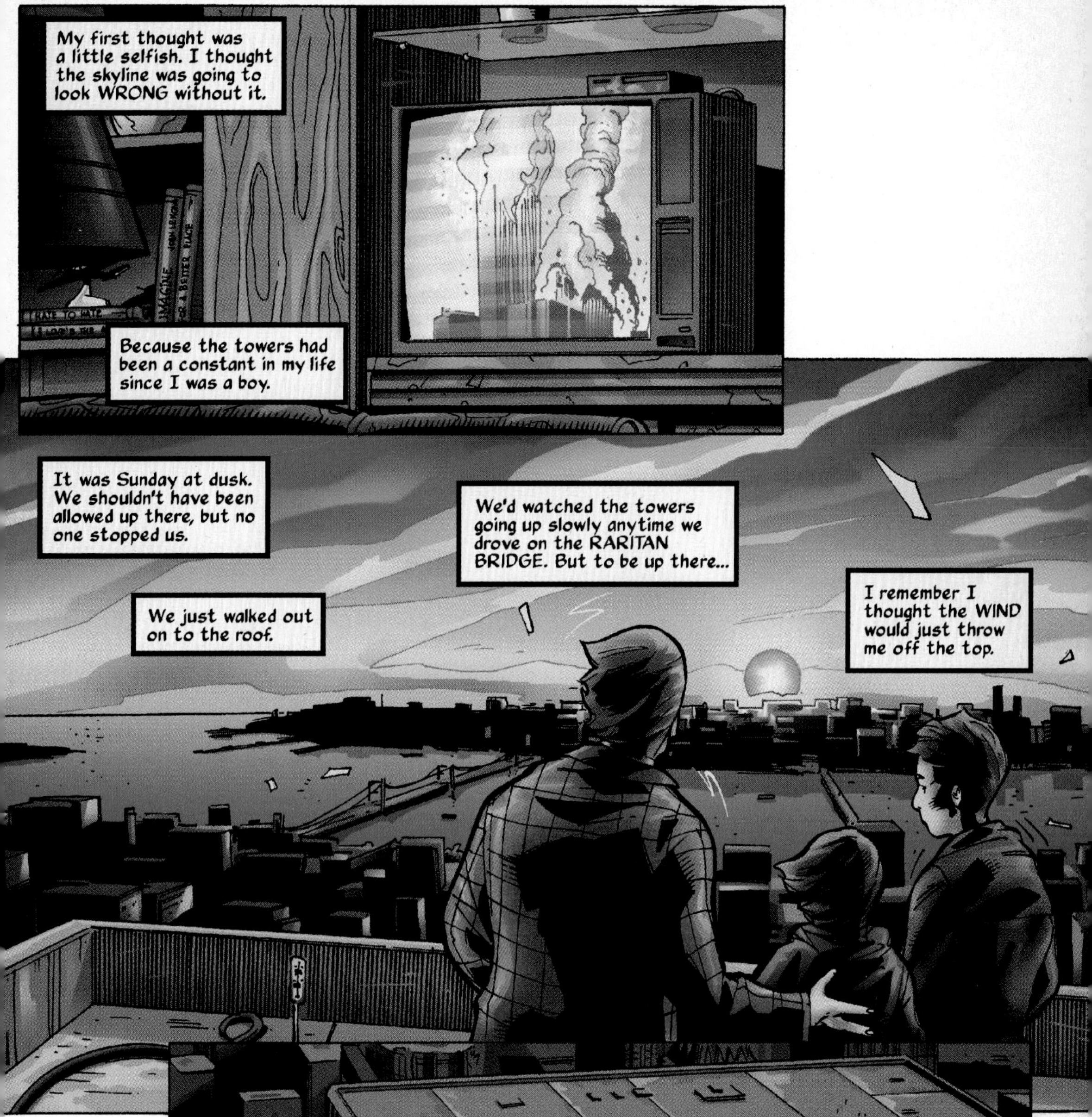

My first thought was a little selfish. I thought the skyline was going to look WRONG without it.
Because the towers had been a constant in my life since I was a boy.
It was Sunday at dusk. We shouldn't have been allowed up there, but no one stopped us.
We'd watched the towers going up slowly anytime we drove on the RARITAN BRIDGE. But to be up there...
We just walked out on to the roof.
I remember I thought the WIND would just throw me off the top.

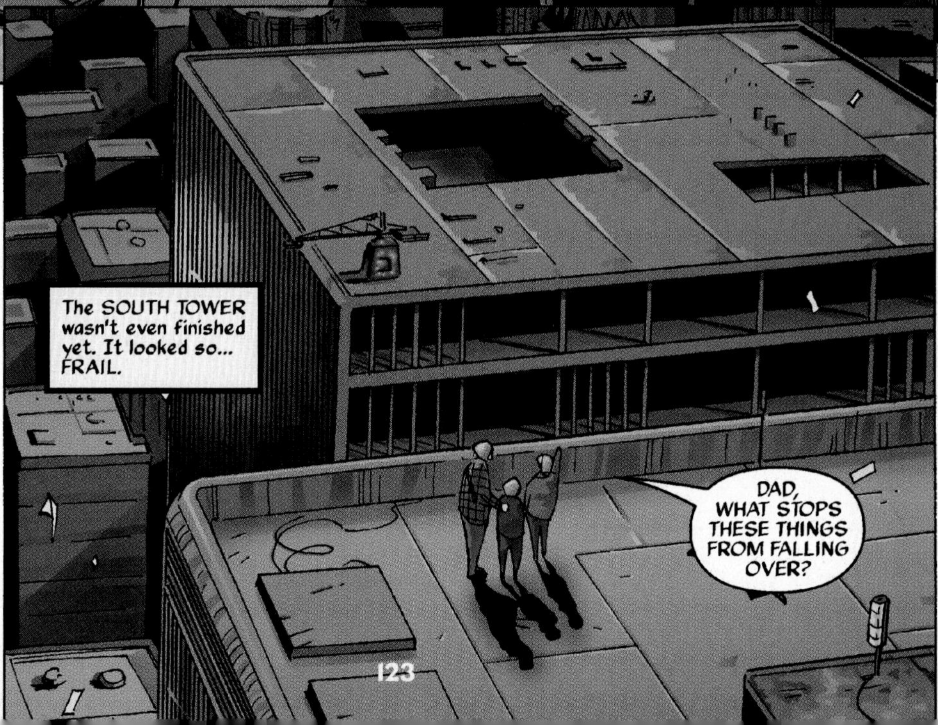

The SOUTH TOWER wasn't even finished yet. It looked so... FRAIL.
DAD, WHAT STOPS THESE THINGS FROM FALLING OVER?

STORY
FABIAN NICIEZA

PENCILS
CLIFF RICHARDS

INKS & COLORS
WILL CONRAD

LETTERS
MICHAEL HEISLER

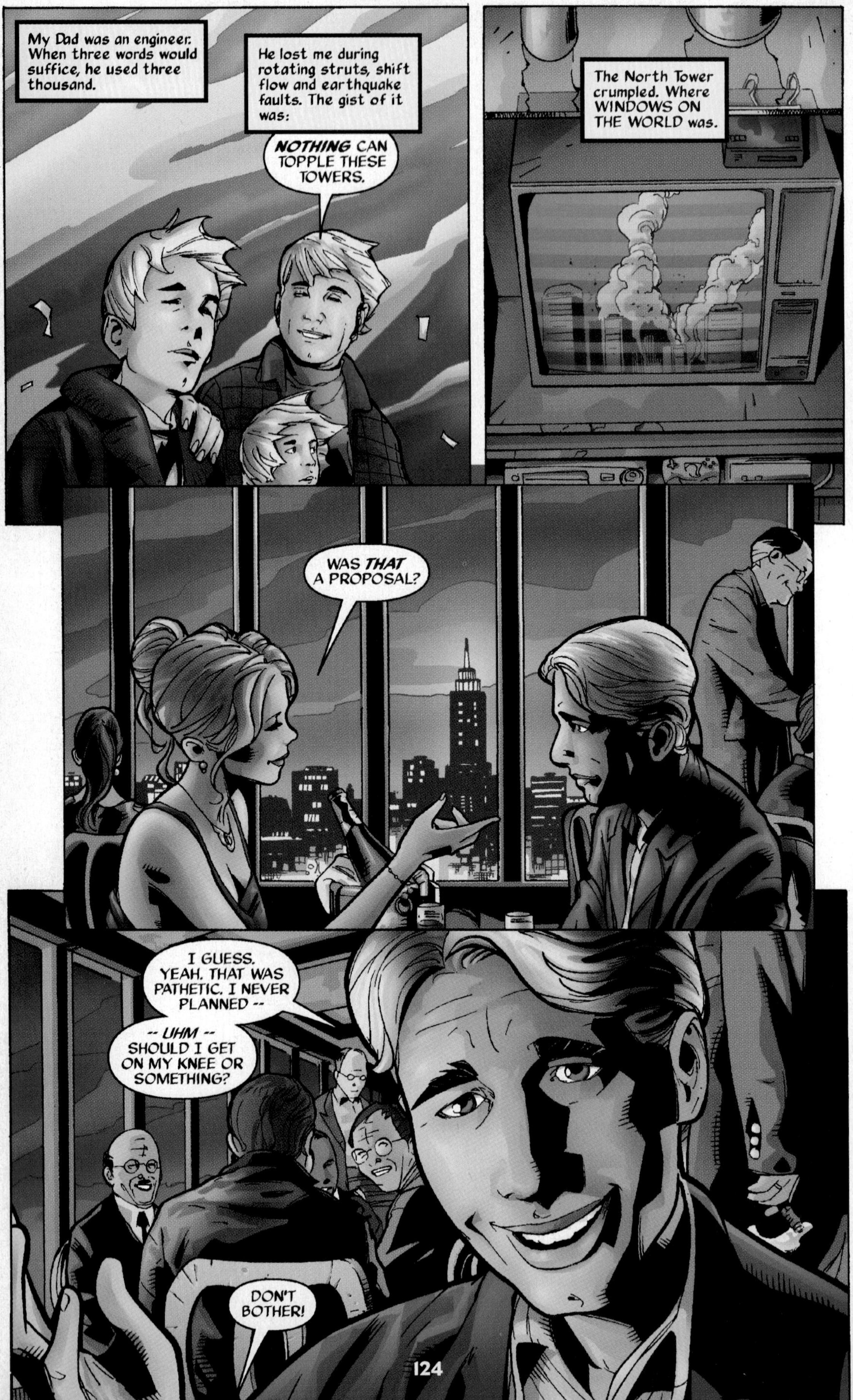
My Dad was an engineer. When three words would suffice, he used three thousand.
He lost me during rotating struts, shift flow and earthquake faults. The gist of it was:
NOTHING CAN TOPPLE THESE TOWERS.
The North Tower crumpled. Where WINDOWS ON THE WORLD was.
WAS THAT A PROPOSAL?
I GUESS. YEAH. THAT WAS PATHETIC. I NEVER PLANNED --
-- UHM -- SHOULD I GET ON MY KNEE OR SOMETHING?
DON'T BOTHER!

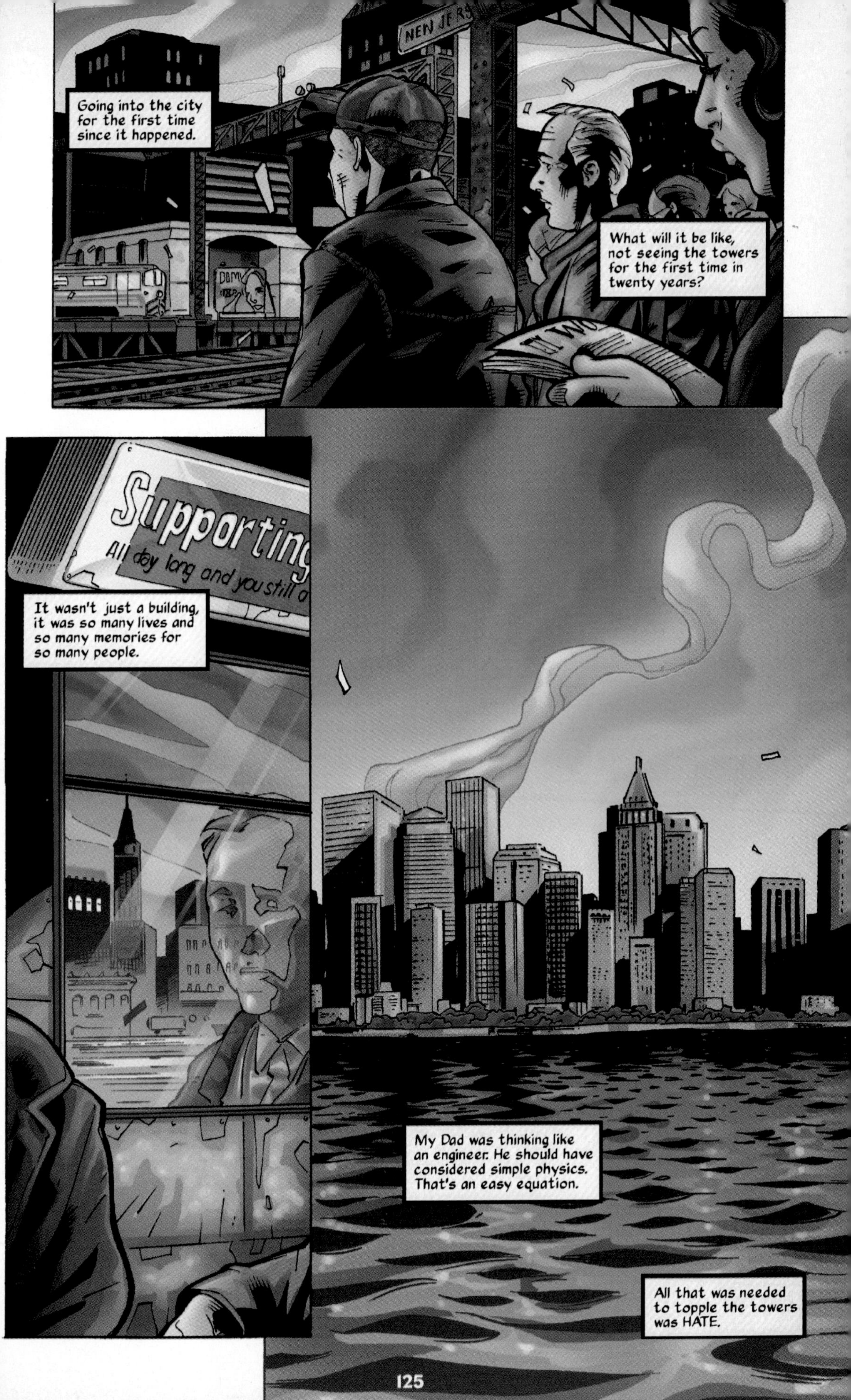
Going into the city for the first time since it happened.
What will it be like, not seeing the towers for the first time in twenty years?
It wasn't just a building, it was so many lives and so many memories for so many people.
My Dad was thinking like an engineer. He should have considered simple physics. That's an easy equation.
All that was needed to topple the towers was HATE.

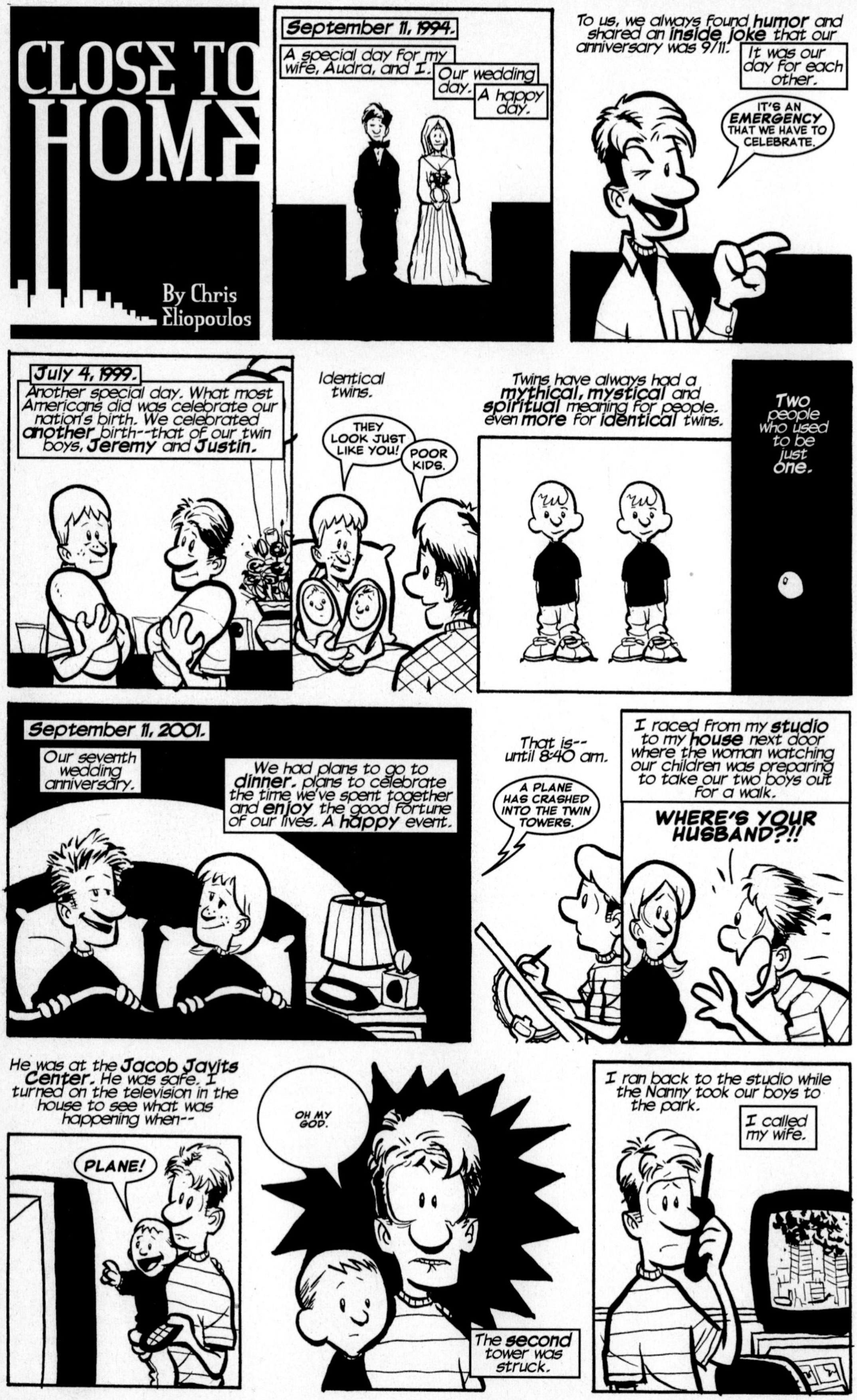
CLOSE TO HOME
By Chris Eliopoulos
September 11, 1994.
A special day for my wife, Audra, and I.
Our wedding day.
A happy day.
To us, we always found humor and shared an inside joke that our anniversary was 9/11.
It was our day for each other.
IT'S AN EMERGENCY THAT WE HAVE TO CELEBRATE.
July 4, 1999.
Another special day. What most Americans did was celebrate our nation's birth. We celebrated another birth--that of our twin boys, Jeremy and Justin.
Identical twins.
THEY LOOK JUST LIKE YOU!
POOR KIDS.
Twins have always had a mythical, mystical and spiritual meaning for people. even more for identical twins.
Two people who used to be just one.
September 11, 2001.
Our seventh wedding anniversary.
We had plans to go to dinner. plans to celebrate the time we've spent together and enjoy the good fortune of our lives. A happy event.
That is-- until 8:40 am.
A PLANE HAS CRASHED INTO THE TWIN TOWERS.
I raced from my studio to my house next door where the woman watching our children was preparing to take our two boys out for a walk.
WHERE'S YOUR HUSBAND?!!
He was at the Jacob Javits Center. He was safe. I turned on the television in the house to see what was happening when--
PLANE!
OH MY GOD.
The second tower was struck.
I ran back to the studio while the Nanny took our boys to the park.
I called my wife.

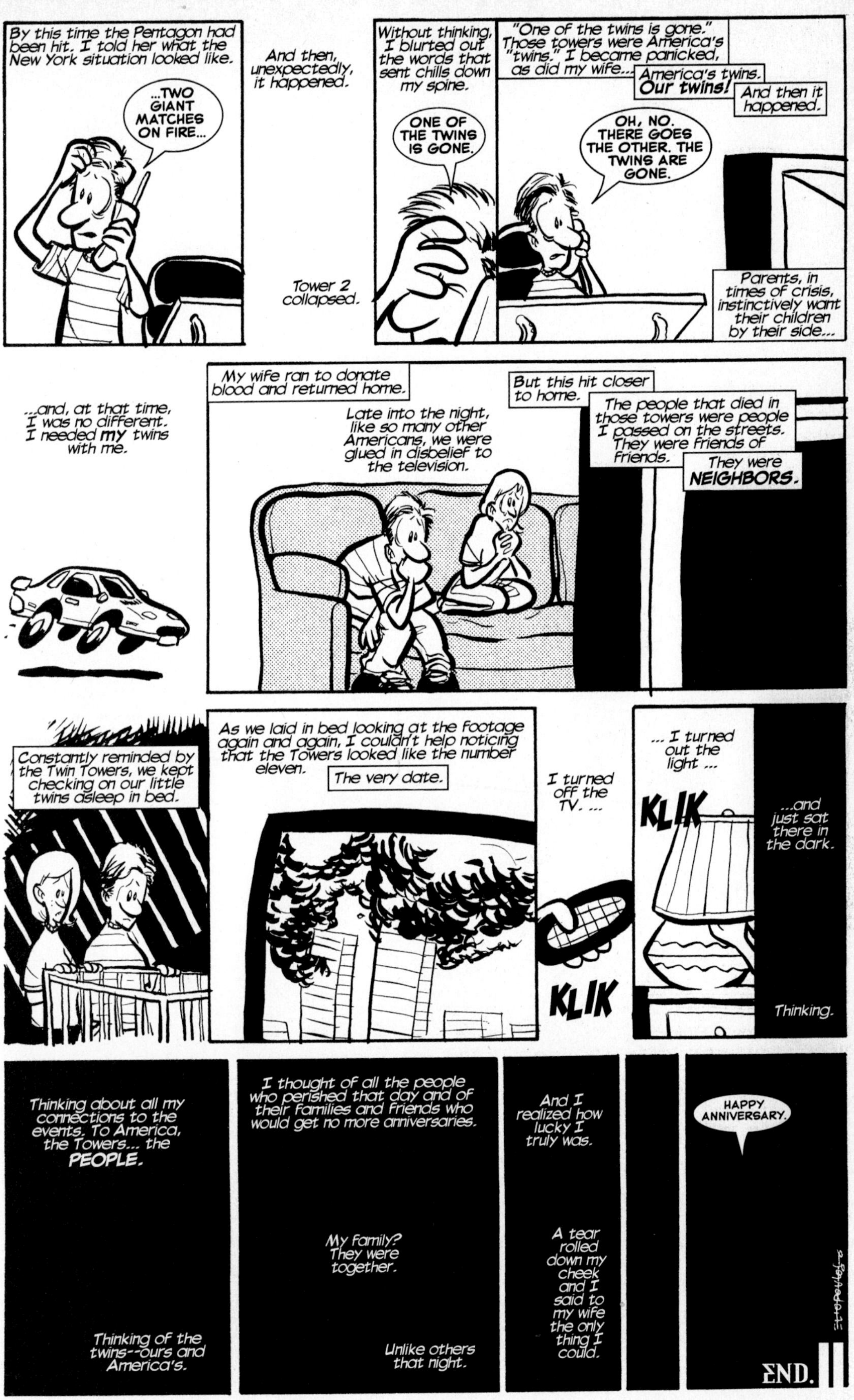

By this time the Pentagon had been hit. I told her what the New York situation looked like.
...TWO GIANT MATCHES ON FIRE...
And then, unexpectedly, it happened.
Tower 2 collapsed.
Without thinking, I blurted out the words that sent chills down my spine.
ONE OF THE TWINS IS GONE.
"One of the twins is gone." Those towers were America's "twins." I became panicked, as did my wife...
America's twins. Our twins!
And then it happened.
OH, NO. THERE GOES THE OTHER. THE TWINS ARE GONE.
Parents, in times of crisis, instinctively want their children by their side...
...and, at that time, I was no different. I needed my twins with me.
My wife ran to donate blood and returned home.
Late into the night, like so many other Americans, we were glued in disbelief to the television.
But this hit closer to home.
The people that died in those towers were people I passed on the streets. They were friends of friends.
They were NEIGHBORS.
Constantly reminded by the Twin Towers, we kept checking on our little twins asleep in bed.
As we laid in bed looking at the footage again and again, I couldn't help noticing that the Towers looked like the number eleven.
The very date.
I turned off the TV. ...
KLIK
... I turned out the light ...
KLIK
...and just sat there in the dark.
Thinking.
Thinking about all my connections to the events. To America, the Towers... the PEOPLE.
Thinking of the twins--ours and America's.
I thought of all the people who perished that day and of their families and friends who would get no more anniversaries.
My family? They were together.
Unlike others that night.
And I realized how lucky I truly was.
A tear rolled down my cheek and I said to my wife the only thing I could.
HAPPY ANNIVERSARY.
END.

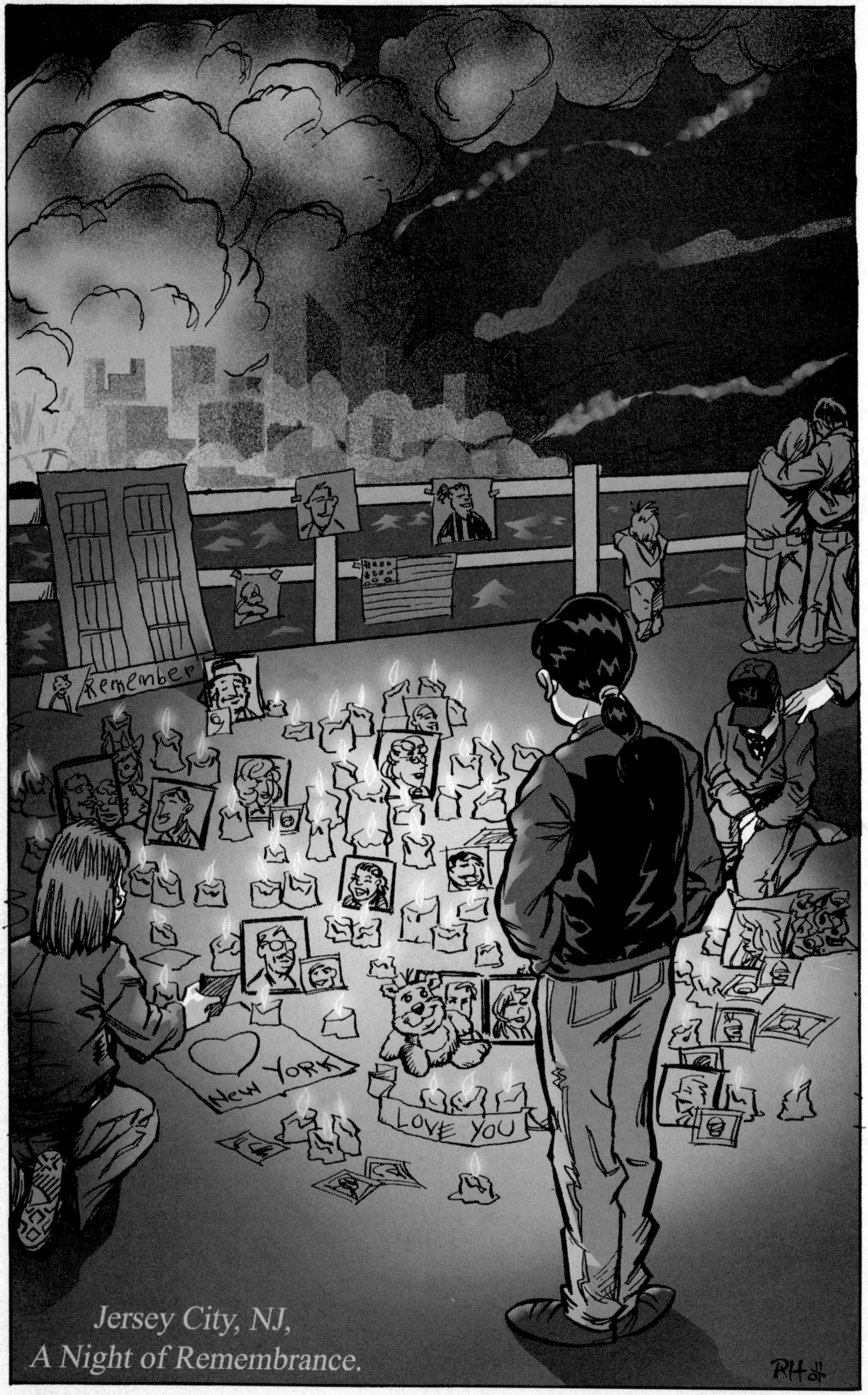
Remember
9
New York
LOVE YOU
Jersey City, NJ,
A Night of Remembrance.
RH 01

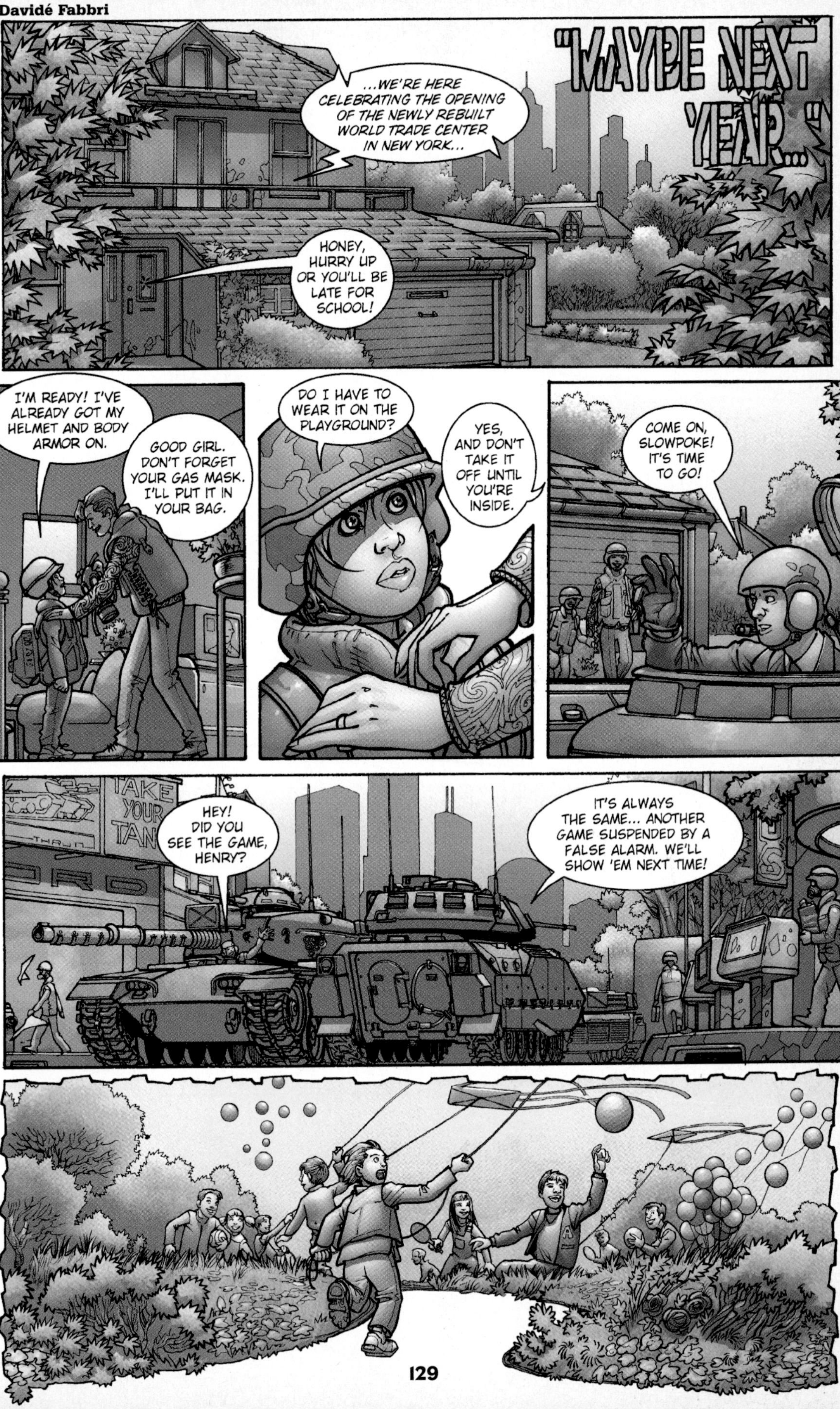
"MAYBE NEXT YEAR..."
...WE'RE HERE CELEBRATING THE OPENING OF THE NEWLY REBUILT WORLD TRADE CENTER IN NEW YORK...
HONEY, HURRY UP OR YOU'LL BE LATE FOR SCHOOL!
I'M READY! I'VE ALREADY GOT MY HELMET AND BODY ARMOR ON.
GOOD GIRL. DON'T FORGET YOUR GAS MASK. I'LL PUT IT IN YOUR BAG.
DO I HAVE TO WEAR IT ON THE PLAYGROUND?
YES, AND DON'T TAKE IT OFF UNTIL YOU'RE INSIDE.
COME ON, SLOWPOKE! IT'S TIME TO GO!
HEY! DID YOU SEE THE GAME, HENRY?
IT'S ALWAYS THE SAME... ANOTHER GAME SUSPENDED BY A FALSE ALARM. WE'LL SHOW 'EM NEXT TIME!

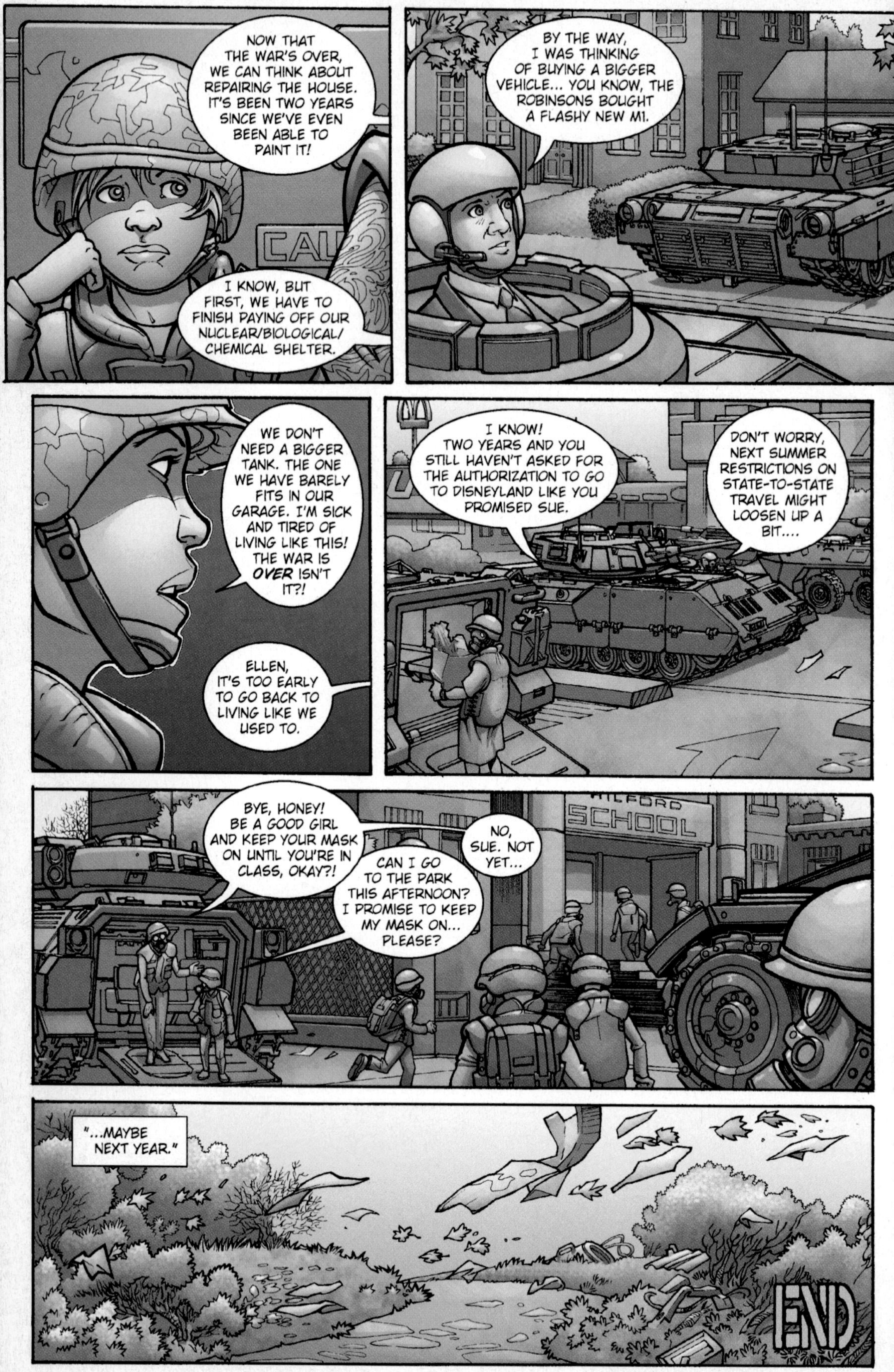
NOW THAT THE WAR'S OVER, WE CAN THINK ABOUT REPAIRING THE HOUSE. IT'S BEEN TWO YEARS SINCE WE'VE EVEN BEEN ABLE TO PAINT IT!
I KNOW, BUT FIRST, WE HAVE TO FINISH PAYING OFF OUR NUCLEAR/BIOLOGICAL/ CHEMICAL SHELTER.
BY THE WAY, I WAS THINKING OF BUYING A BIGGER VEHICLE... YOU KNOW, THE ROBINSONS BOUGHT A FLASHY NEW M1.
WE DON'T NEED A BIGGER TANK. THE ONE WE HAVE BARELY FITS IN OUR GARAGE. I'M SICK AND TIRED OF LIVING LIKE THIS! THE WAR IS *OVER* ISN'T IT?!
ELLEN, IT'S TOO EARLY TO GO BACK TO LIVING LIKE WE USED TO.
I KNOW! TWO YEARS AND YOU STILL HAVEN'T ASKED FOR THE AUTHORIZATION TO GO TO DISNEYLAND LIKE YOU PROMISED SUE.
DON'T WORRY, NEXT SUMMER RESTRICTIONS ON STATE-TO-STATE TRAVEL MIGHT LOOSEN UP A BIT....
SCHOOL
BYE, HONEY! BE A GOOD GIRL AND KEEP YOUR MASK ON UNTIL YOU'RE IN CLASS, OKAY?!
CAN I GO TO THE PARK THIS AFTERNOON? I PROMISE TO KEEP MY MASK ON... PLEASE?
NO, SUE. NOT YET...
"...MAYBE NEXT YEAR."
END

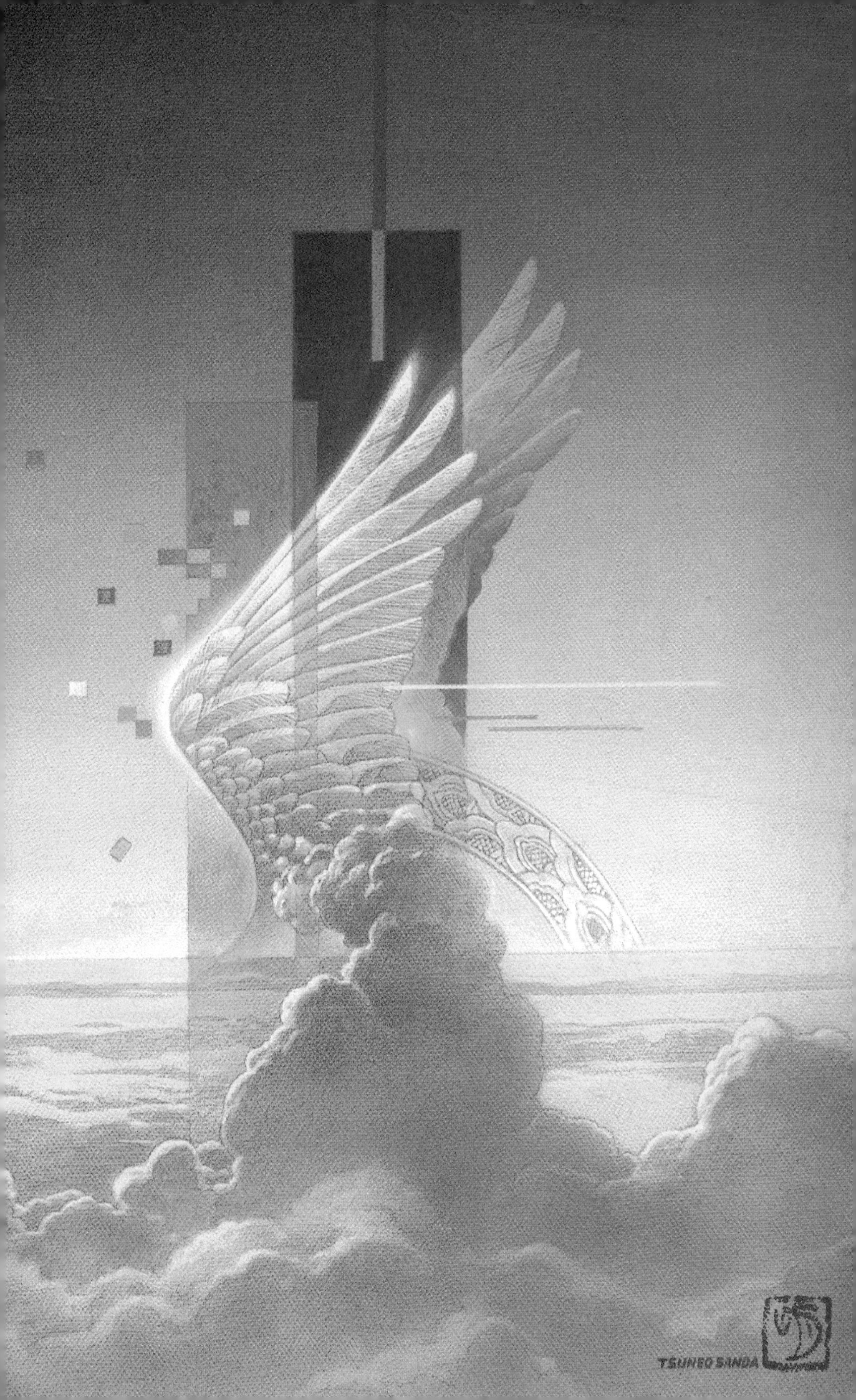
TSUNEO SANDA

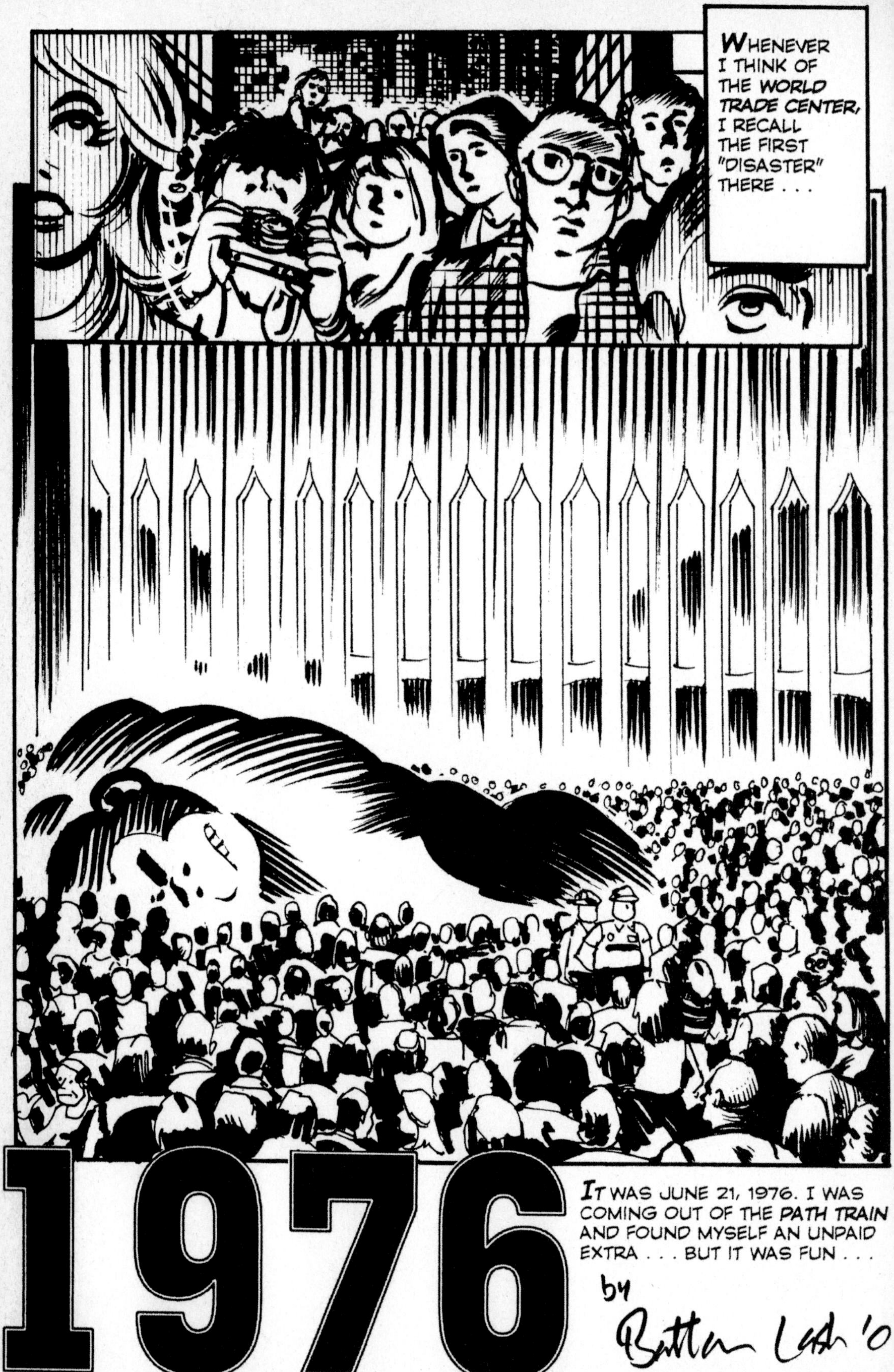
WHENEVER I THINK OF THE WORLD TRADE CENTER, I RECALL THE FIRST "DISASTER" THERE . . .
1976
IT WAS JUNE 21, 1976. I WAS COMING OUT OF THE PATH TRAIN AND FOUND MYSELF AN UNPAID EXTRA . . . BUT IT WAS FUN . . .
by

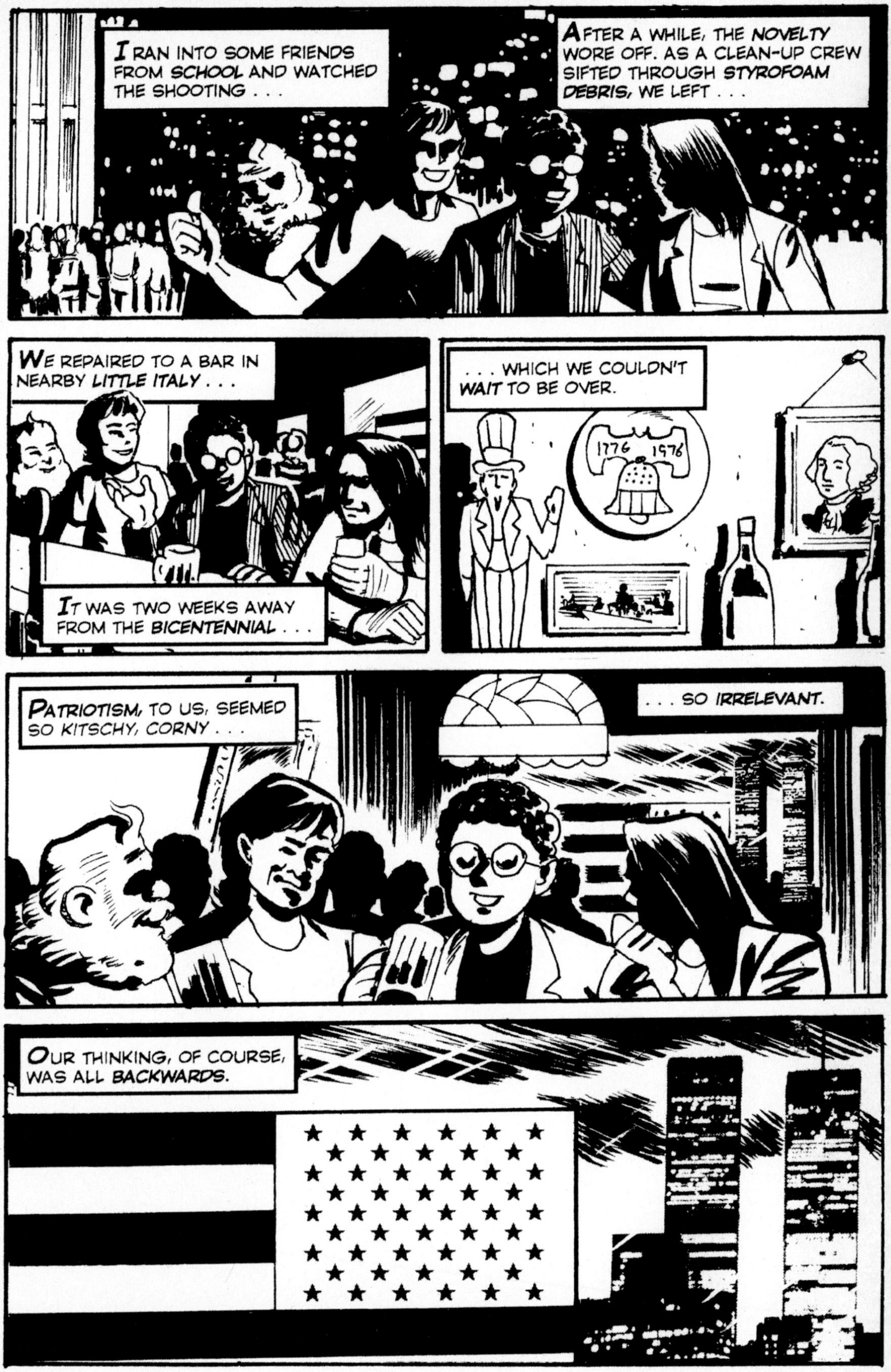
I RAN INTO SOME FRIENDS FROM SCHOOL AND WATCHED THE SHOOTING . . .
AFTER A WHILE, THE NOVELTY WORE OFF. AS A CLEAN-UP CREW SIFTED THROUGH STYROFOAM DEBRIS, WE LEFT . . .
WE REPAIRED TO A BAR IN NEARBY LITTLE ITALY . . .
IT WAS TWO WEEKS AWAY FROM THE BICENTENNIAL . . .
. . . WHICH WE COULDN'T WAIT TO BE OVER.
1776 1976
PATRIOTISM, TO US, SEEMED SO KITSCHY, CORNY . . .
. . . SO IRRELEVANT.
OUR THINKING, OF COURSE, WAS ALL BACKWARDS.

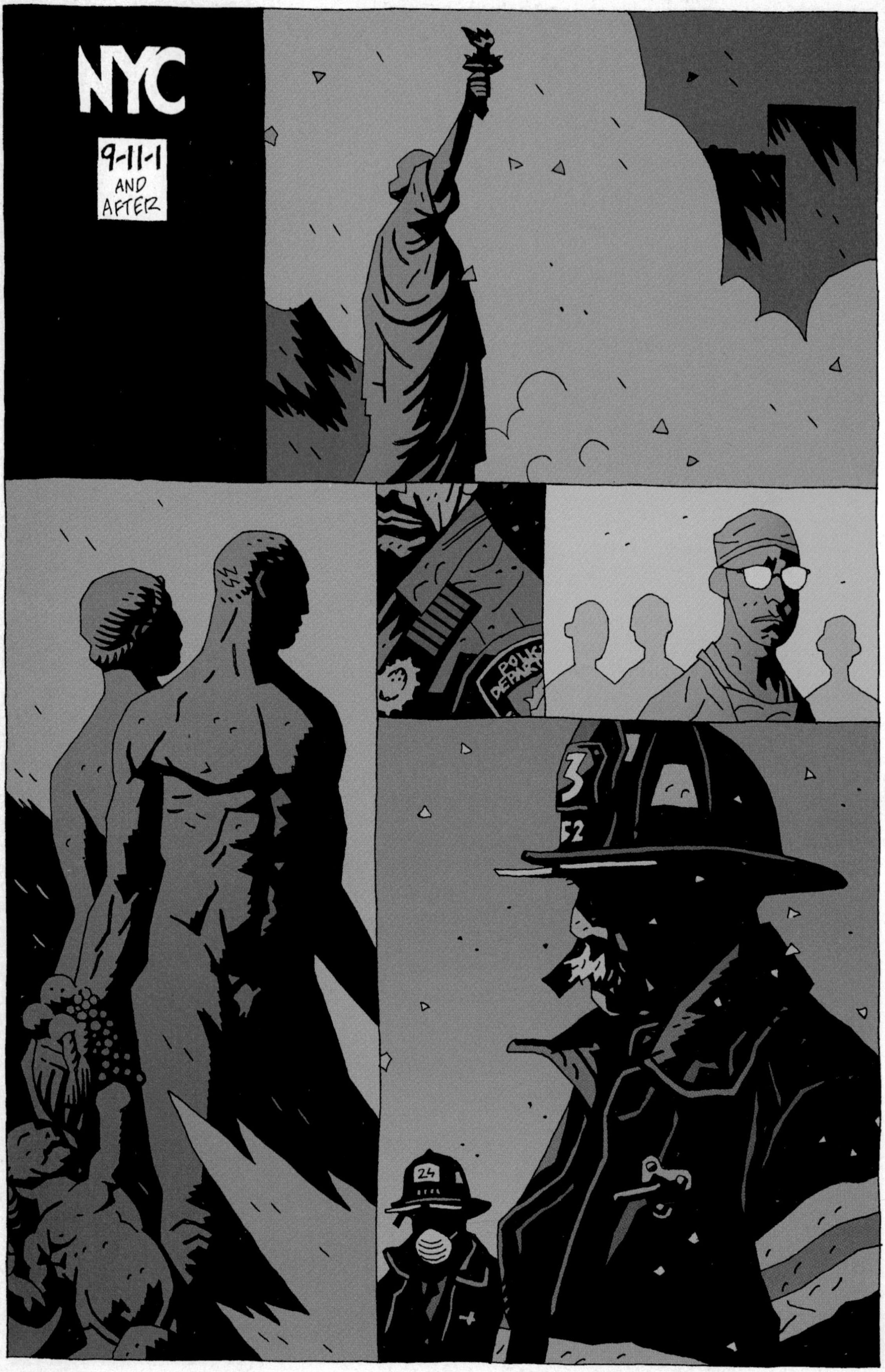
NYC
9-11-1
AND
AFTER

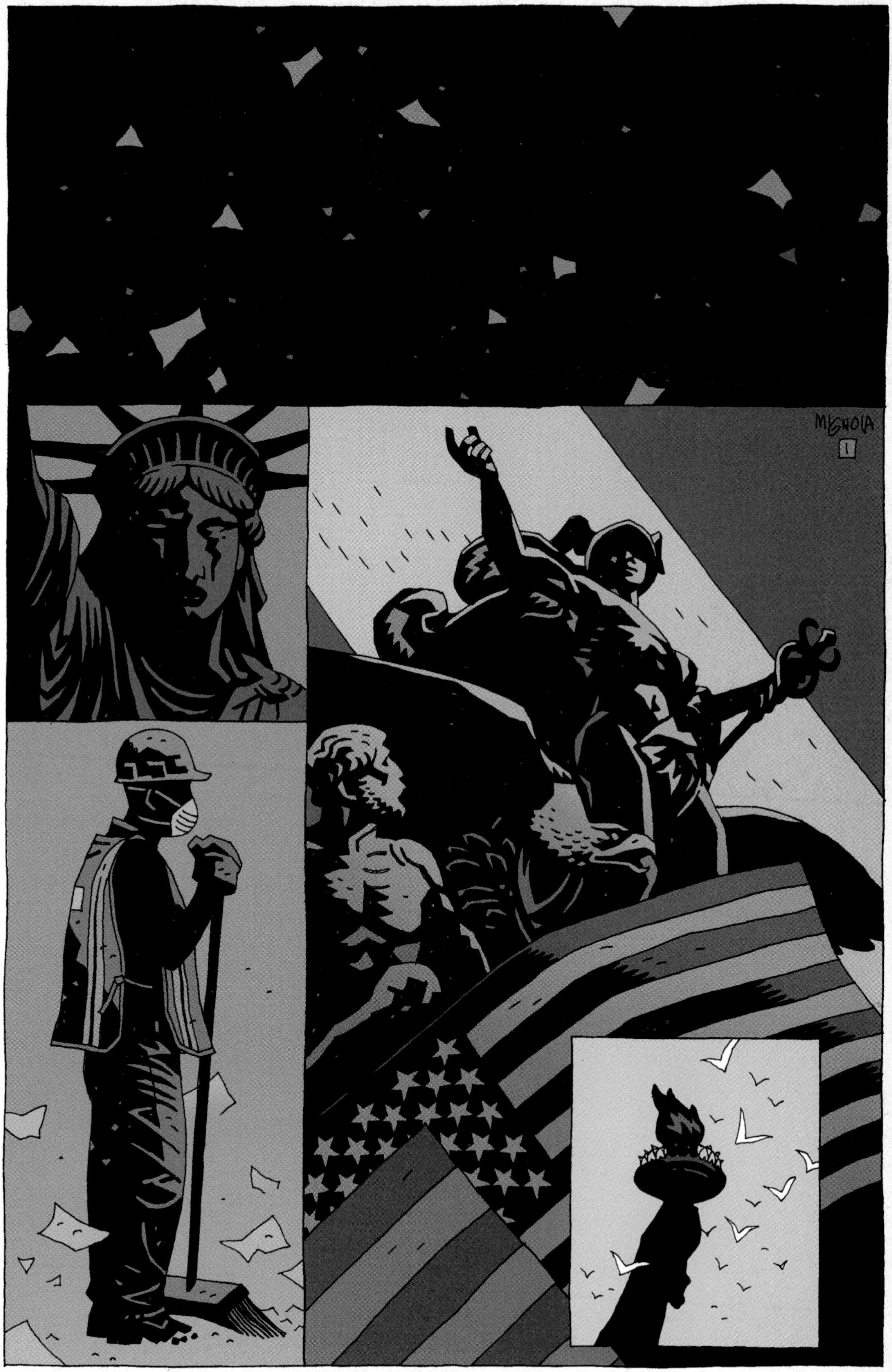
MIGNOLA

Brian Biggs

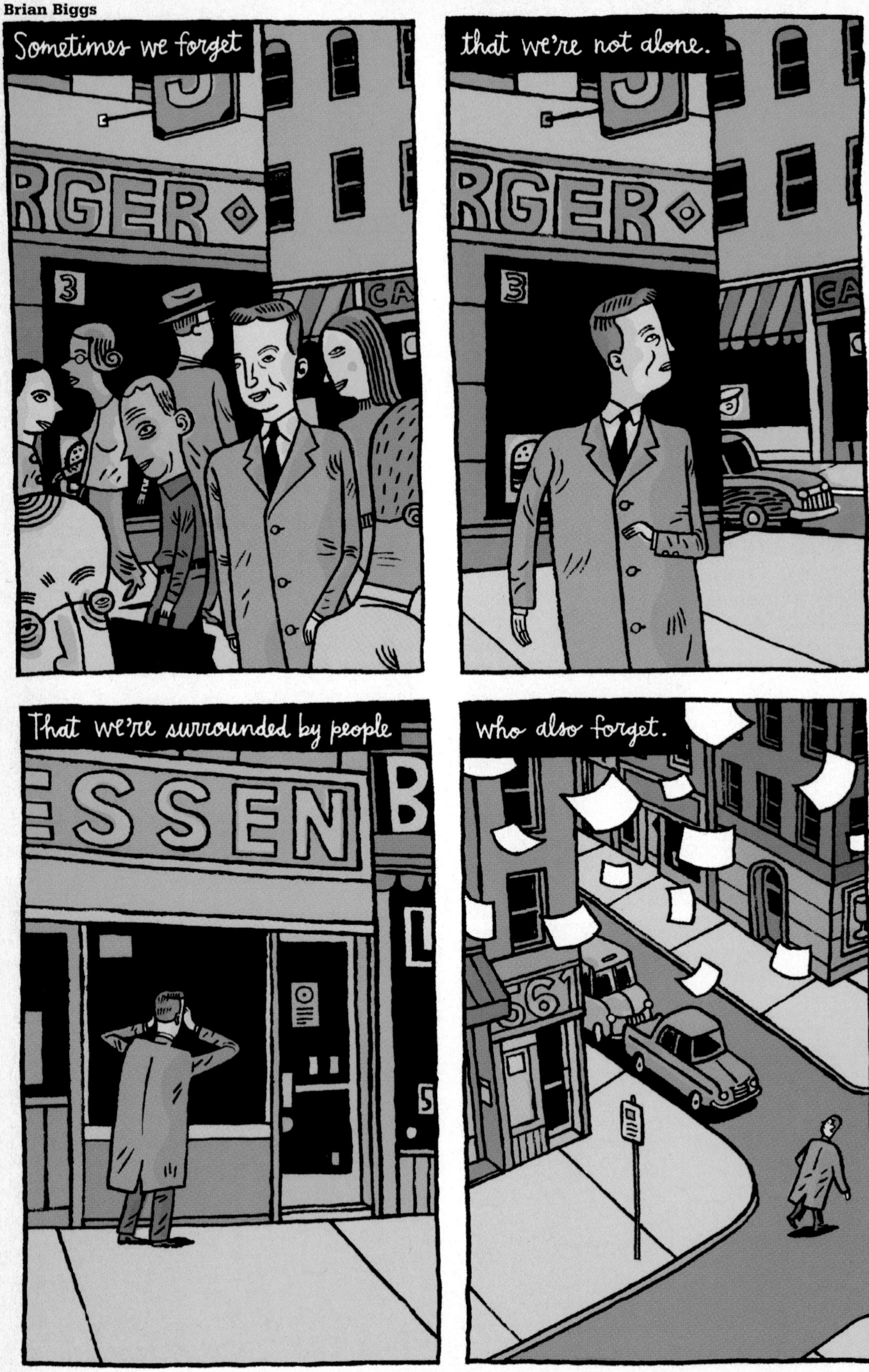
Sometimes we forget
RGER
3
CA
that we're not alone.
RGER
3
CA
That we're surrounded by people
SSEN
B
Who also forget.
561

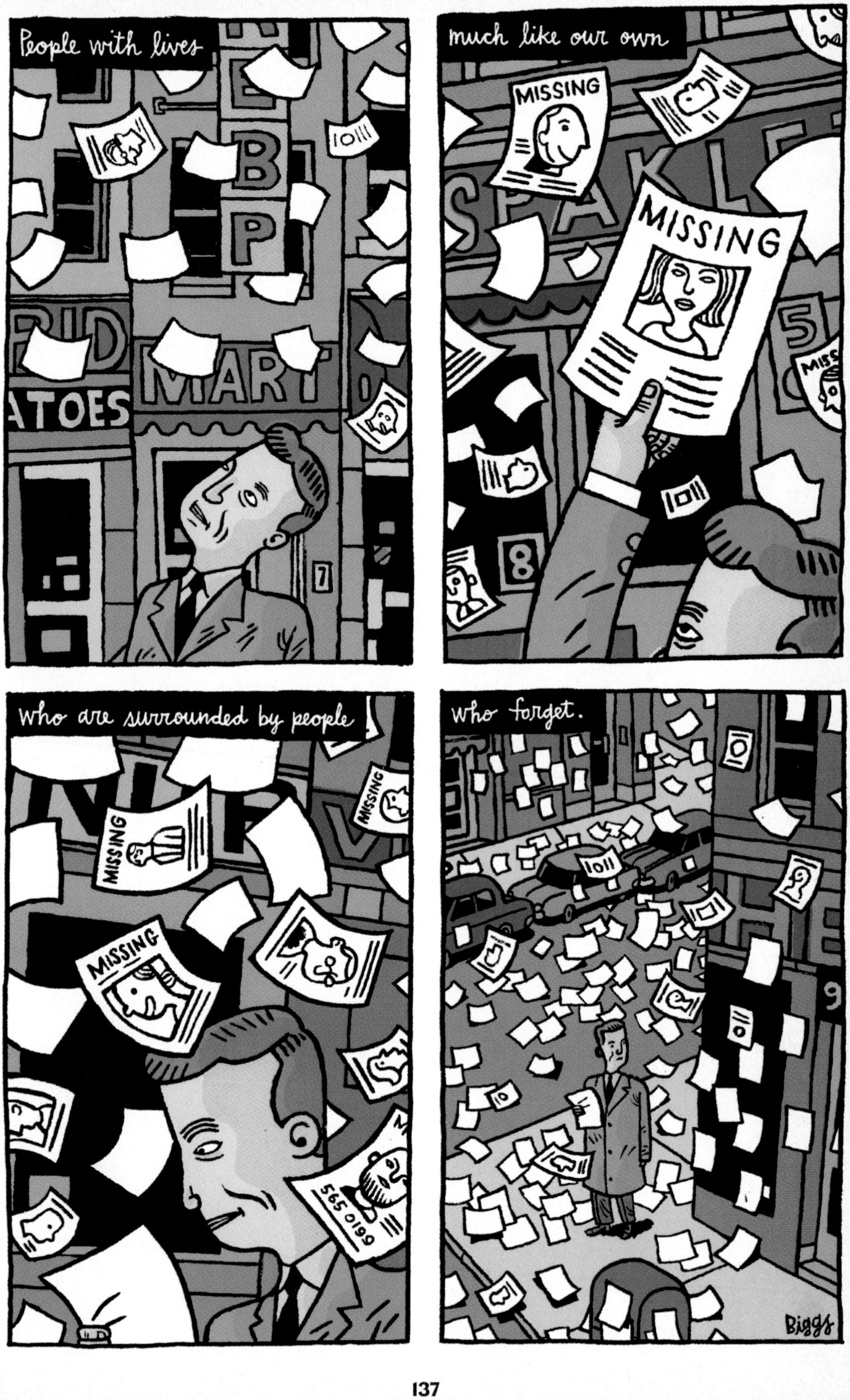
People with lives
ATOES
MART
much like our own
MISSING
MISSING
Who are surrounded by people
MISSING
MISSING
MISSING
who forget.
Biggs

T.V. EXEC VISITS GROUND ZERO

WORDS: ROBERT SMIGEL ART: MICHAEL KUPPERMAN

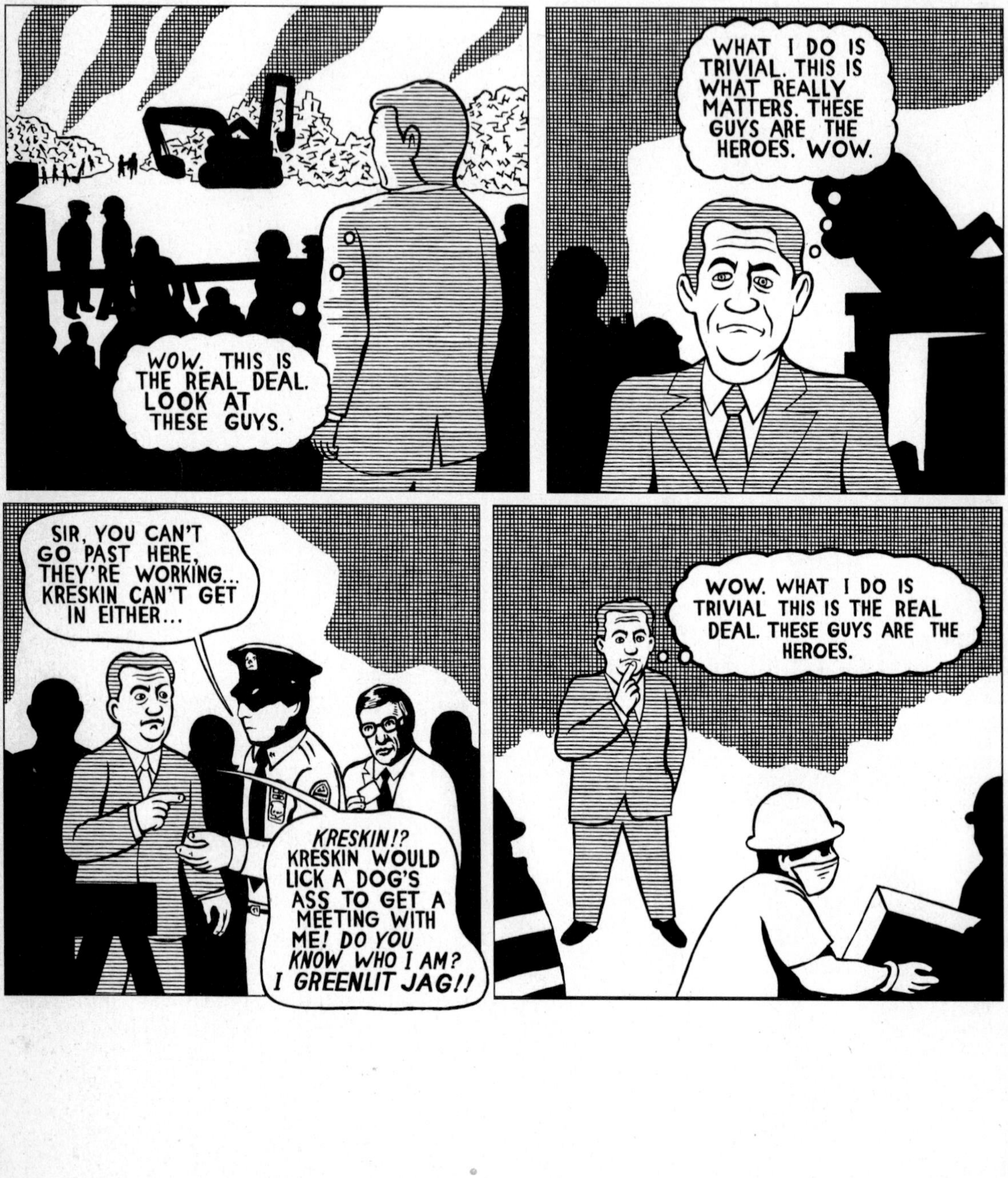
WOW. THIS IS THE REAL DEAL. LOOK AT THESE GUYS.
WHAT I DO IS TRIVIAL. THIS IS WHAT REALLY MATTERS. THESE GUYS ARE THE HEROES. WOW.
SIR, YOU CAN'T GO PAST HERE, THEY'RE WORKING... KRESKIN CAN'T GET IN EITHER...
KRESKIN!? KRESKIN WOULD LICK A DOG'S ASS TO GET A MEETING WITH ME! DO YOU KNOW WHO I AM? I GREENLIT JAG!!
WOW. WHAT I DO IS TRIVIAL THIS IS THE REAL DEAL. THESE GUYS ARE THE HEROES.

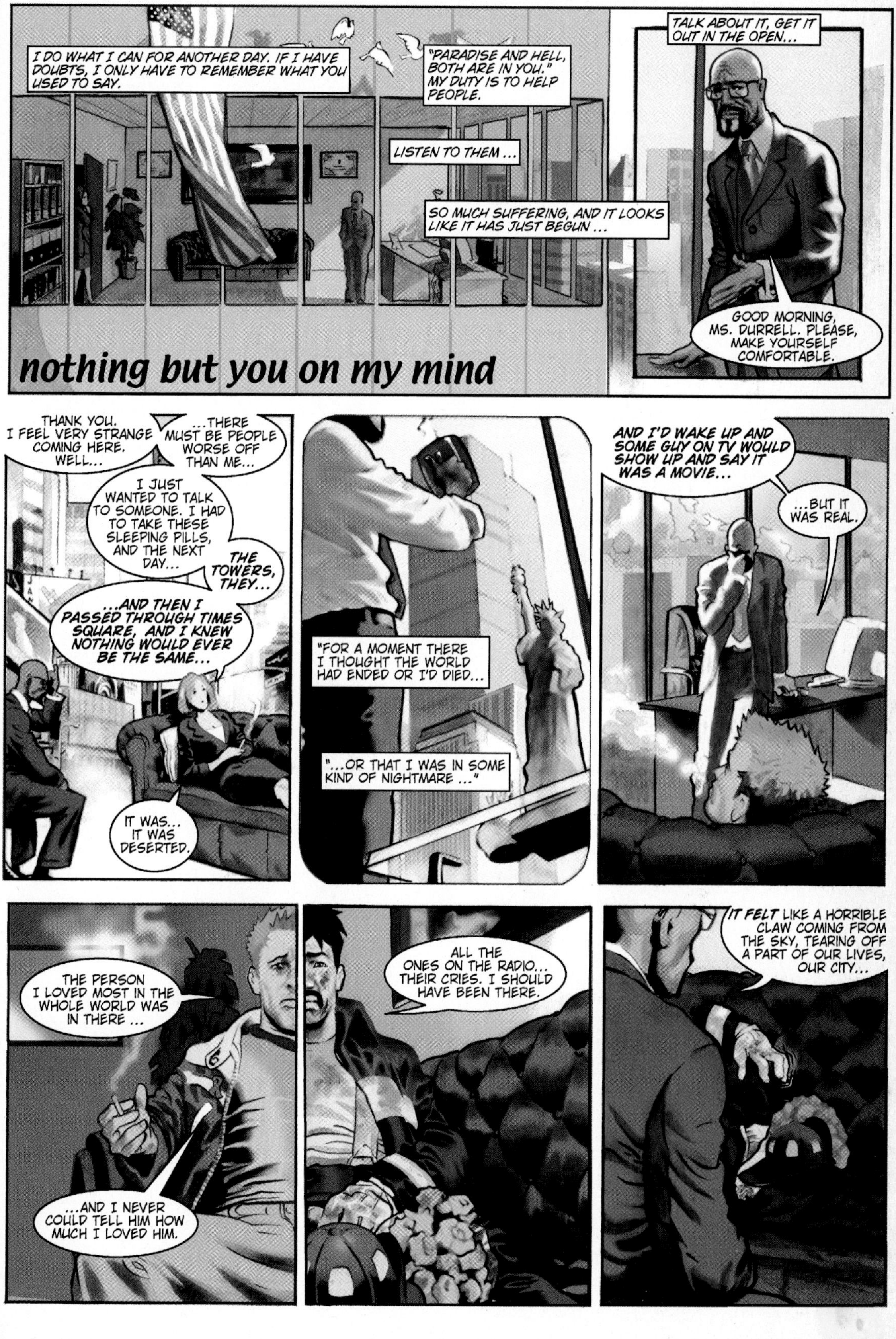
I DO WHAT I CAN FOR ANOTHER DAY. IF I HAVE DOUBTS, I ONLY HAVE TO REMEMBER WHAT YOU USED TO SAY.
"PARADISE AND HELL, BOTH ARE IN YOU." MY DUTY IS TO HELP PEOPLE.
LISTEN TO THEM ...
SO MUCH SUFFERING, AND IT LOOKS LIKE IT HAS JUST BEGUN ...
TALK ABOUT IT, GET IT OUT IN THE OPEN...
GOOD MORNING, MS. DURRELL. PLEASE, MAKE YOURSELF COMFORTABLE.
nothing but you on my mind
THANK YOU. I FEEL VERY STRANGE COMING HERE. WELL...
...THERE MUST BE PEOPLE WORSE OFF THAN ME...
I JUST WANTED TO TALK TO SOMEONE. I HAD TO TAKE THESE SLEEPING PILLS, AND THE NEXT DAY...
THE TOWERS, THEY...
...AND THEN I PASSED THROUGH TIMES SQUARE, AND I KNEW NOTHING WOULD EVER BE THE SAME...
IT WAS... IT WAS DESERTED.
"FOR A MOMENT THERE I THOUGHT THE WORLD HAD ENDED OR I'D DIED...
"...OR THAT I WAS IN SOME KIND OF NIGHTMARE ..."
AND I'D WAKE UP AND SOME GUY ON TV WOULD SHOW UP AND SAY IT WAS A MOVIE...
...BUT IT WAS REAL.
THE PERSON I LOVED MOST IN THE WHOLE WORLD WAS IN THERE ...
...AND I NEVER COULD TELL HIM HOW MUCH I LOVED HIM.
ALL THE ONES ON THE RADIO... THEIR CRIES. I SHOULD HAVE BEEN THERE.
IT FELT LIKE A HORRIBLE CLAW COMING FROM THE SKY, TEARING OFF A PART OF OUR LIVES, OUR CITY...

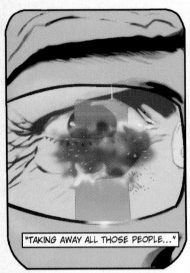

"TAKING AWAY ALL THOSE PEOPLE..."

I DON'T KNOW WHY ALL THOSE PEOPLE HAD TO DIE, BUT I KNOW SOMEONE'S GONNA PAY. YOU JUST WAIT AND SEE...

WHY DO *THEY* HATE US SO MUCH?

WHY SO MUCH HATE?

I LOVE MY RELIGION-- ISLAM IS A PEACEFUL RELIGION. WHOEVER DID THIS WERE INFIDELS, FANATICS.

I'VE ALWAYS WORKED HARD. MY CHILDREN ARE AMERICAN.

NOW WE ARE AFRAID.

THEY ARE NOT TRUE MUSLIMS. THEY ARE KILLERS AND *THEIR RELIGION IS TERROR.*

"OUR HEART IS BROKEN."

HE ALWAYS TOLD ME, "WE OWE OUR HEART TO THE U.S." *IT WAS HARD,* BACK THERE IN THE OLD COUNTRY.

"I'M IN HEAVEN, MAMOCHKA," HE USED TO SAY. HE WAS HAPPY, CLEANING THE WINDOWS OF THOSE BUILDINGS. EVERYBODY KNEW HIM...

SINCE I LOST HIM, I'VE BEEN SHOPPING ALL THE TIME. HE LOVED SHOPPING.

ESPECIALLY THESE BRIGHT TIES...

DO YOU THINK HE'D HAVE LIKED THEM, DOCTOR?

THEY'RE BEAUTIFUL.

HE SAID, "WE HAVE TO PUT COLOR INTO LIFE."

ALWAYS HAPPY AND OPTIMISTIC, ALWAYS THERE FOR US. I DON'T KNOW WHAT I'M GOING TO DO.

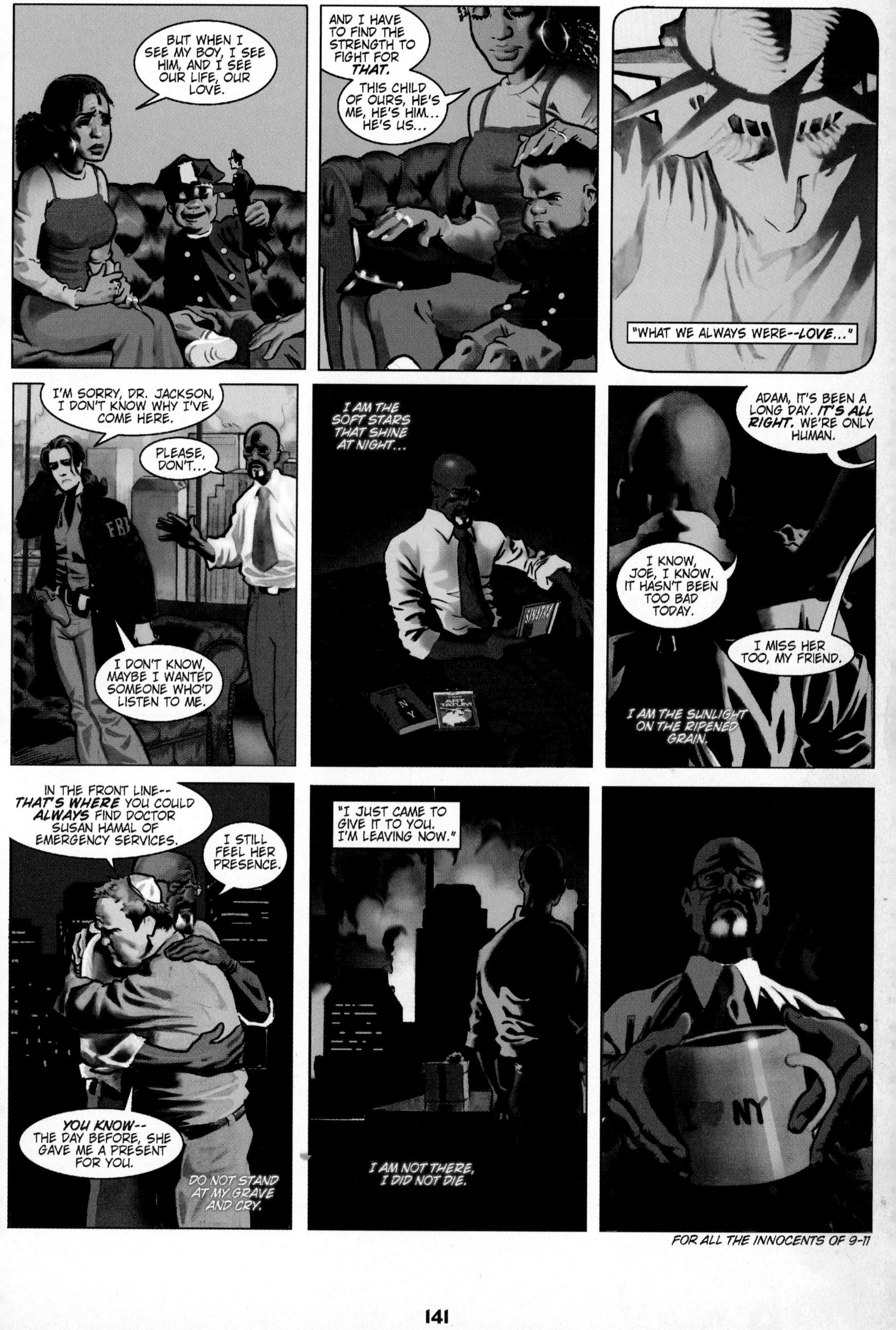
BUT WHEN I SEE MY BOY, I SEE HIM, AND I SEE OUR LIFE, OUR LOVE.
AND I HAVE TO FIND THE STRENGTH TO FIGHT FOR THAT.
THIS CHILD OF OURS, HE'S ME, HE'S HIM... HE'S US...
"WHAT WE ALWAYS WERE--LOVE..."
I'M SORRY, DR. JACKSON, I DON'T KNOW WHY I'VE COME HERE.
PLEASE, DON'T...
I DON'T KNOW, MAYBE I WANTED SOMEONE WHO'D LISTEN TO ME.
I AM THE SOFT STARS THAT SHINE AT NIGHT...
SINATRA
NY
ART TATUM
ADAM, IT'S BEEN A LONG DAY. IT'S ALL RIGHT. WE'RE ONLY HUMAN.
I KNOW, JOE, I KNOW. IT HASN'T BEEN TOO BAD TODAY.
I MISS HER TOO, MY FRIEND.
I AM THE SUNLIGHT ON THE RIPENED GRAIN.
IN THE FRONT LINE-- THAT'S WHERE YOU COULD ALWAYS FIND DOCTOR SUSAN HAMAL OF EMERGENCY SERVICES.
I STILL FEEL HER PRESENCE.
YOU KNOW-- THE DAY BEFORE, SHE GAVE ME A PRESENT FOR YOU.
DO NOT STAND AT MY GRAVE AND CRY.
"I JUST CAME TO GIVE IT TO YOU. I'M LEAVING NOW."
I AM NOT THERE, I DID NOT DIE.
I ♥ NY

FOR ALL THE INNOCENTS OF 9-11

Kellie Strom

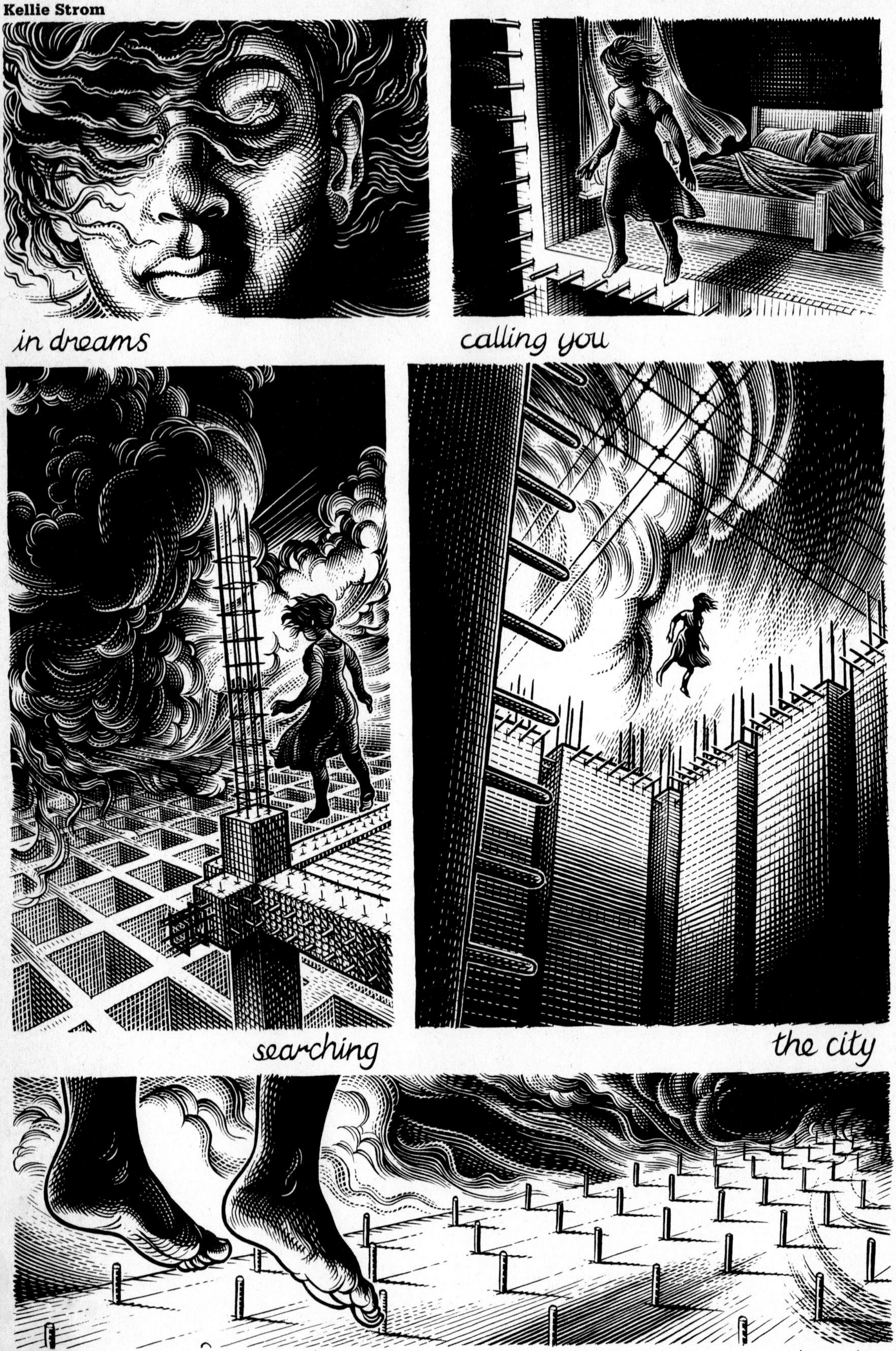
in dreams
calling you
searching
the city
streets

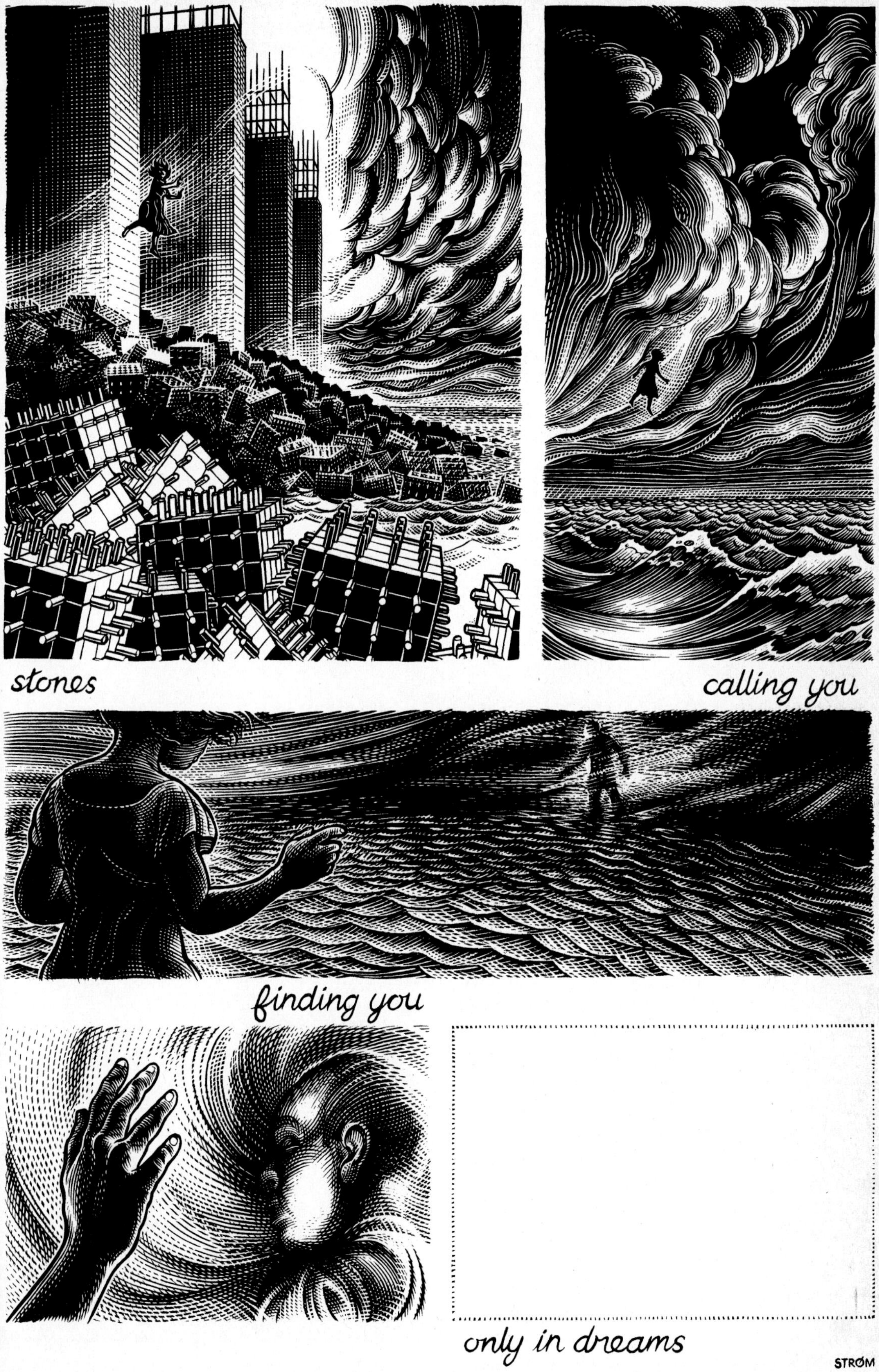
stones
calling you
finding you
only in dreams
STRØM

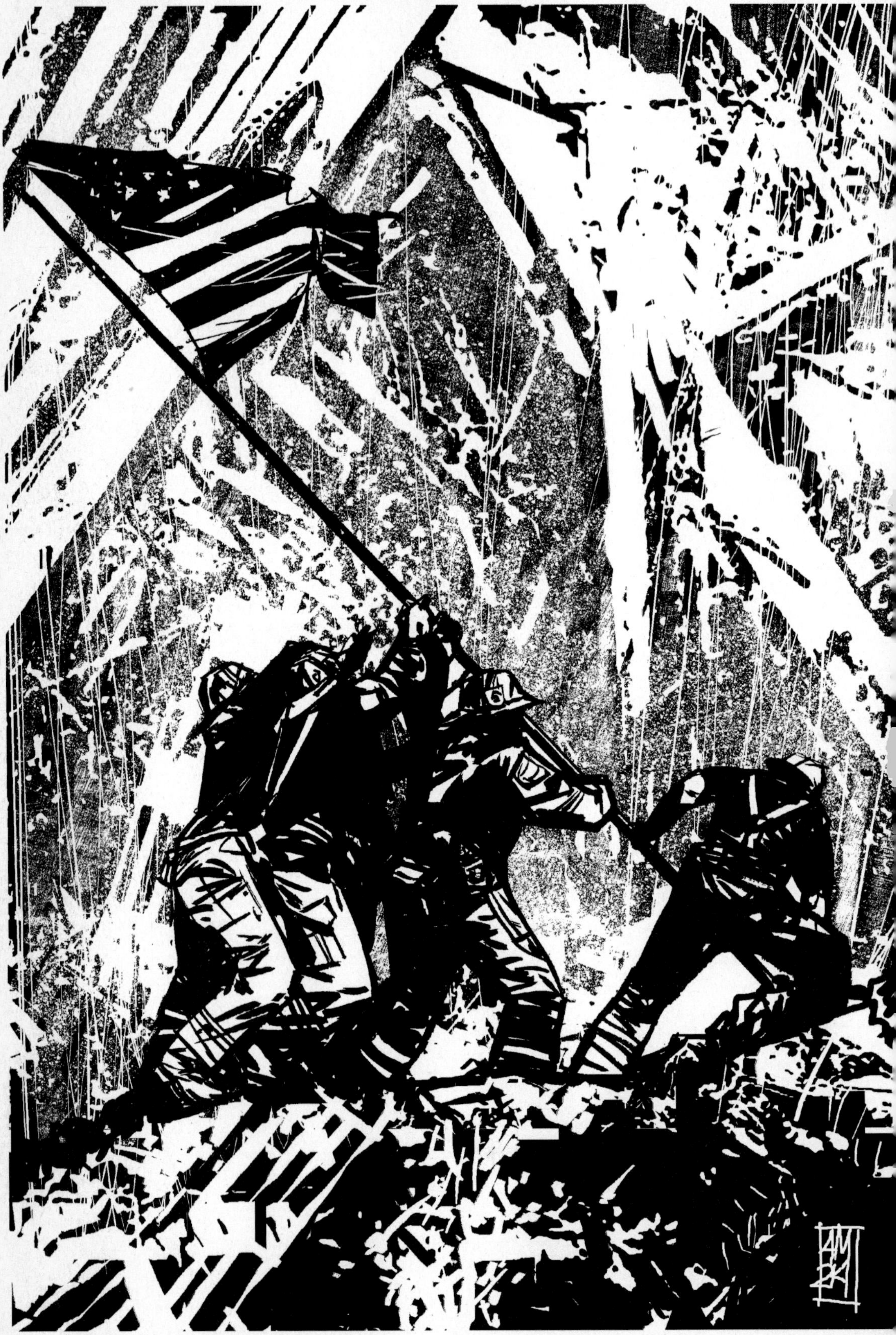

Before THE FALL

By Dean Motter

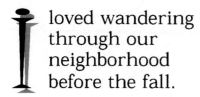 loved wandering through our neighborhood before the fall.

The air was always alive with the sounds, fragrances, and aromas of the season. My companion and I would spend a lot of time walking through the district. When the weather was nice, there was nothing like it.

Perfect place to walk a curious dog.

The area is a unique combination of warehouses and manufacturing concerns that had long ago been abandoned by those tenants and taken over by art galleries, restaurants, and artists' lofts.

Today it is also populated by the families of the artists, writers, actors, musicians, and bohemians that settled in this locale.

The odd thing is how the place blends into the financial section and then into the oldest historic part of the city.

From the most avant garde artists' garrets to Wall Street and the ancient colonial church and graveyard... all in a matter of a few always-interesting blocks.

It is a short, friendly walk down from West Broadway and Reade, where we once lived, past the World Trade Center to Battery Park and South Street Seaport.

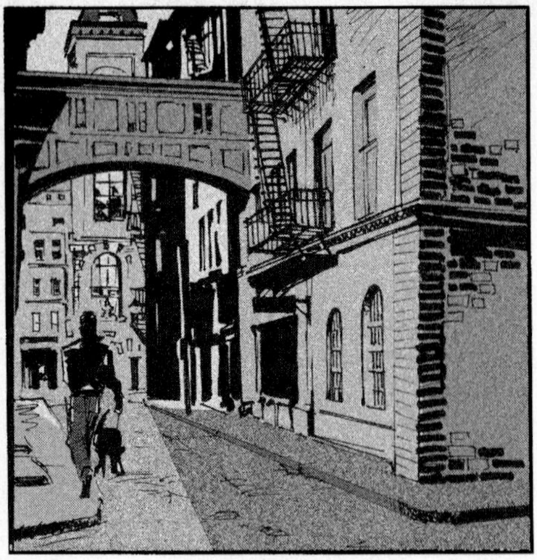

I often wondered what went through his mind when we went on our walks.

I speculated that he might have some secret sense of what might have been in that alley between Greenwich Street and Hudson. It always seemed like it was a link to another time.

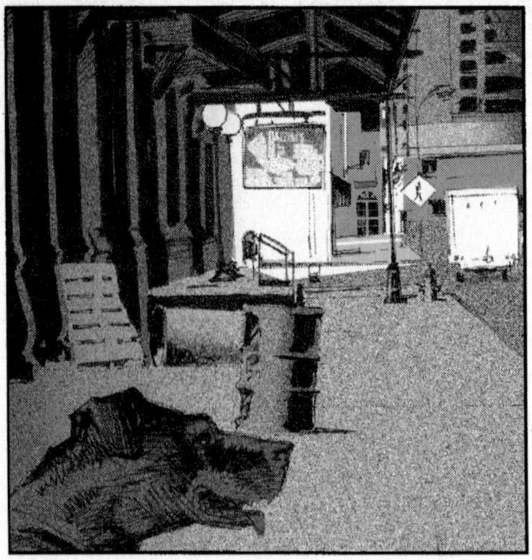

Then there's Bazini's peanut warehouse, just around the corner on Greenwich. It is one of the older tenants in the area. I can still smell the baby elephants they used to bring in for special promotions. I wonder if my companion knows what that scent is. He's a city creature by nature and probably doesn't maintain many instinctive memories from ancestry. Though he does surprise me sometimes.

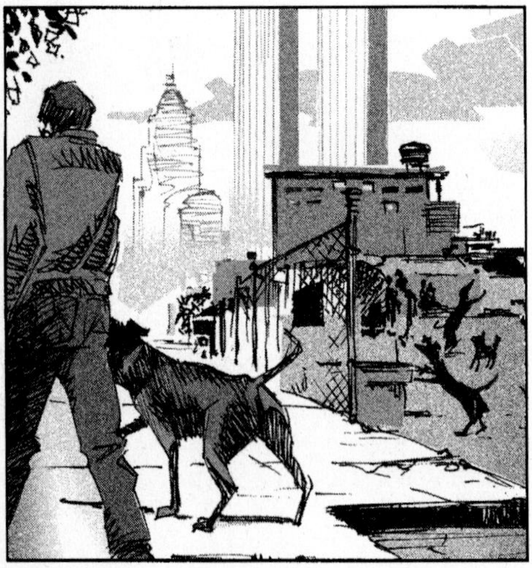

For instance, he always seemed to know when there were local dogs playing down the street at the empty parking lot. They were there with their owners, who were as eager to size each other up as their canine charges. They didn't go as far as sniffing each other's rear ends, but they seemed to be up to the same thing.
Sometimes one wonders who brought whom to the place -- the dogs or the people.

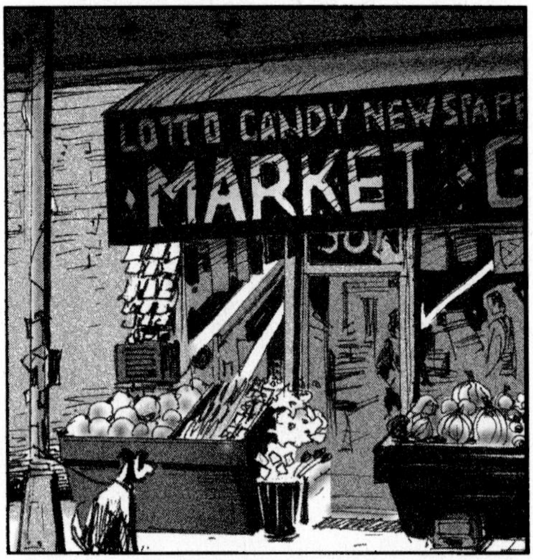
LOTTO CANDY
MARKET

Of course no walk was complete without a quick stop at the bodega for, well, whatever was on the shopping list. But no matter what, it always included dogfood. Not much of a selection - but it was adequate for our needs. I guess the visit somehow made our walk seem productive. Not that he ever saw it that way. His kind, while affectionate are very self-centered. Partly nature, partly breeding. Sometimes there would be fresh cut flowers out front. I knew he could smell those.

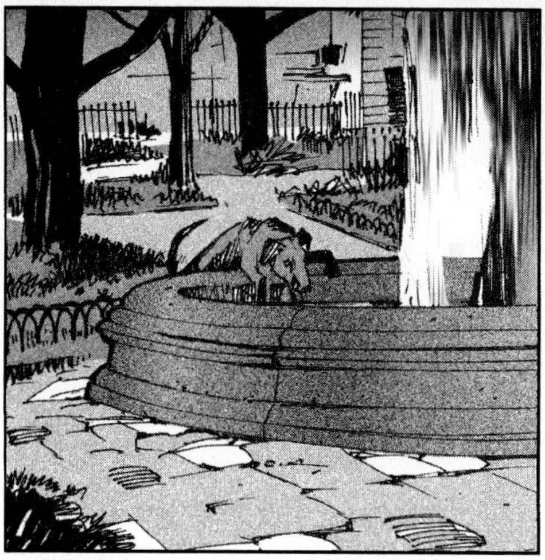

A few blocks away is City Hall. The park there was always busy. And there was enough room to get a good game of fetch-the-tennis ball. There were always other dogs about, but they weren't as important as an invigorating round or two with the ball. By the time I was ready for a break, I could always take a break and get a good long drink at the fountain. Then it was home again.

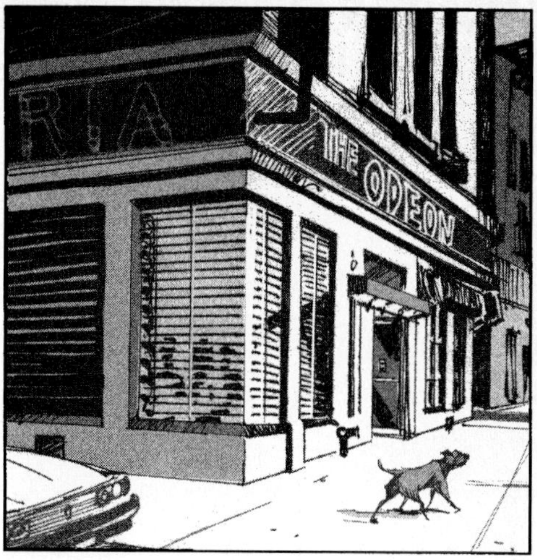
THE ODEON

Occasionally he would let go of the leash and allow me trot to a few blocks ahead. I still don't know if he trusted me that much, or if I had simply worn him out during the ball game. I usually made it a point of not running too far ahead. We'd pass by his favorite hangouts -- El Teddy's, The Odeon, and Riverrun. There we might encounter one of his neighbors or, if we were lucky, one of MY friends.

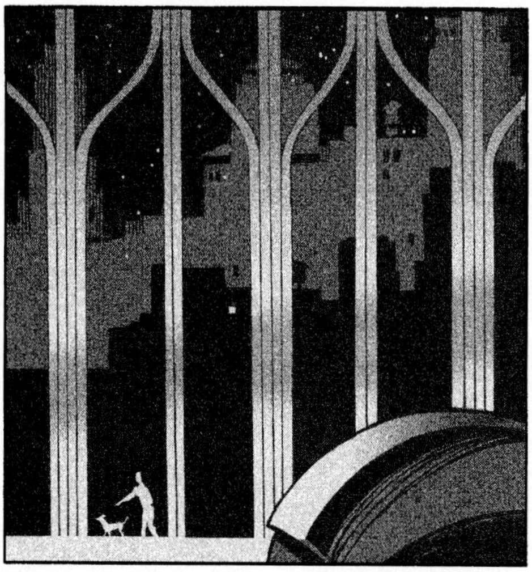

Sometimes in the evening we would take a stroll down to the World Trade Center. It was always quiet and serene. Very few people would be around at that hour. Quite a contrast when one thinks how many people are here during the day... how many people come and go. In the evening the towers were still lit up, but one could sense how empty they were. The combination of the stillness and the cold starkness of the plaza made it very surreal.

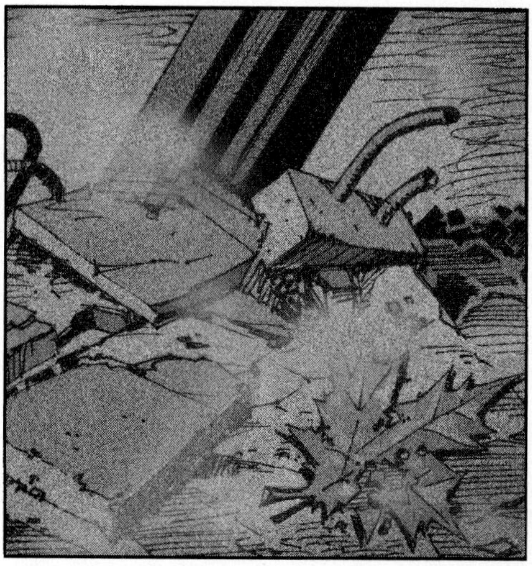

Of course that was before the fall.

Before the environment became more uncomfortable. Before the air changed. Before we moved to a different home.

But the chill is somehow different this season. I sense that things won't be the same the next time I see our old neighborhood. I wonder how much will be gone, and how much will remain.

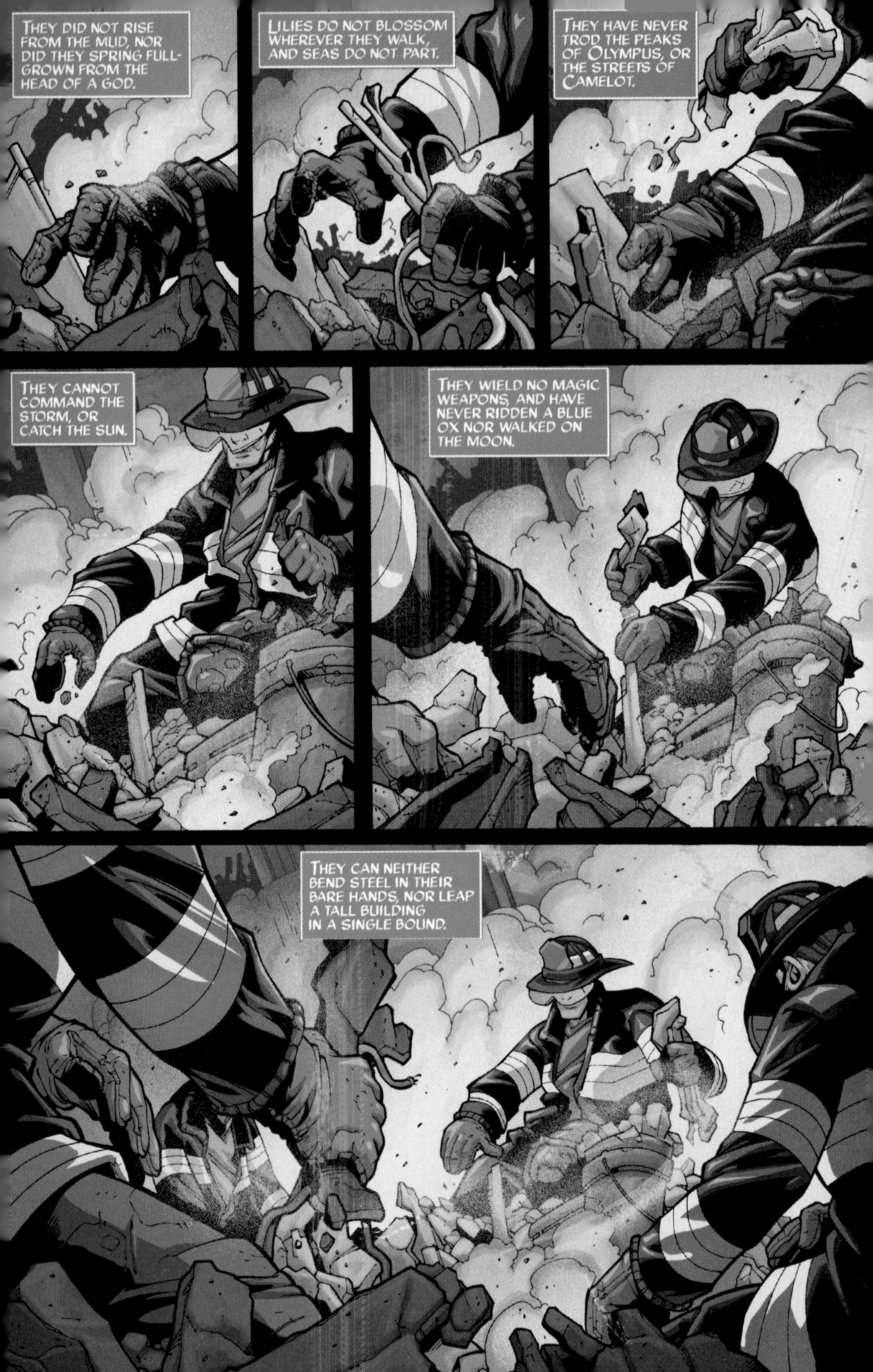
THEY DID NOT RISE FROM THE MUD, NOR DID THEY SPRING FULL-GROWN FROM THE HEAD OF A GOD.
LILIES DO NOT BLOSSOM WHEREVER THEY WALK, AND SEAS DO NOT PART.
THEY HAVE NEVER TROD THE PEAKS OF OLYMPUS, OR THE STREETS OF CAMELOT.
THEY CANNOT COMMAND THE STORM, OR CATCH THE SUN.
THEY WIELD NO MAGIC WEAPONS, AND HAVE NEVER RIDDEN A BLUE OX NOR WALKED ON THE MOON.
THEY CAN NEITHER BEND STEEL IN THEIR BARE HANDS, NOR LEAP A TALL BUILDING IN A SINGLE BOUND.

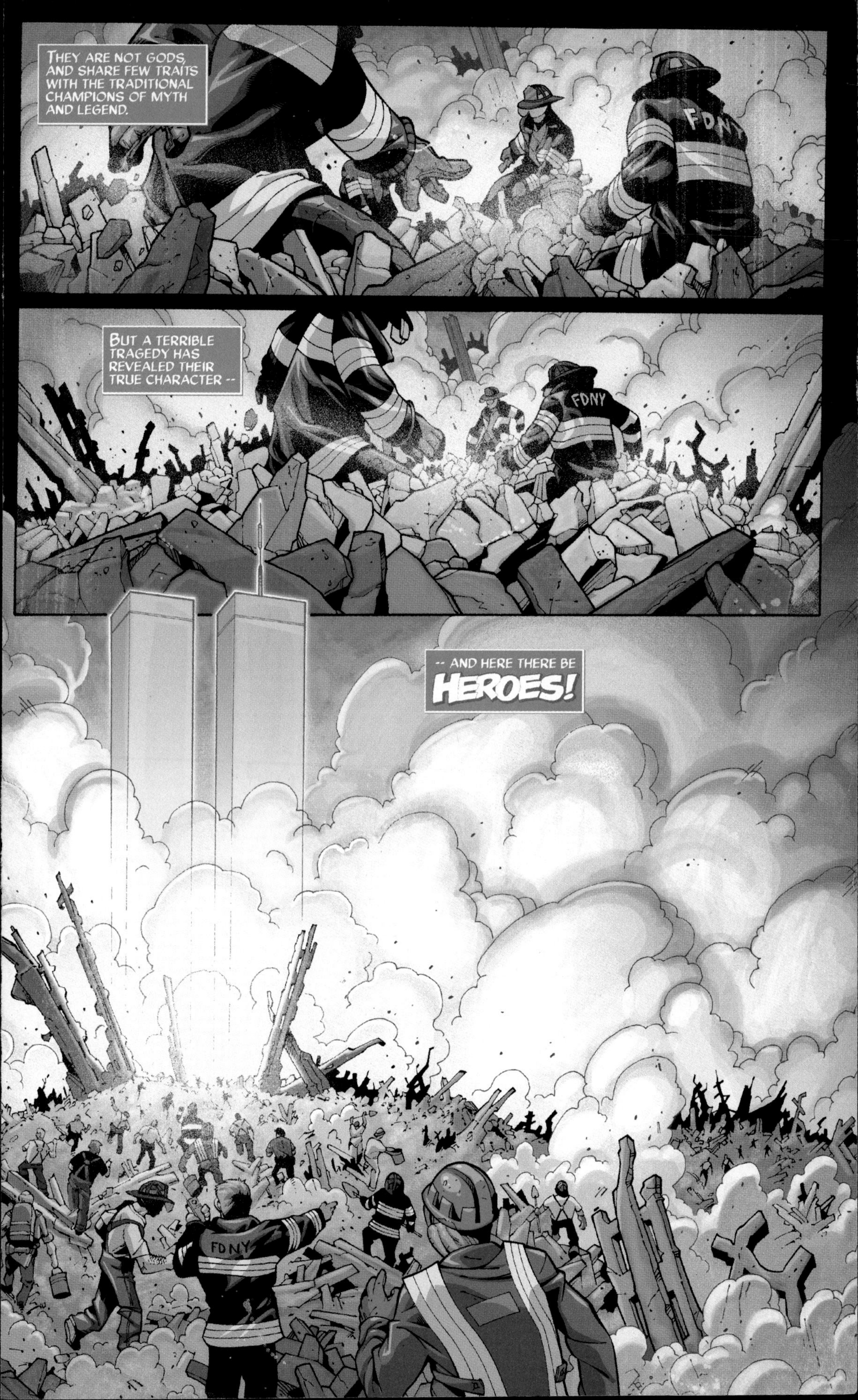
THEY ARE NOT GODS, AND SHARE FEW TRAITS WITH THE TRADITIONAL CHAMPIONS OF MYTH AND LEGEND.
FDNY
BUT A TERRIBLE TRAGEDY HAS REVEALED THEIR TRUE CHARACTER --
FDNY
-- AND HERE THERE BE HEROES!
FDNY

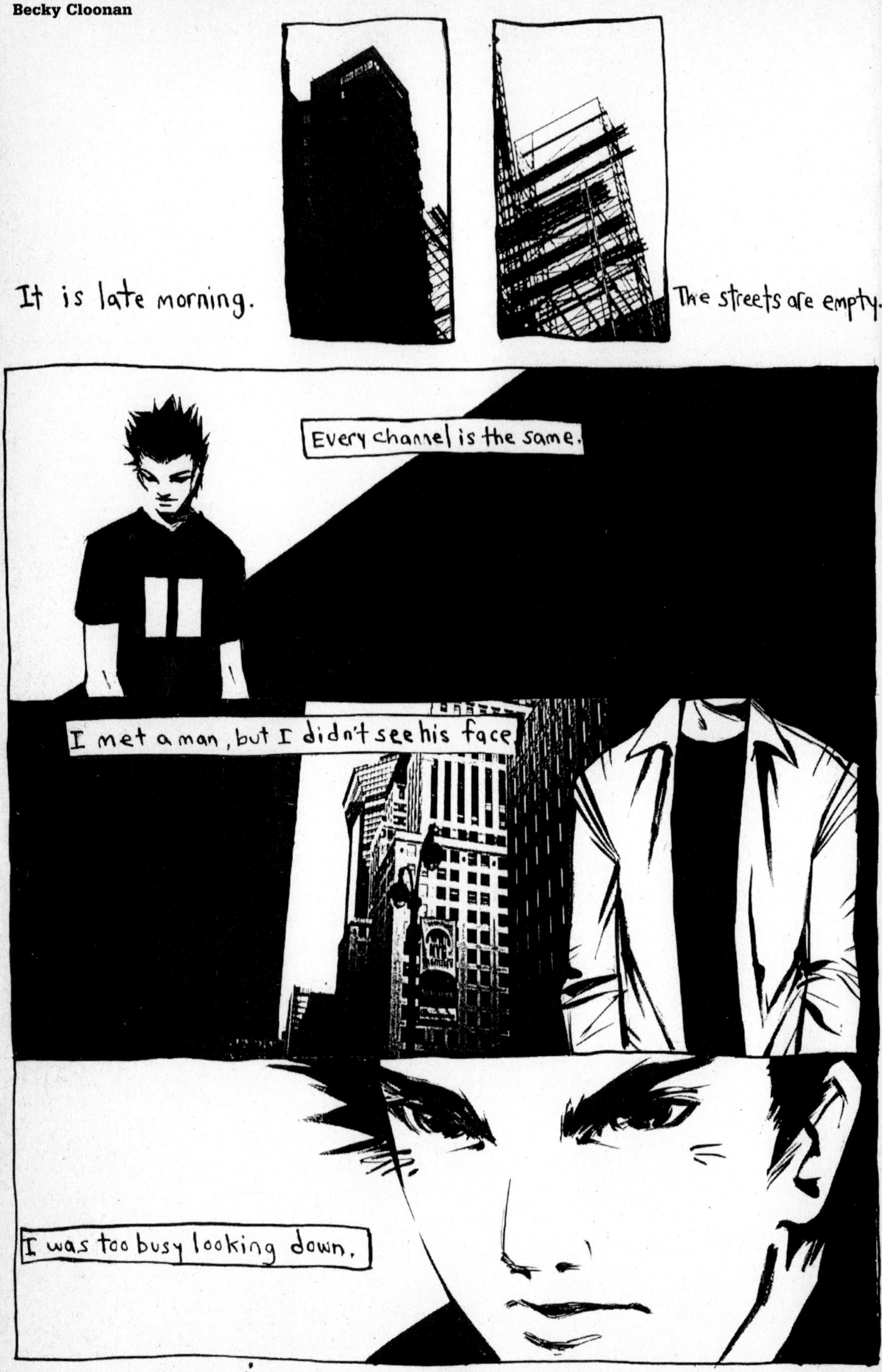
It is late morning.
The streets are empty.
Every channel is the same.
I met a man, but I didn't see his face
I was too busy looking down.

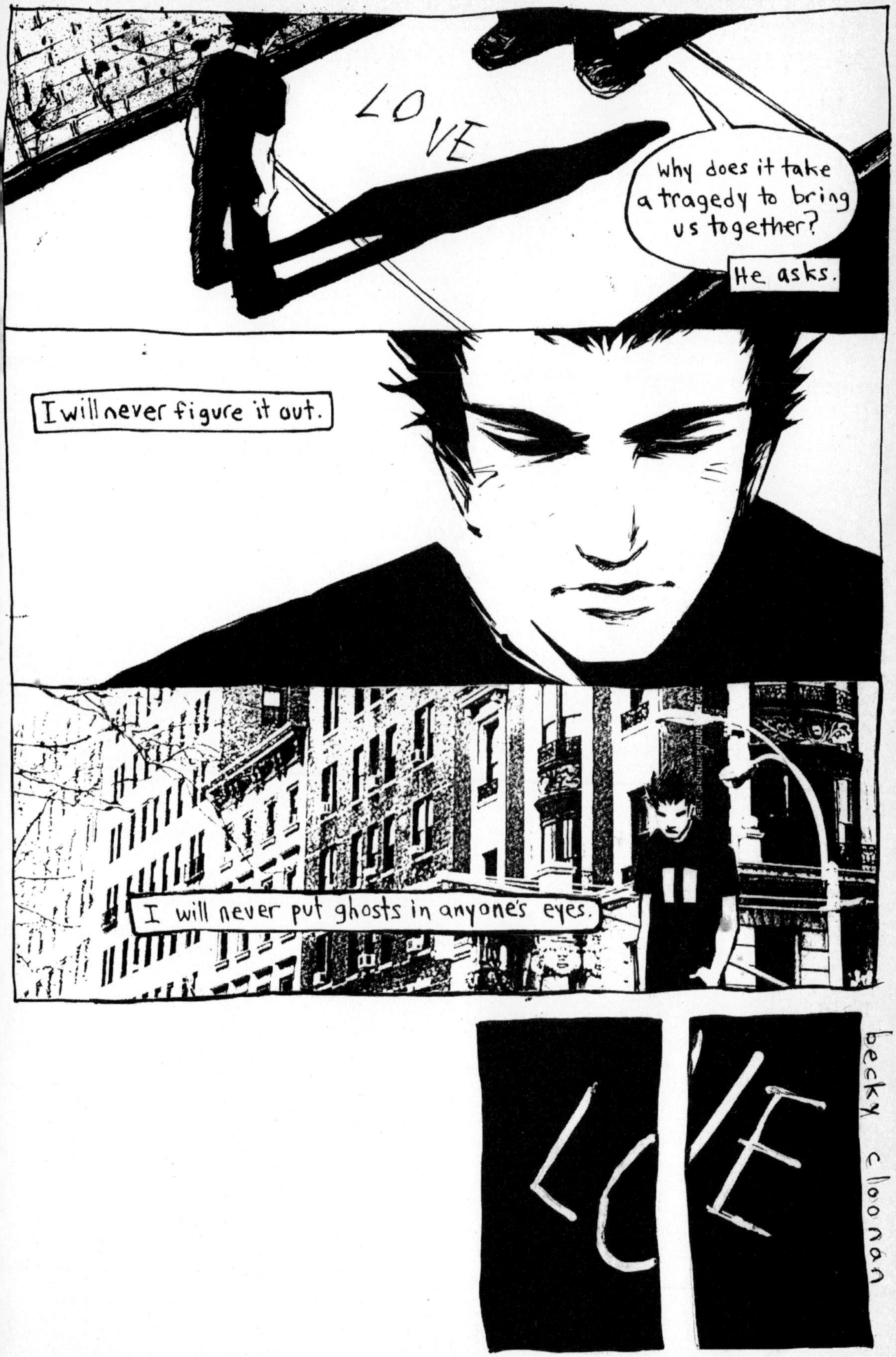
LOVE
why does it take a tragedy to bring us together?
He asks.
I will never figure it out.
I will never put ghosts in anyone's eyes.
LOVE
becky cloonan

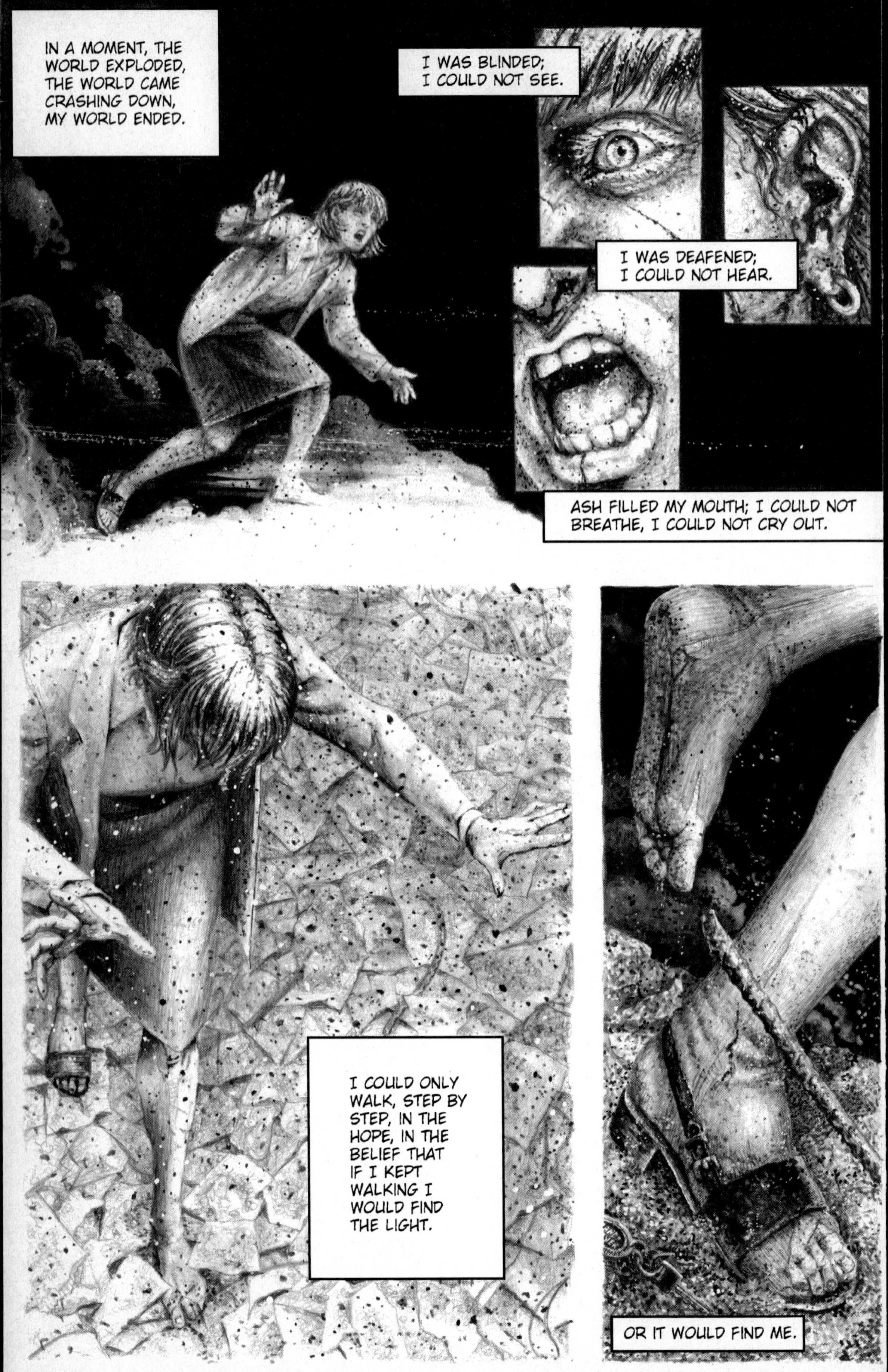
IN A MOMENT, THE WORLD EXPLODED, THE WORLD CAME CRASHING DOWN, MY WORLD ENDED.
I WAS BLINDED; I COULD NOT SEE.
I WAS DEAFENED; I COULD NOT HEAR.
ASH FILLED MY MOUTH; I COULD NOT BREATHE, I COULD NOT CRY OUT.
I COULD ONLY WALK, STEP BY STEP, IN THE HOPE, IN THE BELIEF THAT IF I KEPT WALKING I WOULD FIND THE LIGHT.
OR IT WOULD FIND ME.

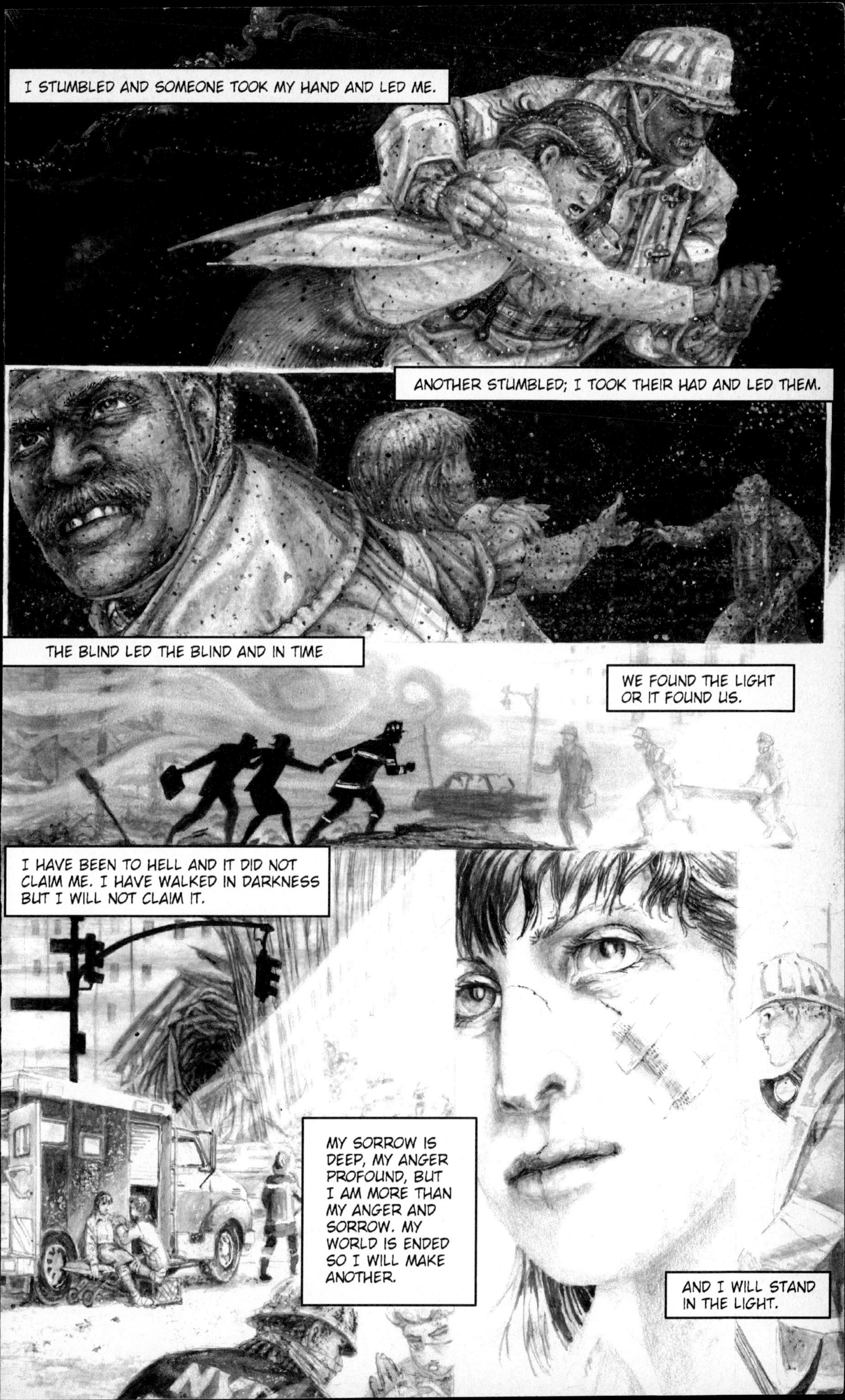
I STUMBLED AND SOMEONE TOOK MY HAND AND LED ME.
ANOTHER STUMBLED; I TOOK THEIR HAD AND LED THEM.
THE BLIND LED THE BLIND AND IN TIME
WE FOUND THE LIGHT OR IT FOUND US.
I HAVE BEEN TO HELL AND IT DID NOT CLAIM ME. I HAVE WALKED IN DARKNESS BUT I WILL NOT CLAIM IT.
MY SORROW IS DEEP, MY ANGER PROFOUND, BUT I AM MORE THAN MY ANGER AND SORROW. MY WORLD IS ENDED SO I WILL MAKE ANOTHER.
AND I WILL STAND IN THE LIGHT.

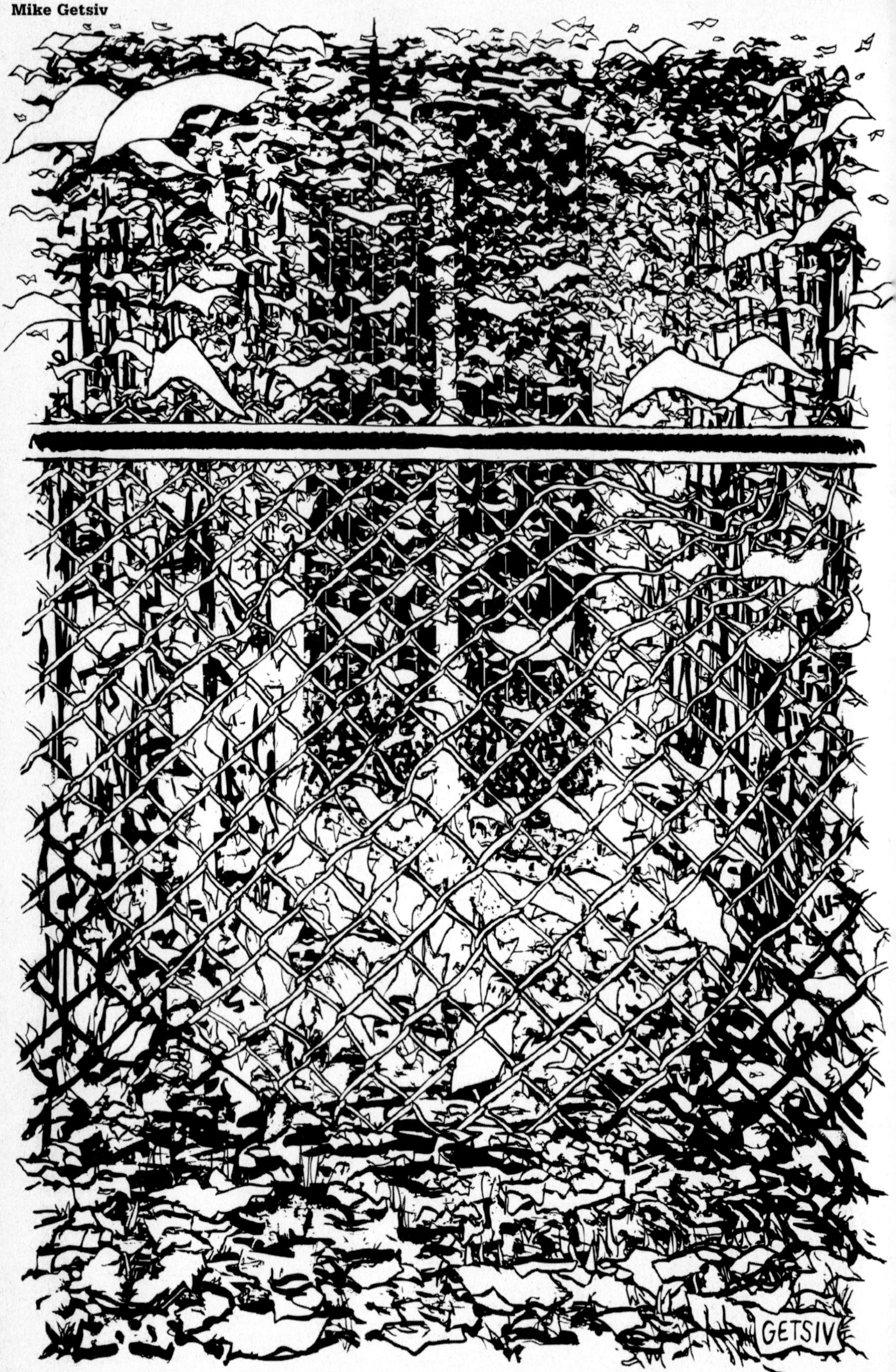
GETSIV

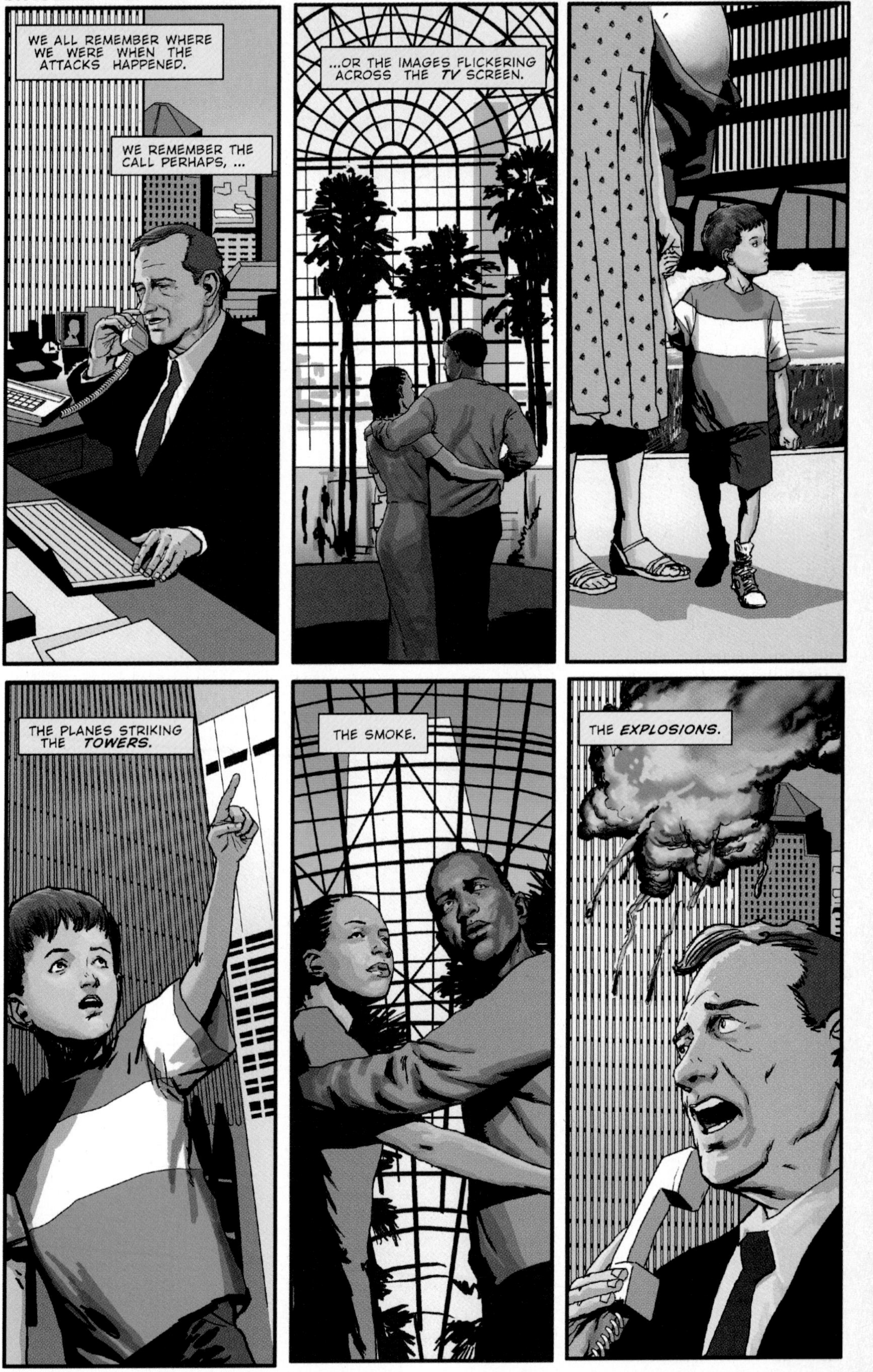
WE ALL REMEMBER WHERE WE WERE WHEN THE ATTACKS HAPPENED.
WE REMEMBER THE CALL PERHAPS, ...
...OR THE IMAGES FLICKERING ACROSS THE *TV* SCREEN.
THE PLANES STRIKING THE *TOWERS.*
THE SMOKE.
THE *EXPLOSIONS.*

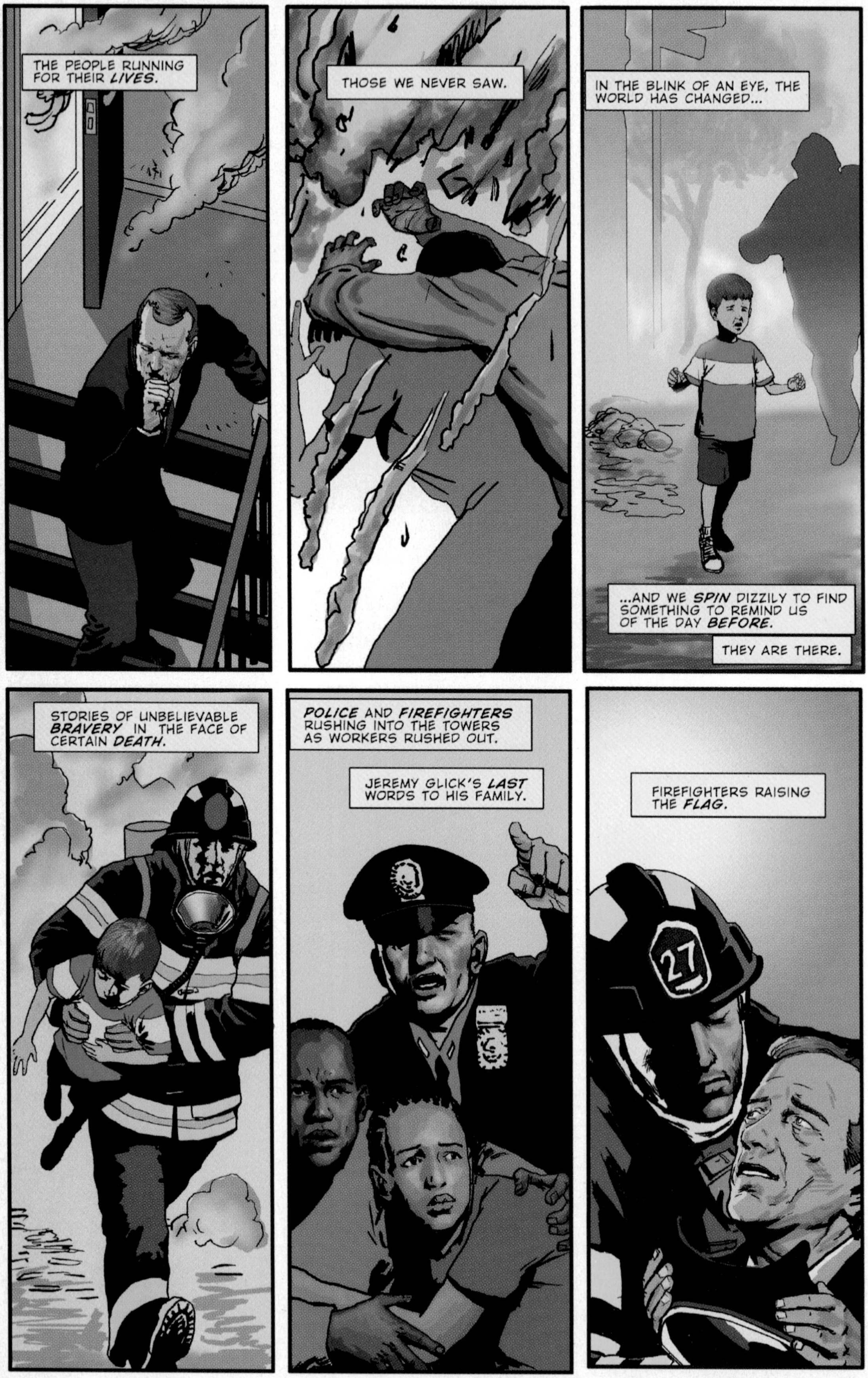
THE PEOPLE RUNNING FOR THEIR LIVES.
THOSE WE NEVER SAW.
IN THE BLINK OF AN EYE, THE WORLD HAS CHANGED...
...AND WE SPIN DIZZILY TO FIND SOMETHING TO REMIND US OF THE DAY BEFORE.
THEY ARE THERE.
STORIES OF UNBELIEVABLE BRAVERY IN THE FACE OF CERTAIN DEATH.
POLICE AND FIREFIGHTERS RUSHING INTO THE TOWERS AS WORKERS RUSHED OUT.
JEREMY GLICK'S LAST WORDS TO HIS FAMILY.
FIREFIGHTERS RAISING THE FLAG.
27

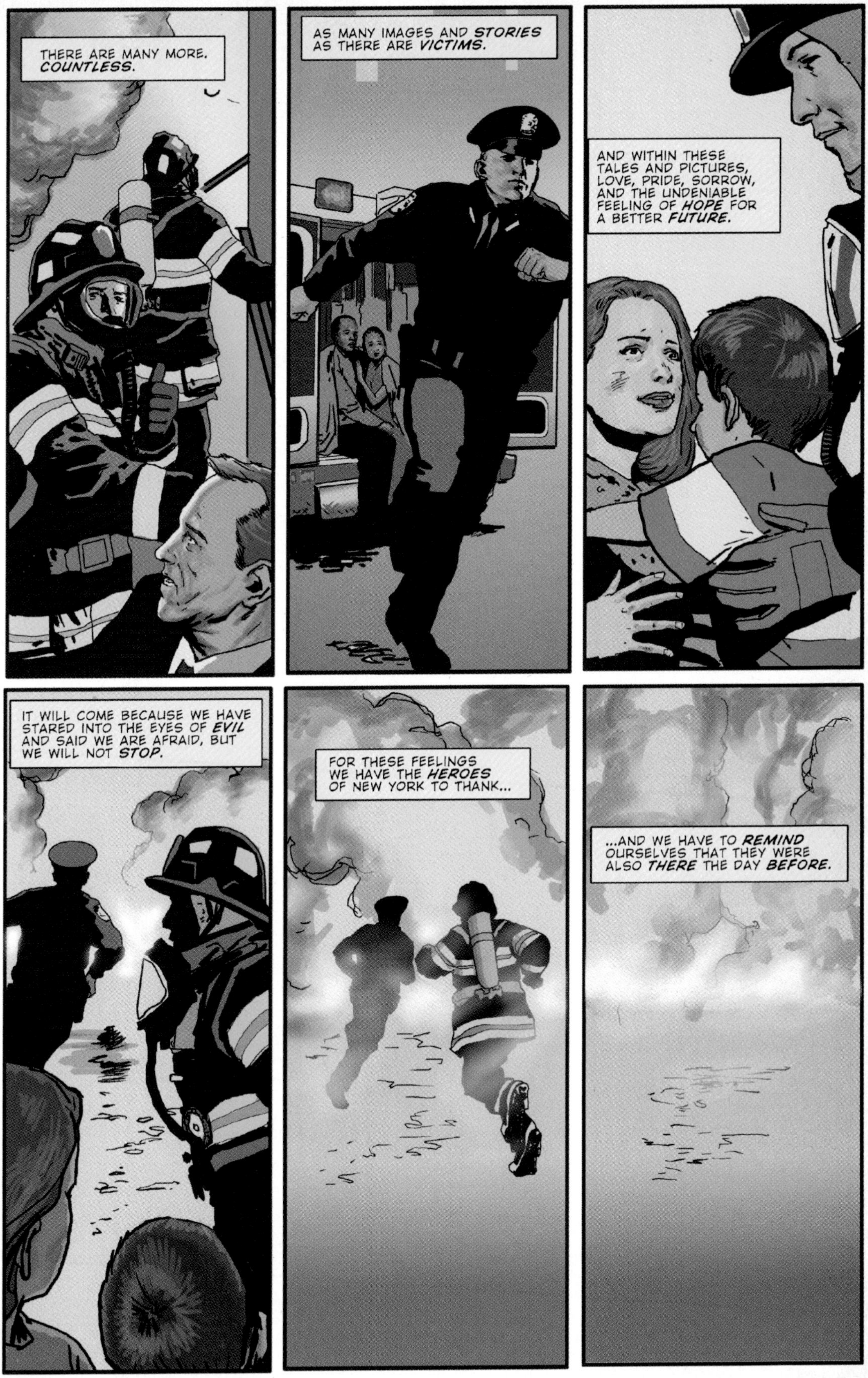
THERE ARE MANY MORE. COUNTLESS.
AS MANY IMAGES AND STORIES AS THERE ARE VICTIMS.
AND WITHIN THESE TALES AND PICTURES, LOVE, PRIDE, SORROW, AND THE UNDENIABLE FEELING OF HOPE FOR A BETTER FUTURE.
IT WILL COME BECAUSE WE HAVE STARED INTO THE EYES OF EVIL AND SAID WE ARE AFRAID, BUT WE WILL NOT STOP.
FOR THESE FEELINGS WE HAVE THE HEROES OF NEW YORK TO THANK...
...AND WE HAVE TO REMIND OURSELVES THAT THEY WERE ALSO THERE THE DAY BEFORE.

ORDINARY HEROES

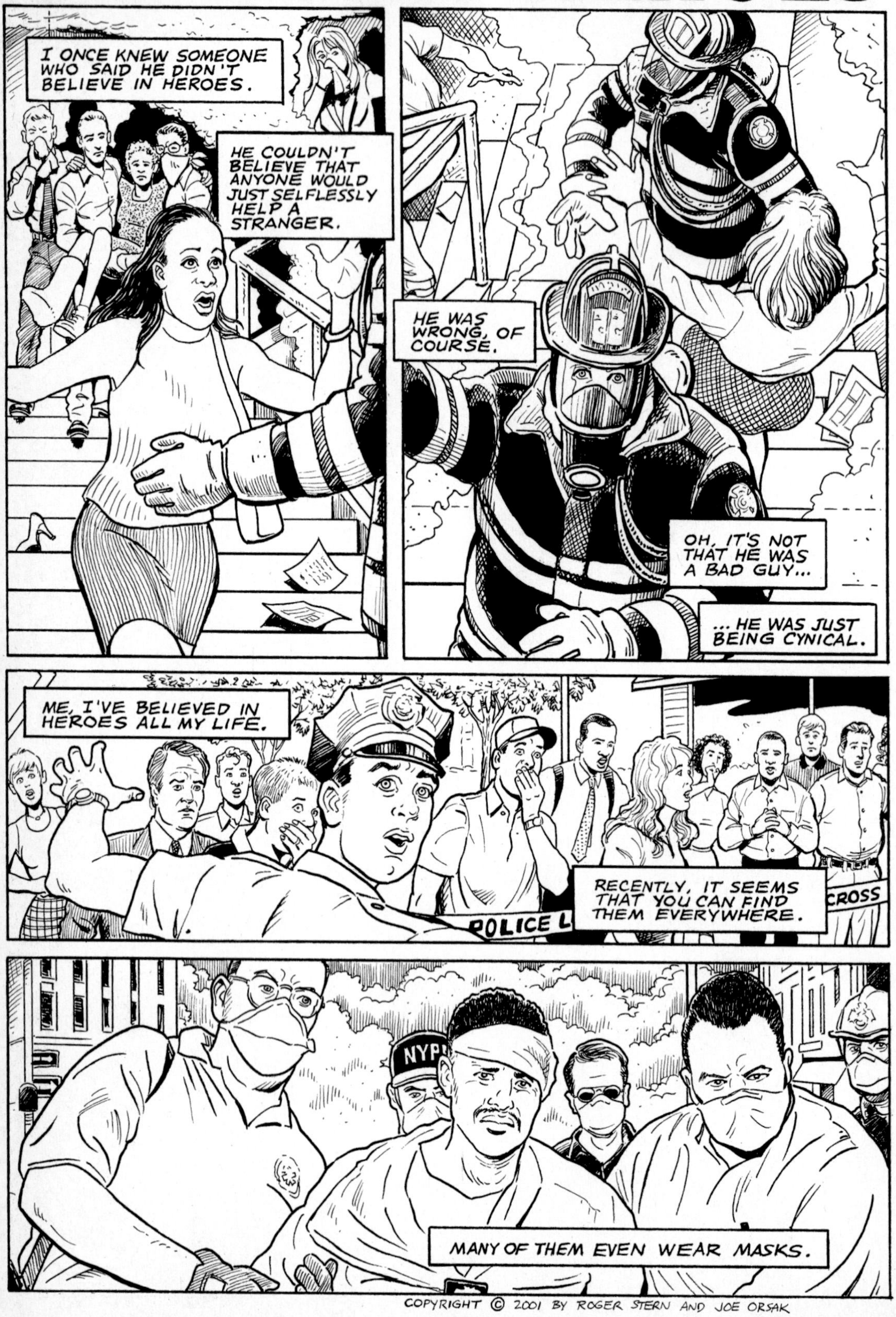
I ONCE KNEW SOMEONE WHO SAID HE DIDN'T BELIEVE IN HEROES.
HE COULDN'T BELIEVE THAT ANYONE WOULD JUST SELFLESSLY HELP A STRANGER.
HE WAS WRONG, OF COURSE.
OH, IT'S NOT THAT HE WAS A BAD GUY...
... HE WAS JUST BEING CYNICAL.
ME, I'VE BELIEVED IN HEROES ALL MY LIFE.
POLICE L
CROSS
RECENTLY, IT SEEMS THAT YOU CAN FIND THEM EVERYWHERE.
NYP
MANY OF THEM EVEN WEAR MASKS.

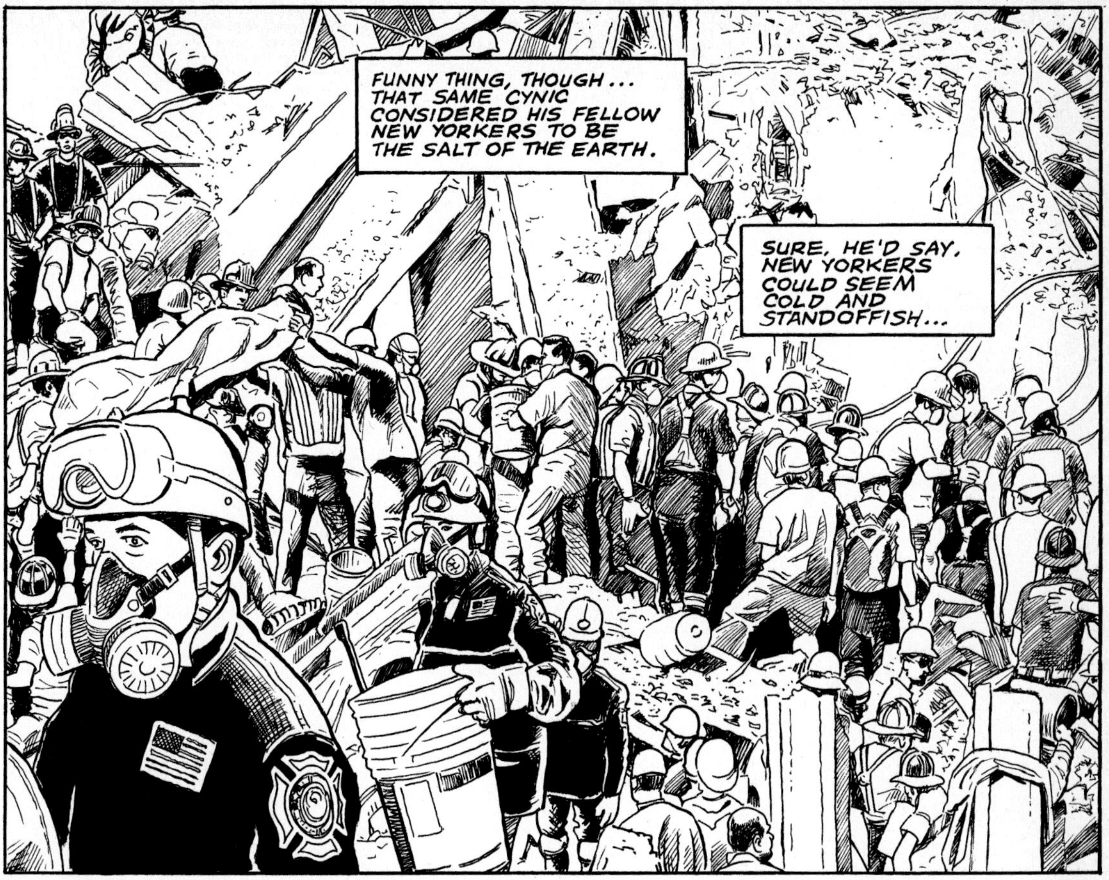
FUNNY THING, THOUGH... THAT SAME CYNIC CONSIDERED HIS FELLOW NEW YORKERS TO BE THE SALT OF THE EARTH.
SURE, HE'D SAY, NEW YORKERS COULD SEEM COLD AND STANDOFFISH...

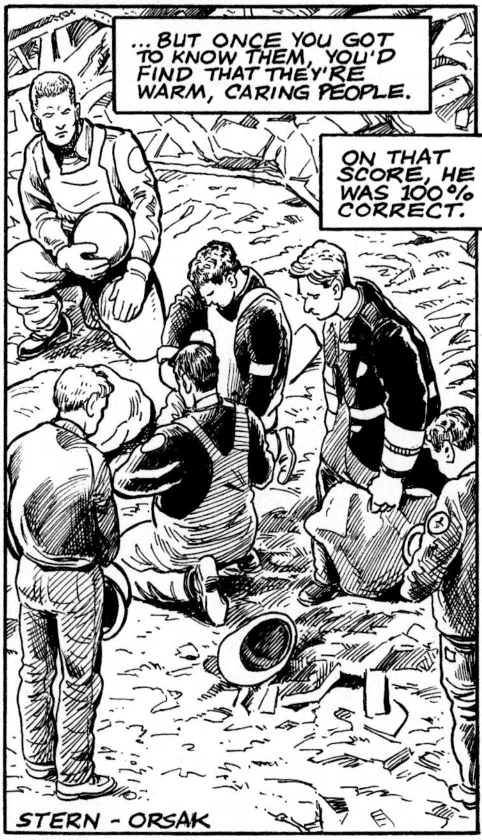
...BUT ONCE YOU GOT TO KNOW THEM, YOU'D FIND THAT THEY'RE WARM, CARING PEOPLE.
ON THAT SCORE, HE WAS 100% CORRECT.
STERN - ORSAK

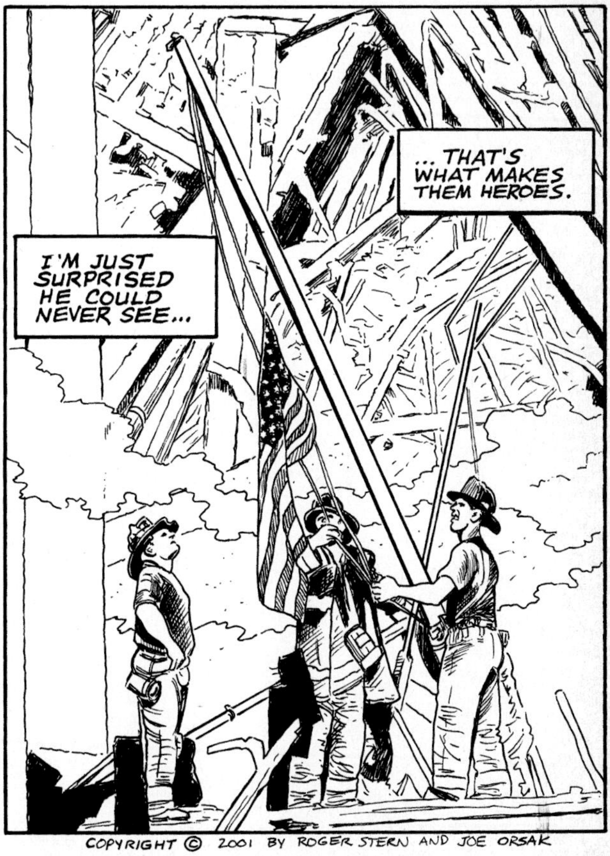
I'M JUST SURPRISED HE COULD NEVER SEE...
...THAT'S WHAT MAKES THEM HEROES.

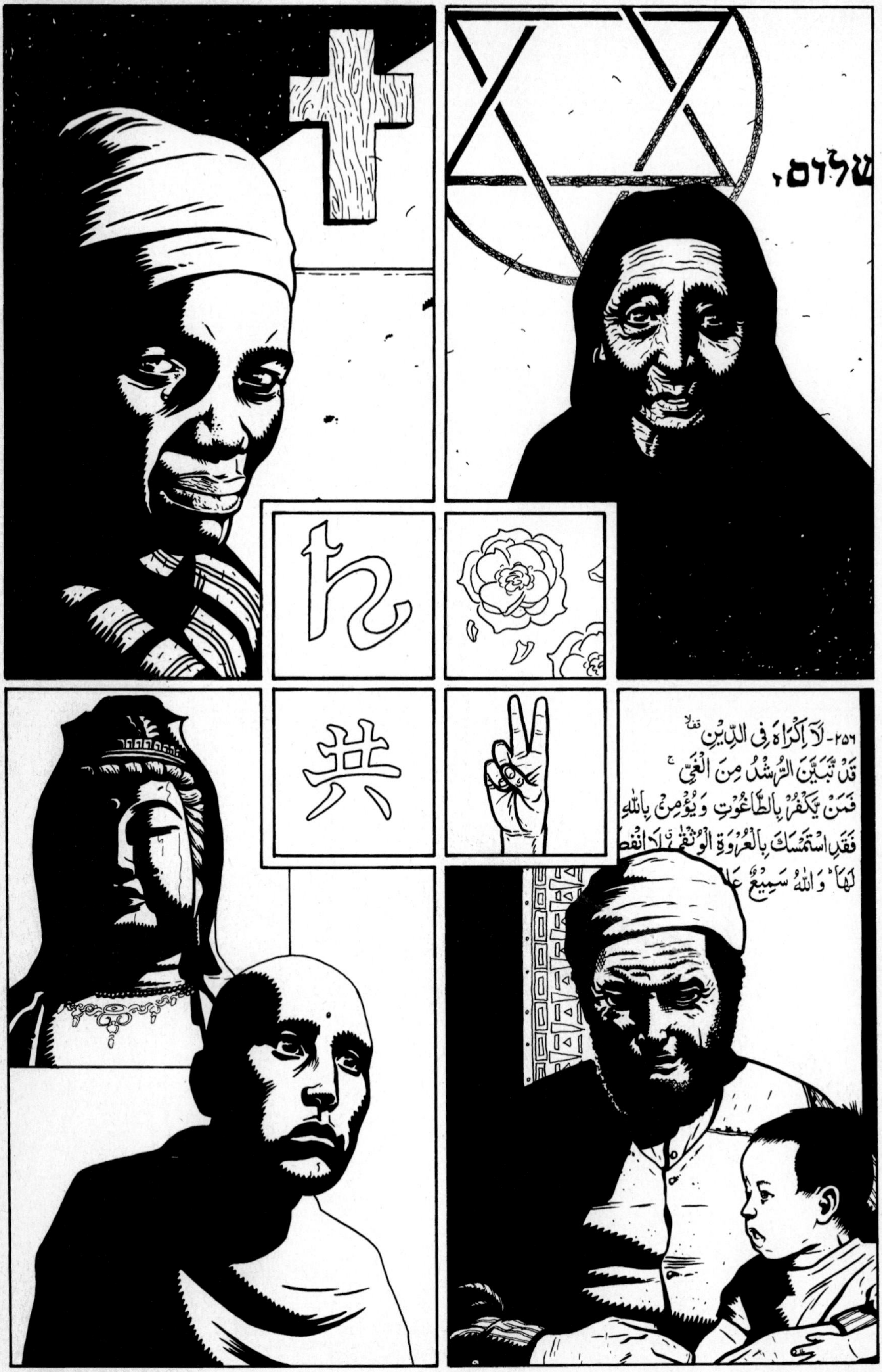
שלום,
共
٢٥٦- لا إكراه فى الدين
قد تبين الرشد من الغى
فمن يكفر بالطاغوت ويؤمن بالله
فقد استمسك بالعروة الوثقى لا انفص
لها والله سميع

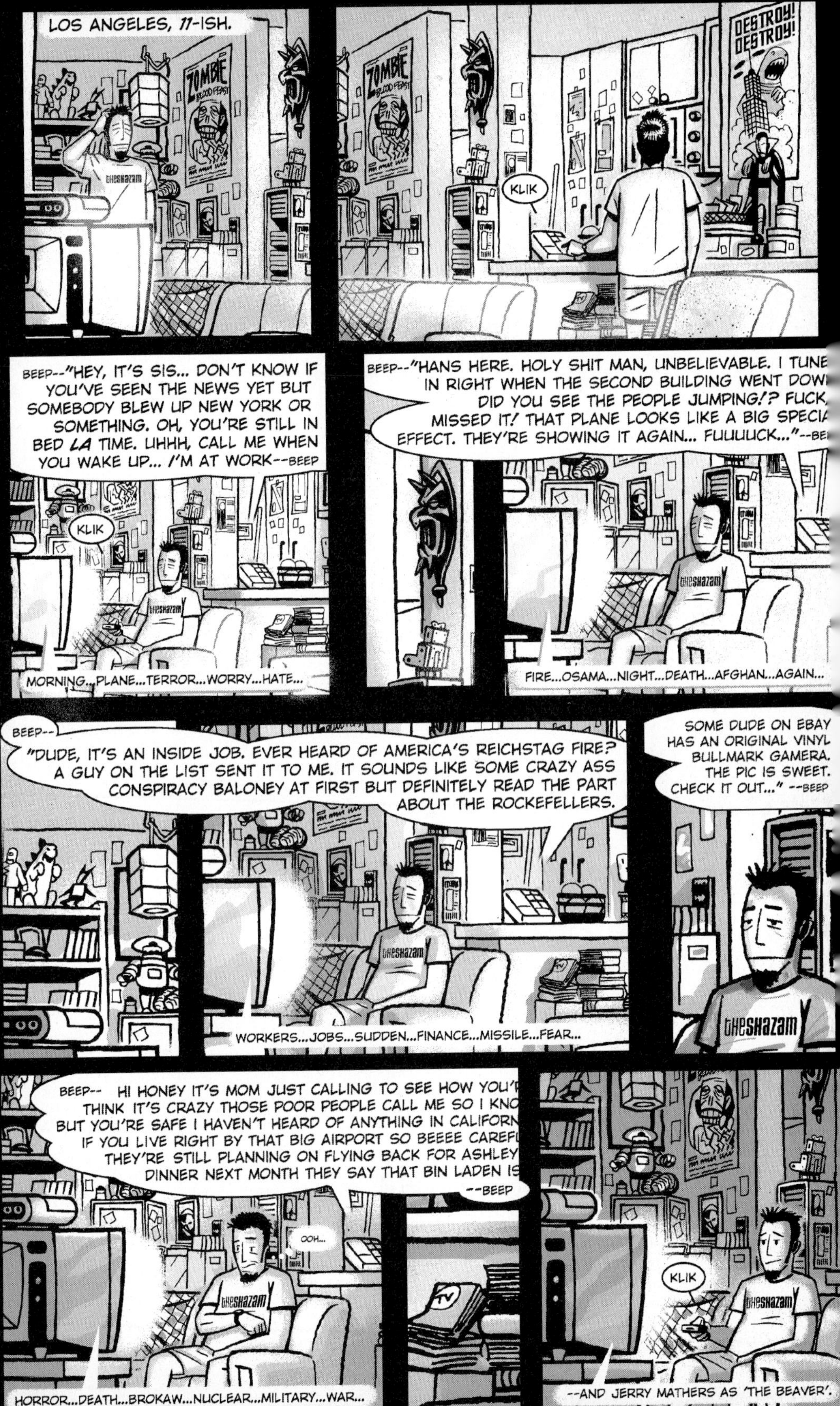

LOS ANGELES, 11-ISH.
ZOMBIE
theSHAZAM
DESTROY! DESTROY!
KLIK
BEEP--"HEY, IT'S SIS... DON'T KNOW IF YOU'VE SEEN THE NEWS YET BUT SOMEBODY BLEW UP NEW YORK OR SOMETHING. OH, YOU'RE STILL IN BED LA TIME. UHHH, CALL ME WHEN YOU WAKE UP... I'M AT WORK--BEEP
KLIK
MORNING...PLANE...TERROR...WORRY...HATE...
BEEP--"HANS HERE. HOLY SHIT MAN, UNBELIEVABLE. I TUNE IN RIGHT WHEN THE SECOND BUILDING WENT DOW DID YOU SEE THE PEOPLE JUMPING!? FUCK, MISSED IT! THAT PLANE LOOKS LIKE A BIG SPECIA EFFECT. THEY'RE SHOWING IT AGAIN... FUUUUCK..."--BE
FIRE...OSAMA...NIGHT...DEATH...AFGHAN...AGAIN...
BEEP--
"DUDE, IT'S AN INSIDE JOB. EVER HEARD OF AMERICA'S REICHSTAG FIRE? A GUY ON THE LIST SENT IT TO ME. IT SOUNDS LIKE SOME CRAZY ASS CONSPIRACY BALONEY AT FIRST BUT DEFINITELY READ THE PART ABOUT THE ROCKEFELLERS.
WORKERS...JOBS...SUDDEN...FINANCE...MISSILE...FEAR...
SOME DUDE ON EBAY HAS AN ORIGINAL VINYL BULLMARK GAMERA. THE PIC IS SWEET. CHECK IT OUT..." --BEEP
theSHAZAM
BEEP-- HI HONEY IT'S MOM JUST CALLING TO SEE HOW YOU' THINK IT'S CRAZY THOSE POOR PEOPLE CALL ME SO I KNO BUT YOU'RE SAFE I HAVEN'T HEARD OF ANYTHING IN CALIFORN IF YOU LIVE RIGHT BY THAT BIG AIRPORT SO BEEEE CAREF THEY'RE STILL PLANNING ON FLYING BACK FOR ASHLEY DINNER NEXT MONTH THEY SAY THAT BIN LADEN IS
--BEEP
OOH...
HORROR...DEATH...BROKAW...NUCLEAR...MILITARY...WAR...
KLIK
--AND JERRY MATHERS AS 'THE BEAVER'.

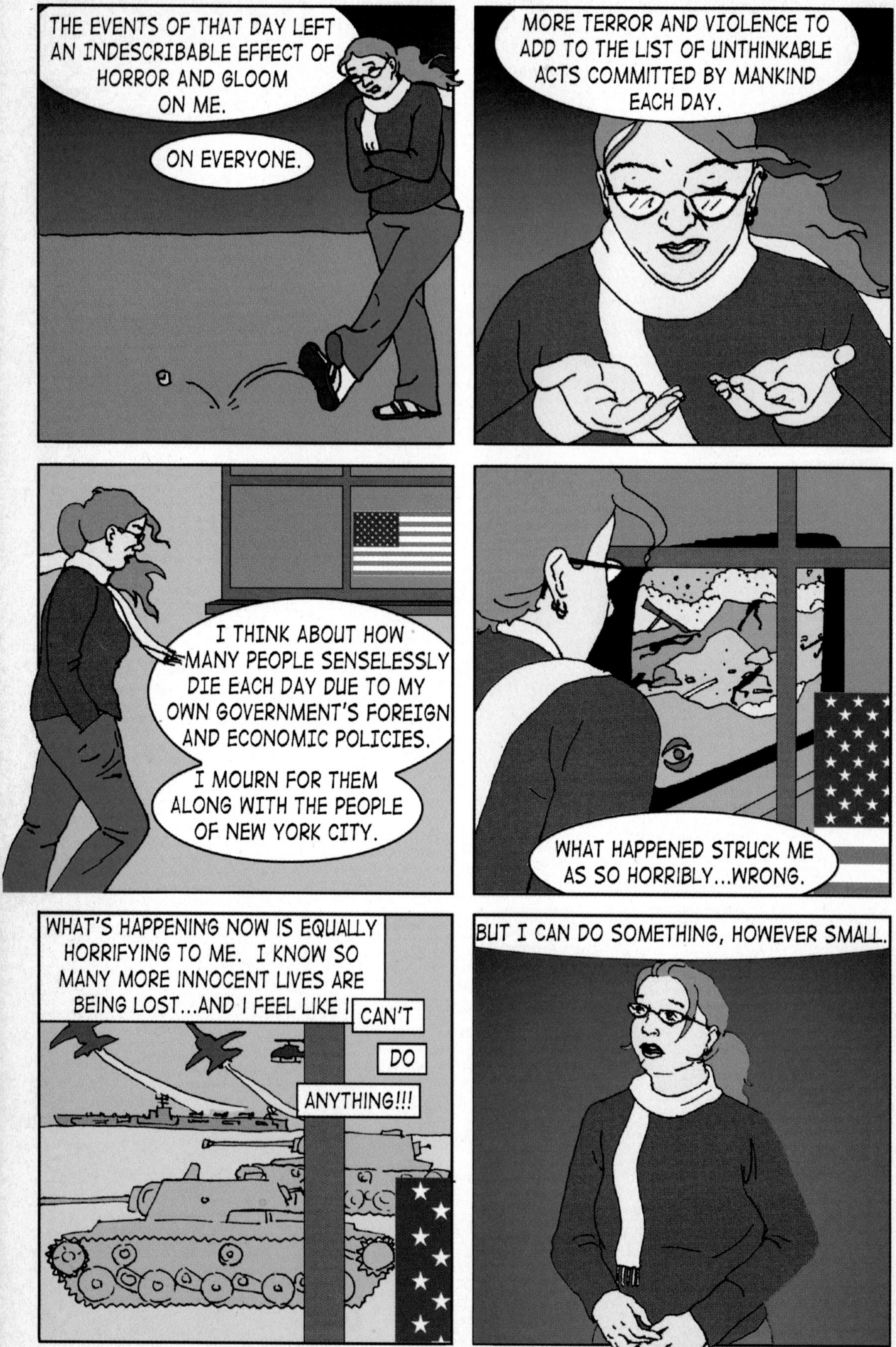
THE EVENTS OF THAT DAY LEFT AN INDESCRIBABLE EFFECT OF HORROR AND GLOOM ON ME.
ON EVERYONE.
MORE TERROR AND VIOLENCE TO ADD TO THE LIST OF UNTHINKABLE ACTS COMMITTED BY MANKIND EACH DAY.
I THINK ABOUT HOW MANY PEOPLE SENSELESSLY DIE EACH DAY DUE TO MY OWN GOVERNMENT'S FOREIGN AND ECONOMIC POLICIES.
I MOURN FOR THEM ALONG WITH THE PEOPLE OF NEW YORK CITY.
WHAT HAPPENED STRUCK ME AS SO HORRIBLY...WRONG.
WHAT'S HAPPENING NOW IS EQUALLY HORRIFYING TO ME. I KNOW SO MANY MORE INNOCENT LIVES ARE BEING LOST...AND I FEEL LIKE I
CAN'T
DO
ANYTHING!!!
BUT I CAN DO SOMETHING, HOWEVER SMALL.

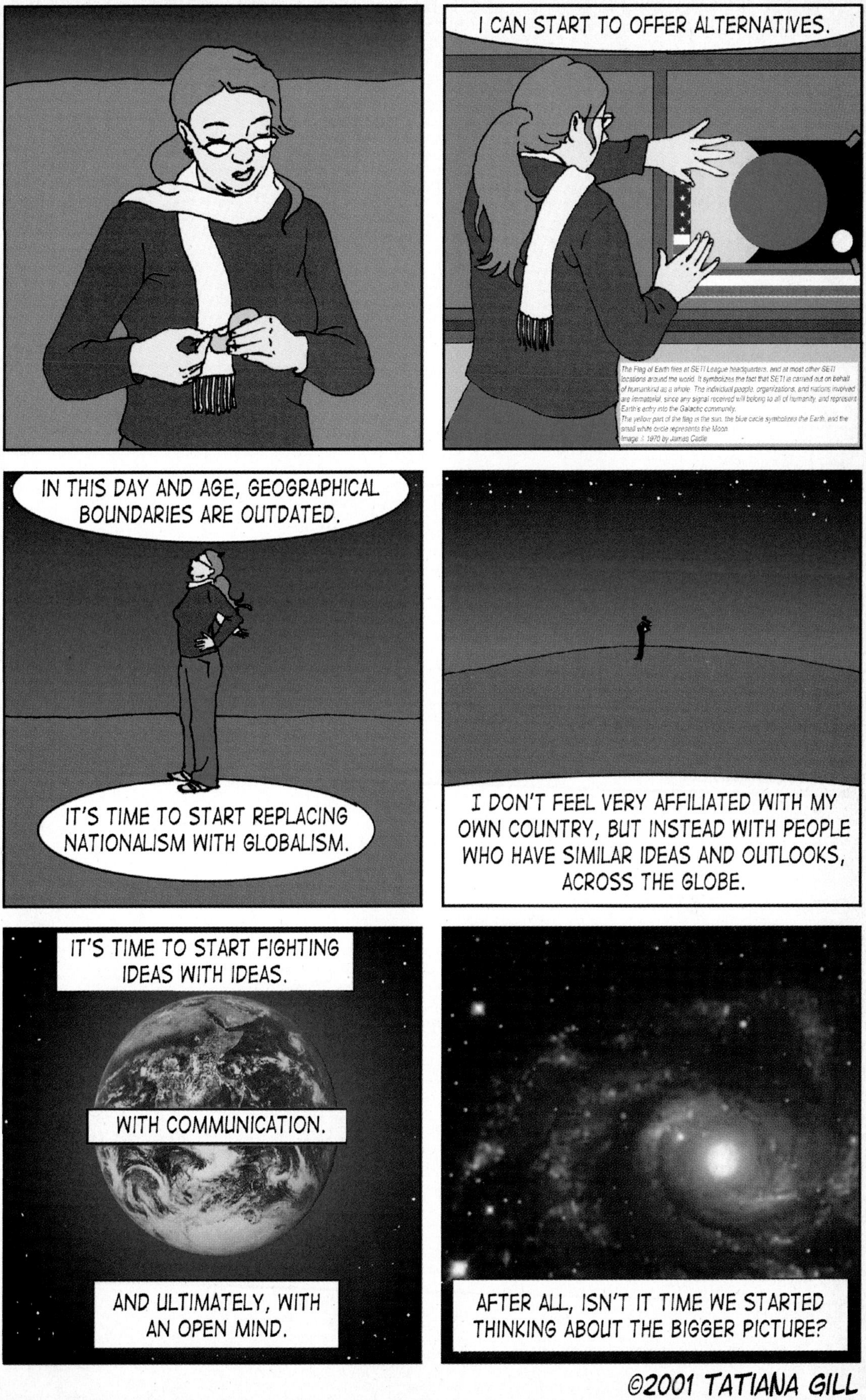

I CAN START TO OFFER ALTERNATIVES.
The Flag of Earth flies at SETI League headquarters, and at most other SETI locations around the world. It symbolizes the fact that SETI is carried out on behalf of humankind as a whole. The individual people, organizations, and nations involved are immaterial, since any signal received will belong to all of humanity, and represent Earth's entry into the Galactic community.
The yellow part of the flag is the sun, the blue circle symbolizes the Earth, and the small white circle represents the Moon.
Image © 1970 by James Cadle
IN THIS DAY AND AGE, GEOGRAPHICAL BOUNDARIES ARE OUTDATED.
IT'S TIME TO START REPLACING NATIONALISM WITH GLOBALISM.
I DON'T FEEL VERY AFFILIATED WITH MY OWN COUNTRY, BUT INSTEAD WITH PEOPLE WHO HAVE SIMILAR IDEAS AND OUTLOOKS, ACROSS THE GLOBE.
IT'S TIME TO START FIGHTING IDEAS WITH IDEAS.
WITH COMMUNICATION.
AND ULTIMATELY, WITH AN OPEN MIND.
AFTER ALL, ISN'T IT TIME WE STARTED THINKING ABOUT THE BIGGER PICTURE?

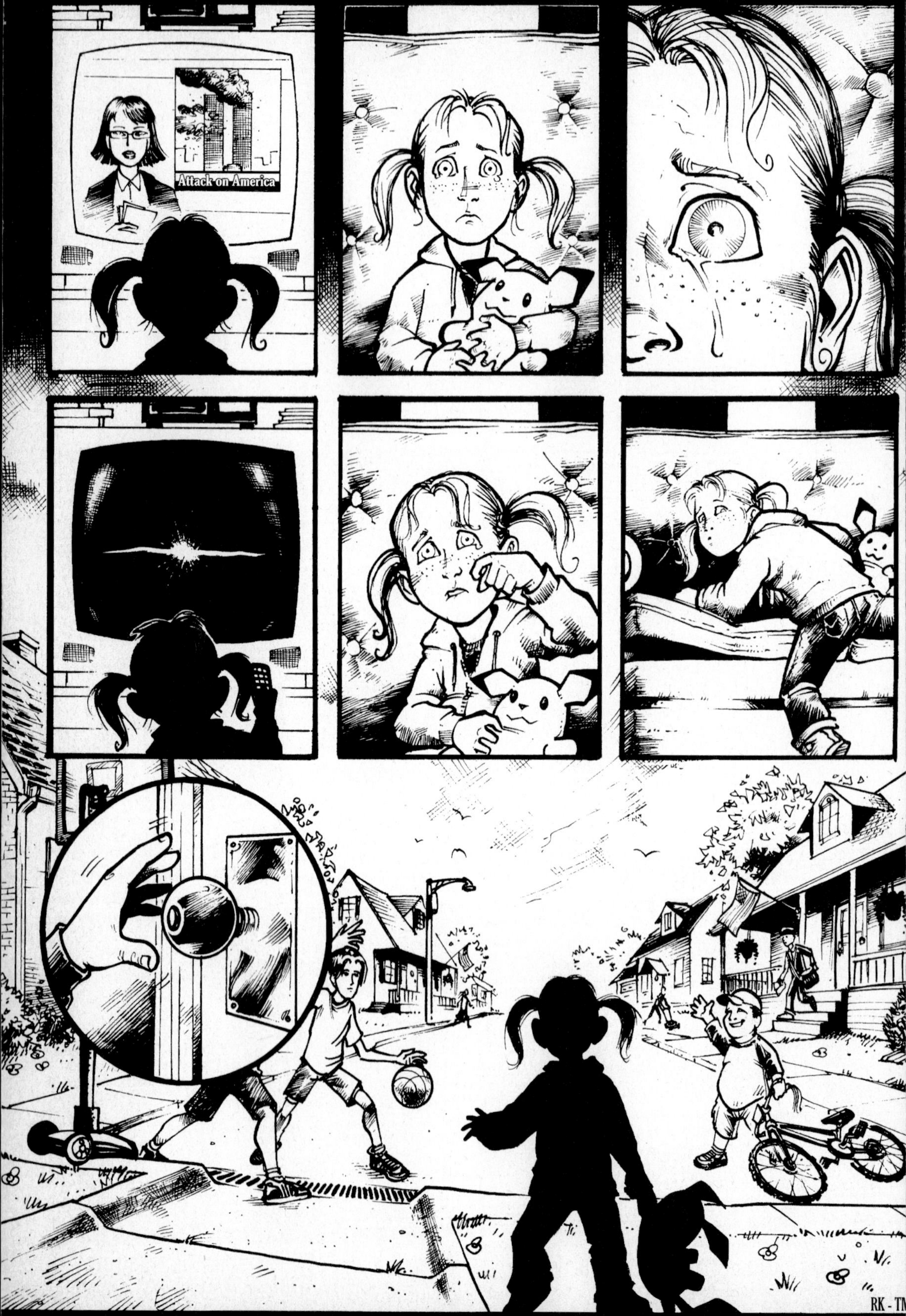

Attack on America
RK - TM

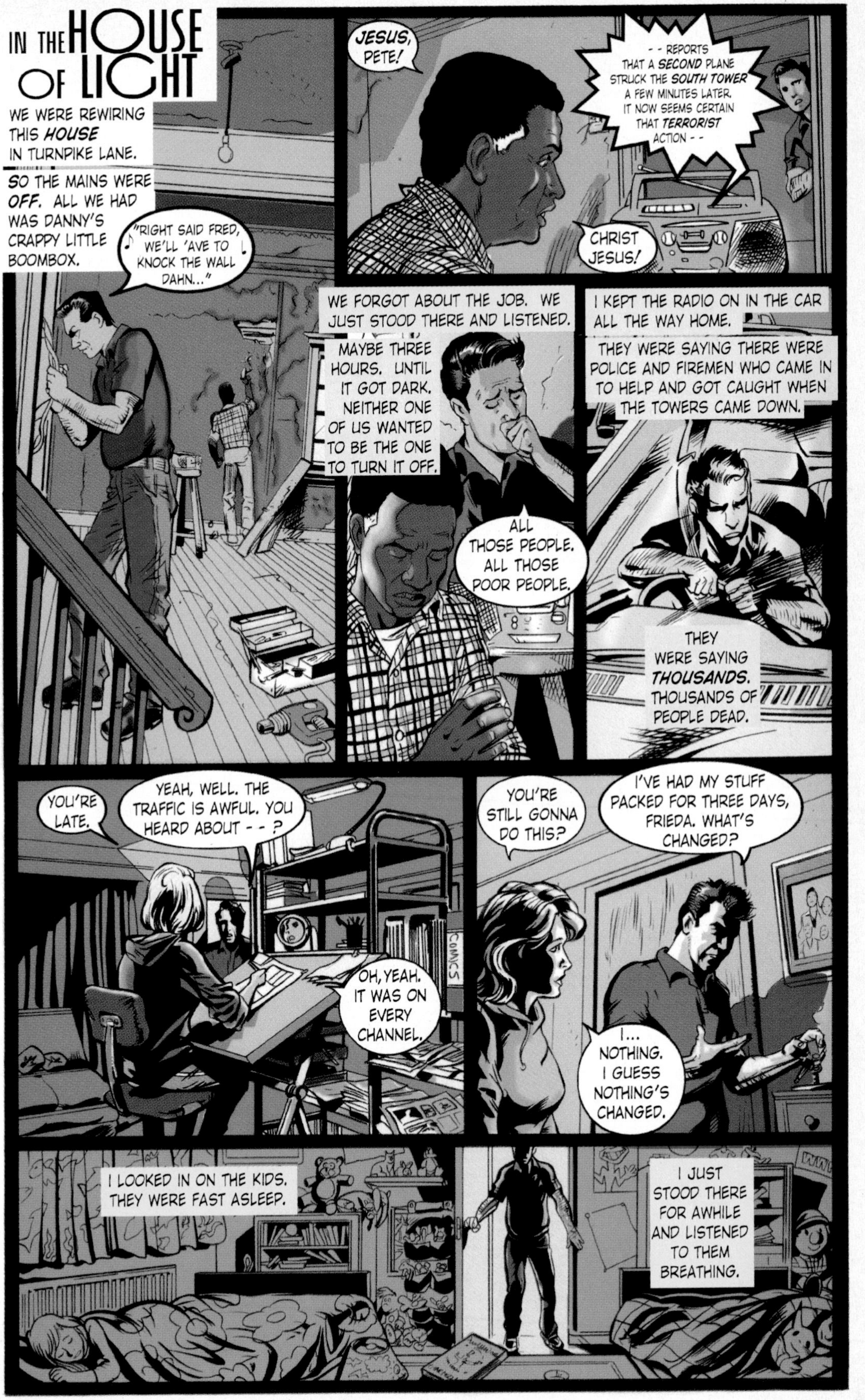
IN THE HOUSE OF LIGHT
WE WERE REWIRING THIS HOUSE IN TURNPIKE LANE.
SO THE MAINS WERE OFF. ALL WE HAD WAS DANNY'S CRAPPY LITTLE BOOMBOX.
"RIGHT SAID FRED, WE'LL 'AVE TO KNOCK THE WALL DAHN..."
JESUS, PETE!
- - REPORTS THAT A SECOND PLANE STRUCK THE SOUTH TOWER A FEW MINUTES LATER. IT NOW SEEMS CERTAIN THAT TERRORIST ACTION - -
CHRIST JESUS!
WE FORGOT ABOUT THE JOB. WE JUST STOOD THERE AND LISTENED.
MAYBE THREE HOURS. UNTIL IT GOT DARK. NEITHER ONE OF US WANTED TO BE THE ONE TO TURN IT OFF.
ALL THOSE PEOPLE. ALL THOSE POOR PEOPLE.
I KEPT THE RADIO ON IN THE CAR ALL THE WAY HOME.
THEY WERE SAYING THERE WERE POLICE AND FIREMEN WHO CAME IN TO HELP AND GOT CAUGHT WHEN THE TOWERS CAME DOWN.
THEY WERE SAYING THOUSANDS. THOUSANDS OF PEOPLE DEAD.
YOU'RE LATE.
YEAH, WELL. THE TRAFFIC IS AWFUL. YOU HEARD ABOUT - - ?
COMICS
OH, YEAH. IT WAS ON EVERY CHANNEL.
YOU'RE STILL GONNA DO THIS?
I'VE HAD MY STUFF PACKED FOR THREE DAYS, FRIEDA. WHAT'S CHANGED?
I... NOTHING. I GUESS NOTHING'S CHANGED.
I LOOKED IN ON THE KIDS. THEY WERE FAST ASLEEP.
I JUST STOOD THERE FOR AWHILE AND LISTENED TO THEM BREATHING.

Mike Carey-**Story** * Mike Collins & Lee Townsend-**Art**

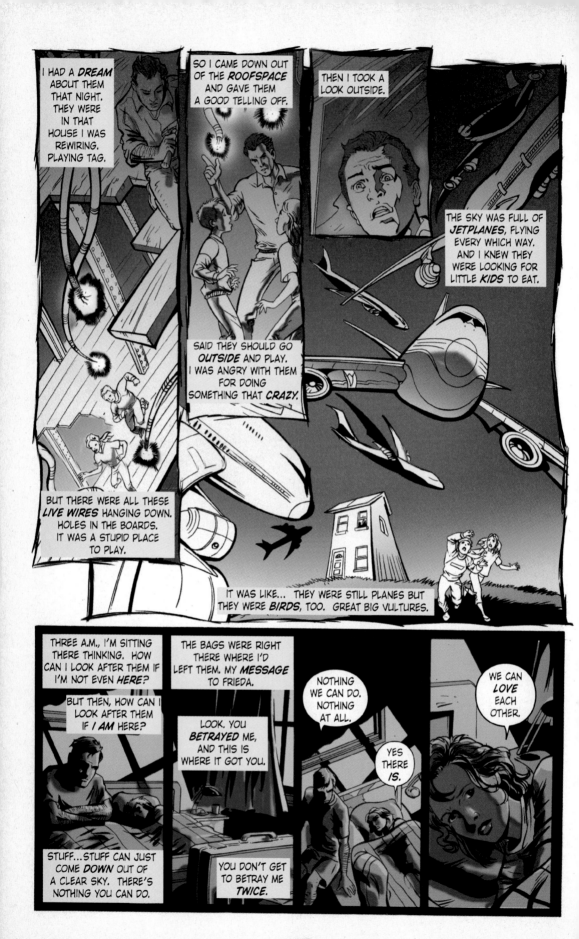

I HAD A *DREAM* ABOUT THEM THAT NIGHT. THEY WERE IN THAT HOUSE I WAS REWIRING. PLAYING TAG.

SO I CAME DOWN OUT OF THE *ROOFSPACE* AND GAVE THEM A GOOD TELLING OFF.

THEN I TOOK A LOOK OUTSIDE.

THE SKY WAS FULL OF *JETPLANES*, FLYING EVERY WHICH WAY. AND I KNEW THEY WERE LOOKING FOR LITTLE *KIDS* TO EAT.

SAID THEY SHOULD GO *OUTSIDE* AND PLAY. I WAS ANGRY WITH THEM FOR DOING SOMETHING THAT *CRAZY.*

BUT THERE WERE ALL THESE *LIVE WIRES* HANGING DOWN. HOLES IN THE BOARDS. IT WAS A STUPID PLACE TO PLAY.

IT WAS LIKE... THEY WERE STILL PLANES BUT THEY WERE *BIRDS*, TOO. GREAT BIG VULTURES.

THREE A.M., I'M SITTING THERE THINKING. HOW CAN I LOOK AFTER THEM IF I'M NOT EVEN *HERE?*

BUT THEN, HOW CAN I LOOK AFTER THEM IF *I AM* HERE?

STUFF...STUFF CAN JUST COME *DOWN* OUT OF A CLEAR SKY. THERE'S NOTHING YOU CAN DO.

THE BAGS WERE RIGHT THERE WHERE I'D LEFT THEM. MY *MESSAGE* TO FRIEDA.

LOOK, YOU *BETRAYED* ME, AND THIS IS WHERE IT GOT YOU.

YOU DON'T GET TO BETRAY ME *TWICE.*

NOTHING WE CAN DO. NOTHING AT ALL.

YES THERE *IS.*

WE CAN *LOVE* EACH OTHER.

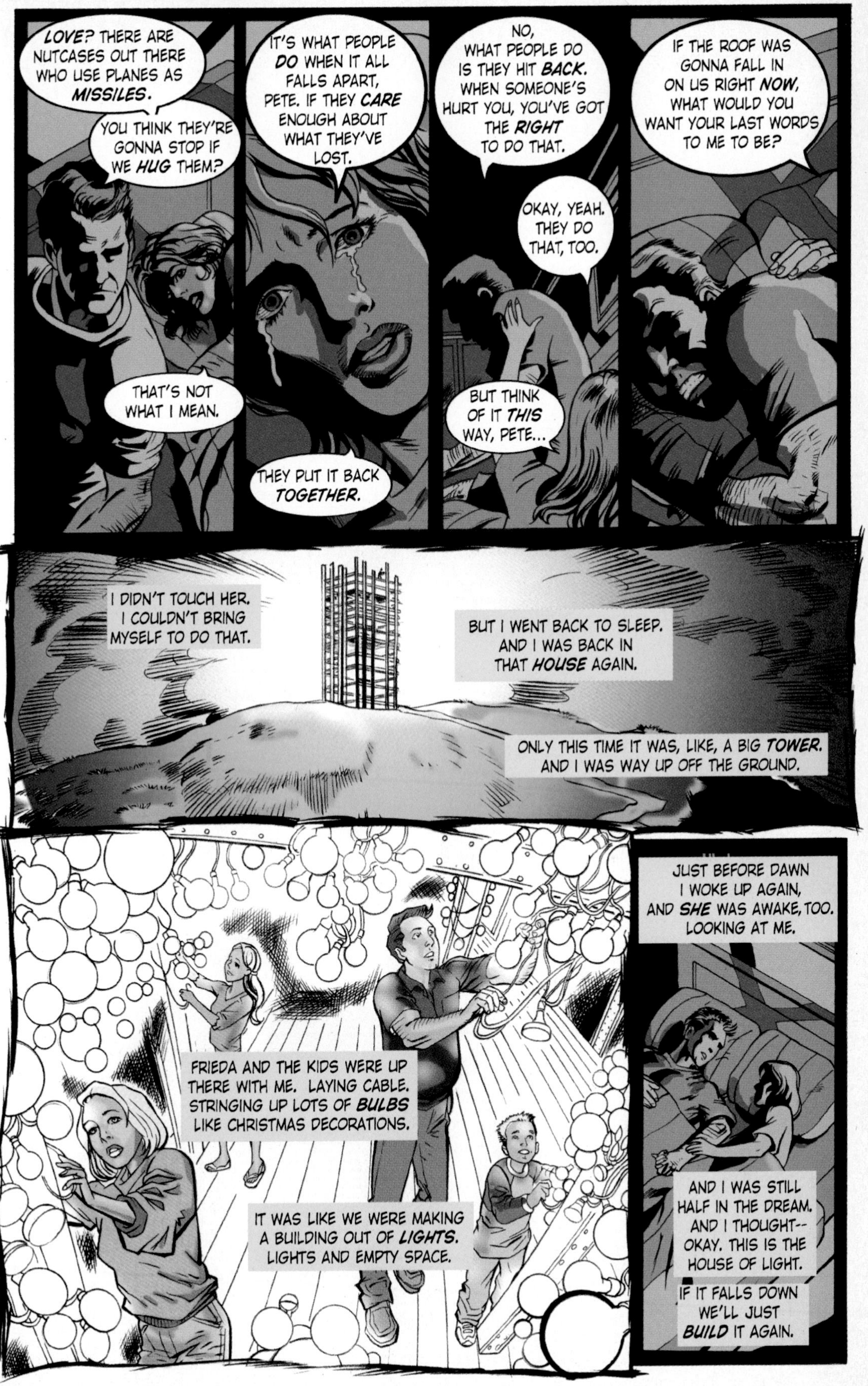
LOVE? THERE ARE NUTCASES OUT THERE WHO USE PLANES AS MISSILES.
YOU THINK THEY'RE GONNA STOP IF WE HUG THEM?
THAT'S NOT WHAT I MEAN.
IT'S WHAT PEOPLE DO WHEN IT ALL FALLS APART, PETE. IF THEY CARE ENOUGH ABOUT WHAT THEY'VE LOST.
THEY PUT IT BACK TOGETHER.
NO, WHAT PEOPLE DO IS THEY HIT BACK. WHEN SOMEONE'S HURT YOU, YOU'VE GOT THE RIGHT TO DO THAT.
OKAY, YEAH. THEY DO THAT, TOO.
BUT THINK OF IT THIS WAY, PETE...
IF THE ROOF WAS GONNA FALL IN ON US RIGHT NOW, WHAT WOULD YOU WANT YOUR LAST WORDS TO ME TO BE?
I DIDN'T TOUCH HER. I COULDN'T BRING MYSELF TO DO THAT.
BUT I WENT BACK TO SLEEP. AND I WAS BACK IN THAT HOUSE AGAIN.
ONLY THIS TIME IT WAS, LIKE, A BIG TOWER. AND I WAS WAY UP OFF THE GROUND.
FRIEDA AND THE KIDS WERE UP THERE WITH ME. LAYING CABLE. STRINGING UP LOTS OF BULBS LIKE CHRISTMAS DECORATIONS.
IT WAS LIKE WE WERE MAKING A BUILDING OUT OF LIGHTS. LIGHTS AND EMPTY SPACE.
JUST BEFORE DAWN I WOKE UP AGAIN, AND SHE WAS AWAKE, TOO. LOOKING AT ME.
AND I WAS STILL HALF IN THE DREAM. AND I THOUGHT-- OKAY. THIS IS THE HOUSE OF LIGHT.
IF IT FALLS DOWN WE'LL JUST BUILD IT AGAIN.

Ron Boyd

AYEKAH

RABBI SPLANSKY SPOKE OF ADAM AND EVE.

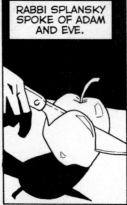

THEIR FALL FROM THE SWEET INNOCENCE OF THE GARDEN.

THEIR BURNING SHAME.

GOD ASKED "AYEKAH?", "WHERE ARE YOU?"

AND THEY HID.

CRUMBLING UNDER THE BURDEN OF KNOWLEDGE.

ROSH HASHANA 2001 Tuesday, September 18

"We'll be home in time for First Night."

"We haven't seen Bubbie in months."

"Don't worry. The flight from Boston's really quick."

RABBI SPLANSKY ALSO SPOKE ABOUT ABRAHAM.

ABOUT HOW GOD ASKED HIM TO SACRIFICE HIS ONLY SON.

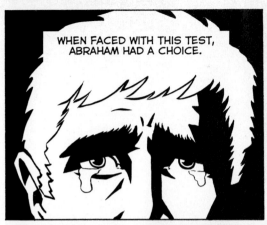

WHEN FACED WITH THIS TEST, ABRAHAM HAD A CHOICE.

IN THAT MOMENT, HIS INNOCENCE WAS LOST.

GOD CALLED OUT TO HIM;

"AYEKAH?", "WHERE ARE YOU?"

ABRAHAM'S FAITH HELD STRONG.

WITH COURAGE HE FACED HIS TEST,

AND BRAVELY ANSWERED "HINEINI",

HERE I AM !!

RON BOYD - OCT '01

J. Torres • Steve Rolston

"CLOSE"

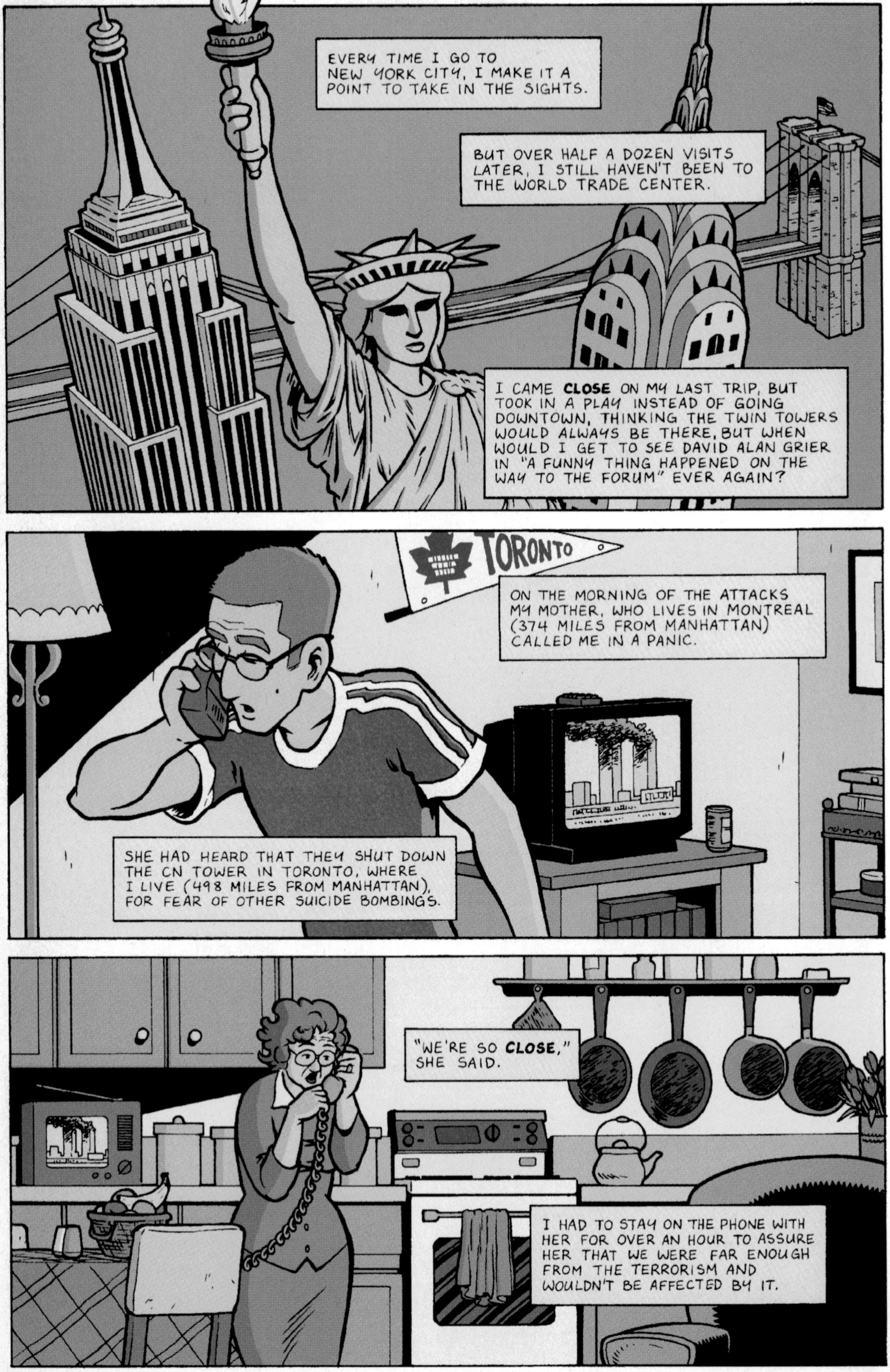
EVERY TIME I GO TO NEW YORK CITY, I MAKE IT A POINT TO TAKE IN THE SIGHTS.
BUT OVER HALF A DOZEN VISITS LATER, I STILL HAVEN'T BEEN TO THE WORLD TRADE CENTER.
I CAME **CLOSE** ON MY LAST TRIP, BUT TOOK IN A PLAY INSTEAD OF GOING DOWNTOWN, THINKING THE TWIN TOWERS WOULD ALWAYS BE THERE, BUT WHEN WOULD I GET TO SEE DAVID ALAN GRIER IN "A FUNNY THING HAPPENED ON THE WAY TO THE FORUM" EVER AGAIN?
TORONTO
ON THE MORNING OF THE ATTACKS MY MOTHER, WHO LIVES IN MONTREAL (374 MILES FROM MANHATTAN) CALLED ME IN A PANIC.
SHE HAD HEARD THAT THEY SHUT DOWN THE CN TOWER IN TORONTO, WHERE I LIVE (498 MILES FROM MANHATTAN), FOR FEAR OF OTHER SUICIDE BOMBINGS.
"WE'RE SO **CLOSE**," SHE SAID.
I HAD TO STAY ON THE PHONE WITH HER FOR OVER AN HOUR TO ASSURE HER THAT WE WERE FAR ENOUGH FROM THE TERRORISM AND WOULDN'T BE AFFECTED BY IT.

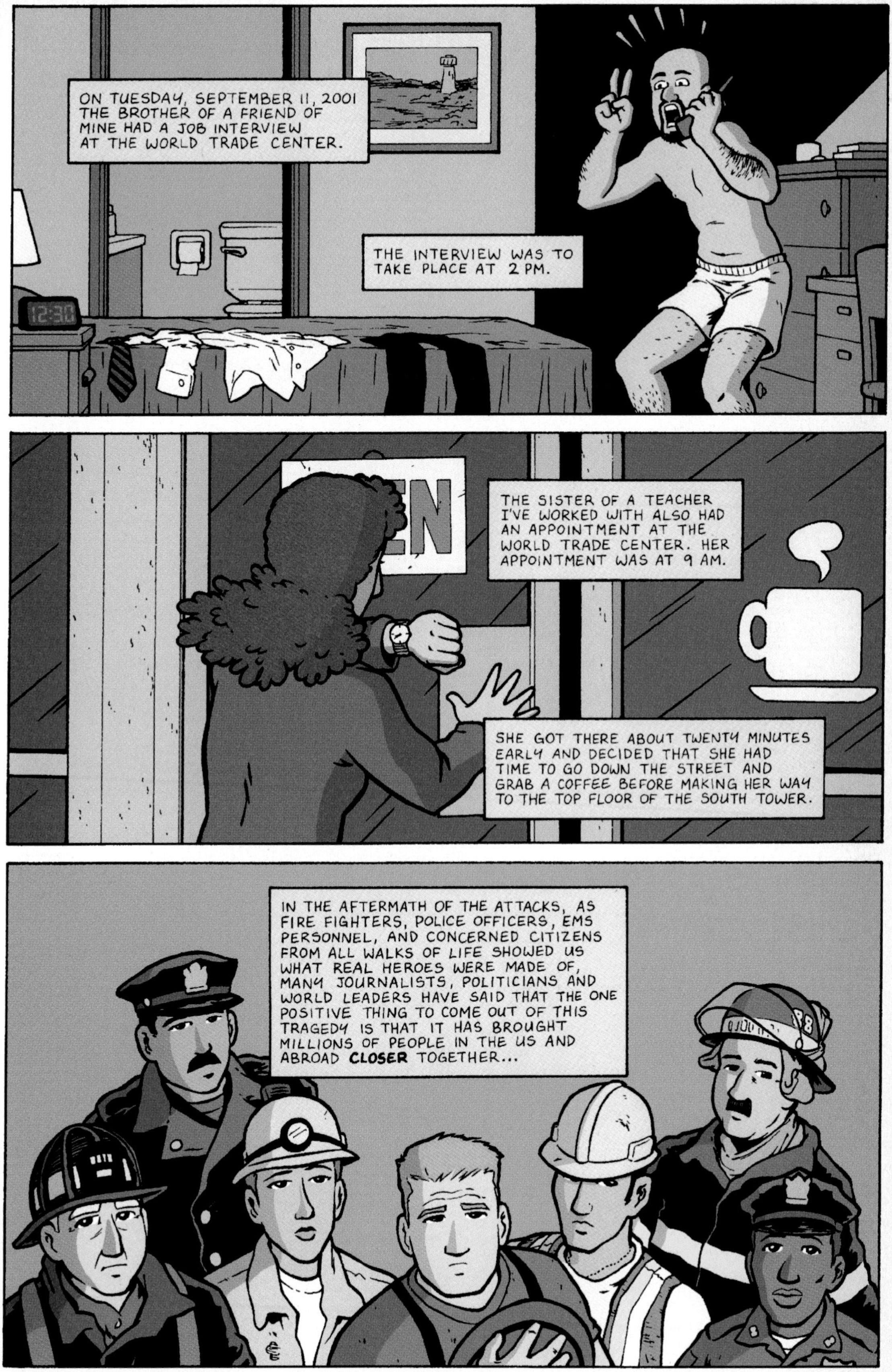
ON TUESDAY, SEPTEMBER 11, 2001 THE BROTHER OF A FRIEND OF MINE HAD A JOB INTERVIEW AT THE WORLD TRADE CENTER.
12:30
THE INTERVIEW WAS TO TAKE PLACE AT 2 PM.
THE SISTER OF A TEACHER I'VE WORKED WITH ALSO HAD AN APPOINTMENT AT THE WORLD TRADE CENTER. HER APPOINTMENT WAS AT 9 AM.
SHE GOT THERE ABOUT TWENTY MINUTES EARLY AND DECIDED THAT SHE HAD TIME TO GO DOWN THE STREET AND GRAB A COFFEE BEFORE MAKING HER WAY TO THE TOP FLOOR OF THE SOUTH TOWER.
IN THE AFTERMATH OF THE ATTACKS, AS FIRE FIGHTERS, POLICE OFFICERS, EMS PERSONNEL, AND CONCERNED CITIZENS FROM ALL WALKS OF LIFE SHOWED US WHAT REAL HEROES WERE MADE OF, MANY JOURNALISTS, POLITICIANS AND WORLD LEADERS HAVE SAID THAT THE ONE POSITIVE THING TO COME OUT OF THIS TRAGEDY IS THAT IT HAS BROUGHT MILLIONS OF PEOPLE IN THE US AND ABROAD **CLOSER** TOGETHER...

WORDS BY J. TORRES   ART BY STEVE ROLSTON   COLOURS BY S. STRUBLE

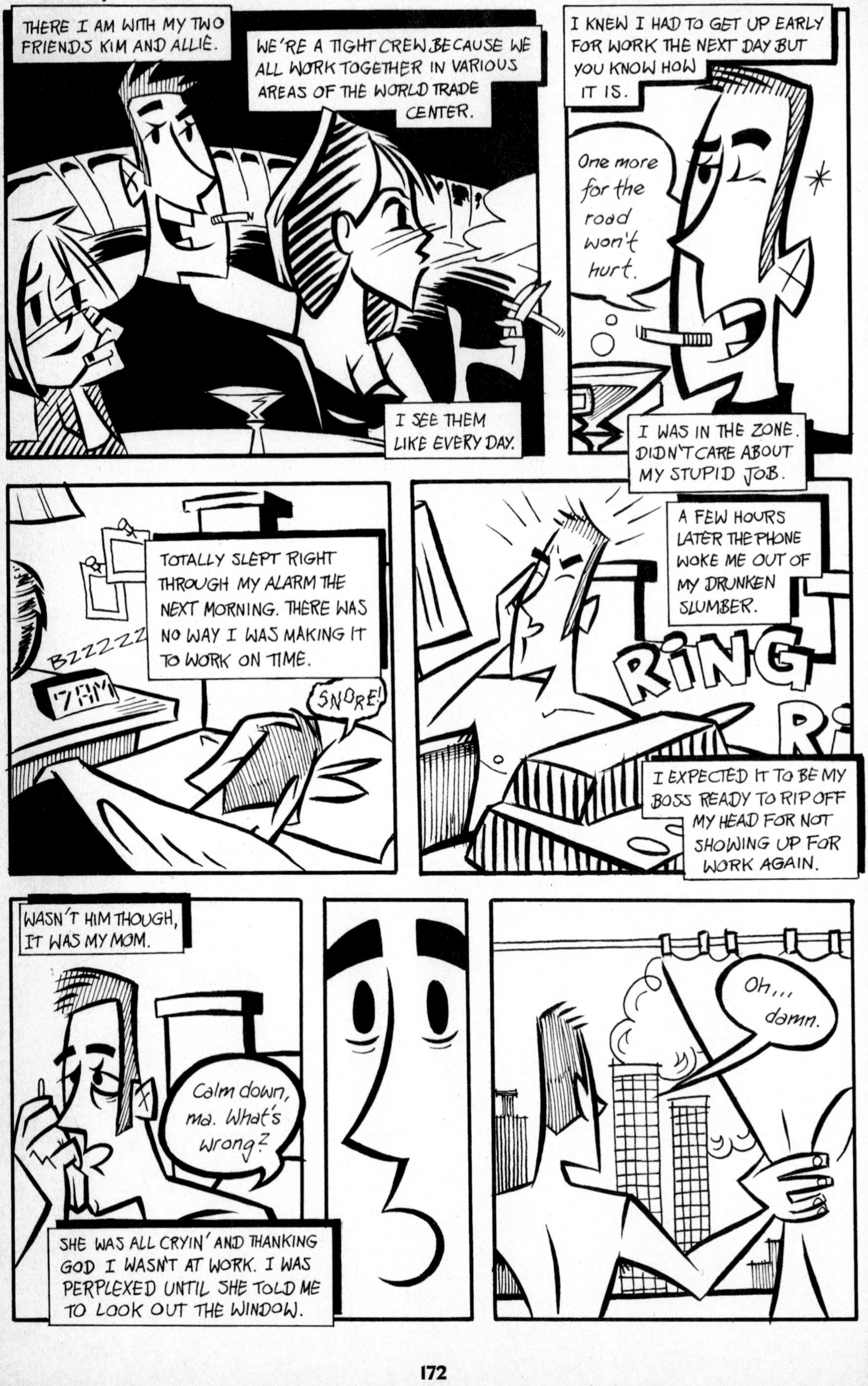
THERE I AM WITH MY TWO FRIENDS KIM AND ALLIE.
WE'RE A TIGHT CREW BECAUSE WE ALL WORK TOGETHER IN VARIOUS AREAS OF THE WORLD TRADE CENTER.
I SEE THEM LIKE EVERY DAY.
I KNEW I HAD TO GET UP EARLY FOR WORK THE NEXT DAY BUT YOU KNOW HOW IT IS.
One more for the road won't hurt.
I WAS IN THE ZONE. DIDN'T CARE ABOUT MY STUPID JOB.
TOTALLY SLEPT RIGHT THROUGH MY ALARM THE NEXT MORNING. THERE WAS NO WAY I WAS MAKING IT TO WORK ON TIME.
BZZZZZ
7AM
SNORE!
A FEW HOURS LATER THE PHONE WOKE ME OUT OF MY DRUNKEN SLUMBER.
RING
I EXPECTED IT TO BE MY BOSS READY TO RIP OFF MY HEAD FOR NOT SHOWING UP FOR WORK AGAIN.
WASN'T HIM THOUGH, IT WAS MY MOM.
Calm down, ma. What's wrong?
SHE WAS ALL CRYIN' AND THANKING GOD I WASN'T AT WORK. I WAS PERPLEXED UNTIL SHE TOLD ME TO LOOK OUT THE WINDOW.
Oh... damn.

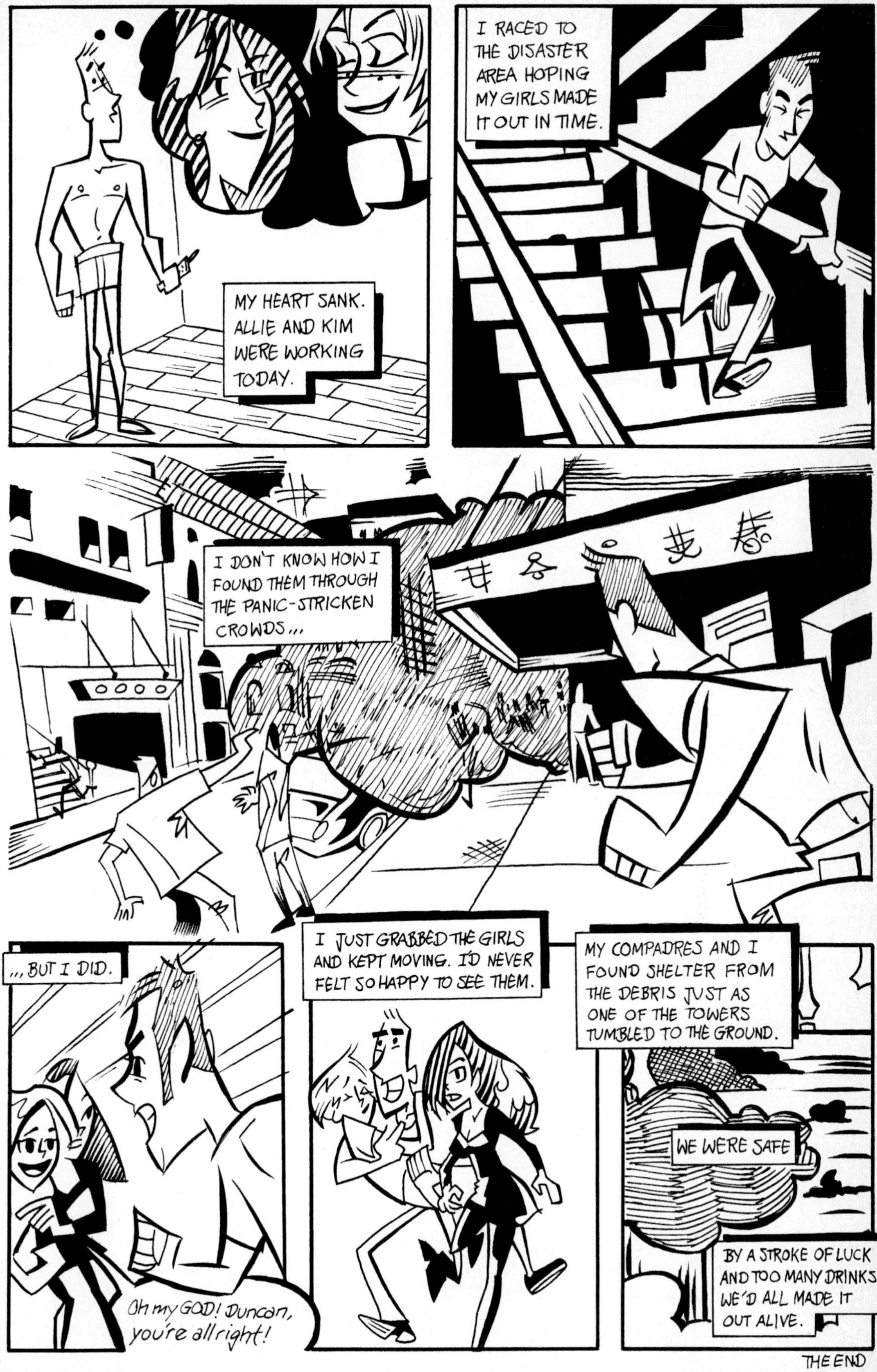
MY HEART SANK. ALLIE AND KIM WERE WORKING TODAY.
I RACED TO THE DISASTER AREA HOPING MY GIRLS MADE IT OUT IN TIME.
I DON'T KNOW HOW I FOUND THEM THROUGH THE PANIC-STRICKEN CROWDS...
...BUT I DID.
Oh my GOD! Duncan, you're all right!
I JUST GRABBED THE GIRLS AND KEPT MOVING. I'D NEVER FELT SO HAPPY TO SEE THEM.
MY COMPADRES AND I FOUND SHELTER FROM THE DEBRIS JUST AS ONE OF THE TOWERS TUMBLED TO THE GROUND.
WE WERE SAFE
BY A STROKE OF LUCK AND TOO MANY DRINKS WE'D ALL MADE IT OUT ALIVE.

THE END

Marc Rosenthal

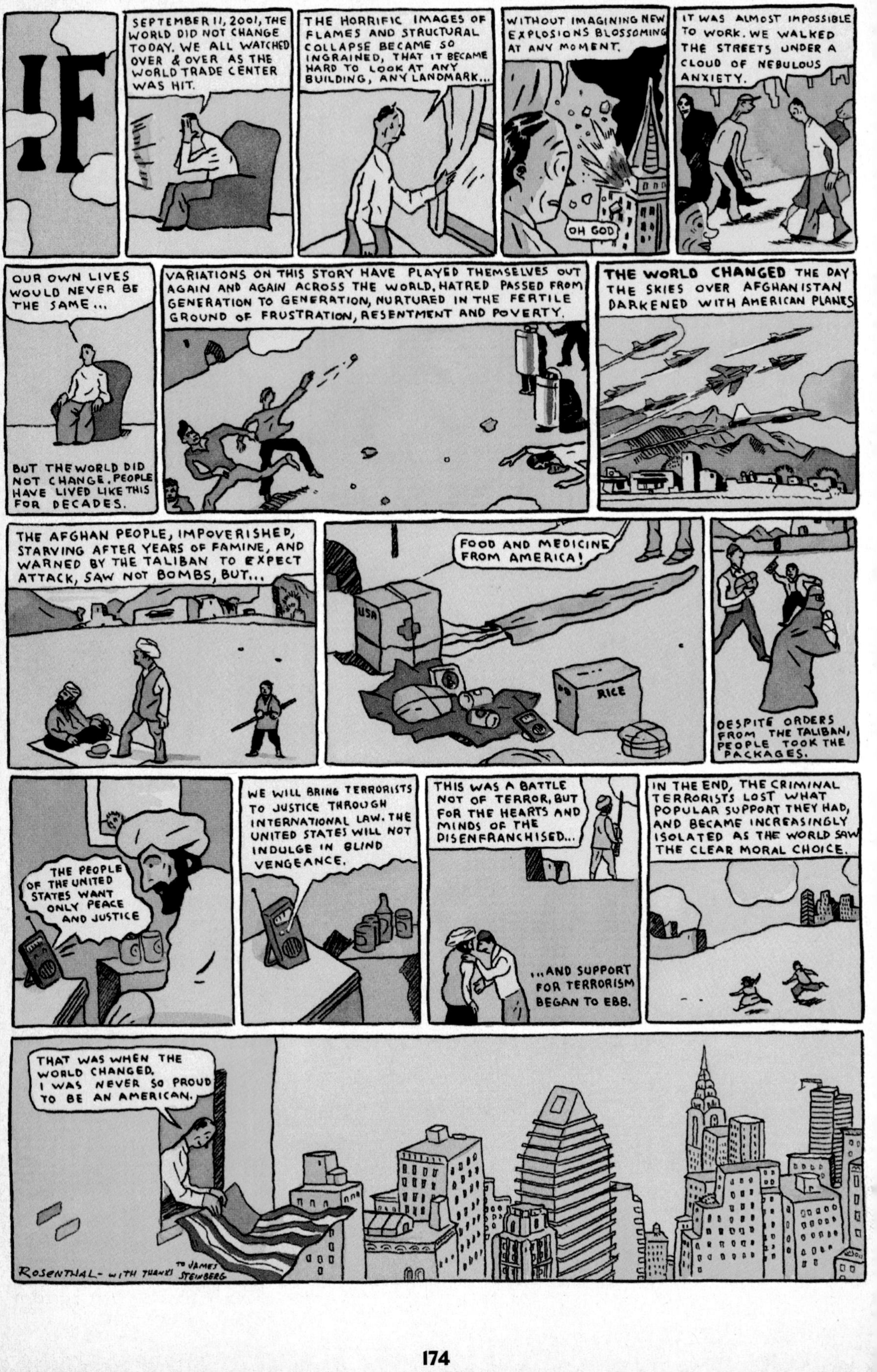

IF
SEPTEMBER 11, 2001, THE WORLD DID NOT CHANGE TODAY. WE ALL WATCHED OVER & OVER AS THE WORLD TRADE CENTER WAS HIT.
THE HORRIFIC IMAGES OF FLAMES AND STRUCTURAL COLLAPSE BECAME SO INGRAINED, THAT IT BECAME HARD TO LOOK AT ANY BUILDING, ANY LANDMARK...
WITHOUT IMAGINING NEW EXPLOSIONS BLOSSOMING AT ANY MOMENT.
OH GOD
IT WAS ALMOST IMPOSSIBLE TO WORK. WE WALKED THE STREETS UNDER A CLOUD OF NEBULOUS ANXIETY.
OUR OWN LIVES WOULD NEVER BE THE SAME...
BUT THE WORLD DID NOT CHANGE. PEOPLE HAVE LIVED LIKE THIS FOR DECADES.
VARIATIONS ON THIS STORY HAVE PLAYED THEMSELVES OUT AGAIN AND AGAIN ACROSS THE WORLD. HATRED PASSED FROM GENERATION TO GENERATION, NURTURED IN THE FERTILE GROUND OF FRUSTRATION, RESENTMENT AND POVERTY.
THE WORLD CHANGED THE DAY THE SKIES OVER AFGHANISTAN DARKENED WITH AMERICAN PLANES
THE AFGHAN PEOPLE, IMPOVERISHED, STARVING AFTER YEARS OF FAMINE, AND WARNED BY THE TALIBAN TO EXPECT ATTACK, SAW NOT BOMBS, BUT...
FOOD AND MEDICINE FROM AMERICA!
USA
RICE
DESPITE ORDERS FROM THE TALIBAN, PEOPLE TOOK THE PACKAGES.
THE PEOPLE OF THE UNITED STATES WANT ONLY PEACE AND JUSTICE
WE WILL BRING TERRORISTS TO JUSTICE THROUGH INTERNATIONAL LAW. THE UNITED STATES WILL NOT INDULGE IN BLIND VENGEANCE.
THIS WAS A BATTLE NOT OF TERROR, BUT FOR THE HEARTS AND MINDS OF THE DISENFRANCHISED...
...AND SUPPORT FOR TERRORISM BEGAN TO EBB.
IN THE END, THE CRIMINAL TERRORISTS LOST WHAT POPULAR SUPPORT THEY HAD, AND BECAME INCREASINGLY ISOLATED AS THE WORLD SAW THE CLEAR MORAL CHOICE.
THAT WAS WHEN THE WORLD CHANGED. I WAS NEVER SO PROUD TO BE AN AMERICAN.
ROSENTHAL- WITH THANKS TO JAMES STEINBERG

Jose Luis Agreda

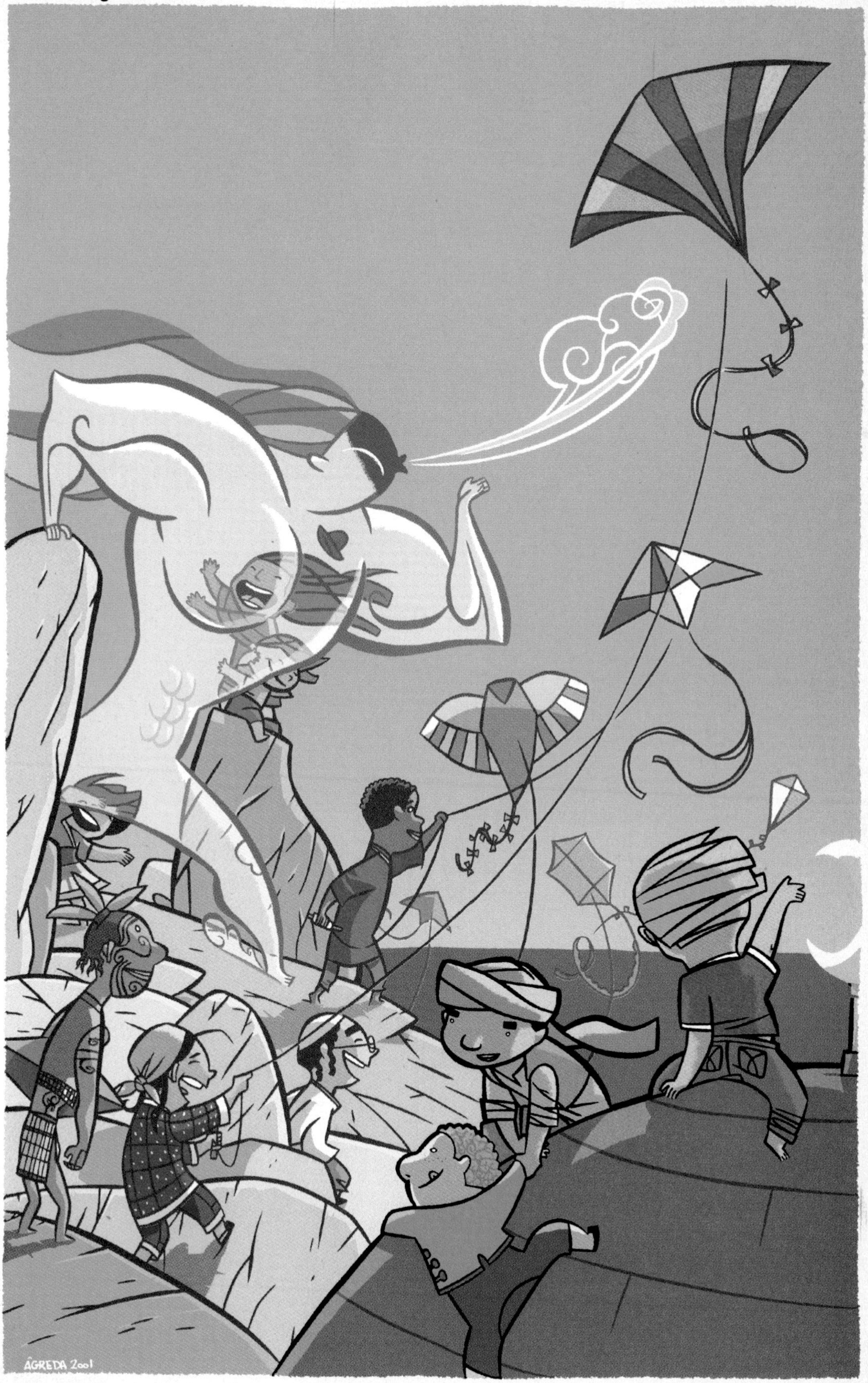
ÁGREDA 2001

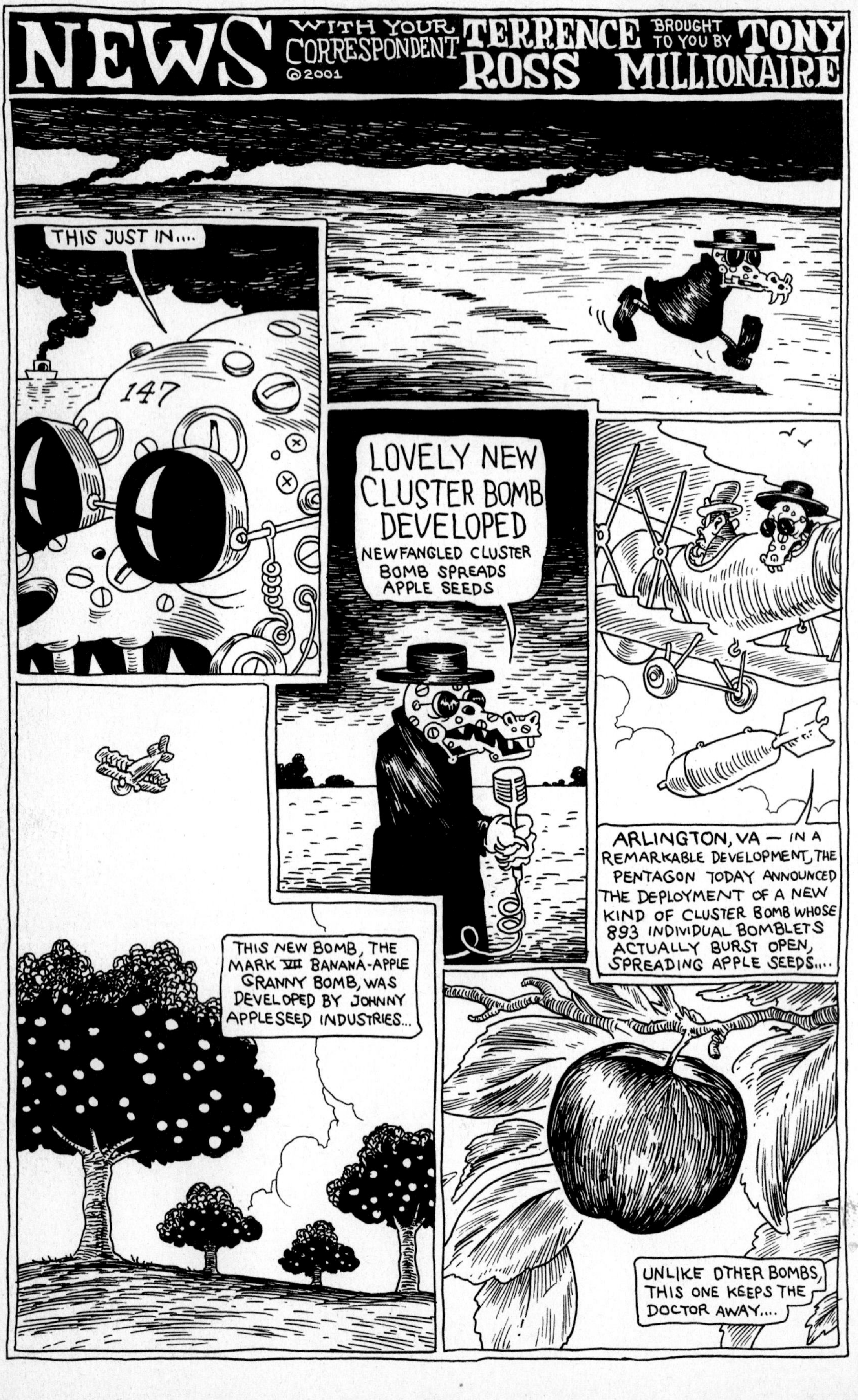
NEWS WITH YOUR CORRESPONDENT TERRENCE ROSS BROUGHT TO YOU BY TONY MILLIONAIRE
©2001
THIS JUST IN....
147
LOVELY NEW CLUSTER BOMB DEVELOPED
NEWFANGLED CLUSTER BOMB SPREADS APPLE SEEDS
ARLINGTON, VA — IN A REMARKABLE DEVELOPMENT, THE PENTAGON TODAY ANNOUNCED THE DEPLOYMENT OF A NEW KIND OF CLUSTER BOMB WHOSE 893 INDIVIDUAL BOMBLETS ACTUALLY BURST OPEN, SPREADING APPLE SEEDS....
THIS NEW BOMB, THE MARK VII BANANA-APPLE GRANNY BOMB, WAS DEVELOPED BY JOHNNY APPLESEED INDUSTRIES...
UNLIKE OTHER BOMBS, THIS ONE KEEPS THE DOCTOR AWAY....

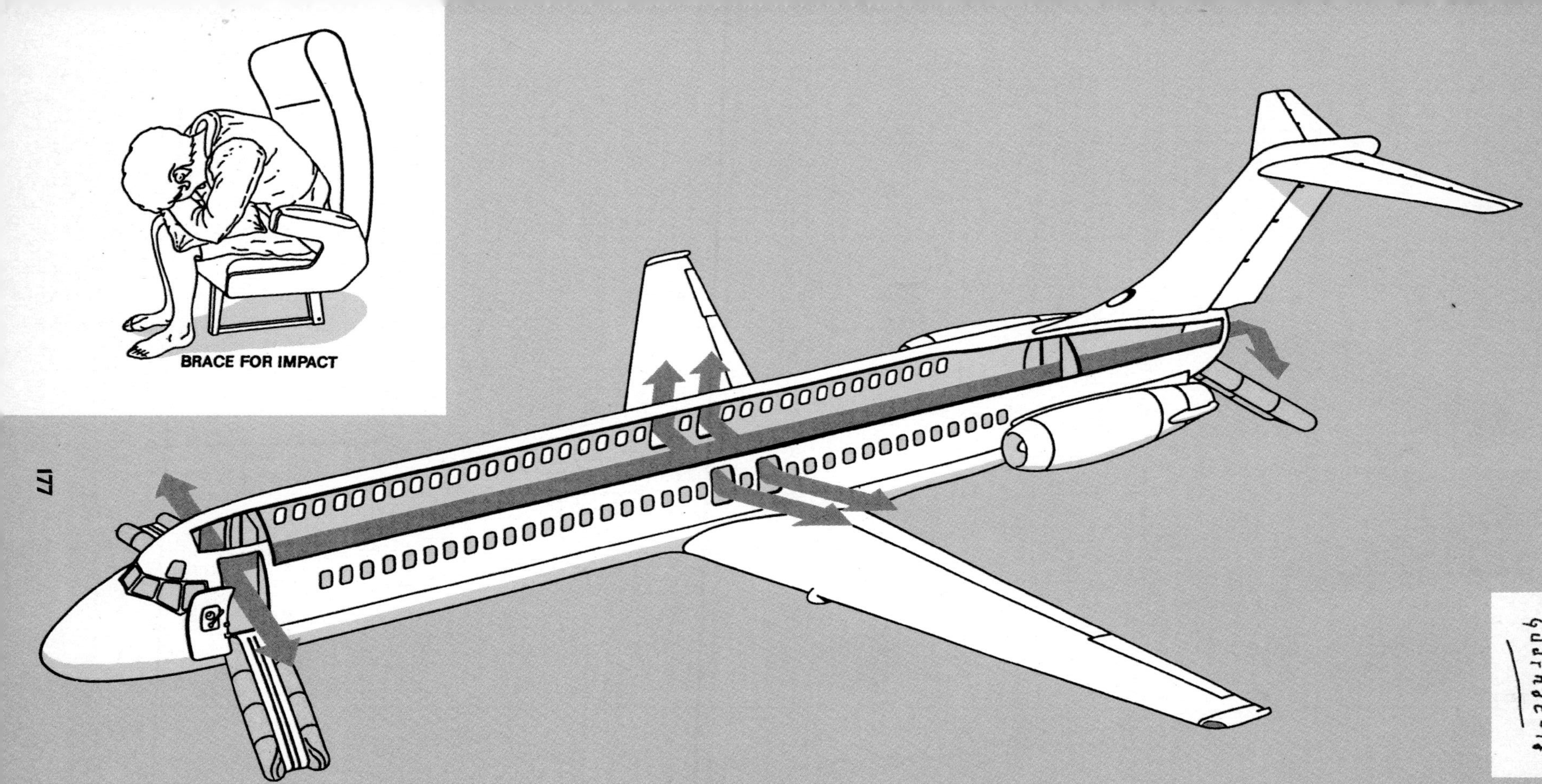
BRACE FOR IMPACT

Guarnaccia

This is not a bomb.

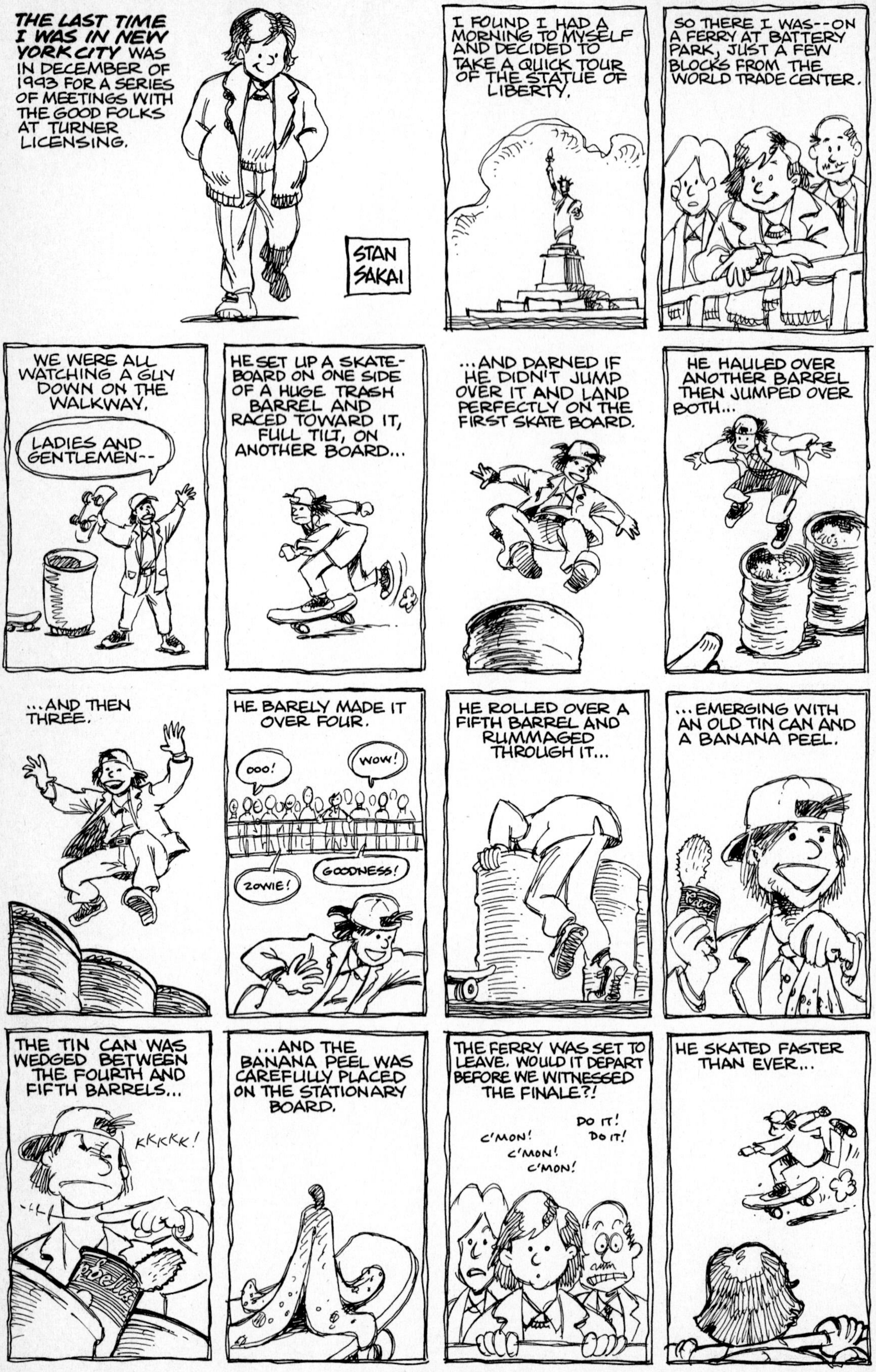
THE LAST TIME I WAS IN NEW YORK CITY WAS IN DECEMBER OF 1993 FOR A SERIES OF MEETINGS WITH THE GOOD FOLKS AT TURNER LICENSING.
STAN SAKAI
I FOUND I HAD A MORNING TO MYSELF AND DECIDED TO TAKE A QUICK TOUR OF THE STATUE OF LIBERTY.
SO THERE I WAS--ON A FERRY AT BATTERY PARK, JUST A FEW BLOCKS FROM THE WORLD TRADE CENTER.
WE WERE ALL WATCHING A GUY DOWN ON THE WALKWAY.
LADIES AND GENTLEMEN--
HE SET UP A SKATE-BOARD ON ONE SIDE OF A HUGE TRASH BARREL AND RACED TOWARD IT, FULL TILT, ON ANOTHER BOARD...
...AND DARNED IF HE DIDN'T JUMP OVER IT AND LAND PERFECTLY ON THE FIRST SKATE BOARD.
HE HAULED OVER ANOTHER BARREL THEN JUMPED OVER BOTH...
...AND THEN THREE.
HE BARELY MADE IT OVER FOUR.
OOO!
WOW!
ZOWIE!
GOODNESS!
HE ROLLED OVER A FIFTH BARREL AND RUMMAGED THROUGH IT...
...EMERGING WITH AN OLD TIN CAN AND A BANANA PEEL.
THE TIN CAN WAS WEDGED BETWEEN THE FOURTH AND FIFTH BARRELS...
KKKKK!
...AND THE BANANA PEEL WAS CAREFULLY PLACED ON THE STATIONARY BOARD.
THE FERRY WAS SET TO LEAVE. WOULD IT DEPART BEFORE WE WITNESSED THE FINALE?!
DO IT! DO IT!
C'MON! C'MON! C'MON!
HE SKATED FASTER THAN EVER...

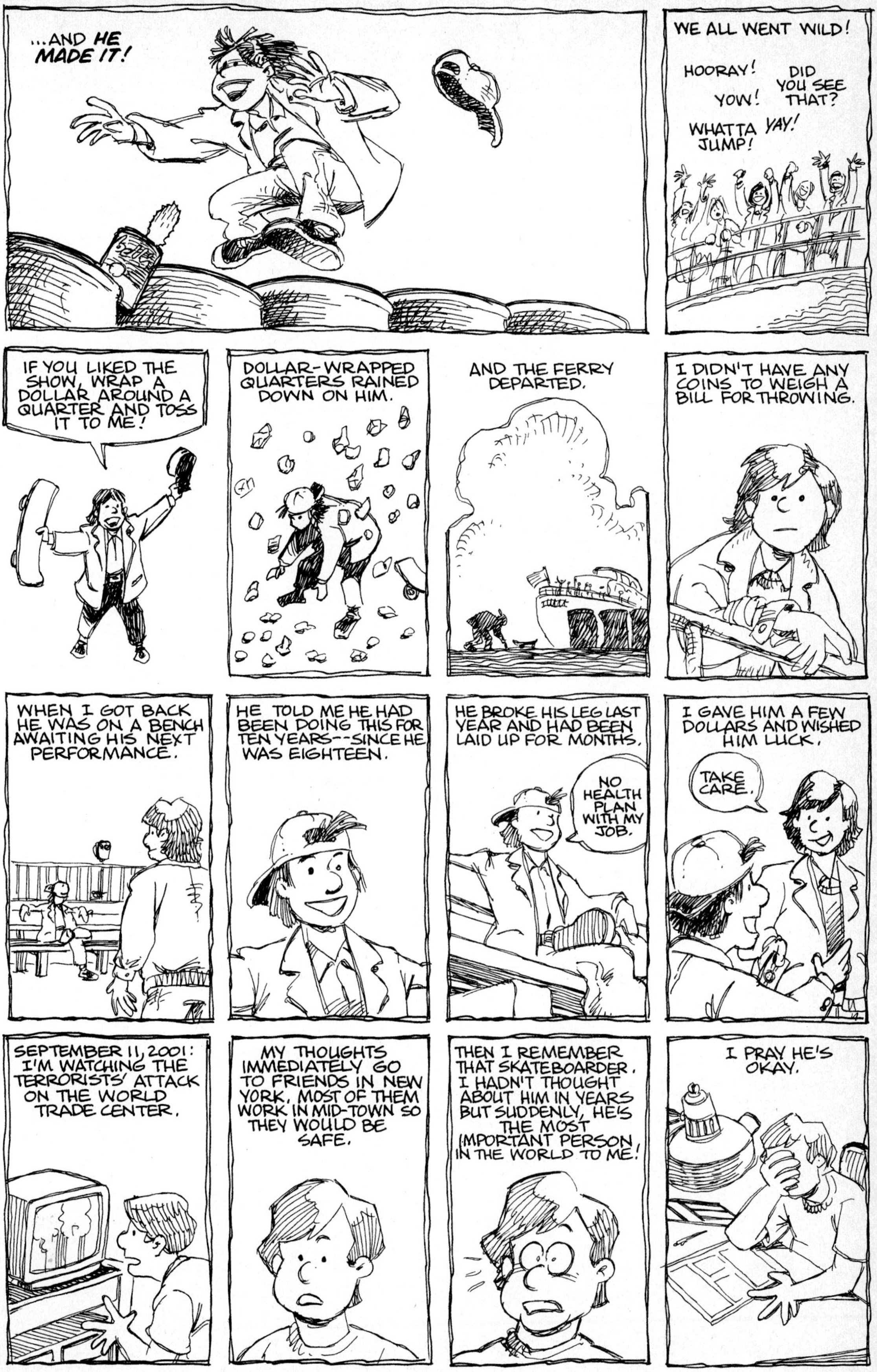
...AND HE MADE IT!
WE ALL WENT WILD!
HOORAY!
YOW!
DID YOU SEE THAT?
WHATTA JUMP!
YAY!
IF YOU LIKED THE SHOW, WRAP A DOLLAR AROUND A QUARTER AND TOSS IT TO ME!
DOLLAR-WRAPPED QUARTERS RAINED DOWN ON HIM.
AND THE FERRY DEPARTED.
I DIDN'T HAVE ANY COINS TO WEIGH A BILL FOR THROWING.
WHEN I GOT BACK HE WAS ON A BENCH AWAITING HIS NEXT PERFORMANCE.
HE TOLD ME HE HAD BEEN DOING THIS FOR TEN YEARS--SINCE HE WAS EIGHTEEN.
HE BROKE HIS LEG LAST YEAR AND HAD BEEN LAID UP FOR MONTHS.
NO HEALTH PLAN WITH MY JOB.
I GAVE HIM A FEW DOLLARS AND WISHED HIM LUCK.
TAKE CARE.
SEPTEMBER 11, 2001: I'M WATCHING THE TERRORISTS' ATTACK ON THE WORLD TRADE CENTER.
MY THOUGHTS IMMEDIATELY GO TO FRIENDS IN NEW YORK, MOST OF THEM WORK IN MID-TOWN SO THEY WOULD BE SAFE.
THEN I REMEMBER THAT SKATEBOARDER. I HADN'T THOUGHT ABOUT HIM IN YEARS BUT SUDDENLY, HE'S THE MOST IMPORTANT PERSON IN THE WORLD TO ME!
I PRAY HE'S OKAY.

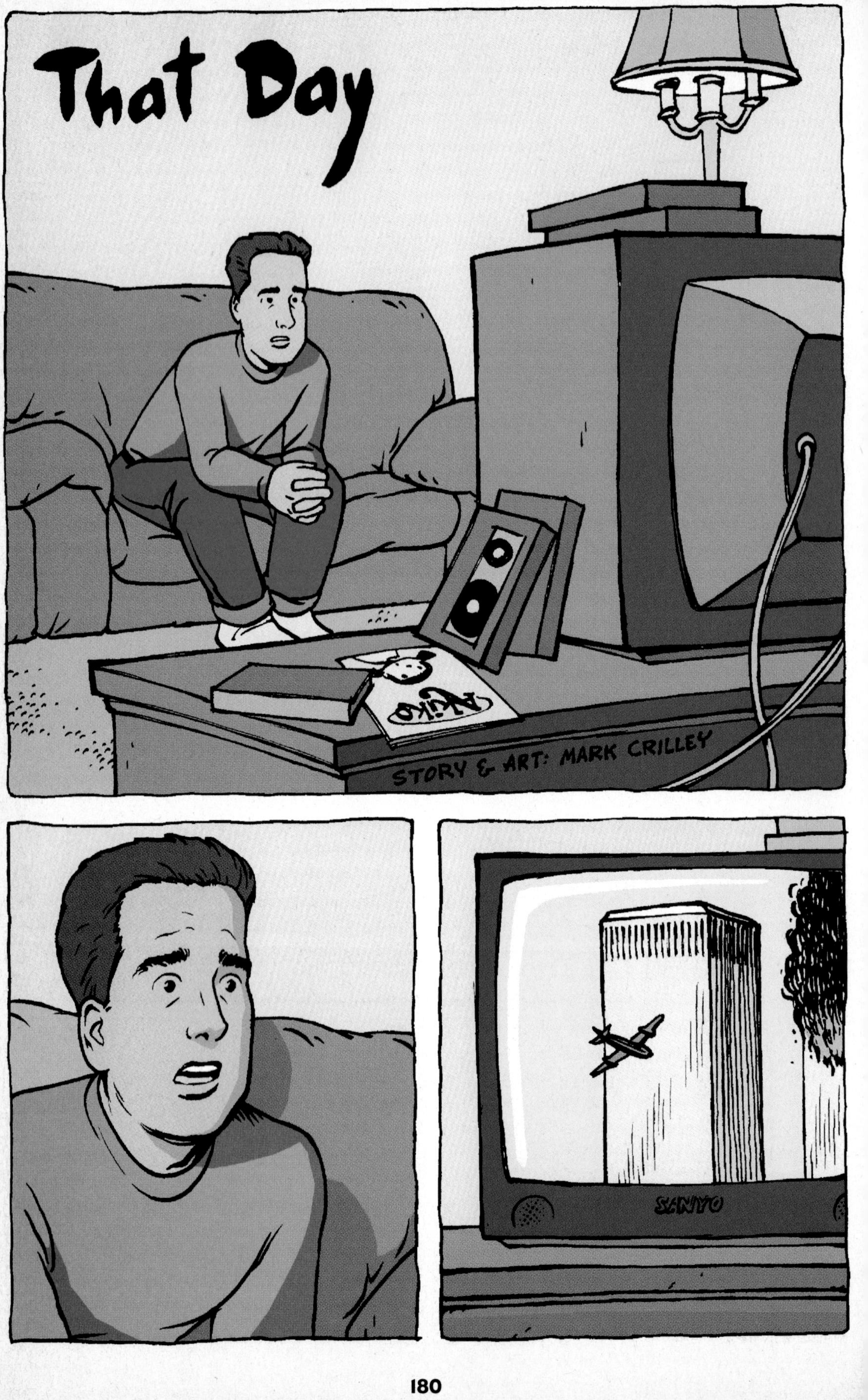
That Day
Akiko
STORY & ART: MARK CRILLEY
SANYO

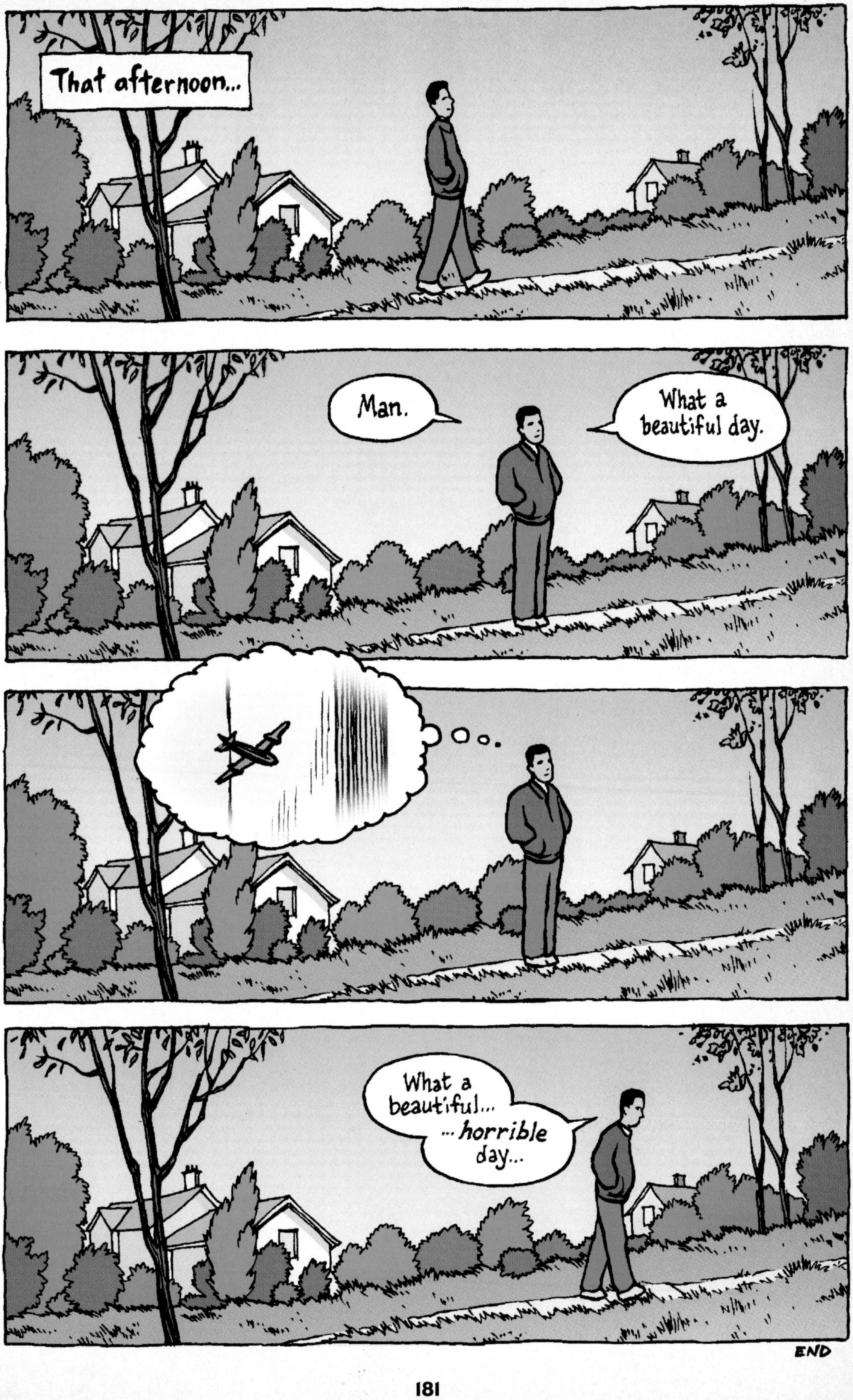
That afternoon...
Man.
What a beautiful day.
What a beautiful...
...horrible day...
END

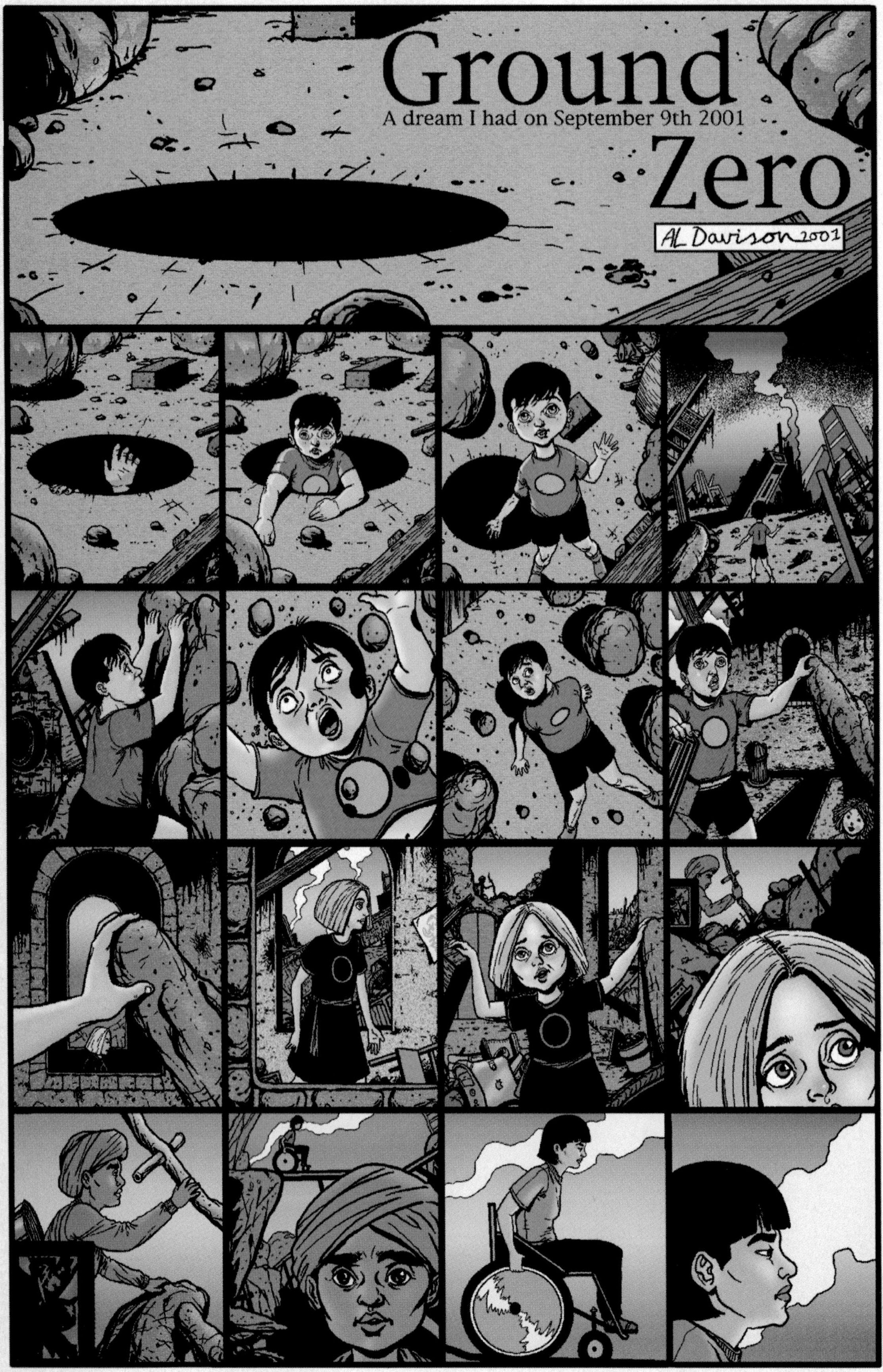
Ground
A dream I had on September 9th 2001
Zero
AL Davison 2001

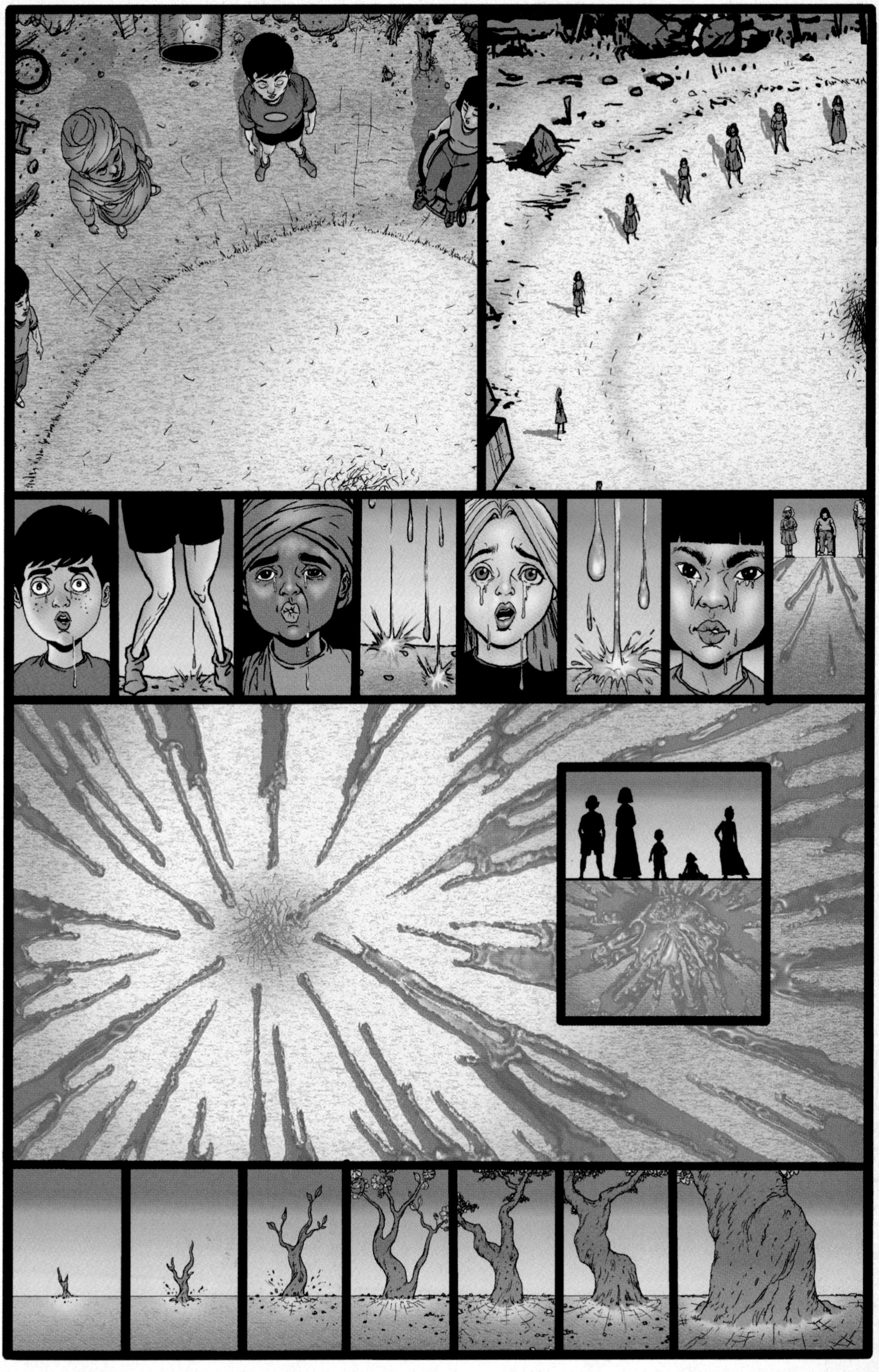

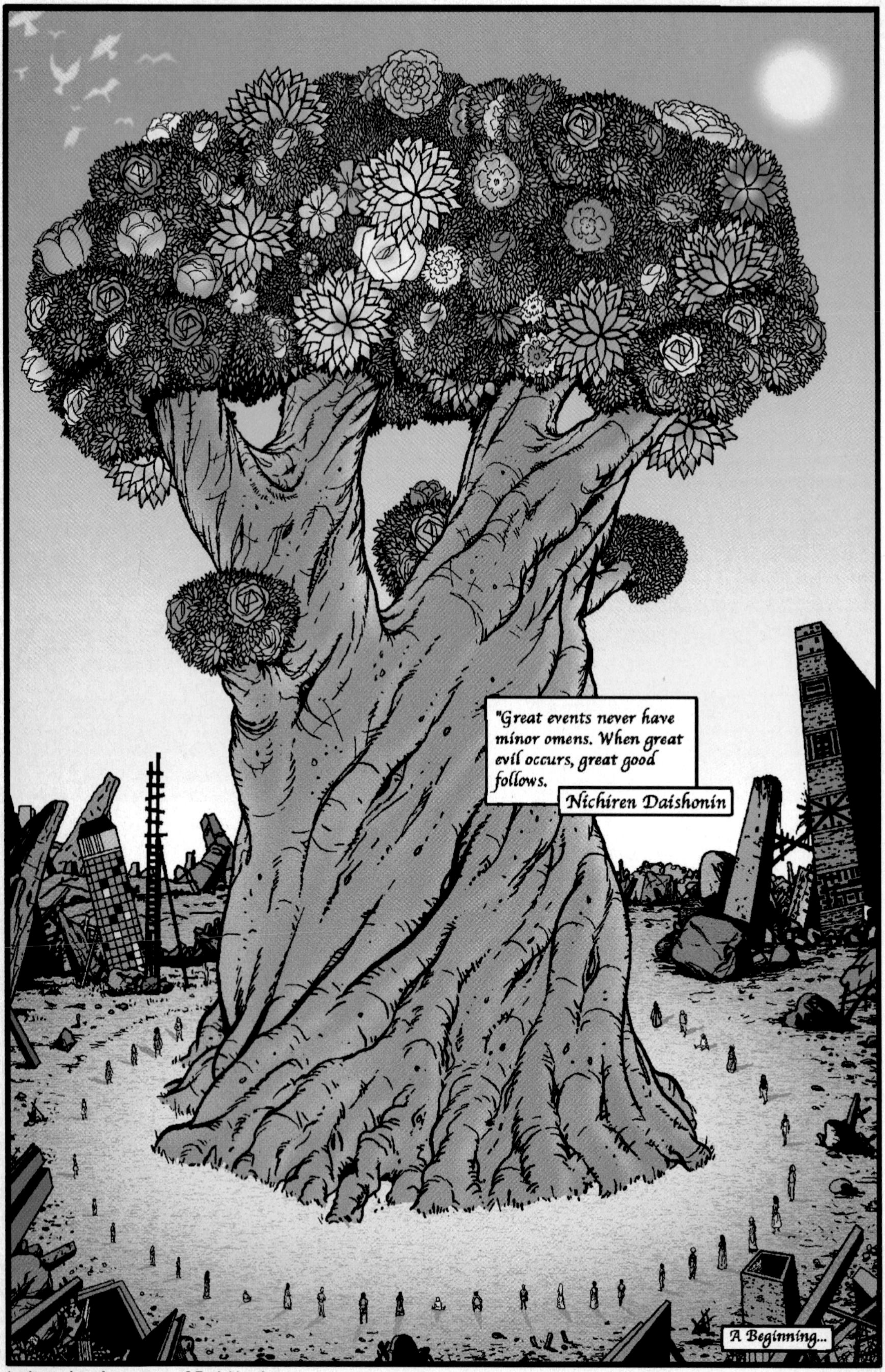
"Great events never have minor omens. When great evil occurs, great good follows.
Nichiren Daishonin
A Beginning...

Dedicated to the memory of Jack Hawthorne.

Alan Moore • Melinda Gebbie

THIS IS INFORMATION

MATTER IS ENERGY. ENERGY IS INFORMATION. EVERYTHING IS INFORMATION.

PHYSICS SAYS THAT STRUCTURES... BUILDINGS, SOCIETIES, IDEOLOGIES... WILL SEEK THEIR POINT OF LEAST ENERGY.

THIS MEANS THAT THINGS FALL.

THEY FALL FROM HEIGHTS OF ENERGY AND STRUCTURED INFORMATION INTO MEANINGLESS, POWERLESS DISORDER.

THIS IS CALLED ENTROPY.

THIS IS WHAT ENTROPY LOOKS LIKE.

NOT MUCH ENERGY.

NOT MUCH INFORMATION.

THE KINETIC ENERGY BOUND UP INSIDE THE STRUCTURE IS RELEASED WITH ITS COLLAPSE, A SINGLE PULVERISING BURST.

COMPLEX INFORMATION IS REDUCED TO DULL SIMPLICITY.

RUBBLE, FOR EXAMPLE, CONTAINS LITTLE INFORMATION. IT ALL LOOKS THE SAME.

THIS COULD BE LONDON, NEW YORK, BAGHDAD, BELFAST, OR KABUL.

OR ANYWHERE.

IT IS THE DISMAL, UNIVERSAL LANDSCAPE OF THE BOMBED.

PICASSO'S GUERNICA. ALL COLOUR GONE. NOTHING BUT BLACK AND WHITE AND GREY. ABOVE ALL, GREY.

LIKEWISE, THE JUTTING HAND HOLDS LITTLE INFORMATION.

DUST-COVERED, ITS RACE, AGE, GENDER, NONE OF THESE CAN BE DETERMINED.

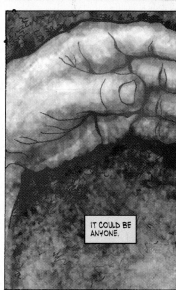

IT COULD BE ANYONE.

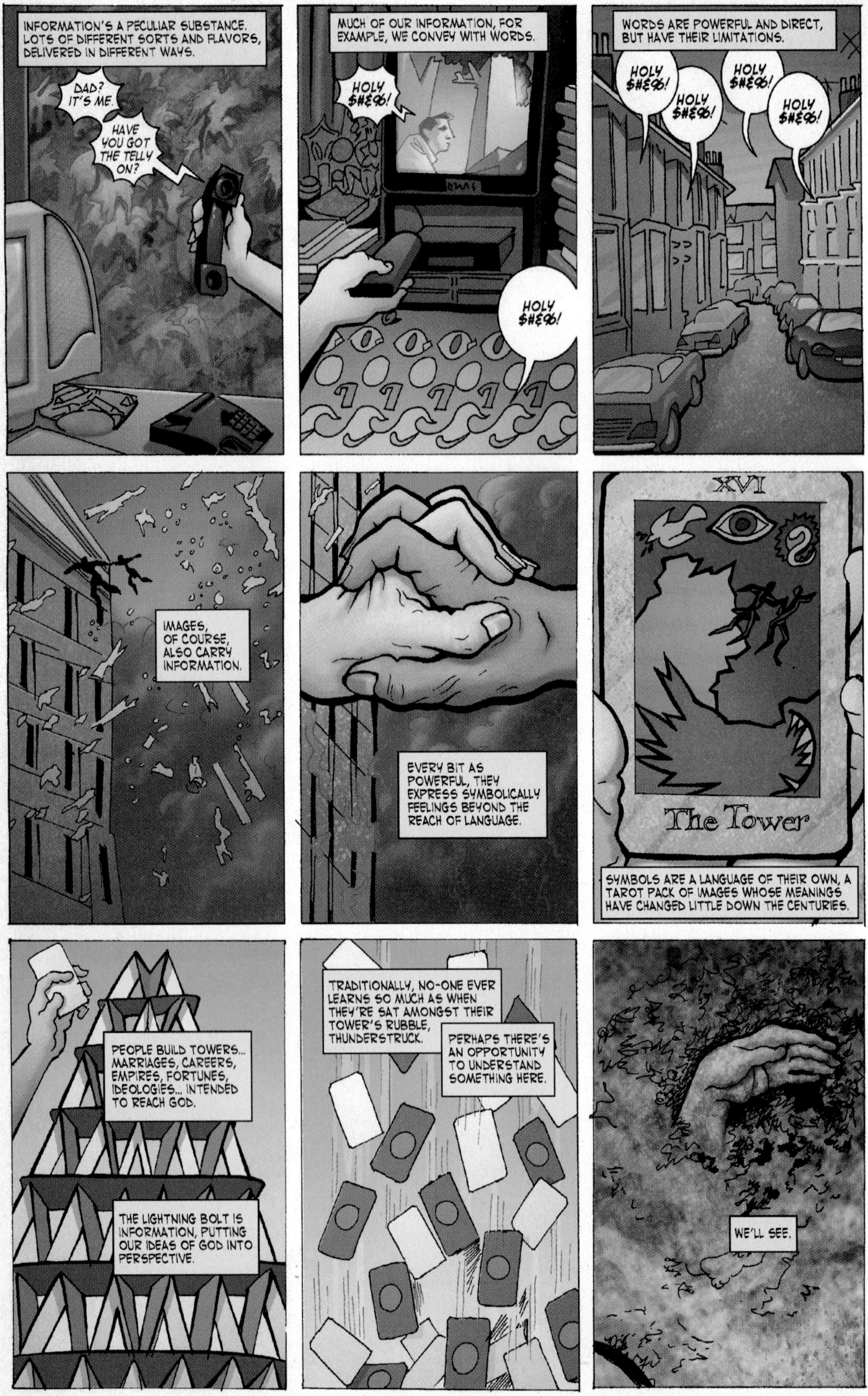

INFORMATION'S A PECULIAR SUBSTANCE. LOTS OF DIFFERENT SORTS AND FLAVORS, DELIVERED IN DIFFERENT WAYS.
DAD? IT'S ME.
HAVE YOU GOT THE TELLY ON?
MUCH OF OUR INFORMATION, FOR EXAMPLE, WE CONVEY WITH WORDS.
HOLY $#£%!
HOLY $#£%!
WORDS ARE POWERFUL AND DIRECT, BUT HAVE THEIR LIMITATIONS.
HOLY $#£%!
HOLY $#£%!
HOLY $#£%!
HOLY $#£%!
IMAGES, OF COURSE, ALSO CARRY INFORMATION.
EVERY BIT AS POWERFUL, THEY EXPRESS SYMBOLICALLY FEELINGS BEYOND THE REACH OF LANGUAGE.
XVI
The Tower
SYMBOLS ARE A LANGUAGE OF THEIR OWN, A TAROT PACK OF IMAGES WHOSE MEANINGS HAVE CHANGED LITTLE DOWN THE CENTURIES.
PEOPLE BUILD TOWERS... MARRIAGES, CAREERS, EMPIRES, FORTUNES, IDEOLOGIES... INTENDED TO REACH GOD.
THE LIGHTNING BOLT IS INFORMATION, PUTTING OUR IDEAS OF GOD INTO PERSPECTIVE.
TRADITIONALLY, NO-ONE EVER LEARNS SO MUCH AS WHEN THEY'RE SAT AMONGST THEIR TOWER'S RUBBLE, THUNDERSTRUCK.
PERHAPS THERE'S AN OPPORTUNITY TO UNDERSTAND SOMETHING HERE.
WE'LL SEE.

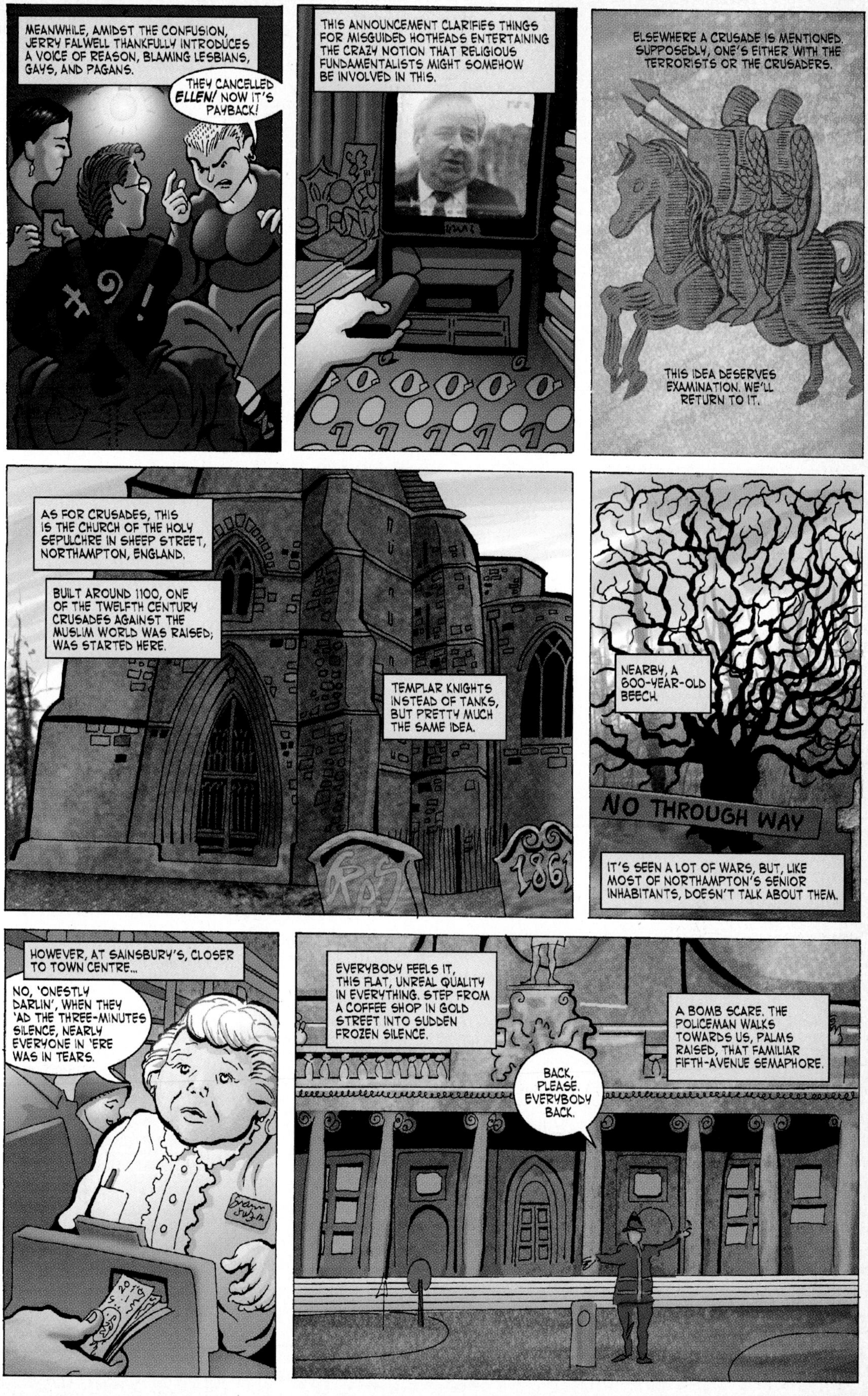
MEANWHILE, AMIDST THE CONFUSION, JERRY FALWELL THANKFULLY INTRODUCES A VOICE OF REASON, BLAMING LESBIANS, GAYS, AND PAGANS.
THEY CANCELLED ELLEN! NOW IT'S PAYBACK!
THIS ANNOUNCEMENT CLARIFIES THINGS FOR MISGUIDED HOTHEADS ENTERTAINING THE CRAZY NOTION THAT RELIGIOUS FUNDAMENTALISTS MIGHT SOMEHOW BE INVOLVED IN THIS.
ELSEWHERE A CRUSADE IS MENTIONED. SUPPOSEDLY, ONE'S EITHER WITH THE TERRORISTS OR THE CRUSADERS.
THIS IDEA DESERVES EXAMINATION. WE'LL RETURN TO IT.
AS FOR CRUSADES, THIS IS THE CHURCH OF THE HOLY SEPULCHRE IN SHEEP STREET, NORTHAMPTON, ENGLAND.
BUILT AROUND 1100, ONE OF THE TWELFTH CENTURY CRUSADES AGAINST THE MUSLIM WORLD WAS RAISED; WAS STARTED HERE.
TEMPLAR KNIGHTS INSTEAD OF TANKS, BUT PRETTY MUCH THE SAME IDEA.
1861
NEARBY, A 600-YEAR-OLD BEECH.
NO THROUGH WAY
IT'S SEEN A LOT OF WARS, BUT, LIKE MOST OF NORTHAMPTON'S SENIOR INHABITANTS, DOESN'T TALK ABOUT THEM.
HOWEVER, AT SAINSBURY'S, CLOSER TO TOWN CENTRE...
NO, 'ONESTLY DARLIN', WHEN THEY 'AD THE THREE-MINUTES SILENCE, NEARLY EVERYONE IN 'ERE WAS IN TEARS.
EVERYBODY FEELS IT, THIS FLAT, UNREAL QUALITY IN EVERYTHING. STEP FROM A COFFEE SHOP IN GOLD STREET INTO SUDDEN FROZEN SILENCE.
A BOMB SCARE. THE POLICEMAN WALKS TOWARDS US, PALMS RAISED, THAT FAMILIAR FIFTH-AVENUE SEMAPHORE.
BACK, PLEASE. EVERYBODY BACK.

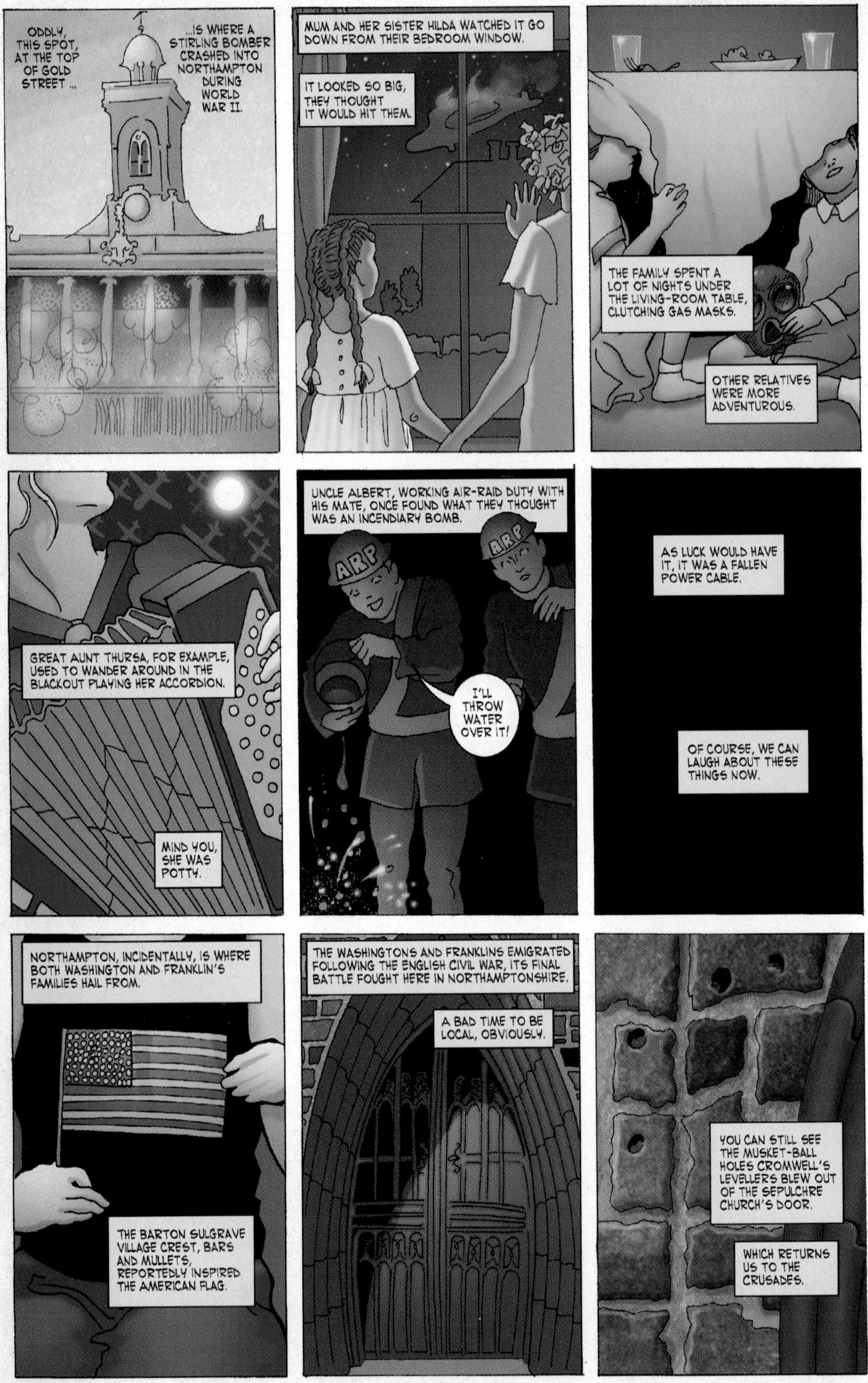
ODDLY, THIS SPOT, AT THE TOP OF GOLD STREET ...
...IS WHERE A STIRLING BOMBER CRASHED INTO NORTHAMPTON DURING WORLD WAR II.
MUM AND HER SISTER HILDA WATCHED IT GO DOWN FROM THEIR BEDROOM WINDOW.
IT LOOKED SO BIG, THEY THOUGHT IT WOULD HIT THEM.
THE FAMILY SPENT A LOT OF NIGHTS UNDER THE LIVING-ROOM TABLE, CLUTCHING GAS MASKS.
OTHER RELATIVES WERE MORE ADVENTUROUS.
GREAT AUNT THURSA, FOR EXAMPLE, USED TO WANDER AROUND IN THE BLACKOUT PLAYING HER ACCORDION.
MIND YOU, SHE WAS POTTY.
UNCLE ALBERT, WORKING AIR-RAID DUTY WITH HIS MATE, ONCE FOUND WHAT THEY THOUGHT WAS AN INCENDIARY BOMB.
ARP
ARP
I'LL THROW WATER OVER IT!
AS LUCK WOULD HAVE IT, IT WAS A FALLEN POWER CABLE.
OF COURSE, WE CAN LAUGH ABOUT THESE THINGS NOW.
NORTHAMPTON, INCIDENTALLY, IS WHERE BOTH WASHINGTON AND FRANKLIN'S FAMILIES HAIL FROM.
THE BARTON SULGRAVE VILLAGE CREST, BARS AND MULLETS, REPORTEDLY INSPIRED THE AMERICAN FLAG.
THE WASHINGTONS AND FRANKLINS EMIGRATED FOLLOWING THE ENGLISH CIVIL WAR, ITS FINAL BATTLE FOUGHT HERE IN NORTHAMPTONSHIRE.
A BAD TIME TO BE LOCAL, OBVIOUSLY.
YOU CAN STILL SEE THE MUSKET-BALL HOLES CROMWELL'S LEVELLERS BLEW OUT OF THE SEPULCHRE CHURCH'S DOOR.
WHICH RETURNS US TO THE CRUSADES.

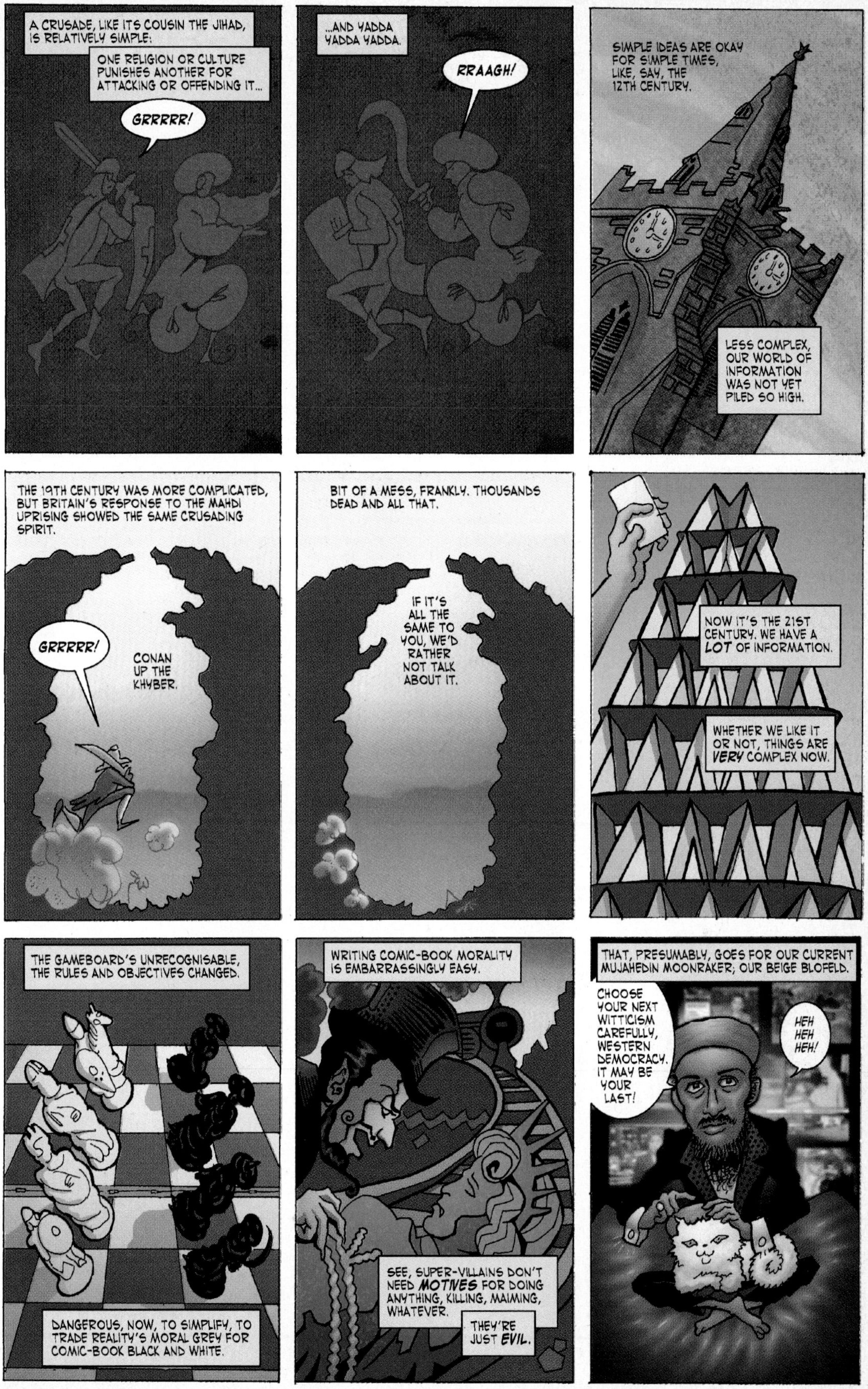
A CRUSADE, LIKE ITS COUSIN THE JIHAD, IS RELATIVELY SIMPLE:
ONE RELIGION OR CULTURE PUNISHES ANOTHER FOR ATTACKING OR OFFENDING IT...
GRRRRR!
...AND YADDA YADDA YADDA.
RRAAGH!
SIMPLE IDEAS ARE OKAY FOR SIMPLE TIMES, LIKE, SAY, THE 12TH CENTURY.
LESS COMPLEX, OUR WORLD OF INFORMATION WAS NOT YET PILED SO HIGH.
THE 19TH CENTURY WAS MORE COMPLICATED, BUT BRITAIN'S RESPONSE TO THE MAHDI UPRISING SHOWED THE SAME CRUSADING SPIRIT.
GRRRRR!
CONAN UP THE KHYBER.
BIT OF A MESS, FRANKLY. THOUSANDS DEAD AND ALL THAT.
IF IT'S ALL THE SAME TO YOU, WE'D RATHER NOT TALK ABOUT IT.
NOW IT'S THE 21ST CENTURY. WE HAVE A LOT OF INFORMATION.
WHETHER WE LIKE IT OR NOT, THINGS ARE VERY COMPLEX NOW.
THE GAMEBOARD'S UNRECOGNISABLE, THE RULES AND OBJECTIVES CHANGED.
DANGEROUS, NOW, TO SIMPLIFY, TO TRADE REALITY'S MORAL GREY FOR COMIC-BOOK BLACK AND WHITE.
WRITING COMIC-BOOK MORALITY IS EMBARRASSINGLY EASY.
SEE, SUPER-VILLAINS DON'T NEED MOTIVES FOR DOING ANYTHING, KILLING, MAIMING, WHATEVER.
THEY'RE JUST EVIL.
THAT, PRESUMABLY, GOES FOR OUR CURRENT MUJAHEDIN MOONRAKER; OUR BEIGE BLOFELD.
CHOOSE YOUR NEXT WITTICISM CAREFULLY, WESTERN DEMOCRACY. IT MAY BE YOUR LAST!
HEH HEH HEH!

IF THE ENEMY IS EVIL, NO MOTIVE IS REQUIRED.

HISTORY, POLITICS, ECONOMICS, ALL OF THESE ARE IRRELEVANT WHEN WRITING SUPER-VILLAINS.

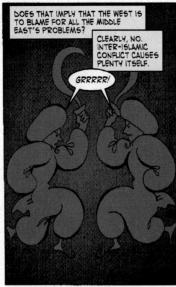

DOES THAT IMPLY THAT THE WEST IS TO BLAME FOR ALL THE MIDDLE EAST'S PROBLEMS?

CLEARLY, NO. INTER-ISLAMIC CONFLICT CAUSES PLENTY ITSELF.

GRRRRR!

DOES SUGGESTING A WIDER CONTEXT JUSTIFY THE SLAUGHTER? INSULT ITS VICTIMS?

CHRIST, NO. WE ALL WEPT.

I'M WEEPING NOW.

ANY SINGLE HUMAN LIFE HAS MORE COMPLEXITY, MORE ENERGY BOUND UP IN IT THAN OUR TALLEST TOWERS.

AND ANY DEATH SIMPLIFIES ALL THAT, HORRIBLY.

DAZED AND CONFUSED AS WE ARE IN THE RUBBLE OF OUR TOWERS, THERE IS AN OPPORTUNITY TO LEARN SOMETHING HERE.

The Tower

PERHAPS JUST ONE OPPORTUNITY.

AND YET WE ARE ALL, SUPPOSEDLY, WITH THE CRUSADERS OR THE TERRORISTS.

(OR, ALTERNATELY, WITH THE GREAT JIHAD OR WITH ISLAM'S ENEMIES.)

WITH ALL DUE RESPECT, WITH ALL SYMPATHY, WITH ALL LOVE, SOME OF US CANNOT MAKE THAT CHOICE.

ARE WE WITH THE TERRORISTS OR CRUSADERS?

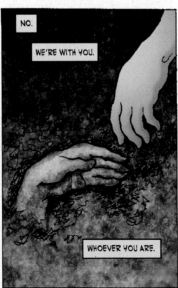

NO.

WE'RE WITH YOU.

WHOEVER YOU ARE.

SQUEEZE ONCE IF YOU UNDERSTAND.

THIS IS INFORMATION.

DEDICATED TO THE MEMORY OF JIM OSBORNE.

Renée French

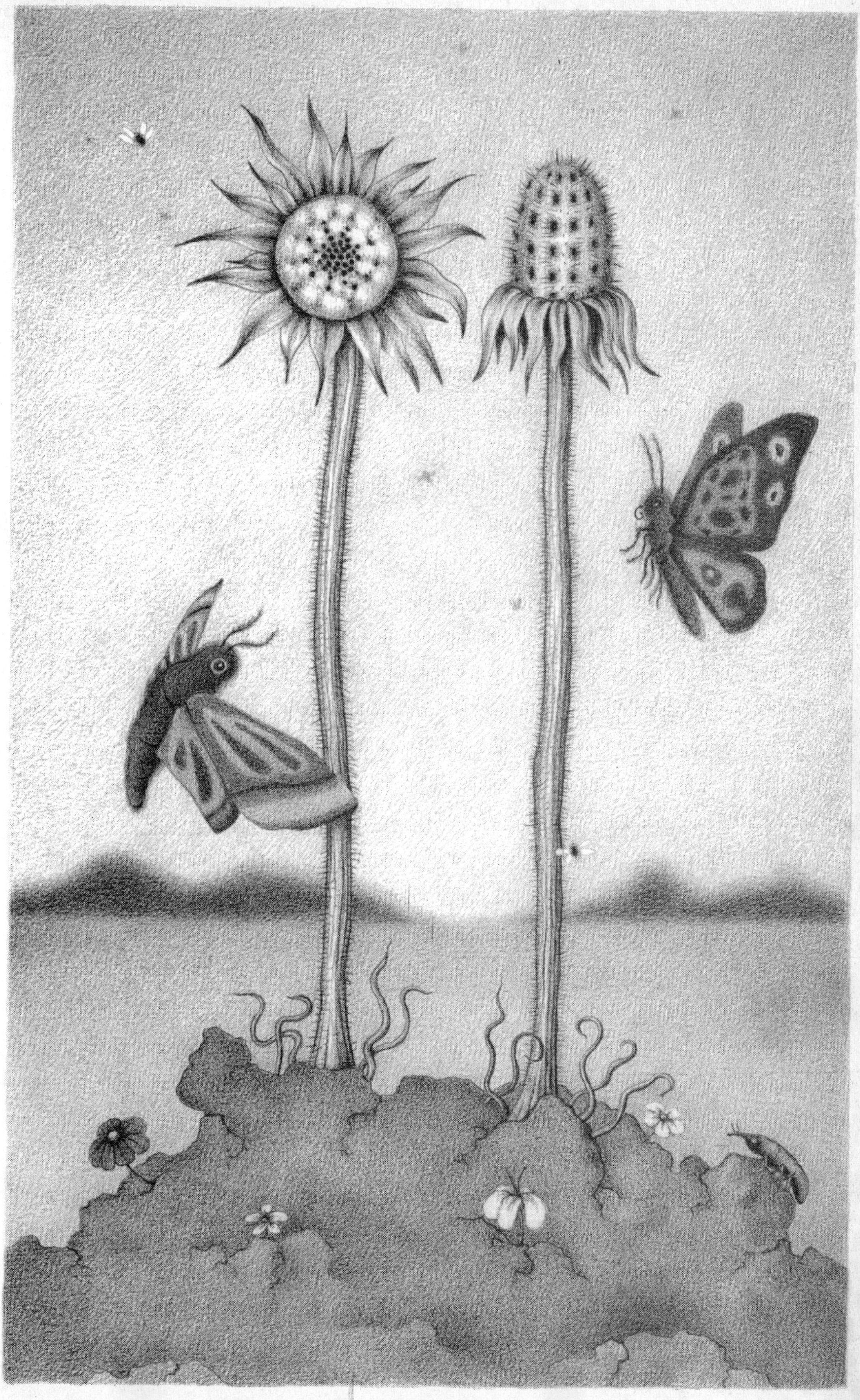

This volume is dedicated
with sympathy and respect to the victims
of the September IIth attacks.

All of the creative talent in this volume have donated
their efforts, as have the suppliers, printer, and distributors
of the book. All of the proceeds from the sale of this book will
be donated to organizations for the benefit and relief of the
victims of the September II, 2001 attacks on America,
their families, and affected communities, including:

New York State World Trade Center Relief Fund

Survivors Fund of the National Capital Region

The September IIth Fund of The New York Community Trust
and the United Way of New York City

———

Twin Towers Fund